POLITICS AND RELIGION IN INDIA

This volume examines how religion is intrinsically related to politics in India. Based on studies from states across the length and breadth of India, it looks at political formations that inform political discourse on the national level and maps the trajectory of religion in politics.

The chapters in this volume:

- discuss contemporary trends in Indian politics, including Hindutva, citizenship bills and mob violence;
- draw on fieldwork conducted across states and regions in India on critical themes, including the role of religion in electoral process, political campaigns and voting behaviour, political and ideological mobilization, and state politics vis-à-vis religion, among minorities;
- focus on the emerging politics of the 21st century.

The book will be a key reference text for scholars and researchers of politics, religion, sociology, media and culture studies, and South Asian studies.

Narender Kumar is Professor at the Centre for Political Science at Jawaharlal Nehru University, New Delhi, India. He has previously taught at three central universities: University of Delhi; Jamia Millia Islamia, New Delhi; and Babasaheb Bhimrao Ambedkar University, Lucknow. He has six authored and edited books to his credit apart from contributing to various journals. His latest volume is *Dr. Ambedkar and Democracy* (edited with Christophe Jaffrelot, 2018). His area of research interest is political institutions and public policy with special reference to group rights. He has been a member of the Indo-European Network, where collaborating institutions included the London School of Economics, King's College London, CERI, Paris, and the Centre for Political Studies, Jawaharlal Nehru University.

POLITICS AND RELIGION IN INDIA

Edited by
Narender Kumar

LONDON AND NEW YORK

First published 2020
by Routledge
2 Park Square, Milton Park, Abingdon, Oxon OX14 4RN

and by Routledge
52 Vanderbilt Avenue, New York, NY 10017

Routledge is an imprint of the Taylor & Francis Group, an informa business

© 2020 selection and editorial matter, Narender Kumar; individual chapters, the contributors

The right of Narender Kumar to be identified as the author of the editorial material, and of the authors for their individual chapters, has been asserted in accordance with sections 77 and 78 of the Copyright, Designs and Patents Act 1988.

All rights reserved. No part of this book may be reprinted or reproduced or utilised in any form or by any electronic, mechanical, or other means, now known or hereafter invented, including photocopying and recording, or in any information storage or retrieval system, without permission in writing from the publishers.

Trademark notice: Product or corporate names may be trademarks or registered trademarks, and are used only for identification and explanation without intent to infringe.

British Library Cataloguing-in-Publication Data
A catalogue record for this book is available from the British Library

Library of Congress Cataloging-in-Publication Data
A catalog record for this book has been requested

ISBN: 978-0-367-33574-8 (hbk)
ISBN: 978-0-367-33787-2 (pbk)
ISBN: 978-0-429-32194-8 (ebk)

Typeset in Bembo
by Apex CoVantage, LLC

 Printed in the United Kingdom by Henry Ling Limited

To
Professor C.P. Bhambhri, the late Dr. R.M. Pal and the likes
For their obstinate credence in human values and secular principles despite coming from the families of victims of the Partition of India

CONTENTS

List of figures ix
List of tables x
Notes on contributors xii
Acknowledgements xvi
List of abbreviations xvii

    Introduction 1
    Narender Kumar

1 Religion, minorities and the Indian state 21
   Himanshu Roy

2 Politics of religious polarization in India: insights from riots in Gujarat (2002), Kandhamal (2008) and Muzaffarnagar (2013) 33
   Mujibur Rehman

3 Sikh politics in Punjab: Shiromani Akali Dal 43
   Ashutosh Kumar and Hardeep Kaur

4 Religion, ethnicity and politics: understanding the BJP's rise in Assam 64
   Dhruba Pratim Sharma, Tarun Gogoi and Vikas Tripathi

5 Church and political action in Mizoram 84
   V. Bijukumar

6 Identity, religion and development: the changing nature of
   political mobilization of Muslims in post-Sachar West Bengal   95
   Abdul Matin

7 Hindutva as a 'sacred form': a case study of Karnataka   108
   Malini Bhattacharjee

8 Nature and dynamics of religion-oriented politics in Kerala   124
   Josukutty C. A.

9 Politics of Hindutva in Maharashtra: actors, causes and
   political effects   139
   Parimal Maya Sudhakar

10 Religion-polity interface in Jammu and Kashmir: an analysis   157
   Muhammad Tajuddin

11 Religion as a tool for political mobilization in Bihar   174
   Umakant

12 Beyond othering: a study of Hindu Political in Gujarat   188
   Dhananjay Rai

13 Indian political space and religion: perspectives and
   exploring alternatives   204
   Y. S. Alone

Index   *216*

FIGURES

4.1	BJP's political performance in the Lok Sabha elections in Assam (1985–2014)	68
4.2	BJP's rise in the Assam Assembly elections (1985–2016)	76
8.1	Vote share of BJP/NDA in Lok Sabha elections in Kerala (1982–2016)	133
12.1	Ideal democracy and Gujarat democracy	199

TABLES

0.1	World Value Survey on religion and its importance for Indians	10
3.1	Summary of Lok Sabha elections in Punjab (1967–2014)	54
3.2	Performance of political parties from 1997 onward: Assembly elections in Punjab	55
4.1	Region-wise BJP political performance in Lok Sabha elections in Assam (1991–2014)	68
4.2	Summary results: seats contested, won and votes secured by major parties in 2014 compared to the Lok Sabha elections (2009)	69
4.3	Political performance of BJP in Assam Assembly elections region-wise (1985–2016)	77
4.4	BJP and other parties' performance in Assam panchayat election (2018)	78
8.1	Population of Kerala by major caste/religious communities (2011)	125
8.2	Caste and religious base of political parties in Kerala	126
8.3	District-religious profile of Kerala	126
8.4	Kerala population religion-wise (1911–2011)	127
8.5	Vote share of BJP/NDA in Lok Sabha elections in Kerala (1982–2016)	133
8.6	Caste/religion and voting behaviour, 2011 and 2016 Assembly elections	134
8.7	District-wise performance of fronts: Kerala elections 2016	134
9.1	Party-wise Lok Sabha seats in Maharashtra (1952–54)	141
11.1	Muslim candidates in Bihar: votes polled, candidates and winners (1952–72)	177

12.1	Major sects (Hindu) in Gujarat	195
12.2	Signposts, dominant vocabulary and vocabulary of political opposition in Gujarat	197
12.3	Dissenting masses in Gujarat	199
12.4	Muslim representation in Lok Sabha from Gujarat	201

CONTRIBUTORS

Y. S. Alone is Professor in Visual Art at School of Arts and Aesthetics, Jawaharlal Nehru University (JNU), New Delhi, India. He completed his Master in Art History at MS University, Baroda and then completed his MPhil and PhD from the Centre for Historical Studies, JNU. He taught at Kurukshetra University before joining JNU in 1996. He has widely published and has visited different countries to deliver lectures in his areas of specialization: Buddhist art, popular visual art, caste studies and interpretations. He was nominated as ICCR Chair, Visiting Professor in Shenzhen University, China, in 2012–13 and continues his academic engagement in China. Currently he is engaged in conceptual formulation of 'protected ignorance'.

Malini Bhattacharjee is Assistant Professor at the School of Policy and Governance at Azim Premji University, Bangalore, India. She teaches and develops courses for the Masters in Public Policy and Masters in Development programmes at the University. Her research interests revolve around the politics of Hindu nationalism in contemporary India and the politics of humanitarianism and disaster relief. She is interested in the intersections emerging between religion, development, governance and public policy in India. She also has an interest in elementary educational policy in India and has spent time in researching on the implementation of the Right of Children to Free and Compulsory Education (RTE) Act in Karnataka.

V. Bijukumar is Associate Professor at the Centre for Political Studies, School of Social Sciences, Jawaharlal Nehru University, New Delhi, India. Previously, he taught at Mizoram University, Aizawl and North Eastern Hill University, Shillong. His areas of specialization include comparative politics, political economy of development, democratization and North East Studies. He has a distinctive academic career with a first rank and gold medal both in his BA and MA in Political Science. He completed his doctoral degree from the Centre for Political Studies, JNU. He is author of the book *Parties and Electoral Politics in Northeast India: Contention of Ethno-regionalism and Hindu Nationalism* and has contributed more than 45 research articles in various journals and 14 articles in edited volumes. He is also a contributor to various regional and national dailies such as the *Mizoram Post, Shillong Times,* and the *Hindu.*

Tarun Gogoi is a PhD scholar at the Centre for Political Studies, Jawaharlal Nehru University, India, and currently doctoral fellow at the Indian Council of Social Science Research (ICSSR). His research interests include Indian politics, federalism, election studies, political parties and Northeast India studies. At present, he is working on the electoral political in Northeast India, understanding the rise of Bharatiya Janata Party (BJP) in Assam, Manipur and Arunachal Pradesh. His doctoral research examines the dominance of national party in the Northeast region and its implication in federal politics.

Josukutty C.A. is Associate Professor and Honorary Director, Survey Research Centre, Department of Political Science, University of Kerala, India. He was Fellow of the Salzburg Global Seminar (2007) and Fellow at Study of the United States Institute at the University of Florida, USA (2010). In 2015, he was awarded the prestigious Fulbright Nehru Academic and Professional Excellence Fellowship. His areas of interest and research include Indian democracy, Kerala politics, India's foreign policy and human rights. He has three books and 24 research articles to his credit. He has participated and presented papers in several seminars and contributes popular articles to newspapers and magazines. He has been serving as general secretary of the Association of Political Scientists, Kerala, since 2011.

Hardeep Kaur is a doctoral candidate at the Department of Political Science, Panjab University, Chandigarh, India. She has been associated with the Lokniti network, Centre for the Study of Developing Societies (CSDS), Delhi. Her research interests include the study of Punjab politics with emphasis on issues related to elections and parties at the state level.

Ashutosh Kumar is Professor, Department of Political Science, Panjab University, Chandigarh, India. Previously he has lectured at the Universities of Jammu and Delhi. He has been associated with the Lokniti network, Centre for the Study of Developing Societies (CSDS), Delhi and has been a visiting faculty member at the University of Tampare, Finland and the Fondation Maison des Sciences de l'Homme, Paris. His research interests and publications include state politics in India, with a focus on issues related to elections, identities and development.

Narender Kumar is Professor at the Centre for Political Science at Jawaharlal Nehru University, New Delhi, India. He has previously taught at three central universities: University of Delhi; Jamia Millia Islamia, New Delhi; and Babasaheb Bhimrao Ambedkar University, Lucknow. He has six authored and edited books to his credit apart from contributing to various journals. His latest volume is *Dr. Ambedkar and Democracy* (edited with Christophe Jaffrelot, 2018). His area of research interest is political institutions and public policy with special reference to group rights. He has been a member of the Indo-European Network, where collaborating institutions included the London School of Economics, King's College London, CERI, Paris, and the Centre for Political Studies, Jawaharlal Nehru University.

Abdul Matin is Assistant Professor at the Department of International Relations, Jadavpur University, Kolkata, India. He completed his MA in Political Science from the University of Hyderabad; his MPhil from the Centre for Political Studies, Jawaharlal Nehru University, New Delhi; and is presently an advanced PhD candidate at the same centre. He has been DAAD Fellow at the Centre for Modern Indian Studies, University of Gottingen, Germany. He has previously been Assistant Professor and Coordinator of the Department of Political Science, Cooch Behar Panchanan Barma University, West Bengal. His research interest broadly includes identity politics in West Bengal, and especially Bengali Muslims, caste, religion and social justice in South Asia, and democracy and inequality in modern India.

Dhananjay Rai is Assistant Professor at the Centre for Gandhian Thought and Peace Studies, School of Social Sciences, Central University of Gujarat, Gandhinagar, India. His books include *Politics: Essays in Tribute to Randhir Singh* (edited, 2018), *Nehru and Adhunikta* (edited, 2016), *Democracy on the Move? Reflections on Moments, Promises and Contradictions* (co-edited, 2013), and *Contemporary Indian Political Theory: A Critical Analysis* (2013). His research articles and reviews have been published in the *Economic and Political Weekly*, *Social Change*, *Social Scientist*, the *Think India Quarterly*, the *Book Review* and the *Indian Journal of Public Administration*.

Mujibur Rehman teaches at Jamia Millia Central University, New Delhi, India. He is currently working on a book on secularism in India. His recently published books include *Rise of Saffron Power: Reflections on Indian Politics* (2018) and a new edition of *Communalism in Postcolonial India: Changing Contours* (2018) with a foreword by Romila Thapar and afterword by Dipesh Chakrabarty. He also writes op-eds and reviews for Indian dailies such as the *Hindu*, *Hindustan Times* and the *Telegraph*. He has received graduate training at the University of Texas, Austin, USA; the University of Heidelberg, Germany; and Indian Institute of Technology (IIT), Delhi. He specializes in development studies and Indian politics.

Himanshu Roy is Senior Fellow, Atal Bihari Vajpayee Fellowship, Nehru Memorial Museum and Library (NMML), Teen Murti House, New Delhi, India. Earlier, he was Fellow, NMML. His recent publications include *Patel: Political Ideas and Policies* (co-edited, 2018) and *State Politics in India* (co-edited, 2017). His forthcoming book is *A History of Colonial India: 1757 to 1947* (co-edited).

Dhruba Pratim Sharma teaches Political Science at Gauhati University, Assam, India. His areas of interest include ethnic politics, public administration and electoral processes. His published papers include 'Demand of "Tea Tribes" for Scheduled Tribe Status in Assam: A Review' in Sandhya Goswami (ed.) *Troubled Diversity: The Political Process in Northeast India* (2015), and 'Saffron Surge in Assam', *Research Journal Social Sciences*, Panjab University (2014).

Parimal Maya Sudhakar is Head of School at MIT School of Government, Pune, India. He is a political commentator and writes regularly in Marathi language newspapers and magazines. He was born and brought up in a small town in eastern Maharashtra and has witnessed the rise of Hindutva politics at the grassroots level. He completed his graduation from Amaravati University in Maharashtra and postgraduation from New Delhi's Jawaharlal Nehru University. He has served as elected joint secretary and vice president of the JNU Students' Union.

Muhammad Tajuddin teaches Political Science at the University of Jammu, India. His broader area of research interest is politics of marginal communities in India. He presently works and supervises research on Jammu and Kashmir politics. Some of his recent works are: 'Review of J&K Language Policy in the Perspective of Nehruvian Language Policy', *South Asian Survey* (2012), 'Freedom from Corruption through Self Governance or Coercive Governance: An Exploration through Political Philosophy', *Mainstream Annual* (2014), 'Scheduled Castes' Reservation in J&K: Promises and Failures', *Indian Journal of Federal Studies* (2012), and 'Dialectic of Peace', *Gandhi Marg* (2012).

Vikas Tripathi teaches Political Science at Gauhati University, Guwahati, Assam, India. He has contributed to academic journals such as the *Economic and Political Weekly* and *Studies in Indian Politics*. His area of interest includes public institutions, and he is currently engaged in research on the Indian Cabinet and the Parliament in India.

Umakant is an independent scholar and completed his MA, MPhil, and PhD in Political Science from Jawaharlal Nehru University (JNU), New Delhi, India. He has been writing on the issues related to Dalit politics, Dalit leadership, and Dalit human rights issues. He has authored several reports on important matters some of which were submitted to UN bodies. He has co-edited a book (with Sukhadeo Thorat), *Caste, Race and Discrimination: Discourses in International Context* (2004). He has also prepared course material for postgraduate-level courses through E-PG Pathshala and also for a new Certificate Programme on Life and Thought of B.R. Ambedkar at the Indira Gandhi National Open University (IGNOU), New Delhi. Apart from human rights issues, he also specializes in the Indian Constitution, Indian government and politics, and other streams in the discipline of political science.

ACKNOWLEDGEMENTS

Many near and dear colleagues support completion of a project. In this regard, first of all, I would like to thank the University Grants Commission–Departmental Special Assistance–II, its Coordinator Gurpreet Mahajan and other colleagues in the Centre for Political Studies, School of Social Sciences, Jawaharlal Nehru University (JNU), New Delhi, for their support in the organization of the National Conference for this study. Second, I am thankful to Vidhu Verma, who has been partner in the project on 'Difference and Identiy: A Study of Minority Rights' supported by the University with Potential of Excellence (UPoE)–II grant at JNU that inspired me to engage on the subject.

I express my gratitude to all those colleagues who have contributed chapters to this volume. Special thanks to those who submitted their chapters soon after the conference and kept working as per suggestions.

I would like to thank scholars Tarun, Pragya, Arvind, Pragya, Vrinda, Ankit, Aishwarya and Shaileja for their support in the process. Thanks to my family members Alyssa, Gautami and Anju for bearing the brunt of my absence from home for long hours.

My special thanks are to Routledge and its editorial team for all the logistical support.

ABBREVIATIONS

AAP	Aam Aadmi Party
AIUDF	All India United Democratic Front
BJP	Bharatiya Janata Party
BJS	Bharatiya Jana Sangh [short form: Jan Sangh]
BSP	Bahujan Samaj Party
CSDS	Centre for the Study of Developing Societies
ECI	Election Commission of India
INC	Indian National Congress
IPC	Indian Penal Code
MNF	Mizo National Front
MP	Member of Parliament
NC	National Conference
NCP	Nationalist Congress Party
NDA	National Democratic Alliance
OBC	Other Backward Castes
PDP	People's Democratic Party
PPOP	People's Party of Punjab
RJD	Rashtriya Janata Dal
RPC	Ranbir Penal Code
RSS	Rashtriya Swayamsevak Sangh
SAD	Shiromani Akali Dal [short form: Akali Dal]
SC	Scheduled Caste
SCR	Sachar Committee Report
ST	Scheduled Tribe
TMC	Trinamool Congress
UPA	United People's Alliance
VHP	Vishwa Hindu Parishad

INTRODUCTION

Narender Kumar

The interaction among social traits and political actors/institutions produces distinct consequences in different societies and nations. These consequences also get transformed in diverse time, space and circumstances. In India, social divisions – caste, ethnicity, religion and so forth – have been devouring their influence on the functioning of the polity in distinctive ways. Moreover, the diverse influence is further complicated in different states/regions. Though the impact of these factors has been studied, there has been a predominance of studies on caste. Even if religion is studied, the focus of majority of such studies predominates the communal or secular lens, and do not look at religion as a factor determining the political outcomes, especially in the electoral process and policy formulation, where the ideology of a party or regime plays a detrimental role in political mobilization or policy initiation. And even parties those claim not to use religion end up employing it implicitly.[1]

In the Western world, modernity marked an almost complete separation of church/religion from state/politics, and the Constitution discerned this separation in India. This distinction between Western and Indian contexts is further distinguished and complicated by the historical processes. In the West, it evolved over a period of time after struggle among church, state and society, but in India it was in some sense imposed by the constitutional development and mandated without a struggle among religious institutions, state and society. And that may be why even the leaders of the national movement against the British had different opinions about this interaction and the future of politics in India.

This difference is also reflected when one looks at the broader Indian history and the interaction of religion and politics therein. One is reminded of some major such events at different intervals of history (the Kalinga War and subsequent emperor Ashoka's conversion to Buddhism in ancient times; Akbar initiating a new religion in the name of *Din-e-ilahi* for inducting secular principles in some way, and Aurangzeb's plunder of Hindu temples and invocation of special religious taxes during medieval times; the well-known British policy of 'divide and rule' that culminated in the partition of India in modern times).

In post-colonial India, Jawaharlal Nehru was in favour of complete separation of state and religion. He went to the extent of arguing that the customs and dogmas of religion were relics of the past and unsuitable to modern situations. He trusted that religious categories would become irrelevant and insignificant in politics and thus remain no longer as an instrument of political contestation (Nehru 1972, 1973). On the contrary, M.K. Gandhi argued vehemently against politics being divorced from religion and went to the extent of saying, 'Those who say that religion has nothing to do with politics do not know what religion means' (Gandhi 2008: 65). Contrary to the dominant Western view, similar to Gandhi's, it has been argued that rejection of religion in democratic societies could lead to absence of ethical wisdom which comes from participation in traditional activities, and such a society is bound to degenerate into tyranny or social and cultural disintegration (Eliot 1936).

B.R. Ambedkar was another who did not reject the relevance of religion as a social and moral value, but he differentiated between religions as he found some fundamental differences in their philosophies. Some religions denied equality among human beings whereas others propagated equality and working to achieve equality. So for Ambedkar, all religions apparently cannot be believed to be having a common philosophy; every individual religion had its own philosophy. Differentiating between Hinduism and Buddhism, he observed that the former was not founded on morality, even if there is little morality that is neither integral nor embedded in religion, rather it functions as a separate force sustained by social necessities; whereas in the Buddhism, morality is embedded in religion in place of God and morality exists, making it different from other religions (Ambedkar 2003: 98). For him, religion was for man and not vice versa and it needs to function in accordance with reason and science, as it is not sufficient to have a moral code but it has to recognize the fundamental tenets of liberty, equality and fraternity (Keer 1994: 421). For him, the philosophy of Hinduism is marked by the tenets of inequality among the individuals, making it non-social. Thus he was for a religion which is social as well as moral and rational, and that is where he defended the conception of Dhamma of Buddha, and not the Buddhism of variant types which had these qualities. One may argue that the secularization theory never blinded him like many of his contemporaries, where secularism took the form of an ideology and was thus completely away from the ground realities.[2]

On the other hand, there were few who argued in favour of Hindu Rashtra and two-nation theory on this interaction.[3] Attributing political meaning to Hinduism, V.D. Savarkar coined the term 'Hindutva' and argued that it encompasses a broader meaning, wherein it needs to be self-realized that it came to 'exercise such imperial sway over the hearts of millions of mankind and won a loving allegiance from the bravest and best of them', and he claimed the term 'Hinduism' was limiting, less satisfactory and essentially sectarian (Savarkar 1969: 4). What we observe in terms of this interaction between religion and politics in the post-independence period is an amalgamation of these views and their outcomes which are reflected in different times, forms and spaces.

Ashis Nandy (1998) in some senses clubs Savarkar, Ambedkar and Jinnah as non-believers in private and believers in public, but looking at Ambedkar's position on religion, one may not be convinced that Ambedkar had something to do with belief, and especially in the existence of God that is fundamental to religion, when he says that he is adopting the Dhamma of Buddha and not the later versions which were manipulated, injected and inoculated over the centuries, ignoring fundamental characteristics of morality and rationality available in the Dhamma (Omvedt 2003).

In the following pages, first we shall discuss the interaction of religion and politics in general, taking the larger context at national level and then coming to the specific contexts of the states in India. Here, an attempt is made to understand the national trends of this interaction in the historical context with reference to the early 20th century till the partition of India and then with a focus on the post-independence period, which also did not have a singular lineage but a varying voyage that observed some important phases of passive and active interaction of religion and politics.

Mapping interaction of religion and politics in modern times

The obvious reflection of religion in politics in modern India could be traced to the advent of British after the Muslim and Hindu rulers faced their onslaughts. Consequently, to maintain their dominance the British manipulated the religious identities of both to serve their own interests. To benefit the Christianity as a religion, Lord Dalhousie, the governor general during the mid-19th century, invoked a law that entitled a convert to Christianity inheritance rights (Sharma 2005: 40). Various such interferences in religious lives led to the revolt of 1857, where there were instances of Hindu-Muslim unity that were considered harmful by the imperialists, leading to the policy of 'divide and rule' and culminating in the first partition of Bengal in 1905 primarily on the religious domination of Hindu and Muslim communities in two separate regions, namely Western and Eastern Bengal.

The beginning of the census and the significance of identities in terms of caste and community brought in the assertion for identities, and the unfolding of the democratic process also marked the significance of numbers. Accordingly, the 20th century's initial years in particular paved the way for the formation of some of the religion-based political and social outfits, including the Muslim League by the dominant Muslim minority, Shri Bharat Dharam Mandal by the dominant Hindus, and Shiromani Gurudwara Parbandhak Committee, the Sikh religious body known popularly nowadays as SGPC.

One could locate more nuanced interface of religion and politics with the British colonial state initiating electoral reforms and consequent politics, especially after the introduction of communal electorates in 1909 in response to an appeal for protection of representation rights of the Muslims in 1906 under the leadership of Aga Khan, who became the first president of the All India Muslim League. It has been viewed as inflicting a formal entry of state-sponsored communal politics on Indian soil. The colonial policies earmarking separate electorates for the religious communities 'reinforced religious identities and made communities the subject of political discourse' (Mahajan 2010: 10).

Not only the British but also different kinds of nationalists, including Bal Gangadhar Tilak and Gandhi, were using religious symbols and sentiments to mobilize people against the British. This trickled down among the Muslim minority as well, and there was a rise of various social, cultural and political organizations amplifying their activities, which led to the partition of Bengal after riots in different areas. This interplay of religion and politics was not new but was in practice in low intensity during the Mughal and Hindu rule, but now it had vast appeal in terms of space and population that culminated in the division of the country – one becoming an Islamic state and the other adopting a secular outlook despite having a Hindu majority population (Sharma 1989: 51).

Promise of constitutional democracy and challenges for secular state

Adoption of a secular Constitution contained communal mobilization in the first few years, as the religion-oriented political parties were relegated to the margins and the secular format of the state forced the religious identities to submerge in the nation-building process. There was almost complete communal peace during the first decade of the republic of India, as Hindu outfits were checked by the leadership and Muslims were left with the choice of accommodation and consensus for the larger goals of the new nation. This was complemented by some cultural and educational rights being termed as fundamental rights by the law of the land.[4]

Thus religion was relegated to a non-significant factor in public life in the initial years, as the partition had left a grave scar that led to the killing of millions of people. It was in this light that religion was given a backseat to political affairs, and religion was treated with neutrality. Nevertheless, one may argue that the selection of candidates in constituencies dominated by minorities used to include candidates from the minority communities, but apart from the selection of candidates on the basis of religion, it was not thought of enough importance to require special attention.

Although, the Constitution of 1950 abolished the system of communal electorates, this did not mean that religion would abstain from having its influence on politics, because politicians depend on votes, and the electoral process almost fascinates them to exploit the religious divisions in society (Weiner 2006: 137). Nonetheless, after a few years, there was a resurgence of communal violence in some parts of the country. It was coterminous with the death of Nehru, who remained committed to the ideas of secularism and communal coexistence. Paul Brass's (1974) study depicts the details of this violence that initiated a new phase of politics interplaying with religious identities.

The 1967 General and Assembly elections brought a major political shift in the electoral map of the country, ending the Congress predominance both in the states and at the centre. It was the first time that Jan Sangh, which was considered to be the political voice of RSS, got 35 parliamentary seats of 520 in this general election, the highest after the partition of India (Graham 1993: 261–2). The Hindu right mobilized Hindu saints in 1967 and those had a demonstration in the national capital favouring a ban on 'cow slaughter' at the all-India level. This could be seen as a major interplay in religion and politics. Interestingly, Indira Gandhi suggested the organizers and the priests not invoke religion-based political mobilization that could become a major threat to the secular and plural ethos of the country. However, despite Mrs. Gandhi's appeal as prime minister, her suggestion was completely ignored and Jan Sangh was successful in making cow protection an important election issue (Sankhdher 1973: 270–1).

On the other hand, the Akali Dal, another party claiming to be representative of another religious community (the Sikhs), formed a coalition government in Punjab in 1967. Thus the 1967 election can be considered not only a watershed in the electoral politics of the country as a whole, where the Congress faced a major challenge from the opposition in many states, but this could also be thought of as the beginning of clear religious influence on the political system.

Thus the seeds of close correspondence between religion and politics that were sown during the British rule could not be dismantled even after the British divided the country and then left. The division of the country in terms of religious identities had a far-reaching impact on the interplay between religion and politics, wherein the majority and minority sentiments based on religion could not be wished away; there could not be complete shifting of religious population from one nation to another, and it has usually not been possible in the history of many nations faced with such eventualities. It was further fuelled by political parties based on religion, and if one goes by the statistics of Election Commission data and formation of such parties, then one realizes that this is not declining but multiplying with successive elections, as the appeal of religious sentiment attracts many (Miller 1987).

Deepening contestation against the secular state and essentialization of religion

Congress enjoyed the support of minorities, especially Muslims, for a longer time. However, at the all-India level, Muslims became disenchanted with the Congress during the Emergency (1975–77), especially over the issue of forced family planning that was perceived to be against the religious sentiments of the community. C.P. Bhambhri, who did fieldwork in the Mewat region of Haryana (dominated by Muslims) during that period, mentions the Muslim masses who would tell him categorically during the post-Emergency election of 1978 that 'they will vote against Congress due to the misdeeds of Sanjay Gandhi', who was considered to be the mastermind.[5]

It was also during this period that the right-wing outfits like RSS and the Vishwa Hindu Parishad raised concerns for scrapping of special constitutional provisions for Jammu and Kashmir under Article 370, doing away with Muslim personal laws, disproportional population growth of Muslims and so forth. During the Emergency, many RSS workers went to jail, which resulted in Janata Party forming the first non-Congress regime at the Centre in 1977 wherein Bharatiya Jana Sangh provided the first chance for a right-wing political party to become a partner in the affairs of the government at the Centre. However, the Janata Party could not survive its full term in office and lost power in 1980. The BJS came in a new form of the Bharatiya Janata Party. It included some Janata Party leaders such as Ram Jethmalani, Shanti Bhushan and Morarji Desai who did not have belief in the staunch form of Hindu nationalism (Jaffrelot 1996: 315).

The BJP did well in the Assembly elections of 1980 in those areas where the RSS network was fairly strong and traditionally the Jan Sangh had a good support base, but interestingly the party suffered heavily in Uttar Pradesh and Bihar – the two strongholds of the so-called cow belt. The emerging strength of the right wing made the Congress Party anxious, and this led to a relatively soft posture towards the right-wing social and cultural outfits. And the Congress leaders realized that having a confrontational position against the two minority groups (Muslims in Kashmir and Sikh extremists in Punjab) might gain them the support of many Hindu. James Manor argues that due to this tactical positioning, numerous activists of the RSS deserted the BJP to support Congress candidates in the elections in the early 1980s (Manor 1998: 111–40).

Now onwards, the Hindu right has continuously been engaged in religious mobilization. But religious mobilization, whether by one religion or the other, has never been merely religious; it has been argued that 'all religious mobilizations are inevitably political' (Marty and Appleby 1991). The religious mobilization becomes political because of the legitimacy it obtains through its connection to morality, a higher truth and knowledge greater than our own. In the absence of the religious belief systems and the communities it creates, the persistence of religion is not possible. And without these beliefs and the mechanisms of religions for legitimating the political actions of the actors involved, religion-based politics is not possible. There is mutual understanding of politicians and religious leaders as politicians seek to use religious identity, institutions and their legitimacy to serve their own ends just like religious leaders and institutions make use of politicians to achieve goals inspired by their religious beliefs and doctrines (Fox 2013: 214).

The electoral politics in Hyderabad, having a considerable number of Muslims, has seen mobilization on the basis of religion. Wilkinson remarks that the religion-based mobilization witnessed through religious festivals in the late 1970s has been responsible for igniting Hindu-Muslim riots during election campaigns in the early 1980s in Hyderabad. Both Hindu and Muslim political parties organized religious events, provoking one community against the other, while the one provoked also became consolidated for its interests (Wilkinson 2004: 48–50).

Before the popularly known Ram Rath Yatra of Lal Krishna Advani in the 1990s, there was another Yatra known as the Ekatmata Yatra ('Pilgrimage of One Soulness') by the VHP in November 1983 with two symbols of Ganga and Bharat Mata and their idols being installed on a *rath* (chariot). It was marked by three processions originating from three places of Hindus: one from Kathmandu in Nepal to Rameswaram in Tamil Nadu; another from Gangasagar in Bengal to Somnath in Gujarat; and yet another from Haridwar in Uttarakhand to Kanyakumari in Tamil Nadu (Jaffrelot 1996: 36). This probably was the first of its kind without the support of any political party contrary to the Rath Yatra of Advani. It aroused the feeling of vulnerability among the Hindus. Jaffrelot argues that it was an effort to construct a 'Hindu vote' to pressure any regime to protect and defend the interests of the majority community. Its objective was obvious when another movement was started in 1984 that was to take back the Ram Janmabhoomi, the birthplace of Ram at Ayodhya (Jaffrelot 1996: 362). However, it was a period when the religious sentiments did not get an active societal response, as it was the beginning of the initiative.

Nevertheless, in such circumstances and due to the assassination of Prime Minister Indira Gandhi in October 1984, the BJP suffered its worst defeat in the 1984 general elections, in which it fetched only two seats. This forced the BJP to take extremist postures towards Hindu nationalism. The fallout was adopting aggressive agitational politics, developing professional electoral strategies, upgrading public relations functions, believing these to be compulsory elements of a majoritarian democracy (*Organiser*, February 1985: 1).

There was no looking back for the BJP thereafter. The main reason for its success was the adoption of an ethno-religious mobilization strategy. These strategies helped BJP in capturing power. Subsequently, the years and decades ahead not only witnessed the growth of social divisions along religious lines but also religion-based politics occupying centre stage, not merely in the electoral process but also in day-to-day public interactions and state policies. It forced the Indian state to grapple with the new form of religion-based politics to safeguard democracy and secularism (Bhambhri 1993: 5). It was not confined to the political parties, which were contesting for the religion-based mobilization, but the state also became entangled in the process (Kanungo 2002).

Therefore, the 1980s and 1990s mark a major shift in Indian politics. The former witnessed the resurgence of religions in Indian politics that culminated in religion-based political mobilization and the later introduced liberal tenets in the economy. The religion-based mobilization in the 1980s continues in one form or the other at present. Some such mobilizations were observed in various forms (i.e. Sikh Secessionism in Punjab; the Shah Bano controversy; the rise of militancy in Jammu and Kashmir; and the Ram Janmabhoomi movement and subsequent demolition of the Babri Mosque in Ayodhya).

Congress, being the dominant party, could not afford to lose popular support among the Hindus, and it started a practice of 'soft Hindutva' against the militant and aggressive Hindutva of the BJP. Though Congress' support base was Muslim, it could not ignore the religious interests of Hindus against the minorities and changed its stance accordingly. It paved the way for the moderate Hindutva standpoint of the Congress that finally culminated in the opening of the Ram Janmabhoomi site to Hindus for worship. Another scholar working on the religion and politics interface argues that both Indira and Rajiv Gandhi compromised with the principles of secularism whenever there was a question of winning elections. They mobilized and formed alliances on communal standing despite the popular claims of being a secular party and condemning communalism of all shapes and forms that stand against the Constitution's statement defining India as secular state (Ludden 2006: 13). Thus the debates around the Congress' conviction with regard to secular ethos after Nehru in particular have been questionable.[6]

The division of Punjab into Haryana, Himachal and of course Punjab (with the Sikh majority residing in Punjab) augmented Sikh Secessionism in the form of a demand for a separate Khalistan in the name of the Sikh religion within two decades of the state's division in 1966. The Indian state resorted to army intervention, popularly known as Operation Blue Star, in the most venerated religious place of the Golden Temple. The anti-Sikh riots of 1984, which saw a major conflict between Hindus and Sikhs in the history of the country, was also the outcome of this same movement. It is argued that the Khalistan movement began with the opposition of the Nirankari sect, but later it was supported for opposing the politics of Shiromani Akali Dal. However, gradually this movement turned into opposing the Indian state per se. The secessionism resulted in the loss of life of ordinary citizens, police officers, Chief Minister Beant Singh, and even Prime Minister Indira Gandhi. It is further argued that killing of Indira Gandhi generated resentment against Sikhs, which culminated into riots against them in various cities. These memories of anti-Sikh riots are time and again invoked against the Congress Party during elections to mobilize Sikh votes.[7] The Khalistan movement and anti-Sikh riots continue to influence politics in the state of Punjab and also in Delhi, even in contemporary India. Commenting on the issues of identity in the Sikh community, Jodhka argues that despite some of the signifiers predominantly indicating towards developmental concerns in the post-colonial period, the impact has not been developmental in nature (Jodhka 2010: 198). Thus religion has been one of the dominant factors in the political mobilization of Sikhs.

On the other hand, in the case of Muslims, the Shah Bano judgment delivered by the Supreme Court (1985) and the mobilization of the Muslim minority against it resulted in the consolidation of this community on the basis of religious identity. The Shah Bano judgment gave the impression that the Indian state was imposing non-religious morality on Muslim community, which might be ending distinctiveness of their identity. In the Shah Bano judgment, the Supreme Court of India ruled that fundamental rights would supersede religious rights. The movement against the judgment portrayed it as a plot to destroy the essential tenets of Islam. This movement consolidated the Muslim minority and sustained its importance in Indian electoral politics. The movement against the Shah Bano judgment forced the government of Prime Minister Rajiv Gandhi to bring special legislation to nullify the judgment, which infuriated Hindu conservatives. To appease Hindu conservatives, the government opened the lock on the controversial Ram Janmabhoomi, where the Babri Mosque also stood. The opening of this controversial site paved the way for Hindu conservatives to build a temple of Lord Rama on the site. Brass argues that Rajiv Gandhi swung 'between the methods of his grandfather and his mother and lacked any distinctive leadership qualities of his own, [and] survived until his assassination in May, 1991 largely on the basis of divine right' (Brass 1994: 26).

In the meantime, the BJP leader Lal Krishna Advani launched a Rath Yatra from Somnath to Kolkata to mobilize the Hindu masses for building the Ram Temple at the controversial site. Lalu Prasad Yadav, who was chief minister of Bihar, stopped this Rath Yatra in Samastipur of Bihar, but it had created such momentum in the masses that Babri Mosque was demolished on 6 December 1992. As a reaction to the demolition of the mosque, riots affected prominent cities across the country. The mobilization around Ram Temple issue enabled the BJP to capture power in many states of north India and finally at Centre in the late 1990s. Atal Bihari Vajpayee, who was considered to be a moderate face in the BJP, was appointed prime minister of India. His own party colleague, K.N. Govindacharya called him a *Mukhauta*, conveying that he was just a mask behind the RSS strategy, controlling the Vajpayee regime pursuing its agenda, whether in terms of change of educational syllabi or similar other attempts to prioritize Hindu interests. However, the regime could not repeat itself despite claims of 'Shining India' during the 2004 general elections. However, Ram Mandir still remains an issue that gets mention in the BJP manifestoes for the electoral mobilization of Hindu voters.[8]

On the other hand, the developments in Jammu and Kashmir, especially migration of Kashmiri Pandits and the autonomy of the Kashmiri Muslims, also remained a dominant narrative in political mobilization. The migration of Kashmiri Pandits has been projected as ethnic cleansing of Hindus from the valley. The resurgence of Islamic fundamentalism in the Kashmir Valley played a very prominent role in the said migration. This terrorism was inspired by Islamic theology, therefore, it targeted non-Muslims of the valley, especially Kashmiri Pandits, leading to their migration. This division became so apparent that over the years Muslims had their Kashmir-centric parties, the National Conference and the People's Democratic Party, and the Jammu region had first the Congress and later the BJP as the dominant party in the region. In recent times, two opposite ideologies representing interests of Hindus and Muslims, namely the BJP and the PDP, even joined together to form the government that could also not succeed for a longer period, and again the regions and religions seem to have been pitted against each other in the state. Indicating towards this kind of phenomenon and its fallout, Verma writes, 'The invocation of religious identities in electoral politics and their privileged position in the public life has polarized Indian society instead of promoting respect for religious difference' (Verma 2017: 226).

Studying the resurgence of religion

If any phenomenon emerges, it obligates the social scientists to study it. And if there is resurgence of such an occurrence, then it becomes much more urgent to analyze it. The post-1980s politics saw a resurgence of religion in India, which was in conformity with similar kinds of phenomena across the world. In other parts of the world, identity-based movements began to play a very important role in social mobilization; religion is one such identity. This period also saw a renewed attempt to study religion and other identities with the help of new tools and techniques called the survey method. Such techniques were used in the World Value Survey,[9] which made an attempt to collect behavioural data on people's opinion and identity.

The World Value Survey began in 1981 with an objective to explore people's values and beliefs, how they have changed over time, and what social and political impact they have. It has an important component for measuring role of religion and changing levels of religiosity. The first survey was exclusively done in developed countries, but later its scope was extended and from the second survey onward India was also included in the survey. The report of the second round of survey was released in 1990.

The response of respondents in four rounds of the survey (1990, 1995, 2001 and 2006) as depicted in Table 0.1 suggests that more than two-thirds of respondents conceded religion remained an important factor in their life. Only in the last round of survey i.e. in 2014, the importance has declined around 50%. But one needs to wait till the next round to conclude definitely the declining role of religion in the lives of Indian people.

However, the data equivocally suggests that religion plays an important role in the lives of people in India, which is reflected in mobilization of voters in the name of religion. This poses an important question as to why such a mobilization did not succeed in promoting fundamentalism in the case of India, whereas in

TABLE 0.1 World Value Survey on religion and its importance for Indians

Values	Years				
	1990	1995	2001	2006	2014
Very important	49.2%	48.2%	55.8%	49.7%	20.4%
Rather important	32.0%	29.5%	23.4%	28.3%	32.4%
Not very important	12.1%	13.9%	11.6%	13.4%	26.9%
Not at all important	6.6%	7.0%	7.1%	5.3%	20.1%
Do not know	0.2%	1.4%	2.0%	3.3%	0.2%

Source: Author's own formulation based on World Value Survey; 1990, 1995, 2001, 2006, 2014.

neighbouring countries, such as Pakistan and Bangladesh, religious fundamentalism led to the overthrowing of democratically elected regimes.

One of the explanations could be that parallel to the religion-based mobilization, other mobilizations have been witnessed, which are also based on traditional identities such as Dalit and Other Backward Classes mobilization. The best example has been the 1993 election in Uttar Pradesh, when despite the religious mobilization of BJP (after the demolition of Babri Mosque in 1992), the Samajwadi Party and BSP were able to form a government in the state, relegating the religious mobilization to insignificance. This could also be observed in the tussle between the Janata Dal government led by V.P. Singh when it went ahead with the implementation of the Mandal Commission Report to dent the attempts by BJP to consolidate the Hindu vote and demand to build a Ram Temple on the existing site of the Babri Mosque in Ayodhya (Brass 1994: 243). This produces a unique situation, where the political influence of Hinduism seems pervasive and contrarily, but its very plurality appears to limit its capacity to dominate politics and thus obstruct the creation of unilinear social and institutional development witnessed in the West (Lannoy 1971: 227). This has further been substantiated by the observation that the 'Hindu majority', both in its liberal and aggressive Hindutva forms, has been continually challenged from socially and economically oppressed groups in an ideological process indicating towards the dialectics of class-caste-gender struggles in India (Omvedt 1990: 728).

Nevertheless, in later elections the religious mobilization spread to various other parts of the country and BJP was in a position to form its governments not only in Uttar Pradesh but also in other states and especially at the Centre in 1999, clearly indicating the benefits of religious mobilization.

Indicating another dimension, Rob Jenkins (1999) observes that political economy has played a major role in religion being invoked in the post-1980 period. The march of marginalized communities for capturing state power to solve their problems created 'governability crises'. To overcome the crises, the state had to surrender economy to the market, as a result of which we see the beginning of liberalization of the economy in the 1980s.[10] The liberalization of the economy has its own discontent, and in order to escape from such discontent, the political elites adopted 'reform by stealth' to push the masses to emotive issues, in the meantime reforming the economy. The government of Rajiv Gandhi introduced the first generation of reforms by engaging masses in Shah Bano by nullifying the Supreme Court order and opening the locks of Babri for the Ram Janmabhoomi movement.

Yet again in the 1990s, economic reforms became successful, though the country has a coalition government as the mass politics of the country was caught up in issue of Ram Mandir on the one hand and the Mandal Commission Report on the other. Rob Jenkins argues that only the elite section of Indian society was concerned with the economic reforms, and religious or other identities were used as an instrument in fulfilling the needs of the economy. However, these interpretations overlook the wider happenings that brought religion to centre stage the world over.

Reasoning the resurgence of religion

The resurgence of religion at the international level is considered to have emerged in the 1990s. The separation of religion and politics in democratic countries of the West had marked a different journey due to the close proximity of church and state. Though religion was relegated to naught in the affairs of the state, religion did exist as an independent entity. The introduction of secularism produced a distinct journey and impacted the relationship in several distinct ways, but the critics argue that the resurgence of religion can be attributed to various factors: (1) secularization theorists ignored the fact that 'religion is a dynamic force that is capable of evolving'; (2) secular ideologies have failed to bring in economic well-being and social justice, especially in the third world countries; (3) secularization has been elite based and was not accepted by the common masses; (4) the end of the Cold War saw religion as a source of a paradigm shift for the world and became the basis of conflict and politics; and (5) religion, in fact, never did disappear and remained a potent political and social force (Fox 2013: 23–5).

Simultaneously, in the Indian context there has also been a resurgence of religion, but it was markedly evident a decade before (i.e. in the 1980s), prior to its resurgence at the international level. The common-sense way to answer this question is to choose some tragic incident and determine religion as the prime cause behind it. However, in recent times, there is deviation from such a mode of study, and scholars have become more focused on structural explanations so as to understand the complexity of the process. Contextualizing this phenomenon in India, Bhambhri enumerates several factors: (1) a break with the past in the form of ending one-party dominance of Congress; (2) unstable and unprincipled coalition governments with the processes of globalization, liberalization and privatization; (3) an upwardly mobile middle class in the absence of larger social goal-projected consumerism, individualism, economic competition and so forth as the goals; and (4) finally and most importantly, this middle class identified itself with Brahmanical, ritualized Hindu religion with a public display of its forms (Bhambhri 2003: 8). Post-colonial India had to negotiate between constitutional secularism and communalism of the Hindu right and also with some elements of Muslim perplexity. Thus as a leader of independent India, Nehru had to in fact 'negotiate with the politics of Hindu fundamentalism as well as Congress majoritarianism', and in some ways he had to 'accommodate the flavours of majoritarian cultural climate with some preferential treatment to Hindu rights' (Doss 2018). The seeds of resurgence of religion through politics were sown in some ways during the initial years of independent India, which was further rooted in the political history of India. It is true that even the Western world is experiencing this resurgence after centuries of practice of secular erudition, probably consequent to ignoring and not addressing it.

Understanding the indispensability of religion

The studies and surveys tell us categorically of the aggregating importance of religion in the lives of people across the world. Thus one is reminded of

Dr. B.R. Ambedkar in this regard, who studied most of the prevailing religions of his times and their influence on the behaviour of human beings. He was consistent in confronting the Hindu religion and its discriminatory tenets deep-rooted in its philosophy. He claimed that having been born in Hinduism was beyond his control, but he would not die as a Hindu. And in 1956, at the end of his life, he converted to Buddhism – in fact, he said that he was going back to his roots. It reveals that for him Dhamma was an essential component of human life, as he made a difference between Dharma (religion) and Dhamma.[11] He looked at every issue from a pragmatic perspective, analyzed it and gave a solution with a vision. He analyzed issues with social, cultural and psychological paradigms and accordingly formed opinion and expressed his ideas. One may argue that he was not an idealist like Nehru, who looked at the secular state and modernity in absolute terms; nor he was utopian like Gandhi, who looked at religion as moral and spiritual without focusing on its limitations. As a pragmatist he could probably visualize the downsides of the Hindu right as well, which over the years has been able to promote the customary tenets and embolden the religious divide among the communities and thus offered an alternative in the form of Dhamma, where the popular basics of religion (personal, individual, superstition and illogic) were transformed into social, scientific and rational.

Haidt (2012) refers to recent research carried out in disciplines of divinity and the neurosciences to find the importance of religion in human life. For him, human decisions are based on the five principles of care, fairness, loyalty, authority and sanctity. In recent times, neurologists have made an attempt to understand the importance of those five moral principles in taking human decisions through mapping the brain. He also refers to neurologists having discovered that the said five principles of moral theory help in activating different lobes of the human brain. Taking his argument further, Haidt argues that conservative leaders remain in an advantageous position because their speeches are able to activate all major lobes of the human brain. On the contrary, progressive leaders are unable to do so because they cannot invoke certain ideas in their speeches that prevent activation of those lobes of the mind and thus fail to attract humans so effectively and efficiently. Thus religion and the values it teaches are *sine qua nons* to the human brain, as a result of which Haidt seems to suggest that religion is indispensable to contemporary politics, especially electoral politics which is based on the universal adult franchise, where the masses become active participants due to invocations of conservative elements in politics. Whether those invocations are right or wrong are the judgments based on various issues, but one needs to understand that religion as a factor of influence is here to stay, and we will have to handle it rather than ignore it. How we do this requires its understanding through empirical and epistemological explorations?

Religion, politics and Indian states

This study looks at the role of religion in politics with a specific focus on different states in India. As discussed previously, religion came to have a major say in Indian politics after the 1970s, and various formations including the political are seen impacting politics of different states in the process. Religion functions as an ideology for mobilization in the case of some political parties, and parties either overtly or covertly use religion as an instrument to influence politics. An attempt has been made to examine how different political formations get ideological support from religion and espouse their politics. Religion has been instrumental in creating a political society where sharp binaries have developed among different communities, as politics has overtaken and influenced societal relations significantly. The politics of Jammu and Kashmir on the one hand and of Gujarat on the other hand indicate this in two different ways, where domination of one community gave rise to polarization against the other. Thus the volume examines the trajectory of the present state of affairs in such and many other cases.

In Chapter 1, Himanshu Roy looks into the history of minority rights in the name of participation and representation. It attributes the emergence of minority rights to the formation of Congress and the legacy of colonial rule and thus argues that the political perpetuation of religious rights is more an outcome of electoral compulsions and power politics than for the development of healthy national life or for allaying the fears of minorities. Then the chapter looks at the specific case of Goa and Mizoram to substantiate its arguments, especially with reference to the Indian Christian minority. On the contrary, Chapter 2 by Mujibur Rehman seeks to explain how the politics of religious polarization are evolving in various parts of India, and contributes to the rise of Hindutva politics at the national level in general and in the states of Gujarat, Odisha and Uttar Pradesh in particular by looking at the three sites of major communal riots. The chapter argues that religious polarization definitely helps the Bharatiya Janata Party (BJP), but how various riots have contributed in the determination of this trend are also discussed and explained.

The states of Jammu and Kashmir and Punjab have apparently observed the interplay of religion and politics, as suggests the political history of these states. One may recognize some commonalities in these cases: (1) a majority of the population belongs to two minorities at the all-India level (Muslims in Jammu and Kashmir and Sikhs in Punjab); and (2) both states have experience with militancy primarily based on religious identity. Looking at the former, Muhammad Tajuddin in Chapter 10 analyzes the politics of state in the constitutional framework and points out that the failure of the state leadership to build the republican democratic polity according to the constitutional process based on consensus or compromise of the religious communities degenerated into an arena of religious rivalry among its different religious communities, and subsequently a battleground of Indian and Pakistani nationalism took away the agency of its citizens. The chapter concludes with the argument of dereligionization of the polity in its internal governance and Centre-state relations as the only rational visible solution of the imbroglio. On the other hand, Chapter 3 by Ashutosh Kumar and Hardeep Kaur observes that Shiromani Akali Dal has been the catalyst behind the major shifts in the politics of the post-partition state of Punjab. Besides being the most successful party apart from the Congress since the state's reorganization in 1966, it has had a state-wide organizational presence since colonial days. Its long-standing alliance with the BJP, an urban Hindutva party, has helped the party broaden its support base that has transformed SAD from ideologically driven religious party to a strategic partner in the political game.

Two chapters on Northeast India bring another dimension to the discussion where ethnicities with religion have influenced the politics of region. Chapter 4, by Dhruba Pratim Sharma, Tarun Gogoi and Vikas Tripathi, asserts that in an ethnically divided milieu like Assam, the rise of religious polarization and consolidation of religious identities may be transient as the dominant social cleavages run more along ethnic-linguistic than religious lines. It further argues that the future of the saffron party like BJP in the state depends on its ability to accommodate regional aspirations within its larger framework of religious nationalism. Chapter 5 on Mizoram, by V. Bijukumar, is an attempt to analyze how the church's role in political action during elections challenge the state's authority in democracy and argues that the undue political action of the ecclesiastical authority during elections counterpoises political institutions and thereby adds to the spirit of political obligation itself.

The chapters dealing with the western parts of India, namely Gujarat and Maharashtra, show how the politics of religion has a deep-rooted presence in these states. Chapter 9 by Parimal Maya Sudhakar analyzes the process of domination of religious identities in electoral politics in Maharashtra, particularly the religious identity of the majority community and its implications on the deprived and marginalized sections of society. It further explores the emerging trends in Maharashtra's politics in the context of the emergence of BJP as the single largest dominant force in the state and its implications in the interplay of religion and politics. Chapter 12 by Dhananjay Rai focuses on the components of the Hindu Political, like sects and dominant caste with identity as guardian, integration without confrontation, political communication, communicating opposition/political opposition, and dissenting masses/critical masses becoming central to the process. It underlines the relationship between Hindu Political and the electoral politics that persists in Gujarat over the decades.

Not only have political formations emerged adhering to majoritarian conceptions of society, but in some states where there is a substantial concentrated population of minorities, political formations have been initiated by the minorities themselves. In some other states, despite a substantial minority population, such initiatives have either not been taken or if taken, did not succeed. Kerala and Telangana are the examples for the former and West Bengal and Uttar Pradesh/Bihar for the latter. Chapter 8 on Kerala by Josukutty C.A. points out that the unique demographic composition of Kerala, with two minority religions (constituting 45% of the total population of the state and their concentration in different locations), compulsions of coalition politics, pressures on the political economy of the state and re-radicalization of the communist parties contribute to the assertion as well as coexistence of various religious identities in politics. The efforts made by the BJP to attract different castes under one common platform of Hindu nationalism by raising religious issues have attracted many castes to BJP, which has helped it to increase its vote share in recent elections in Kerala.

Some states/regimes bring special policies for the members of a particular religious community. The Sachar Committee Report of 2006 on the status of minorities seems to have become a guiding principle for some regimes, and policies have been initiated accordingly, or if not, at least there have been statements for policy initiatives taking inspiration from recommendations of the committee. There have been others who have opposed such initiatives. This volume is an attempt to capture such initiatives bringing the religious component in the politics of the state. Chapter 6 by Abdul Matin looks at the changing pattern of mobilization in West Bengal in the post-left era and argues that the state has witnessed massive Muslim mobilization and assertion by different Muslim organizations. The Trinamul Congress not only attracted large numbers of Muslim clerics but also co-opted many Muslim organizations and religious leaders. The chapter argues that these co-options and fusions have generated new discourse on patron-client relations, electoral mobilizations and identity formations in contemporary West Bengal.

Two chapters on different regions, namely north and south, point out how in one case political dimension of communal riots reduced the influence of other factors, and in another case Hindutva became a 'sacred' form without the component of communal riots. Chapter 11 by Umakant examines the role of religion as a handy and useful tool for garnering support during elections from the 1980s onwards. There may have been several causes (be they economic, social or religious hatred) for communal riots happening in the state of Bihar, but political dimensions of communal riots have overshadowed all other factors. Chapter 7 by Malini Bhattacharjee argues that Hindutva in Karnataka, as elsewhere, operates as a 'sacred form' that is constructed through the help of symbols and discourses relating to issues of 'liberating' Hindu places of worship from the 'other'. The prohibition of cow slaughter, protection of Hindu culture from the onslaught of the 'other' and rejuvenation of Hindu institutions such as *seva* are some other tools functioning in the state for such mobilization.

In chapter 13, Y. S. Alone takes the discussion of the volume on another plank with a critique of major existing formulations on the subject. He explores the possibilities of understandings and interpretations in the Indian politics as a phenomenon analyzed through the Buddhist logic of Pratityasamvutpad (theory of dependent/interdependent) origination through his own conceptual formulation of 'protected ignorance'. He presents a critic of the politicality as being practiced by different political parties, regional or national. It offers to see Indian politics from Ambedkar and anti-Ambedkar perspective where Alone considers 'transformation' and 'enabling process' as critical lenses to understand the nature of Indian politics.

The volume could have benefited from full chapters on Uttar Pradesh and Andhra-Telangana, but owing to some last-minute challenges this was not possible.

Epilogue

The data collected by the World Value Survey shows the increasing importance of religion in the lives of people, and the data from Centre for the Study of Developing Societies/Lokniti, New Delhi, shows that religion plays an important role in campaigning and voting behaviour during the electoral process. The political history of the country reveals that there have been times when the focus has been on the formation and flickering of religious identities, such as from the late 19th to the mid-20th century and in post-1980s India, but religion remained an ancillary factor in the electoral process otherwise as well and therefore requires to be addressed to avoid its cascading effects on the society.

The constitutional mandate of preserving a secular outlook could work only in the few initial years of republican India, and it was probably primarily due to the sentiment of nation-building where communal interests could be pushed to the background. But it could not be sustained for a longer time, as society was primarily possibly communal due to religious divisions. This posed challenges and limitations to the project of secularization of society and polity as the seeds existent in the social milieu of difference of religions brought forth the issue of communal mobilization leading to the politicization of the religion and essentialization of community. The democratic politics gave space to the hitherto overlooked elements of communalism, and the Hindus being relatively in the majority (and the majority being the primary basis of success in democracy) provided impetus to the right-wing mobilization at the all-India level. This was not limited to the Hindu majority, but the Muslim community also mobilized on this basis wherever they formed a majority (in Kashmir, in parts of Kerala, in and around Hyderabad and so forth). This posed a major challenge to the democratic polity and the secular Constitution as the communities having majority in whichever form try to pursue their own community interests at large. But one needs to understand that the politicization of society along religious lines is neither beneficial for Muslims nor for Hindus, and this could be resolved by not merely constitutional means but also combined with the societal initiatives and to be precise with the close association of civil society actors popularly working without communal interests and the constitutional state.

As politicization of caste has had consequences for the democratic polity, so have the implications of essentialization of community in politics. Politicization of caste emerged with the marginalized sections of Indian society at the centre but essentialization of community has at the centre the supposed victims who may not essentially be the marginalized but even the elites of the communities. This makes the issue further complicated, as the supposed victims become beneficiaries and the candid victims of social, cultural and economic order become further marginalized in the process. Essentialization of community emboldens religion and enables the indispensability of religion possible, which may be deep-seated and dormant in the human psyche and society. It became more difficult to essentialize secularism in the Indian context, as the preconditions for discounting religion did not witness acceptance of the idea by the common masses, contrary to the West, where secularism was adopted after its devastating and cascading implications on the society at large that forced separation of state and religion possible through a centuries-long process of struggle between state and religion. The separation of state and religion in India did not run through the similar trajectory but was largely an imposition from the top. One may look for a comparison in the erstwhile Soviet Union, which witnessed this imposition from above much more insolently and failed to keep the promise for a longer time and thus witnessed its resurgence in different modes.

However, it does not mean that the ideals of maintaining a safe distance between religion and state in an institutionalized manner are not desirable, but probably the mechanism needs to be much more nuanced and well-thought-out. Perhaps Ambedkar's understanding could be helpful, where religion is absent in its conventional sense and rooted in sacred morality, logic and rationality, keeping the human being at the centre and not God, that may be expended by selfish men and women.

Notes

1 The Indian National Congress (Congress) and its several offshoots, communist parties like CPI, the CPI(M), the Janata Dal and its variants and many others all claim separation of religion and politics. Nevertheless, compulsions of electoral calculation often compel them to adopt a compromising approach to principles leading to the use of religious symbols and slogans in their political endeavours. The selection of candidates by taking into consideration the religious profile of the constituency remains a dominant factor in this regard. Theoretically and principally, these parties vehemently oppose the use of religion to achieve political goals; they consider religion as a private affair of individuals and do not approve of its intervention in public space.
2 For details on the issue of secularization theory and its implication in different parts of the world, see Peter L. Berger (1996–1997). 'Secularism in Retreat', *The National Interest*, Winter, pp. 3–12; Scot M. Thomas (2005). *The Global Resurgence of Religion and the Transformation of International Relations: The Struggle for the Soul of the Twenty-First Century*, New York: Palgrave Macmillan.
3 V.D. Savarkar and other Hindutva protagonists on the one hand, and Aga Khan, Jinnah and others on the other hand.
4 Articles related with the fundamental rights and freedom of religion from Articles 25–28 on the one hand and providing special rights under Articles 29 and 30 on the other hand.
5 During interaction with the author.
6 This is also reflected in the recent efforts during 2018–19 by Congress president Rahul Gandhi to visit Hindu temples and shrines to counter the BJP efforts to consolidate Hindu votes.
7 The latest being the selection of Kamal Nath as chief minister of Madhya Pradesh in the 2018 Assembly elections.
8 Even the general election of 2014 which was contested primarily on the slogan of *Vikas* (development) had simultaneous reference to construction of the Ram Temple at Ayodhya.
9 I am thankful to Arvind Kumar, former student at the Centre for Political Studies, JNU, and now doctoral candidate in University of London, for having introduced me to the World Value Survey.
10 The command economy discussed by Rudolphs (1986) created a sense among the masses that the Indian state controls enormous power and resources, hence by capturing the power of the state, the problem of marginalization can be solved. The founder of Bahujan Samaj Party, Kanshi Ram, used to refer to political power as the master key and claimed that if captured, marginalized communities can solve their all problems. Such slogans played a very important role in the mobilization of the lower castes for capturing political power in North India.
11 B.R. Ambedkar (1987, 1992) discusses these aspects in his writings 'Buddha and His Dhamma', 'Buddha or Karl Marx' and others.

References

Ambedkar, B.R. (1987). 'Buddha or Karl Marx', in (ed.), Vasant Moon, *Dr. Babasaheb Ambedkar Writings and Speeches*, Volume 3, Bombay: Government of Maharashtra Publications, pp. 441–64.

Ambedkar, B.R. (1992). 'Buddha and His Dhamma', in (ed.), Vasant Moon, *Dr. Babasaheb Ambedkar Writings and Speeches*, Volume 11, Bombay: Government of Maharashtra.

Ambedkar, B. R. (2003). 'Buddha and Future of His Religion', in (ed.), Vasant Moon, *Dr. Babasaheb Ambedkar Writings and Speeches*, Volume 17(II), Bombay: Government of Maharashtra.

Bhambhri, C.P. (1993). *Politics in India 1992–93*, New Delhi: Shipra Publications.

Bhambhri, C.P. (2003). *Hindutva: A Challenge to Multi-Cultural Democracy*, New Delhi: Shipra Publications.

Brass, Paul (1974). *Language, Religion and Politics in North India*, Cambridge: Cambridge University Press.

Brass, Paul (1994). *The Politics of India Since Independence*, Cambridge: Cambridge University Press.

Doss, M. Christhu (2018). 'Sandwiched Nehru: Religious Minorities and Indian Secularism', *Economic and Political Weekly*, 53(29), pp. 38–47.

Eliot, T.S. (1936). *Catholicism and International Order: Essays, Ancient and Modern*, London: Faber and Faber.

Fox, Jonathan (2013). *An Introduction to Religion and Politics: Theory and Practice*, New York: Routledge.

Gandhi, M.K. (2008). *The Essential Writings*, in (ed.), J. Brown, Oxford: Oxford University Press.

Graham, B. (1993). *Hindu Nationalism and Indian Politics*, Cambridge: Cambridge University Press.

Haidt, Jonathan (2012). *The Righteous Mind*, London: Penguin Books.

Jaffrelot, Christophe (1996). *The Hindu Nationalist Movement and Indian Politics, 1925-1990s*, New Delhi: Viking.

Jenkins, Rob (1999). *Democratic Politics and Economic Reforms in India*, Cambridge: Cambridge University Press.

Jodhka, Surinder S. (2010). 'Sikhs Today: Development, Disparity and Differences', in (eds.), Gurpreet Mahajan and Surinder S. Jodhka, *Religion, Community and Development: Changing Contours of Politics and Policy in India*, New Delhi: Routledge.

Kanungo, Pralay (2002). *RSS's Tryst with Politics: From Hedgewar to Sudarshan*, New Delhi: Manohar.

Keer, Dhananjay (1994). *Dr. Ambedkar: Life and Mission*, Bombay: Popular Prakashan.

Lannoy, Richard (1971). *The Speaking Tree*, London: Oxford University Press.

Ludden, David (2006). *Making India Hindu*, New Delhi: Oxford University Press.

Mahajan, Gurpreet (2010). 'Religion, Community and Development', in (eds.), Gurpreet Mahajan and Surinder S. Jodhka Religion, *Community and Development: Changing Contours of Politics and Policy in India*, New Delhi: Routledge.

Manor, James (1998). 'Parties and the Party System', in (ed.), Partha Chatterjee, *State and Politics in India*, New Delhi: Oxford University Press, pp. 111–14.

Marty, Martin E. and R. Scott Appleby (1991). *Fundamentalism Observed, Vol. I*, Chicago: Chicago University Press.

Miller, D. (1987). 'Six Theses on the Question of Religion and Politics in India Today', *Economic and Political Weekly*, 22(30), pp. PE57–63.

Nandy, Ashis (1998). 'The Politics of Secularism and the Recovery of Religious Toleration', in (ed.), Rajeev Bhargava, *Secularism and Its Critics*, New Delhi: Oxford University Press, pp. 321–44.

Nehru, Jawaharlal (1972). *Selected Works of Jawaharlal Nehru, Vol. 3*, in (ed.), S. Gopal, New Delhi: Orient Longman.

Nehru, Jawaharlal (1973). *Selected Works of Jawaharlal Nehru, Vol. 4*, in (ed.), S. Gopal, New Delhi: Orient Longman.

Omvedt, Gail (1990). 'Hinduism and Politics', *Economic and Political Weekly*, 25(14), pp. 723–9.
Omvedt, Gail (2003). *Buddhism in India: Challenging Brahmanism and Caste*, New Delhi: Sage.
Sankhdher, M.M. (1973). *India: Reflections on Indian Politics*, New Delhi: Kumar Brothers.
Savarkar, V.D. (1969). *Hindutva: Who Is a Hindu?* Bombay: SS Savarkar.
Sharma, R.B. (2005). *History of Christian Missions: North Indian Perspective*, New Delhi: Mittal Publications.
Sharma, T.R. (1989). 'Religion and Politics in Modern India: A Historical Overview', in (ed.), Moin Shakir, *Religion, State and Politics in India*, New Delhi: Ajanta Publications.
Verma, Vidhu (2017). 'Secularism in India', in (eds.), Phil Zuckerman and John R. Shook, *Oxford Handbook of Secularism*, Oxford: Oxford University Press.
Weiner, Myron (2006). 'Party Politics and Electoral Behaviour: From Independence to the 1980s', in (eds.), Peter Ronald DeSouza and E. Sridharan, *India's Political Parties*, New Delhi: Sage Publications, pp. 116–54.
Wilkinson, Steven I. (2004). *Votes and Violence, Electoral Competition and Communal Riots in India*, Cambridge: Cambridge University Press.

1
RELIGION, MINORITIES AND THE INDIAN STATE

Himanshu Roy

Contextualizing Muslims as a minority

The minority question (particularly the Muslim question) emerged in post-1857 India. Its social process of emergence, however, had begun from the first decade of the 19th century, when the political sovereignty of the Mughal state was terminated by the British. It had a cascading effect on the traditional elite, particularly on the Muslim elite who were in a dominant position. The failure of the 1857 revolt and the termination of the Mughal dynasty was the final nail in its coffin which had earlier begun to feel the impact of replacement of Persian by English and vernacular languages as the official language of the new colonial state. Combined, these new developments had begun to create fear in them, for the monarchy was the safety box as well as their repository of culture and the centre of patronage. The elite had prided and identified itself with its lineage of Afghans, Persians, Arabs, Turks, Uzbeks, rather than being Indian, whom they had looked down upon.[1] The abolition of dynasty, therefore, deprived them even of emotional support. It made them distraught; the fear of losing their privileges, property and dominance haunted them amidst a Hindu majority bereft of state power.

Under the new colonial state, which had become hostile to Muslims for a while after 1857, there had emerged since the 1870s a section of the pan-Indian political elite that had begun to demand political rights premised on the principles of British liberalism. In other words, it meant to initiate the process of electoral politics and the formation of legislative bodies. Earlier, Rammohan Roy and other civil rights activists had already demanded legalizing civil rights under expanding colonial rule. Such developments had further enhanced their insecurity of being swamped by the Hindu majority; it was felt that a new emerging elite was challenging their dominance. In this socio-political context, we find two Muslim councillors in the Bengal Legislative Council expressing their fear of being a Muslim minority at a legislative-political forum and seeking safety from the colonial state in 1873–74, when Assam was being separated from Bengal as administrative unit.

Colonial state

Subsequently, when the Congress had begun to seek Indian representation in the legislative bodies premised on liberal principle of citizenship as an instrument of political modernity for India based on the British pattern of liberalism, democracy and good governance – which essentially meant focus on individualism and application of rule of law transcending the primordial relations of religion, caste and region – the Muslim elite, particularly a segment led by Sir Syed Ahmad Khan and the Muhammadan Anglo-Oriental Defence Association (M.A.O.) opposed it. It perceived this demand as a medium of Hindu domination and unfit for an unhomogenized population and for an 'unwilling minority'. In fact, they felt 'that the National Congress is strongly opposed and hostile to the political rights of Mohammedans'. In a speech delivered at Lucknow in 1887, Sir Syed Ahmad Khan had remarked they (the National Congress) wanted to copy the English House of Lords and the House of Commons – the elected members were to be like members of the House of Commons and the appointed members like the House of Lords. Now, let us suppose the Viceroy's Council made it this way. And let us suppose first of all that we have universal suffrage, as in the United States, and that everybody, *chamars* and all, have votes. And suppose that all the Mohammedan electors vote for a Mohammedan member and all Hindu electors for a Hindu member, and now count how many votes the Mohammedan members have and how many the Hindus. It is certain the Hindu members will have four times as many because their population is four times as numerous. And now how can the Mohammedan guard his interest? He questioned the audience and then he himself answered it. Let a rule be laid down that half the members are to be Mohammedan and half Hindu and that the Mohammedans and Hindus are each to elect their own men.[2] This questioning and proposal was further supplemented by 'A Mohammedan Manifesto', drafted by the M.A.O. Defence Association, 'dealing with the issue of the representation of Mohammedans on the Legislative Councils and Municipalities'. The Association had sought 'adequate representation . . . for minorities' and had argued that the 'Mohammedan community must be regarded as a political unit with its own interests and sentiments'.[3] Here it must be noted that Sir Syed was the leading member of this Association. In fact, it was at his residence that the initial meeting was held to form this Association and he was one of the members of its rule-drafting committee. In their defence, he had argued that as the first essential for inaugurating any system of government, regulated purely and entirely by the majority of votes (as such systems must necessarily be), it is indispensable that there should be a tangible homogeneity among the voters in point of race, religion, social manners, customs, economic conditions and political traditions of history. In other words the franchise, or the right of voting by the representative system, necessarily presupposes homogeneity, that is similarity among the voters and the population of country in general in regard to the aforementioned points, before the representative system can have any application or be productive of any good.[4] Similarly, their proposal of separate electorate was premised on the logic that Muslims were a separate nation (*Kaum*), which must have equal representatives at par with Hindus. The principle of one man one vote will lead to Hindu domination due to their numerical preponderance and will adversely impact power relations. It was explicitly posited 'that Mahommedans can ever accept Hindus as their rulers' and that they are ready to sacrifice themselves for that glory which they still inherit from their forefathers, who were erstwhile the rulers of India. Sir Syed himself had commented that our nation (Muslims) is of the blood of those who made not only Arabia, but Asia and Europe, to tremble. It is our nation which conquered with its sword the whole of India, although its people were all of one religion.[5] Evidently, they treated Muslims as one homogenized community with shared political traditions of history and Hindus as their subjects. Their subjects becoming their rulers under the representative system of one man one vote haunted them. Inevitably, they opposed it with all their might and counterpoised it with an alternative proposal of a separate electorate. Unfortunately, the British in later years constitutionalized this alternative proposal through the 1909 Act and institutionalized the minority policy. More shockingly, the extremist faction of the Congress accepted this policy of the separate electorate in 1916 at the Lucknow Congress, which was a volte-face of the earlier secular stand of the moderate faction that had consistently opposed the communal electorate of the M.A.O. Defence Association and of the Muslim League. The extremists, in fact, in their zeal to counteract the colonial state after the 1909 Act moved a step ahead: (1) they extended the provision of the separate electorate to a greater number (seven) of provinces, and (2) they empowered the representatives of the Muslim community (three-fourths in number) to block any legislation they felt harmful for the community (clause 4 of section 1 of the Reform Scheme).[6] In other words, they allowed the creation of an Augean stable among them by shutting the doors of reforms on the pretext of safeguarding their cultural-religious identities, which objectively benefited their elite and preserved their feudal cultural desideratum including that of their religious personal laws. In the process, the Congress facilitated the existence of and created the conditions for the emergence of two religious social categories – the minority and majority – which led to the demand for a consolidated Indian Muslim state in the northwest within India[7] (1930), enactment of the Shariat Act (1937) and ultimately the partition of the country. It may be recalled here that prior to the enactment of the Shariat Act, the personal laws of Hindus and Muslims were regional in character and were fused; and it was during the process of their separation (1937) that Iqbal[8] had proposed the formation of 'a free Muslim State' (1937). Derivatively, it was the communal compromise of Lucknow that subsequently catapulted the religious segregation and obstructed the secularization process in the colonial regime and in post-partition India.

Constituent Assembly and minorities

During the transfer of power, the Constituent Assembly classified the minorities in two categories – (1) Anglo-Indians and (2) the rest (Muslims, Christians) – and formulated its policy in two different stages. While the policy for the Anglo-Indians remained consistent in both the stages, the policy for the others changed. In the first stage, which was formulated before the partition, the minorities were granted the (1) social and the (2) political safeguards. In the second stage, which was formulated after the partition, while the political and social safeguards for the Anglo-Indians remained in fact as it was envisaged, the political safeguards for the rest (Muslims, Christians, etc.) were abolished. Only their social safeguards remained intact and were enshrined as their fundamental rights. An analysis of them shall elucidate the logic behind their incorporation, retention or deletion from the constitution. Beginning with the special minority right (fundamental rights) may be the appropriate method.

In the fundamental rights category, there was one specific minority right which was in the nature of education. It was Article 30 that conferred the right to 'establish and administer' their educational institutions. It was different from the rest in terms of certain legal privileges and civil immunities. While the rest of the institutions manifested the philosophy of individualism and of modern citizenship of one category, equal before the law and secular in nature, the minority educational institutions were distinct in terms of being representatives of a 'religious community'. They were separated from the ambit of legal equality to be conferred a special right called their social safeguards to preserve their script, culture, language, religion and so forth. In other words, it meant that they had the right to be separate as a religious community and administer themselves separately in matters of their educational institutions. The specificity was that the educational institutions were (1) free to adopt their own selection procedure for admission of students, (2) free to choose their teachers and members in the management committee/governing body, (3) free not to subject all the appointments and terminations of staff to the prior approval of the Directorate University and (4) free to formulate their religious curriculum. Subsequently, it was added by the 25th Amendment Act, 1971, that in case of compulsory acquisition of properties of minority institutions, they had to be compensated, which was however not applicable in case of the acquisition of property of educational institutions of the majority community. Only one limitation was imposed on it (Article 30) that also evolved through the judicial process after numerous cases came to it for interpretation. It may be stated here that Article 30 itself did not 'lay down any limitations upon the right of a minority to administer its educational institutions'. The judiciary, through numerous interpretations in different cases, evolved a bunch of regulations on the functioning of this Article. It declared that Article 30 was (1) not absolute, that (2) it must be consistent with the national interest and (3) its right to administer educational institutions must not lead to maladministration. It must follow its laid-out procedures and its constitutions, which must be 'for the benefit of the institution' and for the benefit of the minority community. It did not, however, transcend the minority paradigm, and in spite of imposing the regulations on the educational institutions, it juristically recognized them as separate and autonomous bodies and provided them with conditions that facilitated their perpetuation.

Now a question arises as to why the Constituent Assembly did not abolish this special minority right even after the partition, as it had abolished the other minority rights. A plausible, derivative argument may be that the Constituent Assembly might not have perceived this special minority social safeguard as harmful for the polity in the post-1947 period. Instead, it might have perceived it as the safest method to placate the minorities in India even after 1947 without risking the polity. It was more a harmless assurance in the absence of political safeguards which were abolished after the partition. It was also to show that India, despite partition, was a secular state and partition did not deter its character. However, in the process, it proceeded against the views of Gandhi, who had argued that the state should not aid and recognize religious education in educational institutions. It also failed to overcome the fact that the retention of religious personal laws along with the grant of a minority right of education occurred because the Indian bourgeoisie was not in a position to risk the possible antagonism of a large religious population for such 'petty' issues like education and personal laws. Moreover, it was a reflection of the backwardness of a society that treats education and personal laws as low in social ranking in comparison to the importance of executive power of the state. Therefore, the Constituent Assembly abolished the political safeguards for the minorities while retaining the minority education, for the political safeguards were a threat to the executive power of the state. A study of their initial insertion before partition in the constitution and then their subsequent deletion after partition may provide the logic for the changing stance of the members of the Constituent Assembly.

It may be repeated here that Constituent Assembly had appointed an Advisory Committee on 24 January 1947 to submit its reports on minority rights. In the pre-partition Assembly, the Committee formulated its reports as per the then prevailing situation which included (1) the minority right on education and (2) the political rights of minorities. The political rights covered the following points: (1) representation of minorities in legislatures; (2) abolition of a separate electorate; (3) representation of the minorities as per the Convention based on the 1935 Act in the Cabinets of Center and Provinces; (4) the embodiment of an appropriate provision in the constitution for the appointment of minorities in public services; (5) the appointment of special minority officers; and (6) the formation of a Statutory Commission for recommending the steps to be taken for their upliftment. It may be noted here that in spite of recommending such rights, as a matter of general principle, the Committee opposed the weightage for any minority community (CAD Vol. 5: 244), and its recommendations were with utmost restraint. In fact, except for recommending the reservation in legislatures for minorities that, too, after abolishing the separate electorate the Committee did not recommend any kind of reservation for them either in public services or in Cabinets. Instead of reservation, it suggested (1) an inclusion of a directive to the central and provincial governments, an exhortation to them, to pay due regard to the claims of minorities and the (2) the application of the Convention as per the 1935 Act. Both of them were, essentially, to be executive orders in nature rather than mandatory constitutional application (as reservations would have been). In order to make these recommendations applicable, the Committee further recommended the appointment of special minority officers, both at the Centre and in each province, to enquire into the cases if the rights and safeguards of the minorities were violated/infringed upon and to submit the reports to the appropriate legislatures. The Committee was more concerned with their backwardness; and in order to bring them up to the general community, it recommended for the constitution of a statutory commission to investigate the conditions of socially and educationally backward classes, to study the difficulties under which they labour and to recommend to the Union or the unit government, as the case may be, steps that should be taken to eliminate their difficulties and suggest the financial grants that should be given and the conditions that should be prescribed for such grants (CAD Vol. 5: 247). The motive was 'to harmonize the special claims of minorities with the development of a healthy national life'. In fact, the approach was that the state should be so run that minorities should stop feeling oppressed by the mere fact that they are minorities, and that on the contrary they should feel that they have an honourable a part to play in the national life as any other section of the community (CAD Vol. 5: 247).

Keeping in tune with this motive and the general opposition to the principal of weightage to minorities, the committee at the first opportunity after partition debunked its own recommendations and arguments and instead noted that there should be no reservation of seats for religious minorities for their rights and safeguards, which the Committee had earlier suggested. This led 'to a certain degree of separatism' and was contrary 'to the conception of a secular democratic state' (CAD Vol. 8: 311). With the abolition of their political safeguards, only two aspects remained religious, namely the religious personal laws and a fundamental right for minority education. Since personal laws were religious for all communities, the only religious component remained special was the minority education. Both religious rights (personal laws and educational right) remained ingrained in the constitution because, as said earlier, the members of the Assembly were apprehensive in their hearts as to how the people would react once these rights were removed, for these were the inheritances of the past and were difficult to be removed at once. What followed after the partition was at least to remove the political reservations and safeguards which were partly an outcome of reluctant measures and partly out of the initiative taken by a section of the minority themselves (CAD Vol. 8: 329).[9] But this was halfway to the house. The Assembly could not finish its historical agenda of formulating a Common Civil Code and a common secular educational curriculum. Its unfinished agenda, as a result, continues to haunt contemporary India. It left an indelible impression to persist and to perpetuate that religious rights are an integral part of a secular state – which they are not – and that these rights must increase in number and dimension for greater secularization of state. But had these religious rights been part of the secular state, the Assembly would not have abolished the separate electorate or the reservations for religious minorities in legislatures. Since the religious right were not part of the secular state, therefore, Nehru and Patel called these rights 'poison' and 'evils' and considered them as 'one of the main stumbling blocks to the development of a healthy national life'. In fact, they were not in favour of reservation even for the scheduled castes and were relieved when it was conveyed that reservation was intended, initially, only for ten years (CAD Vol. 8: 331).

Post-colonial India

The development of capitalism since 1950 has created two contradictory trends in contemporary India: first, there is a political perpetuation for religious rights as a sacred cornerstone of the secular state; and second, there is a growing secularization of society under the expanding impact of the market. While the first is political in nature, the second is economic. The political perpetuation of the religious rights are more out of electoral politics than for the development of a healthy national life or for allaying the fears of the minorities. No doubt there is one genuine reason for its continuation and that is that the minorities themselves have not come out in the streets against such religious rights, nor have other constituents of society come forward. On the contrary, a section of the elite are demanding more such rights, and they have picked up all such demands for implementation which the Constituent Assembly had proposed for their implementation in its pre-partition sessions and which it had debunked after the partition. It is unquestionable that the majority of the people among the minorities are backward, like the majority of the people among the other constituents, and both need upliftment. It becomes, therefore, all the more necessary to formulate holistic policy measures for the benefit of the poor irrespective of their primordial religious affiliation. The benefit of being minorities with special rights along with the addition of reservation in legislatures, public services or allocation of separate grants and aids are untenable. In fact, minority rights in a secular state are an anachronism. Unfortunately, the possibility of their abolition can only be actuated when the constitutional categorization of majority-minority is abolished, for the very conceptual paradigm of minority and majority creates division among citizens on the basis of religious primordiality, which suits political parties. But ironically, it is argued that for a thorough secularization of society, more special rights should be granted to the minorities as they are more backward in comparison to the majority community. The parameter of the logic is the comparison of economic per capita income between two (minority-majority) religious communities rather than of the secular economic criteria of the class division among the citizens. It is unquestionable that as a religious category, average Muslim families are economically backward in comparison to average Hindu families in terms of per capita income, but then average Hindu families are also backward in comparison to average Christian families in similar terms; and likewise the comparison can be further extended to other religious categories like Parsis, Sikhs and so forth. It can be noted here that an average Muslim family is larger in size than an average Hindu family, which in turn is larger than an average Christian family. In contrast, the percentage of working women in an average Muslim family is far less than that of an average Hindu family, which in turn is slightly less than an average Christian family. As a result, the income per Muslim family is less and expenditure is more. In comparison, an average Hindu family has more income and less expenditure on socially necessary requirements.[10] This leads to the comparative economic backwardness of the religious communities. Analyzed in the light of this background, the logic of extending more special rights to minorities becomes untenable. Moreover, creation of more such special minority/religious rights, instead of the secularization of right, turns the Constituent Assembly on its head, which had secularized the rights to a large extent. The existence of two unsecular rights (the religious civil codes and minority education) had pained Nehru, Patel, Ambedkar and other members of the Advisory Committee and its Sub-Committee.

Minority rights were the creation of the colonial state for its divisive politics. The moderates, akin to the classical liberals of Europe, always opposed this act. Like the French and other revolutionary liberals, which never created a minority-majority paradigm, the moderates argued for modern citizenship and put aside any consideration for primordial affiliations. The subsequent praxis in India, however, not only distorted the interpretations of secularism premised on communal compromise (separate electorate, religious personal laws, minority rights) for realpolitik but also perpetuated it for fruitless argumentative contestation in post-colonial history. Two points are frequently discussed as a result of this perpetuation: it is assumed that (1) minority rights are integral part of secularism and (2) if not secularism, then what? The first assumption has been answered in this chapter and in two other articles[11] of mine, that minority rights are not an integral part of secularism; the second point was answered back in 1948 by M.N. Roy. Roy had argued in an article in *Independent India*[12] that modern secularism in India under capitalism is an integral part of its existence, and it is pointless to argue about it. The important aspect, and the real issue, is what kind of secularism India shall have under the Congress rule.

The fallout of such developments in the last six decades has been the growth and perpetuation of vested interests among minorities. A recent case study of growth of minority educational constitutions in Andhra Pradesh conducted by a citizen group aptly reflects this trend. In Andhra, the percentage of the Muslim population according to the 2001 census is 9.5%. Their number of engineering colleges are 36 (in 2005) – that is 15% in proportion to the population with total seats for 11,000 students. A total of 8,833 Muslim students appeared in the entrance test 2005 (EAMCET 2005) for admission conducted by the Andhra government. Out of this number, 4,000 Muslim students qualified for it. The rest of the 7,000 seats were sold out to other non-Muslim students. Similarly, Christians constitute 1.44% of the population (2001 census), with 22 Christian engineering colleges and 7,430 seats (2005). There were 2,831 Christian students that appeared in the entrance test, 2005 (EAMCET), out of which 2,176 were selected. The rest of the seats (5,254) were sold out to other non-Christian students.[13] These self-evident interests are the root cause for the protection and perpetuation of minority rights which provide minorities legal privileges and civil immunities. However, to be different from the rest on the basis of religion is no pretext for being special. The pretext of social safeguard is essentially a chimera that has turned into a pool of vested interests leading to the emergence of a new segment of non-traditional elite among them. The electoral process has fanned the growth of these segmentary interests under the garb of social justice and secularism.

The antidote to this chimera is the expanding and intensifying secular role of the market which through its economic pressure exerted on citizens' everyday existence secularizes their religious minds. Like the West, where mass Christianity has been secularized and only the priestly Christianity in modified form remains as religion, the religious minds in India are too in the process of becoming citizens. Not only has the market secularized the content of politics as well, as best reflected in the constitution and in its organs. The communal crumbs of the political parties are more a show that results out of their competitive electoral politics. But interestingly, under capitalism even their communal policies no longer remain fruitless. Capitalism sucks the religious minds from the periphery of politics into the whirlpool of democracy and integrates them with the mainstream politics. Or to put it differently, the alienated/rebels are drawn into the expanding bourgeois system from the periphery of the politics and get co-opted into it. It is, however, not to belittle the communal role of the political parties in instigating the religious divide for electoral purposes or for religious bigotry. It may also be simultaneously emphasized that in most cases the communal divide is a manifestation of the political power struggle, economic impoverishment or market domination.[14] Religious hatred purely premised on religious intolerance plays an insignificant role at the grassroots level in its routine existence in normal circumstances. I market has converted the role of religion from being a serious, sacred affair playing a social role in the public sphere to largely a role of social entertainment. In other words, religion has retracted its earlier stand from the public sphere to the private domain, or the serious sacred role of religion has been confined to the private sphere. The standardized attributes of the bourgeois mode have brought the Western features of mass religion to colonial societies trampling the diversities of the feudal mode and of its local production.

Christian minority: Goa and Mizoram

Here we study the electoral politics of two states, Goa and Mizoram, to analyze the actual linkages between religion and politics and the cascading effect of it on politics and society. In both these states, church plays an important and active role in religion, in social development, in the personal domain and in politics. In Goa, the church has existed for centuries and played a pivotal role in providing stability to the colonial state during the Portuguese colonial rule (Roy 2017: 258). It was the ideological state apparatus forging the support base for the state through conversion, education and healthcare. It also mediated between the state and citizens apart from mediating in the personal-family domains of the citizens. In post-colonial Goa, it had picked up the social issues which agitated the local residents, for example damage to the local environment and ecology through Special Economic Zones (SEZ); commercialization of land, hills and forests and their sale to private business; or against minimizing the role of village panchayats in local affairs. This has kept their flock of Catholic Christians together, while being a part of liberal democracy and of electoral politics. This has also facilitated their influence over the local politics through command over the Catholic electorate, party candidates and legislators across parties. The church intervenes and calls the meetings of Christian representatives on issues which it feels are essential and which are obeyed. It also mediates between the electorate and their representatives or between the electorate and the government. In selection of Christian candidates for electoral contests or in blessing them, it plays an equally important role. In the making of the public policy and its execution or prioritizing the issues, the church does play an important role. It does not, however, interfere in the routine functioning of the administration. The church as an institution in its routine functioning interacts with hundreds of citizens, where it cultivates and cements bonds with them, it listens to their grievances and views and it mediates with the political representatives and government to resolve the issues (Roy 2017: 259–61).

Goa has bi-coalitional politics, where one coalitional block is headed by the Bharatiya Janata Party (BJP) and the other is headed by the Congress (Roy 2017: 249–53). In a small legislative assembly of 40 legislators, small parties and independent legislators play an important role in government formation. The growth of the BJP in the state since the 1990s created apprehensions among Catholics, who constitute approximately 25% of the population. The apprehension was of being discriminated against, which was particularly fanned by the church but of late this has substantially dissipated among the electorate due to the presence of Catholic ministers and legislators among the BJP. The church, however, remains wary, as its role with the administration, with the legislators and with the government is becoming marginalized due to the presence of the BJP government. The gradual change in the demography, with the large immigration of non-Goans and emigration of Goans, has also impacted the marginalization of the church.

In contrast to Goa, the church in Mizoram is relatively new. It arrived in the last decade of the 19th century and in the first 30 years (approximately) of its existence, it had converted 50% of the local tribes to Christianity. Today, it has 87% of the Christian population with almost 100% conversion rate of local tribes, resulting in complete destruction of cultural tribal roots. It may here be explained that the tribes had their own mythologies, gods, rituals and social customary practices which were their tribal identities and were an integral part of communitarian existence. Christianity foisted an alien culture and an urban modernity on them which was individualistic and not part of their history. But unconsciously, in its greed for conversion, the church and the missionaries actuated a social process that transformed the tribes irrevocably; it brought in uniformity of one religion, one God, one holy book across different tribes, transcending their customary differences and barriers; in other words, it began a cultural unification process premised on Christianity which also acted as a vanguard, as a tool of the colonial state and the colonial market. And combined, they initiated an urbanization process and a process of modern capitalism which continues to haunt the Mizo society even today.

More than half of the population in Mizoram is urban despite 90% of the territory being hilly and forested, and more than half of the population lives in Aizwal, which is a hill town. The state has a small legislature of 40 members where the Congress and the Mizo National Front have been the ruling party for the maximum number of years in the government. Like Goa, Mizoram has a powerful opposition. Also, like Goa, the church intervenes in all the domains of private and public life of the citizens. It has played a powerful role in stopping the drug and liquor menace and has stopped the insurgency and has kept its re-emergence in abeyance (Roy 2017: 581).

Conclusion

The bourgeois mode of production in India has traversed two different paths in the process of its expansion and existence: the colonial state, for its divisive politics had encouraged and created the majority-minority paradigm and deliberately used the varying social categories against each other to perpetuate the social divisions for self-benefit; and the post-colonial reformist bourgeoisie, which subsequently cast away many features of the divisive paradigm but did not abolish it completely. The unfinished agenda, therefore, continues to linger on even in contemporary times. To circumvent it or to unify the citizenship laws, the state has adopted different methods, sometimes even apparently discriminatory, to co-opt the minorities in a universal bourgeois mode of secularism. Some of its recent acts and attempts have been to (1) establish the Ministry of Minority Affairs; (2) establish a minority commission and financial corporation; (3) broaden the social base of the minorities by incorporating new constituent groups like Kashmiri Pandits, Jains and so fortI(4) modernize madrasas/fortification of burial places; and (5) to register marriages and so forth. All these measures under capitalism facilitate the expansion of the bourgeois laws and encroachment in the affairs of the religious communities and corrode their traditional foundation, or they expand the social base of the minorities to such an extent that they no longer remain a ghettoized block. The bourgeois mode, thus, through gradual social engineering, unlike revolutionary Europe, sucks the traditional communities into its vortex and actuates them towards the process of modernity.

Notes

1 The Muslim elite in India, Ashraf, Sheikh and Syed are approximately 5% of the Muslim population who arrived from outside India over the centuries. The majority (95%) are Arzal and Ajlaf, mainly of Indian subaltern castes who had converted to Islam.
2 The *Aligarh Institute Gazette* on 23 November 1886 had argued that if there is established a parliament for India under the system of one man one vote which the Congress was demanding, 'the Mohomedans would be in permanent minority'. See Shan Muhammad (ed.) (1978). *The Aligarh Movement*, Vol. 3, Meerut: Meenakshi Prakashan, p. 970.

3 See his speech delivered at Lucknow on 28 December 1887 in A.M. Zaidi (ed.) (1975). *From Syed to the Emergence of Jinnah*, Vol. I, New Delhi: Michiko and Panjathan, pp. 39–40.
4 See the minutes of the meeting of the M.A.O. Defence Association and the draft of the 'Manifesto' in Shan Muhammad, *The Aligarh Movement*, pp. 1059, 1063.
5 See his letter to the editor of the *Pioneer* on 22 September 1893 in Shan Muhammad, *The Aligarh Movement*, pp. 1014–15.
6 See his speech in A.M. Zaidi, *From Syed to the Emergence of Jinnah*, p. 43; See *Aligarh Institute Gazette* (editorial), 5 September 1893 in Shan Muhammad, *The Aligarh Movement*, pp. 1122–3.
7 See the Reform Scheme adopted by the Muslim League Reform Committee and The All-India Congress Committee in 1916 in A.M. Zaidi (ed.), *From Syed to the Emergence of Jinnah*, pp. 575–6.
8 In his presidential address (1930), Iqbal had only argued for consolidation of numerous Muslim majority provinces of Northwest India into one province which was earlier rejected by the Nehru Committee on the ground of being very unwieldy in size; see C.M. Naim (ed.) (1979). *Iqbal, Jinnah and Pakistan: The Vision and the Reality*, New York: Syracuse University, pp. 195–6.
9 See the speech of Nehru in the Constituent Assembly on 26 May 1949.
10 See Role of Religion in Fertility Decline – The Case of Indian Muslims (2005). *Economic and Political Weekly*, 29 January; Hindu-Muslim Fertility Differentials (2005). *Economic and Political Weekly*, 29 January.
11 See Himanshu Roy (2006). 'Western Secularism and Colonial Legacy in India', *Economic and Political Weekly*, vol. 41, January; Bombay and The Dharma and Relegere (2005), *Frontier*, Annual Number, Calcutta.
12 M.N. Roy (1948). 'The Secular State', *Independent India*, 1 August.
13 This was stated by T.H. Choudhury, former CMD of VSNL in a Seminar on Minorities and Minority Rights, held at National Museum Auditorium, New Delhi, on 19 March 2006.
14 Asghar Ali Engineer in a series of case studies of communal riots has illustrated these facts. See his *Communal Riots in Post-Independence India* (ed.), 2nd ed., Hyderabad: Sangam Books, 1991.

References

Constituent Assembly Debates (CAD). Lok Sabha Secretariat, Government of India.
Engineer, Asghar Ali (1991). *Communal Riots in Post-Independence India*, 2nd ed., Hyderabad: Sangam Books.
Muhammad, Shan (1978). *The Aligarh Movement*, Vol. 3, Meerut: Meenakshi Prakashan.
Naim, C.M. (1979). *Iqbal, Jinnah and Pakistan: The Vision and the Reality*, New York: Syracuse University, pp. 195–6.
Roy, Himanshu (2005). 'The Dharma and Relegere', *Frontier*, Annual Number, Calcutta.
Roy, Himanshu (2006). 'Western Secularism and Colonial Legacy in India', *Economic and Political Weekly*, 41(2), pp. 158–65.
Roy, Himanshu (2017). *State Politics in India*, New Delhi: Primus.
Zaidi, A.M. (1975). *From Syed to the Emergence of Jinnah*, Vol. I, New Delhi: Michiko and Panjathan, pp. 39–40.

2
POLITICS OF RELIGIOUS POLARIZATION IN INDIA

Insights from riots in Gujarat (2002), Kandhamal (2008) and Muzaffarnagar (2013)

Mujibur Rehman

Ever since Narendra Modi's rise in Indian politics, the word 'polarization' has been employed with far greater frequency in popular, political and academic discourse. The Bharatiya Janata Party's deliberate strategy of polarization has been attributed to its unprecedented electoral success since 2014.[1] The BJP's key objective has been to consolidate the foundation for a majoritarian polity by creating political conditions triggered by the politics of polarization. Like other religious right, the Hindu right is desperate to weave a broader Hindu identity necessary for a majoritarian polity.[2] But the autonomous forms acquired by that politics of Dalits and Other Backward Castes (OBCs) has posed a new challenge to the Hindu right's weaving strategy because it deems necessary to re-weave these increasingly consolidated caste blocks by calling for their dilution into larger Hindu self.[3] Kancha Ilaiah's classic, *Why I Am Not a Hindu*, perhaps articulates the distinct autonomy that the Dalit self is seeking in modern India, often based on the conventional anti-Hindu identity (Ilaiah 2005). The strategy of dilution and re-weaving of its distinct caste groups has motivated the Hindu right to seek out a formidable Other in the Indian Muslim identity, among others. In its political project of the construction of the other from the Muslim self, the Hindu right draws heavily from a distorted historical construction of Muslim identity.[4] In the political and electoral domain, the process of polarization contributes to this enterprise.

Thus polarization could be seen as an attempt to assert the Hindu identity by playing up its victimhood in multiple ways. One such way is the representation of the Muslim kings such as Aurangzeb, Babar or Tipu Sultan as the villains of history while glorifying Hindu kings such as Shivaji or Rana Pratap. According to this narrative of polarization, Muslims are presented as aliens, violent people with ulterior motives, among others, with the clandestine objective to transform India's demography by making Hindu an insignificant minority. Theoretical arguments for such a construction of the Hindu identity are based on a set of imaginary fears with selective stories of atrocities such as destruction of Hindu temples, the rape of Hindu women and other forms of atrocities (Sharma 2015). As Mohammed Mujeeb has convincingly argued in his book, *Indian Muslims*, the so-called Muslim rule was indeed a rule of a handful of Muslim families who often bayed for each other's blood (Mujeeb 2003). This is far from any concerns or representations of the community in India that is widely depicted in major writings of the Hindu right movement – founding thinkers such as Savarkar, Gowalkar, Deendayal Upadhyay and so forth. The Modi government (since 2014) has become an active patron of the publication and distributions of their writings, a major source of propaganda material for politics of polarization. A majority of prominent names of the Hindu right's founding thinkers are drawn from India's upper-caste background, a minority among the Hindus. The Hindutva agenda, therefore, is an ideological formulation of a small minority paraded as a majoritarian agenda. Hence what appears to be a majoritarian agenda is indeed a minority agenda.

On the concept and forms of polarization

The word 'polarization' has been deployed to describe a distinct brand of politics in various parts of the world for quite some time now. However, what is hard to trace is its first use, either in popular or academic discourse in India. James Wilson in his Tanner Lecture on Human Values at Harvard University in 2005 defined polarization in American context as follows:

> By polarization I mean an intense commitment to a candidate, culture, or ideology that sets one group apart from people in rival group. That commitment is revealed when a losing candidate is regarded not simply wrong but as corrupt or wicked, when one culture is seen morally superior or every other one, or when one set of beliefs is thought to be entirely correct – and a rival set wholly wrong.

Polarization so defined was first used by Richard Hofstader in his book, *The Paranoid Style in American Politics* (1965). Hofstader meant not just partisanship or disagreement. What he really meant is that a belief that the other side was managed by a secret conspiracy seemingly uses devious means to obtain complete control (Hofstader 2008). In the US context, polarization has been mainly around race, albeit religion has become a marker in recent years – mainly after 9/11, and more specifically during the Trump presidency.[5] Owing to this similarity about the rise of polarization in both the Indian and US societies, scholars have compared Modi and Trump. According to Martha Nussbaum and Zoya Hasan (2017),

> After the recent meeting between Donald Trump and Narendra Modi, we would all be well advised to pause and reflect about these two men, so similar and yet so different. Both our countries have elected controversial populist strongmen who rode a wave of public anger to great and, to many, alarming, power. As scholars who study political systems both descriptively and

normatively, we have long thought that cross-country comparisons yield insight. Donald Trump and Narendra Modi exemplify different types of the populist strong-man leader, with different potential consequences for democracy's future. Trump and Modi both rose to power as the result of popular rage against longstanding political elites. Corruption, insider politicking, and common people's perceived lack of access to power were prominent themes in both campaigns. Both campaigns fed, as well, on the real distress of the have-nots in our respective societies.

Nonetheless, the Hindu right's politics of religious polarization, I would suggest, could be broadly witnessed in three particular forms. First, there is polarization witnessed in the form of political rhetoric say, for instance, Narendra Modi's statement on 10 December 2017, 'Pakistan wants Ahmed Patel as Gujarat Chief Minister made during the Gujarat Assembly Election campaign in 2017';[6] or Amit Shah's statement on 29 October 2015, 'if BJP loses election in Bihar, crackers will go off in Pakistan during the Bihar election campaign';[7] or Varun Gandhi's statements or hate speech during the Pilibhit campaign in 2009 election campaign where he said, 'If any one raises hand towards Hindus, Varun Gandhi would cut those hands',[8] or 'This is not just a pair of hands. These are hands of Lotus. It would behead Muslims', or 'Hindu Brothers Get United'. Also, Modi government Minister Giriraj Singh, 'if Rastriya Janata Dal (RJD) wins, Araria would become the hub of terrorism on March 15, 2018'.[9] These are a few instances that shows how religious polarization emanates as a political rhetoric.

Second, there is religious polarization as a source of social tension and hostility without leading to large-scale riot. Sudha Pai and Sajjan Kumar describe it as 'institutionalized everyday communalism' (Pai and Kumar 2018). According to them,

> The central feature of this everyday communalism in 2000s is that rather than instigating major and violent state wide riots. The BJP-RSS has attempted to create and sustain constant, low key communal tension. This together with frequent, small, low intensity incidents out of petty everyday issues that institutionalize communalism at the grass roots, keep the 'pot boiling'.
> *(Pai and Kumar 2018: 3)*

Third, religious polarization also plays an active role in engineering major riots and helps pursue the majoritarian project in the post-riot scenarios. Some examples of this form of polarization could be the riots in Gujarat in 2002, Kandhamal in 2008 or Muzaffarnagar in 2013. They contribute to this larger strategy of politics of religious polarization. No doubt, a deep and close interconnection in these three particular forms of politics of religious polarization, driven by a single objective to present religious minorities (such as Muslims and Christians) as the existential threat to the Hindu identity, has been working. However, it is hard to establish a sequence in the operational strategy of the Hindu right. It would only be safe to say each of these forms mutually feeds each other.

While various forms of politics of religious polarization were tried out at different points of time in colonial and post-colonial India, the one during the Ayodhya movement during the 1980s and early 1990s was extremely well organized. It created a political condition that catapulted the BJP into the most dominant political and electoral force in modern India today. One could say that the organized underground campaign, and low intensity violence and major riots, are the most obvious forms of politics of religious polarization operating in India today.

Research on polarization

Some research on polarization has offered crucial insight into this question. In the Indian context, a report appeared in 2014 in the *Economic Times* titled 'BJP Gains after Every Riot, Says the Yale Study',[10] which cited a research article published by a group of young political scientists. The paper argued that political polarization helps the BJP. The title of the research paper is 'Do Parties Matter for Ethnic Violence? Evidence from India' and was jointly authored by Gareth Nellis, Michael Weaver and Steven Rosenzweig.[11] Indeed, the central argument of this research was not whether polarization helps the BJP or not. What drove the research was the following question: Does the partisan identity of elected officials matter for local ethnic conflict? In the Indian context, the question could be reformulated as whether the election of communal politicians enhances the prospect of riots. They study the effect of local-level incumbency of the Congress candidates on Hindu-Muslim riot in India districts from 1962 to 2000. They find that partisanship in general and Congress incumbency has an effect on local ethnic conflict.

According to the study, had Congress lost close elections in the data set – compared to its actual performance – India would have experienced 11% more Hindu-Muslim riots and 46% more riot casualties. Furthermore, riots led to the decrease of vote share and increase of vote share of ethno-religious rivals in subsequent elections, according to this study.

One of the ways we could make sense of this discussion is by asking if the Congress party was perceived as secular. A clear picture of what was unfolding in India since 1947 on communalism or riots or polarization cannot emerge by merely blaming the BJP that came into existence in 1980. What about the pre-BJP era of Indian politics? On the Congress Party's secular credentials there are two rival interpretations: one was by Steve Wilkinson (2004) and other by Ashutosh Varshney (2003). Steve Wilkinson has argued that despite the Congress Party's secular claims, in one time or another, its politicians have participated or fomented or prevented, depending on its political advantage (Wilkinson 2004). On the other hand, Varshney (2003) has argued that the communal harmony in Congress held districts depending on what is the ideological view of the local wings of the Congress Party. In other words, the Congress cannot be certified to be a secular organization from top to bottom because the party had communal leadership at different levels of its organizations. Interestingly, these authors have argued that despite dubious secular credentials, the Congress Party has been able to prevent riots in most cases. What is crucial to note here is that this research does show such polarization does impact electoral outcomes and it favours the Hindu right.

Recent research by Amrita Basu (2016) sheds insights into the relationship between polarization and the Hindu right – specifically into the changing pattern of India's recurrent anti-minority (particularly anti-Muslim) violence. Intrigued by the uneven nature of anti-Muslim violence in India, she embarked on a research project aimed at examining the variation in the violence. Between 1980 to 2008, she noted anti-Muslim violence was limited in Himachal Pradesh and extensive in Gujarat; furthermore, it was not just the extent but timing also varied in Indian states. For instance, there was more violence in the early 1990s in Uttar Pradesh than in 2002 and the trend was just the opposite in Gujarat. She studied anti-minority violence four BJP-ruled states – Rajasthan, Himachal Pradesh, Uttar Pradesh, and Gujarat – to explore the varied patterns of violence, specifically the relationships between the political party, movement and state and national governments. Variations in these relationships influence the magnitude, spatial dimensions, timing and long-term consequences of violence, according to her. The extent of violence, she contends, depends on the nature of ties between the party, movement and the state in the end.

Amrita Basu (2016) has sought to demonstrate that the closer the ties, the worse is the nature of violence. Her line of inquiry included religion, caste and class alignment. The regions in which dominant castes and classes are politically powerful than lower castes and classes, she argues, are more supportive to the Hindu nationalist agenda. Based on extensive fieldwork in various regions of India – particularly in Gujarat, Haryana, Himachal Pradesh and Uttar Pradesh – she explains how the party movement creates new conditions for the violence to grow.

On violence against Muslims, it becomes extensive when the BJP as national ruling party approves the actions of various organizations such as RSS, VHP and other Hindu militant organizations often described as fringe groups. Scholars and journalists who work on these issues have often found that the members of these so-called fringe groups are often active or former members of various Hindu right-wing organizations. The possibility of anti-Muslim violence is also determined by the resistance that it receives from lower castes and classes. These Hindu nationalist forces are most aligned and most militant, according to Amrita Basu, where upper castes and classes fully back up the BJP and the lower caste parties and movements are weak. From the point of view of politics of religious polarization, it is plausible to argue that this politics becomes more effective for the Hindu right and causes optimal damage when party, movement and government are aligned, creating the most favourable conditions for the politics of polarization to flourish.

We might argue that the riots could be an outcome of sustained religious polarization and its impact could continue even after the riot. The post-riot situation could create further conditions for religious polarization, and it could be seen, among others, in the withdrawal of the community to itself to ghettoization. In the political realm, it could contribute to the ideological character of various political structures. For instance, it could take a complete shift to Hindutva polity and transform the governance structure from secular to a saffron system. In the introduction to my volume, *Rise of Saffron Power* (2018), I presented some analysis of how it could happen. Also, I wrote,

> The sharpening of these majoritarian tendencies would grow in both rhetoric and practice without bringing any change to the Constitution and the term secular remining intact. Moreover, the BJP's electoral dominance could contribute to the saffronization of other parties, as they could emulate the BJP's electoral strategies. This is evident in the workings of some of the non-Hindutva political parties. Such development would also aggravate an already fragile polity.
>
> *(Rehman 2018)*

Riots and politics of religious polarization

I would like to reflect on three particular riots and consequently examine how they have contributed to the polity and politics of religious polarization. The three riots are Gujarat (2002), Kandhamal (2008) and Muzaffarnagar (2013). Each of them contributed to the religious polarization in their respective states, and some of them had national reverberations. Among these cases there were different approaches applied to address the post-riot situations. In none of them was the riot alone able to empower the BJP as a ruling party, which is why it cannot be argued that the party could engineer a riot which should be adequate to polarize the voters and catapult the party into victory. Such a reasoning could be deeply over-simplified. In February 2016, a Bharatiya Janata Party (BJP) executive committee member, Umesh Malik, publicly attributed the BJP's massive victory and Prime Minister Narendra Modi in Uttar Pradesh to the Muzaffarnagar riots. This was said in the presence of Central Minister Sanjeev Balyan, also a local MP and an accused in the 2013 violence. The headline in the *Indian Express* quoted Malik as saying, '"Embers from Muzaffarnagar made Narendra Modi PM", Says BJP Leader'.[12] According to Malik, the riot was all planned in the jail where Mr. Balyan was detained as a preventive measure. The parties who pursue this strategy do see political benefits, and the Congress and the BJP are no exceptions.

I would argue that each of these riot cases creates an opportunity to deepen the politics of religious polarization. We come across very distinct trends in each case. In case of Gujarat and Uttar Pradesh, the BJP emerges as the ruling party, but not in Odisha. At the time Kandhamal riots erupted in 2008, the BJP was a coalition partner and had 32 seats with a vote share of 17.11% in the 2004 Assembly election prior to riot. The riot caused a rift between the BJP and Biju Janata Dal (BJD), leading to the collapse of the coalition arrangement (Rehman 2016). In the 2009 election held after the riot, the BJP managed to win only six seats and secure 15.11% of the votes, resulting in a significant decline of seats and also some decline in vote share. In 2009, the BJP's performance was even worse than what it had been in 1995. The details of BJP's seats and vote share in Odisha has been 1995 (9/7.88%);

2000 (38/18.20%); 2004 (32/(17.11%); 2009 (6/15.11%); 2014 (10/17.99%). But riots of these kinds could present an opportunity to deepen the politics of religious polarization. Both the cases of Gujarat in 2002 and Muzaffarnagar in 2013 are also seen as attempts to 'defang the Muslim community', or something often expressed as an attempt to 'teach Muslims a lesson' kind of experiment.

In the case of Gujarat, there was barely any attempt to bring reconciliation between the state and the victims, and between the majority and minority communities. It could be argued that Gujarat state contributed to the deepening of polarization, and the election that followed was considered by scholars as one of the most polarized state elections in Indian history. While Modi returned to power in successive elections and prepared himself to be Indian prime minister, it would not be entirely convincing to argue that the Gujarat riot in 2002 alone contributed to his victory in each of the ensuing elections. I would rather argue that polarization in the face of a very weak, reluctant opposition helped Mr. Modi seal his successive victory. It is instructive to note here that future electoral benefits arising out of the politics of polarization depends on how much resistance the party faces. The seats and vote shares of the BJP are as follows: 1990 (67/26.69%); 1995 (121/42.51%); 1998 (117/44.81%); 2002 (127/49.85%); 2007 (117/49.12%); 2012 (115/47.85%); 2017 (99/49.10%) (and in the parliamentary election of 2014 (26/60.11%)).

But Modi's decision not to visit the relief camps or not to rebuild the shrines destroyed during violence could be seen as efforts to deepen the politics of religious polarization. Such politics of religious polarization takes different shapes and forms. For instance, according to surveys, there was a huge rise of religiosity in Gujarat during this period:

> The rise of religiosity is to some extent validated by the fact that Gujarat recorded construction of highest number places of religious worships during the 1991–2000 Census, which beat the national decennial average. In towns and cities of Gujarat, one often sees either renovation of old, hitherto neglected, dilapidated religious structures like cremation places, graveyards of Muslims and Christians, shrines, temples, majars.
>
> *(Patel: 168 in Shastri and Yadav, Oxford 2009)*

In Kandhamal in Odisha, the religious polarization that followed after the anti-Christian violence in 2008 was limited to few districts – particularly the regions where Christians or tribal Christians were living. Its political impact remained limited so far as its electoral implications are concerned. The ruling BJD decision to end its alliance with the BJP and fight the election of 2009 alone and return to power fails to support the argument that only by engineering a riot a party could generate adequate polarization for electoral victory. While BJP managed to wrest power in the region, the Kandhamal violence did not contribute to its expansion. Compared to Gujarat, there was more organized resistance to the politics of polarization in Odisha that perhaps contributed to checkmate the BJP.

The Muzaffarnagar violence in 2013 has been seen as a more convincing case of politics of religious polarization. Scholars have argued that the riot did disturb long-established caste alliances in favour of Hindutva politics and contributed to the victory of the BJP (Pai and Kumar 2018). In the case of Uttar Pradesh, an interesting connection between the politics of religious polarization and electoral outcomes could be established. During the Ayodhya movement, the BJP saw a significant rise in its electoral power. There was a systematic rise between 1989 to 1996 with minor fluctuations in different elections in Uttar Pradesh. For instance, in 1989, it had 57 seats (11.61%), which in 1991 became 221 (31.45%) and in 1993 became 177 (33.30%). In 1996, the BJP had 174 seats (32.52%), but then there was a remarkable decline in 2002, when the BJP won only 88 seats (20.08%); by 2007, the BJP won only 51 seats (16.97%), which is less than the seats in 1989, although the vote share is greater. In 2012, the BJP won only 47 seats with 15.00%, but in 2014 in the parliamentary election the vote share was 42.65% with 71 seats and in 2017, the vote share was 39.67% with 312 seats.

Conclusion

While in the case of Gujarat, the state's complicity in deepening religious polarization was far greater than in Uttar Pradesh or Odisha, though in all cases the state contributed to varying degrees. Odisha state under Naveen Patnaik perhaps played a relatively more positive role in addressing the issues of victims and restoring normalcy as opposed to Uttar Pradesh and Gujarat. All three states fell short of expectations. With these conditions, one could argue that each of these states not only undermined secular polity in their respective domain but they also contributed to creating conditions for a post-secular polity, and pushing the polity towards the saffron system. Among all of these, the Gujarat has been a more effective case of the saffron system, which has clearly purged minorities from sharing the power structure. I analyzed this in an op-ed in the *Hindu* thusly:

> Though the BJP has a few symbolic Muslim faces in New Delhi, its decision not to field Muslim candidates in Uttar Pradesh in 2014 and 2017, and in Gujarat in 2017, and now in Karnataka only confirms that this exclusion is indeed a carefully crafted campaign strategy. In December 2017, in Gujarat, the Vijay Rupani-led BJP government was sworn in with no Muslims in its ranks. U.P.'s BJP government has the same story, and it will be so in Karnataka too if the BJP manages to form the government. When India's largest political party pursues such a strategy and finds it electorally rewarding, it may be emulated by other political parties. What does this exclusion from legislatures imply for the Indian polity or for Muslims? One implication is that Muslims will not be part of the political elites and consequently command their own political voice. Such a vision of denial has been ingrained in the Hindutva narrative and in the writings of its founding fathers. Indeed, it is a necessary process for any majoritarian polity that hopes to force minorities to live according to its terms.[13]

It seems Uttar Pradesh is following it up with considerable speed, and although in Odisha the condition is relatively less hospitable for this at this point, it faces serious competition from the BJP.

Acknowledgement

I am grateful to Dwaipayan Bhattacharya for his comments on the chapter.

Notes

1 Some would argue – and rightly so – the rise of the BJP in the 1980s is also owing to its strategy of polarization employed during the Ayodhya movement; see Jaffrelot (1998).
2 On the idea of majoritarian polity, some of the important works would include Sharma (2015), Sud (2012), Anderson and Damle (1987), Anderson and Damle (2018), and Rehman (2018).
3 These autonomous forms have taken the shape of party formations such as Bahujan Samaj Party (BSP) and also various forms of movements in various parts of India championing the cause exclusively of Dalits. See Pai (2013).
4 On the construction of the other, see Mujibur Rehman (2017).
5 For an interesting take on the Trump presidency and its inner contradictions, see Cohen (2019).
6 'Why Does Pakistan Want to Make Ahmed Patel Gujarat CM, Asks Modi', *Hindu Business Line*, 10 December 2017. Retrieved 24 December 2018 from www.thehindubusinessline.com.
7 ' If BJP Looses Election, Cracker Will Go Off in Pakistan: Amit Shah', *Economic Times*, October 2015. Retrieved 24 December 2018 from www.theeconomictimes.indiatimes.com.
8 See the report, 'Maneka Gandhi Refuses to Comment on Son Varun', *Hindustan Times*, 17 March 2009. Retrieved 24 December 2018 from www.thehindustantimes.com.
9 'Araria Would Turn into a Terror Hub, Says Union Minister Giriraj Singh', *Times of India*, 16 March 2018. Retrieved 24 December 2018 from www.timesofindia.com.
10 *Economic Times*, 5 December 2014. Gareth Nellis, Michael Weaver, and Steven C. Rosenzweig (2016), 'Do Parties Matter for Ethnic Violence? Evidence From India', *Quarterly Journal of Political Science*, 11(3), pp. 249–77.
11 It was published in the *Quarterly Journal of Political Science* (QJPS) and first was presented at the 2015 American Political Science Association.
12 www.indianexpress.com, 4 February 2016. Retrieved 24 December 2018.
13 'Quests of Representations', *Hindu*, 19 May 2018. Retrieved December 2018.

References

Anderson, Walter and Sidharth Damle (1987). *Brotherhood in Saffron*, New York: Westview Press.
Anderson, Walter and Sidharth Damle (2018). *RSS: A View From India*, New Delhi: Viking.
Basu, Amrita (2016). *Violent Conjectures in Democratic India*, New Delhi: Cambridge University Press.
Cohen, Eliot A. (2019, January–February). 'America's Long Goodbye', *Foreign Affairs*. Retrieved April 15, 2019, from www.foreignaffiars.com.
Hofstader, Richard (2008). *American Style of Paranoid Politics*, New York: Vintage.
Ilaiah, Kancha (2005). *Why I am Not a Hindu: A Sudra Critique of Hindu Philosophy, Culture, and Political Economy*, New Delhi: Samaya, Sage Publications.

Jaffrelot, Christophe (1998). *The Hindu Nationalist Movement*, New York: Columbia University Press.
Mujeeb, Mohammad (2003). *Indian Muslims*, New Delhi: Munshiram Manohar Lal Publishers.
Nussbaum, Martha and Zoya Hasan (2017, July 24). 'India and US: Spot the Difference', *Indian Express*. Retrieved May 19, 2019.
Pai, Sudha (2013). *Dalit Assertion: A Short Introduction*, New Delhi: Oxford University Press.
Pai, Sudha and Sajjan Kumar (2018). *Everyday Communalism: Riots in Contemporary Uttar Pradesh*, New Delhi: Oxford University Press.
Rehman, Mujibur (2016). *Communalism in Postcolonial India: Changing Contours*, New Delhi: Routledge.
Rehman, Mujibur (2017). *Reading the Past, Rewriting the Present*, Seminar, No. 698.
Rehman, Mujibur (2018). *Rise of Saffron Power: Reflections in Indian Politics*, New Delhi: Routledge.
Sharma, Jyoti (2015). *Hindutva: Exploring the Idea of Hindu Nationalism*, New Delhi: Harper Collins.
Shastri, Sandeep and Yogendra Yadav (2009). *Electoral Politics in India: Lok Sabha Elections in 2004 and Beyond*, New Delhi: Oxford University Press.
Sud, Nikita (2012). *Liberalization, Hindu Nationalism and the State: A Biography of Gujarat*, New Delhi: Oxford University Press.
Varshney, Ashutosh (2003). *Ethnic Conflict and Civic Life: Hindus and Muslims in India*, New Haven: Yale University Press.
Wilkinson, Steve (2004). *Votes and Violence*, Cambridge: Cambridge University Press.

3
SIKH POLITICS IN PUNJAB
Shiromani Akali Dal

Ashutosh Kumar and Hardeep Kaur

This chapter provides an overview of Sikh politics in Punjab as it has evolved from the vantage point of Shiromani Akali Dal (SAD), which is one of the oldest surviving state parties in India along with the National Conference and DMK.[1] It argues that the SAD has been instrumental in effecting the paradigmatic changes and development in state politics. This would more be the case after state underwent territorial remapping, with religion playing a major role both times. Significantly, though not being a winnable party due to the minority status of the Sikhs in communally volatile pre-partition Punjab, the party even then had a considerable political support base among the rural Sikh community and had committed cadres. After the reorganization of Punjab on a linguistic basis in 1966, the SAD has been the only other winnable party apart from the Congress, especially with the support of the other two important Sikh institutions, Shiromani Gurdwara Parbandhak Committee (SGPC) and the Akal Takht. As a 'Panthic' party, it has always claimed to be the custodian of the Sikh community's religious and cultural interests, not only its political interests, whenever perceived to be under threat in the state or elsewhere.

This chapter is structured broadly into three parts. In the first part, the chapter takes up a discussion about making the Sikhs into a modern political community, narrating political developments that led to the formation of the three Sikh bodies, namely the SAD, SGPC and the Akal Takht, which formed both the religious and political agendas that shaped in a significant way the Sikh politics in colonial Punjab. The second part of the chapter refers to the emergence of the SAD as an electoral party in post-colonial India having a definitive political agenda. The third part refers to the post-militancy period, which has been witness to a perceptible change in the party in both ideological and organizational terms. It argues how, post-militancy, the party that was once an ideological party that emanated out of an ethnic movement has now sought to transform itself as an electoralist/catch-all party seeking support on the basis of development and governance.

Making of the Sikhs as a political community

The Sikh political life began with the sixth Sikh Guru Hargobind linking religion and politics by wearing two swords (Miri and Piri). While the former symbolized spiritual power, the latter referred to temporal power. The process culminated with the tenth Guru Gobind Singh, who established the 'Khalsa Panth' by mandating all Sikhs to carry weapons, invoking the image of 'saint-soldiers' (Singh 2007: 557). The tenth Guru established the Akal Takht (seat of the immortal) in front of Sri Harmandir Sahib in 1666. Wielding supreme authority in religious matters, it also became the sacred space for political assemblage of the community. This way the Sikh tradition of linking politics with religion was established (Chima 2018). Distinctiveness of Sikh identity was further consolidated as the tenth Guru established Khalsa, the martial order of the Sikhs, on 30 March 1699, the Baisakhi day. Sikhs were collectively designated as belonging to the Khalsa Panth. Khalsas belonged to Waheguru, the Supreme Lord. Ordained to carry the five symbols, Sikhs were to reject all forms of caste- and gender-based discrimination and follow a prescribed/codified way of life as per the Sikh Rehat Maryada. Sikhs were to be moral and embody virtues like humbleness, truthfulness, enlightenment, valour, justice, sacrifices, service and fraternity. The disciples were to protect the religious places and guard the helpless with all their might (Mukherjee 1985: 108; Singh 1993: 211). For enabling the community, the tenth Guru also formed the Khalsa army. In his lifetime, he conferred guruship upon the Adi Granth (Primal Scripture), popularly referred as Guru Granth Sahib (Singh, Pashaura 2014: 125; Singh, Ajit 2005: 32).[2] The Guru is also credited with establishing the institution of Panj Pyare, any five initiated Sikhs reputed to be strictly following the Rehat Maryada (Sikh discipline/code of conduct) to provide a collective leadership.[3] As Sikhism does not approve of a caste system, Panj Pyares were to come from different castes (Singh and Fenech 2014: 1; Dilgeer 1978: 43).[4]

The Sikhs witnessed the height of their political power when Maharaja Ranjit Singh (Sarkar Khalsaji) established an empire, bringing reality to the tenth Guru prediction about Raj Karega Khalsa. After annexation of the Sikh kingdom to the British in 1849, however, the community defined by the trinity of 'Guru, Granth, and Gurdwara' perceived existential crisis as it found its distinct identity being subsumed by the rise of Hindu Mahasabha and Arya Samaj in the state. Arya Samaj had launched the Shuddhi movement, which aimed to bring Sikhs and Christians back to the Hindu fold.

The community was also concerned with the way Sikh gurdwaras were being managed by mahants who disregarded Sikh traditions (keeping idols in the premises) and were siphoning off the gurdwaras' properties for their own benefits (Narang 2014: 339). The late 19th and the early 20th centuries witnessed incidents of conversion of the Sikhs to Christianity under the influence of the Christian missionaries in the Doaba region. Mission schools were established in whole of Punjab, 'whose pedagogic ethos was coloured by a proselytizing agenda' (Mandair 2014: 73).

In 1873, the Singh Sabha came into existence under the leadership of Thakur Singh Sandhanwalia along with Giani Gian Singh and Khem Singh Bedi to protect and resurrect the distinctive religious identity and traditional values of the Sikhs (Dilgeer 1978: 45). Subsequently, Singh Sabhas were established in other cities in different parts of India and abroad. In 1879, Gurmukh Singh, a college teacher by profession, along with Giani Ditt Singh, editor of *Khalsa Akhbar*, founded the 'Lahore Singh Sabha', which took it upon itself to issue general directions regarding the religious matters concerning the Sikh community. Intellectuals from the community, mostly having Western education and urban roots, gave a call to 'a return to an original Sikh consciousness' that was to be based on the distinctive vision of the Gurus as envisaged in the Khalsa tradition. The proponents of this school of thought known as Tat Khalsa with their influential writings attempted 'a specifically Sikh discourse' that would lead to 'the erasure of extraneous cultural influences', especially a 'clean break from the priestly tradition of Hinduism' to invoke the Sikh orthodoxy (Mandair 2014: 74).

Khalsa College was established in Amritsar in 1892, which contributed to the creation of cultural and political awareness among the Sikhs. As a part of the ongoing Akali Lehar, the Singh Sabhas also opened a number of schools and colleges with the word 'Khalsa' prefixed to their names. It was during this period, facing an increasingly communalized Punjab that had much larger Muslim and Hindu communities, that different Singh Sabhas that had spread all over Punjab and beyond came together, forming Chief Khalsa Diwan (CKD) in 1902 to promote the study of Guru Granth Sahib and to adjudicate over the social and religious matters of the Khalsa Panth (Tutleja 1984: 9; Mandair 2014: 77). For the next two decades till the formation of the SAD, it served as the representative body of the Sikhs, striving to build up a consistent image of Sikh identity as had been attempted by the Tat Khalsa movement. The CKD launched two newspapers, *Khalsa Samachar* and *Khalsa Advocate*, for the purpose of wider propagation of its ideas.

The British, however, wary of growing feeling of nationalism among the community, reconstructed the management of Khalsa College, raising Sikh resentment.[5] In 1913, a serious conflict had arisen between the colonial regime and the Sikhs over the Gurdwara Rakab Ganj issue, as the government dismantled a part of the wall of the gurdwara to construct a link road to the vice-regal lodge (Grewal 1996: 29). The CKD aimed to unify the Sikh community by prescribing a definitive way of life and also by bringing together all the Singh Sabhas as well as different castes, including the lower-caste Sikhs and also Sahajdhari (clean shaven), by emphasizing the principle of equality by birth. One of the aims behind the unifying effort was to demand a reserved electorate of 30% of all seats for the Sikh community in the legislative bodies of Punjab. The demand was not met by the colonial regime, citing the lesser demographic proportion of the community. What also added to the dissatisfaction among the community was the Lucknow Pact concluded in 1916 between the Congress and the Muslim League, which was criticized for ignoring the interests of the Sikhs. The influence of the CKD dwindled due to its failure to get the community demands accepted and also its perceived loyalty to the empire[6] and over-reliance on the constitutional process. At this time, a new political formation called the Central Sikh League (CSL) was established on 29 December 1919. The League was committed to the agenda of Tat Khalsa established by the Singh Sabhas to unify all the Sikh institutions including the important gurdwaras. Besides establishing a standardized form of the community identity and code of conduct to be followed by all the Sikhs, the CSL wanted the administration of gurdwaras, especially the Golden Temple, to be passed on to a representative body of the Sikhs, replacing the mahants who had the support of the British (Grewal 1996: 18; Mandair 2014: 78).[7]

Gurdwara reform movement

It was in the aforementioned context that the CSL launched a movement. Due to the British unwillingness to remove the mahants, it soon acquired an 'anti-imperialist tone' (Singh G. 2000: 83). The agitators forced the Akal Takht authorities to issue a Hukamnama (order) summoning a general meeting of the representatives of Amritdhari (initiated) Sikhs across the world in front of the Akal Takht for the purpose of electing a representative committee to control the administration of the Golden Temple. In response to the popular demand, the then Punjab governor was forced to constitute a 36-member provisional advisory committee. The committee members were persons of moderate views and were loyalists to the empire. The Akali leaders, however, were not dissuaded and went ahead with the General Assembly (Sarbat Khalsa) as pre-planned on 15–16 November 1920. It was attended by over 12,000 Sikh representatives. The Assembly elected a bigger committee on its own consisting of 175 members and named it the Shiromani Gurdwara Parbandhak Committee (SGPC). Members of the managing committee constituted by the British were also included in the enlarged committee to avoid any controversy with the moderates (Singh Kashmir 2014: 329).

SAD was formed on 20 December 1920 as the political arm of the SGPC. It was originally tasked with the aim to lead the movement to bring about reforms in the gurdwaras. The word 'Akali' is derived from the word 'Akal', which has its origin from the Sanskrit word *kal* (time). Thus 'Akal' literally means one who does not die and belongs to the immortal/God (Sidhu 1994: 24). Guru Gobind Singh first used the term 'Akali' for those of his followers who were prepared to risk their lives for the protection of religion. Thus all those Sikhs who supported the Gurdwara Reform Movement and were prepared to sacrifice their lives to achieve their objectives came to be addressed as Akalis.[8]

The SAD was to have four declared objectives: to bring the Sikh religious places under Panthic control; to abolish the institution of mahants; to utilize the property and resources of the gurdwaras for just purposes; and to practice a way of life according to the teachings of the Sikh Gurus and sacred scriptures (Singh, Ajit 2005: 32).

Despite the popular sentiment for reforms, the mahants, having tacit support of the British, were not ready to leave the control of the gurdwaras. Only a few mahants voluntarily gave up the control of the gurdwaras to the SAD leadership (Grewal 1996: 34). Morchas led by Jathas comprising Akali cadres were sent to occupy the control of the gurdwaras. The participants faced repressive action by both the private armies of the mahants and the imperial police.[9] The movement led to the forcible 'liberation' of over 300 large and small gurdwaras (Singh, Mohinder 1988: 19). The British finally relented and the Gurdwara Act was passed on 1 November 1925. Elections for the central board to manage the gurdwaras were conducted on 18 June 1926. In this first election, out of 120 seats, the SAD candidates secured 85 seats. The first meeting of the Central Board was held on 4 September 1926 in Amritsar. On 2 October 1926 the board members passed a resolution renaming itself as SGPC, which was accepted by the British government (Dilgeer 1978: 99). All the important Sikh gurdwaras were placed legally under the control of the SGPC under the 1925 Act. Local gurdwaras were to have their own elected bodies for management of the shrines with one nominee on its committee. The central body, the SGPC, consisted of 151 members, out of which 120 were to be elected and 12 were nominated by the Sikh princely states. Fourteen members were to be co-opted and five were to represent the four chief shrines of the faith (Singh, Ajit 2005: 26). Emerging as 'a sort of parliament' of Sikhs, it has been argued that SGPC decisions

> acquired the sanctity of the ancient gurmata, . . . and the income from gurdwaras . . . gave it financial sustenance . . . disbursement of this income in the management of shrines, patronage in the appointment of hundreds of granthis, sevadars (temple servants) teachers and professors for schools and colleges which were built, arrangements for the training of granthis and for missionary activity outside the Punjab, all made the (SGPC) . . . a government within the government.
>
> *(Singh 1977: 213–14)*

The gurdwara reform movement was significant not only in establishing the SAD as the foremost Sikh political organization but also had a wider national impact. First, it gave confidence to the Indians that the colonial regime could be put under pressure to meet their demands by resorting to non-violent mass movement – an idea that was already put into practice by Gandhi during the noncooperation movement in the early 1920s. Second, the movement brought the two parties' leadership close to each other, which led to an intensification in the nationalist movement in the large Punjab province, though the SAD leadership did not allow the Congress workers to participate in the movement as it treated struggle for reforms as religious and non-political in nature. Third, the SGPC and the SAD as two institutions responded to the social and political aspirations of the Sikh community.

The SGPC and the SAD since their inceptions as two pillars of the Sikh politics have always been closely linked to Punjab politics as it has unfolded till today. While the supremacy of the SGPC in the religious affairs was established after the movement success, the SAD became the leading political organization of the Sikhs (Verma 1987: 262; Tutleja 1984: 123). To underline the role of the SGPC in the faction-ridden SAD, only the party faction which wins majority of seats in the SGPC election is considered by people as the 'official' Akali Dal.[10] Due to its access to the gurdwara priests, workers, Sikh social, cultural and educational organizations and resources, the SGPC has remained the most important non-government bureaucratic organization and the pre-eminent institution of the Sikh Community, dubbed as the mini-parliament of the Sikhs – a 'state within a state' in Punjab (Brass 1974: 311; Puri 1995: 35; Nayar 1966: 77).

Political representation

The Akali confrontation with the British during the reform movement, though dubbed as non-political by them, did help in turning the Sikh community into a political community. The movement helped in bringing to fore the Panthic issues in Punjab politics. Thus after the success of the gurdwara reform movement, the party focused now on securing adequate political representation to the Sikh community in the legislative bodies of colonial India. For the purpose, the party sought to enter into the mainstream electoral politics. The party sought political power for the Sikhs as a separate ethnic entity. It was in line with party's avowed claim of being the political mouthpiece of the Sikhs.

The inadequate share of representation given to the community in the Punjab Legislative Council under the Montague-Chelmsford Scheme was the triggering factor for the SAD to enter into political battle (Tutleja 1984: 135). The Muslim community had secured 50% of the non-official seats of the Council. In continuity with the demand raised by the CKD, the SAD demanded a 30% share of representation for the Sikhs in the Punjab Legislative Council and also in the Central Legislative Assembly based on the principle of joint electorate in case its demand for the abolition of the communal representation was not accepted (Verma 1987: 262). Akalis like the Congress boycotted the Simon Commission, which was set up by the British in 1927 to review the working of the constitutional reforms of 1919. However, the SAD at that time was demanding independence rather than the Congress demand for dominion status. Baba Kharak Singh termed the dominion status as equivalent to 'semi-slavery' and dissuaded Sikhs from participating in the civil disobedience movement, though he was opposed by another influential Akali leader, Master Tara Singh (Verma 1987: 265).

The Simon Commission in its report recommended the continuation of the separate communal electorate and reservation of seats in the legislative bodies. In case of Punjab, it did not recommend 30% reservation for the Sikhs who constituted 15% of the overall population. SAD joined an all parties' conference in Delhi convened by the Congress to discuss the formulation of a constitutional proposal for India. Consequently the Nehru Committee Report, 1928 recommended the abolition of a separate communal representation. However, an exception was made in the case of the Muslim community on the ground that their relative economic and education backwardness would come in the way of their representation in the legislative bodies. This recommendation was rejected by Akalis. The party demanded complete abolition of communal representation in India. The Akali position was that if communal representation was to be given to any minority, then the same concession was to be extended to the Sikh minority in the Punjab as well (Singh, Ajit 2005: 28). The first round table conference held in 1930 included the representatives of every community and every organization in India including the princely states, except the Indian National Congress, which had launched a civil disobedience movement with the most important of leaders courting imprisonment. The Central Sikh League refused to participate, but the moderate Sikh leaders (i.e. Ujjal Singh and Sampuran Singh) represented the Sikh community at the conference. The Sikh representatives presented a memorandum asking for the same treatment (30% reservation in the legislative bodies) in Punjab as the Muslim minority had received in other provinces (Singh, Ajit 2005: 28–9). Ramsay McDonald announced the communal award in 1932. Seat distribution remained in the favour of the Muslims, who were given 86 out of 175 seats in the Punjab Legislative Assembly, whereas 33 out of 175 seats were reserved for the Sikh community. In the North-West Frontier Legislative Council, 3 seats out of 50 were reserved for the Sikhs. In The federal Legislative Assembly, 6 seats out of 250 and in the Council of States 4 seats out of 150 were reserved for the community (Singh, Ajit 2005: 30). The communal award was rejected by the miffed SAD leadership as a 'scrap of paper' to be 'buried' along with the Nehru and Simon Commission report (Tutleja 1984: 151).[11] The Sikh leadership also complained that by accepting universal adult suffrage, the Nehru committee had attempted to establish Muslim rule in Punjab as Muslims commanded a numerical majority in the Punjab province (Singh, Ajit 2005: 28). Baba Kharak Singh expressed his anguish by resigning from the Congress and exhorted the Sikhs to throw the Nehru report into the 'dustbin' (Gulati 1974: 48). Despite the bitterness, the SAD leadership allowed for dual membership and also agreed to contest the 1937 election in alliance with the Congress (Narang 2014: 340). The alliance could be explained in the fact that the two parties were pitted against the Unionist Party, which enjoyed the support of the powerful landed peasantry and was viewed as collaborating with the British government. In the 1937 elections, the Unionist Party secured the majority by getting 96 out of 175 seats of the Punjab Legislative Assembly. The Congress obtained 18 seats and the Muslim League got only 2 seats. Among the Sikhs, Khalsa National Party, considered moderate, won 18 out of 33 seats reserved for the Sikh community in the Assembly (Kapoor 1986: 52). With the absolute majority of the Unionist Party in the Legislative Assembly, Sir Sikander Hayat Khan formed a ministry in the Punjab, joined by Sunder Singh Majithia belonging to the CKD in the cabinet. Only one urban non-agriculturist Hindu was included in the cabinet underlining the hold of the rural landed peasantry over the politics of Punjab (Singh 1977: 234).

More than the Unionist Party, the SAD was opposed to the Muslim League. The party perceived the Muslims having a disproportionate share of power in the state legislative body. While it saw the Muslim League as a communal party, it was willing to have truck with the Unionist Party, a secular party having a support base among all religious communities (Narang 2014: 340).[12] It was under pressure from the Akali leadership that the Congress modified its stand by drafting a resolution which stated that the Congress would not accept any constitutional setup which did not give equal and fair treatment to all minorities, particularly to the Sikhs (Gulati 1974: 50). However, the gap between the SAD and the Congress gradually widened as the latter too had a support base among the Sikhs (Verma 1987: 266). It came particularly under strain on the eve of the Second World War in 1939, as SAD supported the British in the war efforts, contrary to the Congress (Verma 1987: 267). Akalis took this position as the Sikhs were being recruited in large numbers in the imperial army. The party also did not join the Quit India movement, though a faction jointly led by Giani Gurmukh Singh Musafir, Partap Singh Kairon, Darshan Singh Pheruman and Udham Singh Nagoke among others supported it and offered themselves for arrest (Nayar 1966: 81).

Opposition to the demand for Pakistan brought the Congress and the SAD closer (Singh Ajit 2005: 34). Condemning the resolution for a separate Muslim state, the Akali leader Master Tara Singh in his letter to Stafford Cripps, dated 1 May 1942, made it clear that the Sikhs and the Hindus of Punjab did not support the partition.[13] In their opposition to the idea of Pakistan, the Sikh leaders did not hesitate even to share a platform with the leaders of the Hindu Mahasabha, which stood for India as a single political unit. The reason for the opposition to the partition was the party's apprehension about the future of the Sikhs in the Muslim majority western Punjab where the Sikhs had settled in the wake of the establishment of the canal colonies. To thwart the Muslim League design, SAD even raised the demand for Azad Punjab, which was to have the mixed population of Punjabi-speaking people belonging to different religions. It was to be a buffer state covering much of the area between the Chenab and the Yamuna Rivers (Grewal 1996: 65–6; Narang 2014: 341).

Provincial elections results held in 1946 reflected the entrenched communal divides. The Muslim League succeeded in winning 75 seats reserved for the Muslims and the SAD won 22 Sikh seats. The Congress could win majority of Hindu seats only (40 out of 51). The once dominant Unionist party could now win only 20 seats, and those in rural Punjab only, as the party continued to retain support among the influential landlords. In the case of a fractured verdict, the SAD entered into an alliance with the Unionist party and the Congress to form the coalition government after its initial negotiations with the Muslim League failed over the Akali demand of reserving 25% of the cabinet positions and also the government posts for the Sikhs. As the Cabinet Mission proposals were accepted by both the Congress and the Muslim League and partition loomed large on the horizon in 1946, the SAD made a last-ditch effort to have an understanding with the Muslim League seeking the safety of Sikhs. After the talk failure, Akalis threw in their lot with the Congress and its promise of a secular India, where minority rights would be protected in post-partition India. Soon, a fissure emerged once again as the Congress refused to support the separate communal electorate in the constituent assembly (Narang 2014: 341).

Demand for Punjabi Suba

Once partition happened, SAD leadership raised two demands: to ensure adequate representation of the Sikhs in the legislative bodies and promotion of the Punjabi language in Gurumukhi script (Grewal 1996: 74). The non-acceptance of demands led the party leadership to start a movement. The communalization of the language issue resulted in the rejection of the demand for Punjabi Suba by the State Reorganisation Commission. In the 1961 census, Punjabi was reportedly not recorded as their mother tongue by the non-Sikhs in the state. To the Akali leadership, it was that the non-Sikhs conspired to reduce the Sikhs, 'a minority people by religion . . . a minority by language as well' (Brass 1974: 327, 298). Not only the language but even the script of Punjabi language (Gurmukhi or Devnagari) became the bone of contention (Sarhadi 1970: 211). The Punjabi Suba movement in this context could be symptomatic of a 'deeper quest for recognition and power' on part of a now sizable Sikh community in the form of their own homeland (Deol 2000: 94; Oberoi 1994: 416; Lamba 1999).

The Congress did not support the demand of Punjabi Suba, dubbing it as communal. Here mention can be made of the Arya Samaj appeal to the Hindus to register Hindi as their mother tongue in the census. It also emphasized on preaching Hindus to follow the Vedic tradition and maintain distance from the Sikh traditions. All this helped in sowing the seeds of a communal division which was reflected in the state's politics. The demand resurfaced of securing a 'self-determined political status' for the Sikh community, ostensibly on the basis of language (Anand 1976: 263; Nayar 1966).

Besides the language and reorganization issues, what further added to the ire of Akalis was the emergent electoral dominance of the Congress in the now Hindu majority post-partition Punjab. The Congress took advantage of the newly introduced simple plurality electoral system winning the first three Assembly elections held in 1952, 1957 and 1962 with robust majority. Due to the Congress electoral dominance, the SAD leadership decided to merge the party with the Congress on the eve of the 1957 elections. The party hoped that it would bring the Congress government to accept the demand of reorganization. However, as the state Congress leadership continued to oppose the demand, Akalis decided to revive the party. However, many erstwhile Akali Members of Legislative Assembly as a part of the Congress government refused to resign and rejoin the parent party. As a result, a truncated Akali Dal performed badly in 1962 Assembly elections. The growing Hindu-Sikh divide helped Bharatiya Jana Sangh, which was able to win nine seats in 1962 elections, up from two seats in the 1952 elections.

Electoral support base

Since the colonial days, SAD as a self-projected farmer party has been getting significant electoral support from rural Punjab, inhabited mostly by the Sikhs.[14] Reference can be made in this regard of the Assembly elections held since 1967 up to 2007.

In all these elections, the SAD had a consistent lead in 28 of the state's rural assembly constituencies (Kumar 2014: 226).

The SAD leadership's inability to win a majority of seats despite succeeding in getting a Sikh majority state could be explained in the Sikh community being heterogeneous in terms of castes and sects and the party being closely identified with the Jat Sikhs. The gains of the green revolution going mainly to the landowning Jat community further increased the class divide (Puri 1995: 49; McLeod 2000: 109–12). Significantly, since its formation, the Akali leaders mainly belonged to the urban upper-caste/middle-class Sikhs. The shift to Jat Sikh party leadership began with the emergence of Sant Fateh Singh, who succeeded Master Tara Singh (Bajwa 1979: 25). In regional aspect also there was a gradual shift of the Akali leadership base from the Doaba and Majha regions to the larger Malwa region. Prominent leaders from the region included Sant Fateh Singh, Giani Kartar Singh, Master Tara Singh, Udham Singh Nagoke, Giani Bhupinder Singh.[15] The ascendance of Jat Sikhs as dominant community was due to their numerical predominance along with their land ownership and the prosperity that came with the green revolution (Jodhka 2000a: 392).

The political and economic dominance of the Jat Sikhs also became visible in the Congress party by the 1970s.[16] This is reflected in the social profiles of the lawmakers. Out of the 1,248 Legislative Assembly members elected from the state from 1967 to 2012, a sizable 44% of them belonged to the Jat Sikh community whereas Khatris/Aroras constituted 22%.

The reorganization of the state resulted in a perceptible communal divide in electoral terms. It enabled SAD to emerge as a contender of power in the now Sikh majority state. However, the Akali leadership realized soon that it would be difficult to come to power alone because the Congress retained its support base across the castes and communities (Kapur 1986: 216). Congress succeeded by projecting itself as a secular party, holding the middle ground in its effort to 'cut off the support base of all other political parties, instead of seeking to accommodate them' (Sharma 1986: 640).

Assembly elections held just after the reorganization in 1967 gave an early indication about the rural-urban, regional and religious divides in terms of the electoral choices of the people that were going to persist in the state's politics even today, though in diminished form. SAD could receive only one-fifth of the votes and 24 seats in the assembly of 104 members. The broader social constituency of the Congress was evident, as it succeeded in getting more Sikh candidates elected than SAD. The electoral support of Scheduled Caste voters having different religious allegiance remained uncertain, even in the case of Sikhs. Akali Dal also suffered from internal differences over agenda and leadership.

In the Assembly elections held in 1969 and 1977, the party won 43 and 58 seats, respectively, which was an improvement. Bharatiya Jana Sangh (BJS), another ethnic party, secured a segment of the urban Hindu upper-caste vote as the party was viewed as supportive of Hindu trading and business classes' interests. Besides having a complementary support base, the two parties have contested on the plank of 'anti-Congressism' and thus are 'natural allies'. The SAD-BJS alliance set the pattern of sharing of power to strike a kind of social balance, which neither community could establish on its own (Deol 2000: 100). At the same time, the interparty ideological divide was reflected in the BJS treating 'the Sikhs as part and parcel of the Hindu society' (Brass 1974: 333). In order to sustain the partnership, SAD and BJS agreed to have a three-language policy in 1969. Punjabi was made the compulsory language and medium of instruction in the government schools. Hindi and English became second and third languages to be introduced from classes 4 and 6, respectively. The need to not only retain the core social constituency support but also to remain in a coalitional arrangement was reinforced by the massive win of the Congress in the 1972 Assembly elections. The SAD-Janata Party victory in 1977 was helped by the alliance.

The stable alliance and voting pattern has imparted a stability of the traditional support base of both the Congress and the SAD across the three electoral regions.[17] Elections therefore have always been close, even when the elections have been plebiscitary in nature, like in post-Emergency 1977 elections or also in 1985 after historic the Longowal–Rajiv Gandhi Accord.[18] This trend explains why there has always been very intense campaigning and high turnout in the elections (Tables 3.1 and 3.2).

Anandpur Sahib resolutions

The party's need to consolidate the Sikh majority vote led the SAD to raise the demand for state's autonomy. This was expressed in the form of the Anandpur Sahib Resolutions of 1973 and 1978. The dismissal of Parkash Singh Badal led the Akali Dal-Janata Party (mainly constitutive of the former BJS members) government and the subsequent attempt by the Congress leaders like Giani Zail Singh to encourage factionalism[19] within SAD by encouraging the radical elements to vitiate the atmosphere in the state. Personalized and centralizing politics of Indira Gandhi that attempted to stifle the local voices gave rise to anti-centre sentiment in the state.

The core of Akali demands relating to the political, economic and social relationship between the centre and the state of Punjab was reflected in the Anandpur Sahib Resolutions adopted by the working committee of the Shiromani Akali Dal in October 1973. The resolutions incorporated seven objectives aimed to establish the 'pre-eminence of the Khalsa through creation of a congenial environment and a political set up' (Singh 1981: 346). The demands raised included among others, transfer of the federally administered city of Chandigarh to Punjab; the readjustment of the state boundaries to include certain Sikh majority Punjabi-speaking territory, presently outside but contiguous to Punjab; demand for autonomy to all the states of India with the centre retaining jurisdiction only over external affairs, defence and communications; introduction of land reforms as well as the subsidies and loans for the peasantry as well as the measures to bring about heavy industrialization in Punjab; the enactment of an all-India gurdwara act to bring all the historic gurdwaras under the control of the SGPC; protection for the Sikh minorities

TABLE 3.1 Summary of Lok Sabha elections in Punjab (1967–2014)

Year	Total seats	Turn out in %	Congress Seats	Congress Vote %	BJP (1984–)/JNP (1977–80)/BJS (1967–72) Seats	BJP/JNP/BJS Vote %	CPI Seats	CPI Vote %	State Party I Party	State Party I Seats	State Party I Vote %	State Party II Party	State Party II Seats	State Party II Vote %
1967	13	71.13	9	37.31	3	12.49	0	4.28	ADS	1	22.61	ADM	0	4.42
1971	13	59.90	10	45.96	0	4.45	2	6.22	SAD	1	30.85	NCO	0	4.48
1977	13	70.14	0	34.85	3	12.50	0	1.65	SAD	9	42.30	CPM	1	4.94
1980	13	62.65	12	52.45	0	9.97	0	1.27	SAD	1	23.37	INCU	0	2.56
1985	13	67.36	6	41.53	0	3.39	0	3.84	SAD	7	37.17	CPM	0	2.98
1989	13	62.67	2	26.49	0	4.17	0	2.10	SAD (M)	6	29.19	JD	1	5.46
1992	13	23.96	12	49.27	0	16.51	0	1.57	SAD	0	2.58	BSP	1	19.71
1996	13	62.25	2	35.10	0	6.48	0	1.60	SAD	8	28.72	BSP	3	9.35
1998	13	60.07	0	25.85	3	11.67	0	3.40	SAD	8	32.93	BSP	0	12.65
1999	13	56.11	8	38.44	1	9.16	1	3.74	SAD	2	28.59	BSP	0	3.84
2004	13	69.7	2	34.7	3	10.48	0	2.55	SAD	9	34.28	BSP	0	7.65
2009	13	70.6	8	45.23	1	10.6	0	0.33	SAD	4	33.85	BSP	0	5.75
2014	13	70.61	3	33.05	2	8.6	0		SAD	4	26.4	AAP	4	24.5

Source: Centre for the Study of Developing Societies (CSDS) Data Unit.

Note: In the 1989 elections, one seat was won by the Bahujan Samaj Party, which secured 8.62% of the vote; independents won three seats. In 1998, the Janata Dal won one seat and secured 4.18% of the vote.

TABLE 3.2 Performance of political parties from 1997 onward: Assembly elections in Punjab

Party name	\multicolumn{3}{c	}{1997}	\multicolumn{3}{c	}{2002}	\multicolumn{3}{c	}{2007}	\multicolumn{3}{c	}{2012}	\multicolumn{3}{c	}{2017}
	Seats contested	Won	Votes polled	Seats contested	Won	Votes polled	Seats contested	Won	Votes polled	Seats contested	Won	Votes polled	Seats contested	Won	Votes polled
BJP	22	18	8.33%	23	03	5.67%	23	19	8.28%	23	12	7.18%	23	03	5.4%
INC	105	14	26.59%	105	62	35.81%	116	44	40.90%	117	46	40.9%	117	77	38.5%
BSP	67	01	7.48%	100	00	5.69%	115	00	4.13%	117	00	4.29%	111	00	1.5%
CPI	15	02	2.98%	11	02	2.15%	25	00	0.76%	14	00	0.82%	–	00	0.2%
SAD	92	75	37.64%	92	41	31.08%	93	48	37.09%	94	56	34.73%	94	15	25.4%
IND	244	06	10.87%	274	09	11.27%	431	05	6.82%	418	03	6.75%	303	00	2.09%
PPOP	–	–	–	–	–	–	–	–	–	87	00	5.04%	–	–	–
AAP	–	–	–	–	–	–	–	–	–	–	–	–	112	20	23.72%
LIP	–	–	–	–	–	–	–	–	–	–	–	–	06	02	1.23%

Source: CSDS data unit.

living outside the state; reversal of the new recruitment policy of the centre, under which the recruitment quota of Sikhs in the armed forces fell from 20% to 2% (Singh 2005: 111–25; Kumar 2009: 173). The party added two new demands to the Anandpur Sahib Resolutions in February 1981, after which a set of 45 demands were submitted to the centre in September in the same year. These included, among others, the halting of reallocation of available waters of riparian Punjab to non-riparian states (Pettigrew 1995: 5).

Radical Sikh politics

Akali leadership failure to get the centre conceding to its demands gradually undermined the position of the moderate leadership within the party. In 1981 there was intensification of the second phase of Akali agitation as radical elements within the party assumed leadership. Armed militancy that came up with the active support of Pakistan received a boost by the support of these radical elements. The militancy-related violence and the failure of the centre to meet the demands of moderate Akalis and absence of democratic forums ultimately led to the military action in the Golden Temple, followed by the armed forces state-wide search for the militants causing human rights violations (Dyke 2009). The anti-Sikh riots that followed in Delhi and elsewhere in 1984 further distanced the Sikh community, as the accused remain mostly unpunished. What followed was the rise of the radical autonomist forces as the moderate forces became marginalized in a surcharged atmosphere that brought back the wounded memory of Sikh persecution. It took some time for moderate Akali leadership to overcome the tumult and trauma of these events and to make a political comeback after they were released in March 1985. The Longowal–Rajiv Gandhi Accord between the moderate Akali leadership and the Gandhi-led Congress government signed on 24 July 1985 was an attempt to bring peace. However, the SAD government led by Surjit Singh Barnala, which came to power on 25 September 1985, was unable to get any of the demands fulfilled by the centre under the accord. Even after agreeing to the transfer of Chandigarh to Punjab by 26 January 1986, the Congress government, fearful of losing votes in the neighbouring Hindi-speaking state of Haryana, backed out. Pro-militant organizations came together, forming United Akali Dal and weakening further the Barnala government. The incidents of human rights violation by the state police and paramilitary forces also underlined the weakness of the government. Entry of the state police in April 1986 to flush out the militants from the Golden Temple premises under Operation Black Thunder saw the desertion of the Badal- and Tohra-led Akali factions from the government. The Barnala government was dismissed and a state of emergency was imposed in the state in May 1987. The state remained under the president's rule for close to five years, even necessitating a constitutional amendment.[20] During this turbulent period, the party came under the firm control of the extremists and the elements supportive of militancy. The situation remained the same even after the victory of SAD (Mann) in November 1989 parliamentary elections on six out of eight seats contested, securing 29.19% of the votes. The

SAD now clearly stood for the right to self-determination that subsequently found expression in the form of the Amritsar declaration. The marginalization of the two moderate factions of Akali Dal, led by Parkash Singh Badal and Surjit Singh Barnala, was evident as the two factions managed to win only 6.65% of the votes and could not win a single seat.

Return to mainstream politics

The cessation of militancy happened only after the restoration of the democratic process. The process started with the holding of Assembly elections in 1992 under the shadow of militancy. Akalis boycotted the elections resulting in low turnout. The Congress government led by Beant Singh that came to power managed to flush out militancy with the active support of the Narasimha Rao–led minority Congress government at the centre. The state action was helped by growing antipathy towards militants due to their criminal acts. The normal competitive politics returned with panchayat elections held in 1995 that witnessed 82% voting (Verma 1995: 1325). As the moderates gained within the party, the radicals formed SAD (united) in 1994, uniting as many as six factions of SAD, namely SAD (Panthic), SAD (Mann), SAD (Kabul), SAD (Babbar), SAD (Talwandi) and SAD (Manjit Singh 2012). Since the urge for peace and Hindu-Sikh unity had been strong, SAD (Badal) emerged as the dominant faction and was able to integrate almost all the constituents of United Akali Dal with the notable exception of SAD (Mann).

The factional politics, however, soon returned. Typical of the person-centred politics in the party, the split soon happened again as the faction led by Gurcharan Singh Tohra, president of the SGPC for close to two decades, separated. Sarb Hind Shiromani Akali Dal (SHSAD) was formed on 30 May 1999.[21] It formed an electoral alliance with other factions, namely SAD (Mann), SAD (Panthic) and SAD (Democratic). The SHSAD-led alliance contested both the Lok Sabha and the Assembly elections in 1999 and 2002 held in the state, thus dividing the traditional Akali vote. The result was dismal performance of both. Congress, which had a poor run in the 1996 and 1998 Lok Sabha and 1997 Assembly elections held in the state, made a comeback in the 2002 Assembly elections. Since then, despite the SAD (Badal) becoming official Akali Dal under the colossal figure of Badal as undisputed topmost leader, different factions have continued to exist like SAD (Amritsar), SAD (1920) and others. However, they all have remained electorally marginal just like Dal Khalsa, another Sikh right-wing party. SAD (Taksali) emerged as a new party in 2018 after the Badal leadership was accused of pressurizing the Akal Takht in pardoning the Guru of Dera Sacha Sauda or impersonating the tenth Guru.

Symptomatic of long-term shift in the SAD ideology, even as the 1990s saw emergence of a sharp and shrill politics of identity veering around caste and religion, the party desisted reverting back to its ethnic/autonomist agenda, sticking to an agenda of 'peace, brotherhood, and communal harmony' (Jodhka 2000a).[22] Formations of successive coalition governments having both the national and the state parties which saw SAD as a constituent of Vajpayee- and Modi-led NDA governments has also brought a turnaround in the party mindset, making Akalis aware about the benefit of sharing power at the national level. The dire financial situation of the state also makes it imperative for the SAD when in power not to take cudgels with the centre.

On the flip side, last two decades have witnessed the rise of person-centric leadership in the party, as the Badal family has wrested control over not only the party but also over the SGPC and the Akal Takht, the two institutions which always enjoyed autonomy vis-à-vis the party. SGPC has been used as the major source of funding for the party and also for serving the political purpose of the SAD leadership. Once a cadre-based/ideologically driven party is now reduced to a 'family party'.

Electoral shift

The 'mainstreaming' of the SAD is visible as governance and development figure prominently in the party manifestos and the campaigns. Besides the popular disenchantment with extremism among the masses who do not want a revival of radicalism, the shift in the Akali agenda can also be due to the emergence of new generation of voters and leadership. Both have little memory of the gruesome events that had taken place in the state during militancy and have very little concern with the '*gurdwara* politics/*dharma yudh morcha* politics' or the affairs of SGPC. On the part of older leadership, the realization is there that the party has become once again relevant and even winnable only with the revival of the democratic process. However, the political scenario in the state can quickly change if the SAD-BJP alliance breaks down. BJP state unit leadership has been consistently looking for a greater number of seats than the 4 and 23 seats allotted to it in the Lok Sabha and Assembly elections, respectively. However, such a decision can strengthen the position of the Congress in the state. Breakup would also reinforce the image of the BJP of being a Hindutva party. SAD would also be inclined to increase emphasis on its Panthic agenda.

Arguably, electoral alliance with the BJP has benefited SAD more than it has helped the BJP. SAD gets a higher number of seats in the coalition and also plays a decisive role in allotting the seats in the state in accordance with the party's strength across the regions, especially in the Malwa region.[23] BJP, on the other hand, has not gained much from the electoral alliance in terms of spreading its support base across the regions and social groups/communities. The party has been viewed as an ineffective partner in the coalition government and thus unable to benefit its traditional urban social constituency. In fact, the SAD heading the coalition government for a decade sought to take credit for all the governmental initiatives for urban constituencies. BJP has also been constrained to underplay its ideological thrust, thus alienating its social constituency. SAD with its state-wide organizational reach and leadership has been able to retain its core Panthic support base and broadens its appeal by vowing to work for 'Punjab, Punjabi and Punjabiyat' (Moga Declaration, 25 February 1996).

Summing up

The end of militancy and subsequent revival of democratic institutions has witnessed newfound Akali focus on its identity as a party for Punjabis and not only the Sikhs. In addition, the party is adhering to the idea of cooperative federalism and also is moving from a politics of communal harmony rather than its earlier Panthic agenda (Verma 1999). Such a swing in the agenda of the Akali Dal helped bring normalcy to the once troubled state. It reflects the yearning of people to break away from 'gurdwara politics' and look for lasting peace and prosperity (Jodhka 2000a). The new breed of Akali party workers has little to do with Panthic politics, unlike those of the past. These 'new' leaders under Sukhbir Badal are gradually replacing Taksali leaders in the party organization.[24] As the memories of Operation Bluestar and anti-Sikh riots fade and new generations of youth emerge, the secular criteria such as governance and economic policies have taken precedence over the identity politics. It is reflected in the SAD-BJP uniform emphasis on 'peace, brotherhood, communal harmony, socio-economic welfare, all round development and sustainable and profitable agriculture through diversification'.

In an effort on the part of the SAD leadership to expand its support base while retaining its core-voting constituency, the party has put up Hindu candidates in the last two Assembly elections. Hindus have also been inducted in the party organization. Dubbed as an 'agriculturalist' party, it has also made conscious efforts to cater to the urban constituency. SAD has been showing inclination to fight more and more urban bodies' elections. In addition, the party is aiming to expand its spatial base beyond Punjab. It won an assembly seat in the 2014 elections in Haryana.

The dismal result in the 2017 elections, when the party suffered the humiliation of winning a smaller number of seats than the debutant Aam Aadmi Party, has put a question mark over the longevity of the bipolar system in the state – especially as both the SAD (in alliance with the BJP) and the Congress cannot absolve themselves of their responsibility of bringing the state to such a sorry state of affairs with massive unemployment, tainted politicians, politicized administration, rampant mafia-style corruption, massive drug addiction and heinous crimes often targeting the marginal communities. The promises made of diversification of agriculture and industrialization remain confined to successive manifestos and public rally speeches. The electoral outcomes in the 2014 and 2019 Lok Sabha elections and the 2017 Assembly elections show decisively that the state even now may be headed for a third credible alternative in the form of the AAP or newly founded alliance of small parties like SAD (Taksali), Punjabi Ekta Party, Lok Insaf Party and Punjabi Manch, if their party leadership is able to strengthen their parties organizationally. The Congress, despite winning a record number of seats in 2017, has once again failed to fulfil its poll promises. Worse, the Amrinder Singh government is being seen complicit in saving the culprits involved in the nefarious activities in the state like drugs and mining. As for the SAD, the senior leaders of late have raised voice against the Sukhbir Badal leadership on the issue of seeking support from the *deras* and also the undermining of the importance of the SGPC and the Akal Takht.

The inability of the SAD-BJP government in checking the repeated incidents of desecration of the Holy Granth in 2015 also weighs heavily on the party. There is a perception issue, as the party leadership is viewed as corrupt and not concerned with farmers or Panthic issues. The party leadership needs to take corrective measures by reviving the party's original cadre-based character.

Notes

1 This chapter draws from some of the earlier published work in Kumar (2004, 2017, 2018) with substantial modifications.
2 Guru Nanak handed over a 'single codex of his writings' referred as a 'pothi' to Guru Angad, who with the successive Gurus – Guru Arjan being most prolific – continued updating this earlier scriptural corpus till Guru Gobind Singh brought closure to the process (Singh, Pashaura 2014: 128).
3 In Sikh theology, as in the Indian classic tradition, *panj*, the numeral five, holds a special place. Guru Nanak in 'Japji Sahib' refers to five stages in spiritual development.
4 Panj Pyare are chosen by the Sikh assemblage. They preside over important ceremonies such as laying the cornerstone of a gurdwara building or inaugurating Karsewa (i.e. cleansing by voluntary labour) of a sacred tank, or leading a religious procession.
5 In 1909 Master Sunder Singh Lyallpuri wrote one pamphlet, 'Ki Khalsa College Sikha da Hai?' (Does Khalsa College Belong to the Sikhs?). *Khalsa Akhbar* was renamed as *Akali Akhbar* in 1920 by the publisher/editor Harchand Singh Lyallpur. Another newspaper, *Khubsoorat Akhbar*, was started by Sardar Mangal Singh, Giani Hira Singh Dard and Sohan Singh Josh. These newspapers supported the demand to reform the Sikh gurdwaras (Dilgeer 1978: 51).
6 CKD actively mobilized the Sikhs to join the imperial army in order to retain the support of the colonial regime.
7 Hurting the popular sentiment, Arur Singh, then manager of the Golden Temple, had organized Akhand Path to celebrate the victory of the British in the First World War. He also presented a *siropa* to General Dyer after the Jalianwala Bagh tragedy (Dilgeer 1978: 49–50).
8 Every Sikh who joined the party had to take vows in the presence of the holy book, committing himself to participate in the efforts for gurdwara reforms, and also that he would follow the orders of Jathedars and would refrain from using derogatory language or resorting to violence (Dilgeer 1978: 53).
9 During the movement, 4,000 died, 2,000 were wounded and 30,000 people were jailed (Singh G. 2000: 83).
10 For almost two decades now, the dominant SAD faction that has controlled almost all the seats in the SGPC body is the SAD (Badal) led by Parkash Singh Badal. The other factions like the SAD (Amritsar) have no influence over the SGPC.
11 On 24 July 1932, a Sikh conference was held at Lahore representing the SAD and the Central Sikh League. It 'voiced its grim determination not to allow the successful working of any constitution which does not provide full protection to the Sikhs by guaranteeing an effective balance of power to each of the three principal communities in the Punjab' (Singh, Ajit 2005: 30–1).
12 Another rival of the SAD was the CKD, which had changed its name to the Khalsa National party and was also a contestant in 1937 provincial elections.
13 Master Tara Singh, Giani Kartar Singh and Giani Sher Singh were among the prominent Akali leaders who declared that Pakistan would be formed on their dead bodies (Gulati 1974: 91)
14 A sample survey of party activists of the SAD in 2004 showed that an overwhelming majority (85%) were Sikhs, and the majority of them were in the farming sector (Talbot 1980).

15 Unlike the SAD, the Congress leadership in post-independence Punjab came from all three regions. Bhim Sen Sachar, Lala Jagat Narain, Shri Yash and Comrade Ram Kishan came from the Doaba region, while Pratap Singh Kairon, Probodh Chandra and Pandit Mohan Lal came from the Majha region, and Brishbhan, Gian Singh and Gurmukh Singh Musafir were from the Malwa region (Sharma 1986: 650–1).
16 Agrarian prosperity that followed the green revolution 'celebrated the Jatness of Sikh farmers and in many ways helped them capture the centre stage of the social and political life in the state' (Jodhka 1997: 279).
17 The three historically cultural regions have also emerged as a distinct electoral region with their own specificities.
18 SAD support base has mainly been in the Malwa region, where the party has won an impressive 20 to 48 seats from the 1967 to 2017 elections (except in the 2007 and 2017 elections when the numbers were 18 and 8, respectively).
19 Sharma (1986: 635) argues that while the Congress in the state has been 'defusionist in its inter-party behaviour and accommodationist in intra-party relations', SAD has been 'accommodative in inter-party relations, while defusionist about intra-Akali relations'. Congress is thus the 'opposite' or 'mirror image' of Akali Dal.
20 Assembly elections to be held in 1991 were abruptly cancelled by the Election Commission followed by the extension of central rule, a move supported even by the CPI(M) but opposed by the SAD (Editorial 1991: 2271).
21 Dissolved in 2003, like most of the breakaway SAD factions, it was also short-lived.
22 The Hindu–Sikh unity was common to the agenda of the Akali–Jan Sangh coalition government way back in 1967 (Singh 1981: 103–4).
23 Organizationally, the party is divided into five different zones. Among these five zones, the larger Malwa region is subdivided into three zones. The zonal units are further divided into districts, circles and villages.
24 Most of these youthful leaders were sent outside the state during the militancy, and as such they remained away from the contentious politics of the day.

References

Anand, J.C. (1976). 'Punjab: Politics of Retreating Communalism', in (ed.), Iqbal Narain, *State Politics in India*, New Delhi: Meenakshi Prakashan.

Bajwa, Harcharan Singh (1979). *Fifty Years of Punjab Politics (1920–1970)*, Chandigarh: Modem Publishers.

Brass, Paul (1974). *Language, Religion and Politics in North India*, Cambridge: Cambridge University Press.

Chima, Jugdeep Singh (2018, June). 'The Shiromani Akali Dal and Emerging Ideological Cleavages in Contemporary Sikh Politics in Punjab: Integrative Regionalism versus Exclusivist Ethno-Nationalism', *Journal of Punjab Studies*, pp. 143–74.

Deol, Harnik (2000). *Religion and Nationalism in India: The Case of Punjab*, London: Routledge.

Dilgeer, Harjinder Singh (1978). *Shiromani Akali Dal: Ikk Itihas*, Chandigarh: Modern Publisher.

Dyke, Virginia Van (2009). 'The Khalistan Movement in Punjab, India, and the Post-Militancy Era', *Asian Survey*, 49(6), pp. 975–97.

Editorial (1991, October 5). 'Election Game in Punjab', *Economic and Political Weekly*, 26(40), p. 2271.

Grewal, J.S. (1996). 'Sikh Identity, the Akalis and Khalistan', in (eds.), J.S. Grewal and Indu Banga, *Punjab in Prosperity and Violence*, New Delhi: K.K. Publishers, pp. 65–103.

Gulati, Kailash Chander (1974). *The Akalis Past and Present*, New Delhi: Ashajanak Publication.

India Today. (1996, March 31). 'Akali Dal Led by Parkash Singh Badal Break from the Past to Forge a Moderate Agenda'. Retrieved May 18, 2018, from www.indiatoday.in/

magazine/special-report/story/19960331-akali-dal-led-by-parkash-singh-badal-break-from-the-past-to-forge-a-moderate-agenda-834735-1996-03-31.
Jodhka, Surinder S. (1997). '"Crisis of the 1980s and Changing Agenda of Punjab Studies": A Survey of Some Recent Research', *Economic and Political Weekly*, 32(6), pp. 273–79.
Jodhka, Surinder S. (2000a).'Decline of Identity Politics', *Economic and Political Weekly*, 35(11), pp. 877–79.
Jodhka, Surinder S. (2000b, July–December). 'Prejudice Without Pollution? Scheduled Castes in Contemporary Punjab', *Journal of Indian School of Economy*, XII(3&4), pp. 381–402.
Kapur, R.A. (1986). *Sikh Separatism: The Politics of Faith*, London: Allen and Unwin.
Kumar, Ashutosh (2004, April 3–10). 'Electoral Politics in Punjab: Study of Akali Dal', *Economic and Political Weekly*, XLIV(39), pp. 1515–20.
Kumar, Ashutosh (2009). 'Punjab Dissonance Between Governance and Electoral Process', in (eds.) Sandeep Shastri, K.C. Suri and Yogender Yadav, *Electoral Politics in Indian States: Lok Sabha Elections in 2004 and Beyond*, New Delhi: Oxford University Press.
Kumar, Ashutosh (2017). 'Electoral Politics in Indian Punjab: A New Phase?' *South Asia Research*, 37(1), pp. 223–34.
Kumar, Ashutosh (2018). 'Electoral Politics in Punjab: A Study of Shiromani Akali Dal', *Japanese Journal of Political Science*, Cambridge: Cambridge University Press, 19(1), pp. 1–20.
Kumar, Pramod (2014). 'Coalition Politics in Punjab: From Communal Polarisation in Catch-All Parties', in (ed.), E. Sridharan, *Coalition Politics in India: Selected Issues at the Centre and the States*, New Delhi: Academic Foundation, pp. 219–316.
Lamba, G.K. (1999). *Dynamics of Punjabi Suba Movement*, New Delhi: Deep & Deep Publication.
Mandair, Navdeep S. (2014). 'Colonial Formations of Sikhism', in (ed.), Pashaura Singh and Louis E. Fenech, *Oxford Handbook of Sikh Studies*, Oxford: Oxford University Press, pp. 282–97.
McLeod, W.H. (2000). *Sikhs and Sikhism*, New Delhi: Oxford University Press.
Mukherjee, Partha N. (1985). 'Akalis and Violence', in (ed.), Amrik Singh, *Punjab in Indian Politics*, New Delhi: Ajanta Publications, pp. 71–122.
Narang, Amarjit Singh (2014). 'The Shiromani Akali Dal', in (eds.), Pasaura Singh and Louis E. French, *The Oxford Handbook of Sikh Studies*, Oxford: Oxford University Press, pp. 339–49.
Nayar, Baldev Raj (1966). *Minority Politics in the Punjab*, Princeton: Princeton University Press.
Oberoi, Harjot (1994). *The Construction of Religious Boundaries: Culture, Identity and Diversity in the Sikh Tradition*, New Delhi: Oxford University Press.
Pettigrew, J.J.M. (1995). *The Sikhs of the Punjab: Unheard Voices of State and Guerrilla Violence*, London and New Jersey: Zed Books.
Puri, Harish (1995). 'Akali Politics: Emerging Compulsions', in (ed.), Virendra Grover, *The Story of Punjab: Yesterday and Today*, New Delhi: Deep & Deep Publications.
Sarhadi, Ajit Singh (1970). *Punjabi Suba: The Story of the Struggle*, New Delhi: UB Kapoor and Sons.
Sidhu, Lakhwinder S. (1994). *Party Politics in Punjab*, New Delhi: Harman Publication.
Singh, Ajit (2005) *Shiromani Akali Dal Religio-Political Study (1947–90)*, Kaputhala: Armann Publications.
Singh, Dalip (1981). *Dynamics of Punjab Politics*, New Delhi: Palgrave Macmillan.
Singh, Devinder (1993). *Akali Politics in Punjab*, New Delhi: National Book Organisation.
Singh, Gurharpal (2000). *Ethnic Conflicts in India: A Case Study of Punjab*, London: Palgrave Macmillan.

Singh, Kashmir (2014). 'Shiromani Gurdwara Parbandhak Committee: An Overview', in (ed.), Pashaura Singh and Louis E. Fenech, *Oxford Handbook of Sikh Studies*, Oxford: Oxford University Press, pp. 328–38.

Singh, Khushwant (1977). *A History of Sikhs*, Vol. II, Delhi: Oxford University Press.

Singh, Manjit (2012, March 31). 'A Re-Election in Punjab and the Continuing Crisis', *Economic and Political Weekly*, XLVIL(13), 21–3.

Singh, Mohinder (1988). *The Akali Struggle*, New Delhi: Atlantic Publishers and Distributors.

Singh, Pashaura (2014). 'The Guru Granth Sahib', in (eds.), Pasaura Singh and Louis E. French, *The Oxford Handbook of Sikh Studies*, Oxford: Oxford University Press, 339–49.

Singh, Pashaura and Louis E. Fenech (2014). *Oxford Handbook of Sikh Studies*, Oxford: Oxford University Press, pp. 282–97.

Singh, Pritam (2007). 'The Political Economy of the Cycles of Violence and Non Violence in the Sikh Struggle for Identity and Political Power: Implications for Indian Federalism', *Third World Quarterly*, 28(3), pp. 555–70.

Sharma, T.R. (1986). 'Diffusion and Accommodation: The Contending Strategies of the Congress Party and Akali Dal in Punjab', *Pacific Affairs*, 59(4), pp. 634–54.

Talbot, A. (1980). 'The 1946 Punjab Elections', *Modern Asian Studies*, 14(1), pp. 65–91.

Tutleja, K.L. (1984). *Sikh Politics, 1920–40*, Kurukshetra: Kurukshetra University Press.

Verma, P.S. (1987). 'The Akali Dal: History, Electoral Performance and Leadership Profile', in (ed.), Gopal Singh, *Punjab Today*, New Delhi: Intellectual Publishing House.

Verma, P.S. (1995). 'Zilla Parishad and Panchayat Samiti Elections in Punjab: Revival of Political Activity', *Economic and Political Weekly*, 30(22), pp. 1321–5.

Verma, P.S. (1999). 'Akali-BJP Debacle in Punjab Wages of Non-Performance and Fragmentation', *Economic and Political Weekly*, 34(50), pp. 3519–31.

4
RELIGION, ETHNICITY AND POLITICS

Understanding the BJP's rise in Assam

Dhruba Pratim Sharma, Tarun Gogoi and Vikas Tripathi

Democracy creates the ideal conditions for the formulation and expression of political identity. The electoral process encourages groups to identify themselves politically and bestows real political meaning on the concepts of majority and minority, reinforcing the existing cleavages in society. The Northeast Indian state of Assam provides an example of politics being influenced largely by issues concerning ethnic identity. The unusually large rate of migration into the state since the heyday of British rule and the varied array of ethnic groups, each striving to preserve its identity and its interests through the political process, led to a situation of ethnic conflict in the post-independence period, as politics became centred on issues of immigration and ethnic identity (Sharma 2002: 1). The state underwent various political shifts ranging from a situation of Congress dominance till the mid-1970s to the rise of regionalism in the mid-1980s, and gradually moving towards a largely bipolar contest between two national parties in the 21st century.

Issues relating to ethnic and religious identity came to the fore as the state held one of its most keenly contested State Assembly elections in early April 2016. Against the backdrop of three successive wins by the Congress in the Assembly polls since 2001 and of the BJP's upsurge in the 2014 Lok Sabha polls and the 2015 municipal elections, the polls promised to be a clash of titans in a largely bipolar scenario between two national parties with active intervention of ethnic-regional players. This chapter seeks to understand the relatively recent rise of the BJP, a party representing Hindu nationalism at the national level, in a state that has traditionally witnessed the dominance of ethnic politics based on linguistic and tribal identities. Specifically it will look at the salience of religion as a political factor in an ethnically divided milieu and examine the trends towards religious consolidation where the issue of illegal immigration from across the international border emerges as a main factor of religious polarization.

The socio-political setting

The state of Assam consists of three main regions:

1 The Brahmaputra Valley, the traditional homeland of the Assamese-speaking people and of indigenous tribes such as the Bodos, covering as many as 106 of the state's 126 Assembly constituencies and 11 of the state's 14 Lok Sabha constituencies;
2 The Barak Valley in southern Assam, predominantly Bengali speakers, with 15 Assembly constituencies and covering two Lok Sabha constituencies;
3 The two hill districts of Karbi Anglong and North Cachar (Dima Hasao) in central Assam, which are dominated by hill tribes and are governed by Autonomous Councils, constituting five Assembly constituencies and one Lok Sabha constituency.

According to the 2011 census, 61.5% of the state's population was Hindu by religion, 34.22% was Muslim, and 3.7% was Christian, the percentage of Muslims being the second-highest among the Indian states (Census of India 2011). Nine out of the 32 districts of Assam are Muslim majority according to the 2011 Census of India, of which two (Karimganj and Hailakandi) are in the Barak Valley and seven (Dhubri, Goalpara, Barpeta, Morigaon, Nagaon, Darrang and Bongaigaon) in the Brahmaputra Valley. The share of the Assamese speakers in Assam was 48.80% in the 2001 census. Assamese-speaking Muslims, also known as Khilonjia Muslims and including groups such as Goria and Moria, are estimated to be around 40 lakhs out of a total population of 1 crore Muslims in Assam (The Indian Express 2016). Scheduled Tribes account for around 13% of the population in Assam, of which Bodos are estimated to constitute about 40% (Census of India 2011).

Electoral politics in Assam since independence

The state witnessed uninterrupted Congress rule for over three decades since 1946, enabled by the charismatic presence of the Freedom Movement leaders and by the forging of a strong base among Muslims, Scheduled Castes and tea workers. The notorious statement of the All India Congress Committee (AICC) president preceding the 1977 polls – implying that as long as the Muslims and tea workers in Assam were with the Congress, the party need not worry about elections – symbolized the trend of vote bank politics (Borpujari 1995). The Assembly elections of 1978 heralded the end of Congress dominance in the state and brought a newly formed coalition led by the Janata Party to power (Deka et al. 1987: 240).

A Janata ministry assumed office in 1978, followed a year later by another non-Congress ministry. In 1980, amidst the turmoil of the Assam Agitation, an eight-member Congress ministry assumed office. Six months later, president's rule was imposed for the first time in the state due to political disturbance. The elections of 1983 were marred by large-scale ethnic violence in the Brahmaputra Valley and the voter turnout was ridiculously low in most constituencies, excepting those dominated by religious and linguistic minorities and tea workers. The Congress ministry that came to power lasted till 1985.

The Assam Accord signed in 1985 between the central government and the leaders of the Assam Agitation brought about a sea change in the state's political situation. A new regional party, the Asom Gana Parishad (AGP) formed by the erstwhile leaders of the Assam Movement with the slogan 'Unity, Peace, Progress' came to power riding a huge wave of popular support from diverse ethnic groups that strove to identify with the 'greater Assamese community'. The emergence of the United Minorities' Front (UMF), a joint forum of religious and linguistic minorities bitterly opposed to the Assam Accord, was another feature of the 1985 elections, and it bagged many seats in the Muslim-dominated areas; it failed, however, to sustain its momentum in subsequent elections as the Congress soon regained influence over the minorities. In a state where Congress dominance lasted uninterrupted till 1978, the erosion of its support among various ethnic groups meant that the party increasingly came to rely for votes on the tea workers who by and large remained loyal supporters (ACMS 2000).

The AGP ministry led by P.K. Mahanta that was formed in 1985 lasted till 1990. Despite making its mark on the national political scene as a 'regional party with a national outlook' and becoming a part of the 'National Front' coalition government at the Centre in early 1990, the AGP did not seem to satisfy the high expectations of the multitude that had voted it to power. The multifarious constituents of the 'greater Assamese community' now began to perceive the AGP as a party representing Assamese caste-Hindu interests, and this created unrest among members of various tribes and backward castes, who saw their respective community interests as being threatened by an assimilative tendency of the ruling group (Thapa 2002). The period of AGP rule witnessed the rise of ethnic agitations and insurgency on an unprecedented scale, and in late 1990, the ministry was dismissed and president's rule imposed on the state in order to curb militancy. Within a year, elections were held in the state and the Congress returned to power following a pre-poll split in the AGP that had left the regional party in a severely battered condition. The non-Congress parties, especially the AGP, made an issue of human rights violations during the military anti-insurgency operations in the 1991 elections and managed to get some sympathy on this count in many constituencies. But this could not cut much ice with the tea workers and migrant Muslims, who voted heavily for Congress. The Congress government in the state that came to power in 1991 lasted its full term.

The 1996 elections witnessed the victory of an AGP-led alliance that included the CPI and the CPI(M). The Lok Sabha elections of 1998 and 1999 led to the victory of Congress candidates in most of the seats in the Brahmaputra Valley and weakened the AGP's hold. A significant feature of these elections was the emergence of the BJP as an influential party in Assam. The United Liberation Front of Assam (ULFA)'s call for poll boycott on both occasions had its effect on the Assamese voters but not on the tea workers or on the migrant Muslims who voted in large numbers as usual. The Assembly elections in 2001 resulted in another change of the state's ruling party and the Congress was back in power, with Tarun Gogoi as the chief minister. The collapse of the alliance between the AGP and the left parties, and the hastily patched AGP-BJP combine on the eve of the 2001 Assembly elections proved to be a godsend for the Congress, as the electorate rejected the non-Congress parties for their perceived opportunism and shifting stances, and voted overwhelmingly for the Congress. The 2001 elections were followed by more than a decade of Congress dominance, a period marked by the decline of the AGP, the strengthening of the BJP, and the emergence of the AIUDF as a strong force among religious minorities, and of the Bodo Peoples' Front (BPF) as the dominant party among the Bodos. An important feature since 2009 has been a decline in militancy due to severe losses borne by major insurgent outfits.

The verdict of 2014

In 2014, Assam was among the few states where the Congress Party had been confident about pulling off a good performance based on Chief Minister Tarun Gogoi's performance and the fact that the party had retained its alliance with the Bodoland Peoples Front (BPF) that had proved successful in the 2009 Lok Sabha and the 2011 Assembly elections. The other main parties in the state, namely the Asom Gana Parishad (AGP), the Bharatiya Janata Party (BJP) and the All India United Democratic Front (AIUDF) contested the 2014 election on their own. However when the final results came, it turned out to be an embarrassing loss for the Congress and Gogoi himself.

Although traditionally BJP had significant support base in the Barak Valley and Lower Assam since the 1991 general and Assembly elections, alliance with regional party like AGP helped them to expand their support base in other parts of Assam. The even, regional spread of the BJP witnessed in 2014 can be dubbed as a precursor to the BJP's rise in the state as it upset the electoral balance previously tilted towards the Congress across regions in Assam (Goswami and Tripathi 2015). BJP's phenomenal rise in Assam is significantly remarkable only after the 2014 general election and the 2016 Assembly election continues the significant trend of BJP's unprecedented expansion in largely Assamese speaking Upper Assam along with Lower Assam and Barak Valley.

In 2014 election, BJP won 7 out of 14 seats with the highest ever vote share of 36.5%. Figure 4.1 shows the significant increase of vote share and seat numbers of BJP in Lok Sabha elections since 1985 where BJP has a steady growth of vote share from 9.6% in the 1991 election with two seats to highest ever 36.86% vote share with seven seats in the 2014 election. In Assam region-wise, BJP has made a significant electoral presence in the Barak Valley since 1991. BJP had significant presence in the Karimganj and Silchar of the region. In the 2014 election BJP could not win either of the two seats. From Lower Assam, Gauhati and Mangaldoi had been the two main constituencies where BJP has dominated for a long time. In Upper Assam the BJP only had a significant support base in Nowgong constituency from 1999

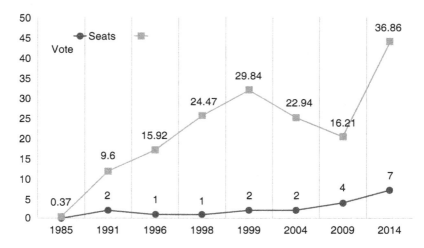

FIGURE 4.1 BJP's political performance in the Lok Sabha elections in Assam (1985–2014)

Source: Based on Election Commission of India's statistical report on general election from 1985–2014, available at https://eci.gov.in/statistical-report/statistical-reports/.

TABLE 4.1 Region-wise BJP political performance in Lok Sabha elections in Assam (1991–2014)

Region	Years						
	2014	2009	2004	1999	1998	1996	1991
Upper Assam (6)	5	1	1	1	0	0	0
Lower Assam (5)	2	2	1	1	0	0	0
Barak Valley (3)	0	1	0	0	1	1	2
Total seats (14)	7	4	2	2	1	1	2

Source: Author's own calculation based on Election Commission of India's statistical report on general election from 1991–2014, available at https://eci.gov.in/statistical-report/statistical-reports/.

Note: The classification into Upper Assam, Lower Assam and Break Valley is based upon distribution of Vidhan Sabha seats in respective Lok Sabha constituencies.
The Upper Assam region includes Lakhimpur, Dibrugarh, Jorhat, Tezpur, Nowgong, and Kaliabor Lok Sabha seats.
The Lower Assam region includes, Mangaldoi, Gauhati, Barpeta, Kokrajhar and Dhubri Lok Sabha seats.
The Barak Valley region includes Autonomous Districts, Silchar and Karimganj Lok Sabha seats.

onwards. Table 4.1 and Figure 4.1 show the increasing presence of BJP in different regions of Assam.

The state, which recorded a massive voter turnout of 80% – an 11 percentage point jump since 2009 – threw up a big surprise. The BJP finished in the top winning half of the state's 14 Lok Sabha seats – its highest ever tally in the state (Table 4.2). In terms of changeover from 2009, when it had contested in alliance

TABLE 4.2 Summary results: seats contested, won and votes secured by major parties in 2014 compared to the Lok Sabha elections (2009)

Party/Alliance	Seats contested	Seats won	Seat change since 2009	Vote (percent)	Vote change since 2009 (percentage points)
Congress	13	3	−4	29.61	−5.27
BPF	2	0	−1	2.19	−3.22
BJP	13	7	3	36.51	20.30
AUDF	10	3	2	14.83	−1.27
AGP	12	0	−1	3.83	−10.77
Others	126	1	1	13.03	0.23

Source: ECI data recomputed by CSDS Data Unit.

with the AGP, it was a gain of three seats for the BJP. The party also notched up an impressive vote share of 36.5% (up by over 20 percentage points since 2009). The Congress, with a vote share of 29.6% (down by 5 percentage points from 2009), managed to win only 3 of the 13 seats on which it contested. Its ally, the BPF, lost the only seat it had won in 2009. The other gainer apart from the BJP was the AIUDF, which retained its hold over the state's heavily Muslim-dominated areas, winning three seats – an addition of two since 2009. The party managed to secure 15% of the votes, down marginally by 1 percentage point. The AGP could not win on any of the 12 seats that it contested and polled merely 3.8% of the total vote.

Dissidence and intra-party infighting within the state unit of the ruling Congress, which enjoys overwhelming majority in the state legislature and had performed splendidly in the panchayat and municipal polls held a year earlier, took its toll and contributed heavily to the party's defeats. Its main losses were in the Brahmaputra Valley where it won just one seat (Koliabor, won by the chief minister's son, a political newcomer) and lost four of the seats it won in 2009, three of them (Lakhimpur, Dibrugarh and Jorhat) to BJP and one (Barpeta) to AIUDF. In the Bengali-speaking Barak Valley, the Congress wrested one seat (Silchar) from the BJP but lost its other seat (Karimganj) to AIUDF (Sharma 2014a). The partial erosion of Congress's hold over its traditional bastions (i.e. the Muslims and tea workers) impacted the poll outcome. While the party's support among Assamese Muslims remained largely intact, the division of Bengali Muslim votes between the Congress and AIUDF contributed to losses for Congress and gains for both BJP and AIUDF. Among the hill tribes, the Congress mustered strength through the support of its local units for their demand for statehood and retained the lone seat in the tribal hill areas. The Congress' alliance with the Bodoland Peoples Front (BPF), a party seen as patronizing tribal militants in their bloody anti-non-tribal campaigns, seemingly irked Muslim voters who had been targeted by the militants; the Congress-BPF alliance broke down after the polls.

The AIUDF, by giving voice to their grievances, became the preferred choice for the Bengali-speaking Muslims in Lower Assam; it secured an equal number of seats as the Congress with just half the vote share as the Congress, indicating the concentrated nature of its support base limited to a few constituencies in both valleys of the state. Its founder-president and his brother emerged victorious in the Lower Assam constituencies of Dhubri and Barpeta, respectively, the other seat for the party coming from the Barak Valley. A surprise element was the victory of an independent candidate, a tribal ex-ULFA cadre claiming support of the non-tribal population in the trouble-torn Kokrajhar (ST) constituency, wresting the seat from the BPF representing the Bodo tribes against the backdrop of severe communal (Bodo versus non-Bodo) tensions. Here Bodo militants unleashed massive post-poll anti-Muslim violence seemingly in retaliation for their voting for the non-Bodo candidate. As per the NES-2014 (Lokniti-CSDS National Election Study) survey, 15% of the Muslim votes went to 'others' (candidates not belonging to the four main parties); presumably, a large chunk of these went to the winning candidate in Kokrajhar. The events indicate the state's blunder in creating the Bodoland Territorial Council in areas inhabited mostly by non-Bodos and in subsequently tolerating the surge of militancy.

The BJP attracted mainly the Hindu votes including those of the Assamese Hindus who had once constituted the AGP's backbone, through its consistent stand against Bangladeshi Muslim immigrants. Its gains were in the Brahmaputra Valley, retaining its three seats and wresting four more, while losing its lone Barak Valley seat to the Congress. The tea workers constituting a major chunk of population in Upper Assam decisively ensured BJP's win in Dibrugarh and Jorhat where the party put up candidates belonging to the tea worker community that had traditionally backed the Congress. The leadership crisis in AGP (which had twice assumed power in the state but had been on a decline since 2001) led to a shift of its traditional voters towards the BJP. The regional party failed to stem the demoralization and subsequent exodus of its cadres towards the BJP in the run-up to the polls; its lacklustre campaign and intra-party squabbles sealed its fate. Most of the top state BJP leaders are ex-stalwarts of the AGP, which also worked in the BJP's favour. This unprecedented growth of BJP in 2014 became possible, partly owing to the existence of a regional vacuum owing to the decline of AGP and partly because the Congress faced severe anti-incumbency. Mahanta analyzed the emergence of the BJP in the 2014 election as a phenomenal one, which marks a new phase of polarized politics in Assam (Mahanta 2014). In his words, 'first time ethnic, regional and identity-based issues have been sidelined and questions of governance and religion played a more important role in mobilizing voters' (Mahanta 2014: 19).

The 2016 State Assembly Polls: Social Polarisation and Appropriation of Ethnic Space

The changing political dynamics in the state became even more pronounced in the 2016 State Assembly elections, in which the Congress party led by Chief Minister Tarun Gogoi contested largely on its own, allying only with a minor tribe-based party in four seats. The other national party, the Bharatiya Janata Party (BJP), contested in alliance with the main regional party, the Asom Gana Parishad (AGP), and with the largest tribe-based party, the Bodoland Peoples Front (BPF), which till mid-2014 had been in alliance with the Congress. The BJP also made an understanding with some tribal leaders representing the Rabhas and Tiwas respectively in some constituencies. The second largest party in the State Assembly, the All India United Democratic Front (AIUDF), based almost exclusively among Bengali-speaking Muslims in both valleys of the state, contested in 74 seats largely on its own, having an inconsequential alliance with two parties (RJD and JD(U)) with no significance in the state. In the sense that BJP had only a marginal presence in most of the AIUDF strongholds and vice versa, the contest was largely bipolar in many constituencies between Congress on one hand and either BJP or AIUDF on the other. In fact, during the campaigning, BJP leaders had publicly discounted the possibility of the party's or its alliance's win in at least 35 Muslim-dominated constituencies. The left parties, CPI and CPI(M), together put up candidates in 34 seats.

The state witnessed its highest-ever voter turnout in State Assembly elections at 84.72%, with 82.2% in the first phase and 87% in the second phase, crossing the previous record of 79.21% in the 1985 elections. The BJP alliance, with 41.5% of the votes, swept the 2016 State Assembly polls, winning 86 seats out of 126 seats in the Assembly. The BJP alone, with 29.5% of the votes, bagged 60 seats, 12 times the number it had won in 2011; its alliance partners, the AGP, with 8.1% of the votes, and the BPF, with just 3.9% of the votes, won 14 and 12 seats, respectively. The alliance won convincingly in both valleys as well as the hill districts of the state, and even in constituencies with high Muslim populations, including indicating a split in Muslim votes between the Congress and AIUDF. The Congress alliance, with 31% of the votes, won 26 seats and was reduced to exactly a third of its strength in the previous Assembly; it was the second-worst performance for the party in the state, the worst being in 1985 when it got 25 seats. The AIUDF, with 13% of the votes, got 13 seats, losing nearly a third of the number of seats that it had won in the last Assembly elections, including the seat contested by its chief and held earlier by his son, but significantly gaining a seat (Naoboicha) for the first time in Upper Assam, considered the Assamese heartland. It may be noted that parties having localized influence confined to a few constituencies, such as the AIUDF, and parties contesting in only a few constituencies as a result of electoral alliances, such as the AGP and the BPF, could secure relatively more seats with far lesser proportions of the vote share, than a party like the Congress having wider influence spread across the state. This also partly explains the paradox of BJP with a 1.5% lesser vote share securing more than twice the number of seats as the Congress.

As argued earlier, the issues of indigeneity and illegal migration have dominated the electoral politics of Assam. The rise of BJP as the major political force by replacing Congress marks a political trend of the co-option of ethno-regionalism and indigeneity by a party with explicit Hindu nationalist aspirations. The victory of BJP in 2016 Assam assembly enabled the party to shed its image of the North-India Hindi Heartland party. Based on his observation of BJP's electoral expansion from other Indian states to northeastern states, Mehta (2016) defined it as a moment of a 'BJP Dominant System' in Indian Politics. The 2016 election in Assam for the first time marked the significant growth and consolidation of BJP as a dominant political force across regions by winning 60 seats out of total contested 90 seats with 29.51% vote share. The 2016 election remains significant owing to the emergence of a

Hindu nationalist party as an alternative to Congress that for the first time formed a government in Northeast India. However, the dominance enjoyed by the party remains quite distinct from other parties that had dominated the politics in Assam during different moments. Thus it becomes imminent to interrogate the nature and pattern of dominance that came to characterize the BJP and its underlying causes. One has to understand the reasons that enabled a party like BJP representing Hindu nationalism to become a dominant political force in Assam. These reasons assume centre stage because traditionally ethnicity and identity politics rather than religion had been the dominant axis of political mobilization in Assam. Palshikar (2017a) analyzes the rise of BJP in Indian politics as a 'second dominant party system' in India. He further argues,

> besides the electoral ascendance of the Bharatiya Janata Party (BJP) (the steadiness of which is rather incontrovertible), political developments also indicate the gradual shaping of a new hegemony in India. Thus, the 'second dominant party system' is more than a mere party system; it is a moment of the rise of a new set of dominant ideas and sensibilities that would provide ideological sustenance to the dominant party system.
>
> *(Palshikar 2018: 36)*

BJP emerged as a major political force only after 2014 election and further consolidated its position in the 2016 Assembly election (Palshikar 2014; Mahanta 2014; Goswami and Tripathi 2015; Tripathi et al. 2018). Scholars depict this political change as localization of BJP or victory for identity politics or inorganic growth or 'saffronization' of Northeast India (Misra 2016; Tripathi et al. 2018; V. Bijukumar 2019). Assam is considered as the gateway to enter the electoral politics of Northeast India. As a party with a Hindu nationalist agenda, it was very difficult for the BJP to establish its dominance, as Assam is a complex society with diverse ethnic, religious and linguistic communities. Among all communities, the Assamese Hindus are dominant in the Brahmaputra Valley while Bengalis are dominant in the Barak Valley.

Initially, BJP was not a strong force in Assam but gradually it could make its support base in the Barak Valley by winning seats in both Lok Sabha and Assembly elections from 1991 onwards (Srikanth 1999). Although the rise of BJP in Assam and other states in the northeast region is a relatively new phenomenon, in this political journey of BJP the Hindutva forces led by RSS, which had its active presence since the pre-independence era in part, facilitated the emergence of BJP. Scholars argue that it is only due to the quiet and determined hard work of the RSS cadre that BJP could make inroads in this region for the very first time after independence (Firstpost 2017). In this context, Malini Bhattacharjee points out that the BJP's political experiment in making inroads into Assam over the past decades has been given so much attention, but at the same time it is important to understand the contribution of the social and cultural wings of its *parivar* over the past 60 years in Assam in deepening the roots of Hindutva in Assam (Bhattacharjee 2016: 80).

While discussing the emergence and consolidation of Hindutva in Assam, Bhattacharjee argues, 'local histories, myths and idioms often become the vehicle for Hindutva to promote and entrench itself' (Bhattacharjee 2016: 80). While referring to L. Pachuau, Bhattacharjee further points out how the ideologues of Hindutva tried to mark a connection between Assam and 'Bharat' by referring to Vedic, Puranic and epic texts, as they could impart a strong Hindu identity to Assam in their narrative (Bhattacharjee 2016: 81). The RSS has been active in the region since 1946 and played a significant role in promoting Hindutva through its different organizational activities, from humanitarian activities such as providing relief during disaster and providing targeted services to marginalized groups such as women, tribal and Hindu lower castes and helping the Hindu refugees find employment opportunities (Bhattacharjee 2016: 83). Simultaneously, it could make the halting of conversion by Christian missionaries and checking the infiltration by Bangladeshi Muslims a central agenda of its various organizational activities. In this regard, the RSS established many affiliated bodies including Pahari Sewa Sangh and Vanavasi Kalyan Ashram to facilitate different social welfare works like establishing schools, hospitals, hostels and medical dispensaries in tribal-dominated districts of Udalguri, Diphu, North Lakhimpur and so forth for the 'economic, moral and social upliftment' of tribals (Bhattacharjee 2016: 84).

Another grand strategy of RSS in this context was to appropriate Sankardev. While discussing the BJP's strategy pertaining to its Hindu nationalist discourse in the context of 2016 Assam election, Christophe Jaffrelot (2016) pointed out how BJP has adjusted to the local variant of Hindu culture as part of their project of vernacularization process by appropriating Sankardev, a 16th-century socio-religious reformer of Assam who was against the Brahminical orthodoxy. RSS's primary education wing, Shishu Shikha Samiti, established in 1979, started a series of schools in different parts of Assam and named it after Sanakerdev as 'Sankardev Shisu Kunj'. It served the larger project of the Hindutva imagination. The Shankardev Sangh, a Vaishnava devotees' organization, shared the platform as part of the Hindutva project (Gohain 2003). In January 2016, Prime Minister Narendra Modi attended the 85th conference of the Srimanta Sankar Sangh in Sivasagar. Modi also visited Majuli, the epicentre of Assamese Vaishnavite culture with over 30 satras (Tripathi et al. 2018). So, Bhattacharjee observes, 'Sankardev is thus projected as a torch bearer of Hinduism who successfully arrested Christian proselytization amongst tribal people' (Bhattacharjee 2016: 82). Further, she writes:

> Hindutva activists have therefore, from the very beginning, adopted novel strategies for navigating through the complex particularities of this region in order to establish itself in the cultural and political imagination of the people. Moving away from its standard techniques of mobilising support through the invocation of Hindu stereotypes like 'Ram' or 'Ayodhya', it instead focuses on adapting local cults and symbols such as those associated with Kamakhya and Sankardev – Sattra traditions. Coupled with this, it also consolidates support

by providing welfare services in the realm of education, health and cultural development, through a range of affiliate bodies.

(Bhattacharjee 2016: 86–7)

The parental organization of BJP became quite instrumental in gathering support for BJP. In this context while talking with *First Post* regarding this, RSS Pranta Pracharak of Assam, Shankar Das talked about the contribution of RSS in BJP's rise in Assam:

> We are helping the BJP either directly or indirectly. Although the BJP runs the government today at the Centre, the credit has actually indirectly gone to the RSS. In Assam, BJP had no organization before. Even though we have not claimed credit, it is because of the RSS, that the BJP won in the state.
>
> (First Post 2017)

In January 2018, RSS organized a mass contact and expansion programme in Assam named Luit Poriya Hindu Sammelan, wherein RSS chief Mohan Bhagwat, Assam Chief Minister Sarbananda Sonowal, Finance Minister Himanta Biswa Sarma and former Chief Minister from AGP Prafulla Kumar Mahanta also joined the several heads of village bodies, 20 tribal kings from Karbi, Naga, Khasi, Hajong, Tiwa, Garo, Jayantiya and Mishing communities and all the Satradhikars of satras of Assam – more than 35,000 Swayamsevak participated in the programme (News18 2018; Guwahati Plus 2018). The *sammelan* was mainly organized for the purpose of bringing the Sangh closer to the citizens of Northeast India. While addressing the gathering of 40,000 Swayamsevak from the Northeast in Luitporiya Hindu Sammelan, RSS chief Mohan Bhagwat said that Hindutva (Hindu culture) and Bharat (India) remain inseparable. In Bhagwat's words, 'Bharat is not possible without Hindutva. Whenever divisive forces have tried to separate, they got separated from India' (Guwahati Plus 2018). Though there is a complex relation between the BJP and its parent organization, by observing the recent state elections in different states including Northeast India, it could be argued that BJP has a 'ready-made apparatus of voluntary organizations' that works as election machine for the party by 'supplying man power and generates support for the regimes' (Palshikar 2017b: 13). While discussing the relation between BJP and its parent organization, Palshikar argues:

> The RSS connection is not important for proving or accusing the BJP of its Hindutva. The BJP, in any case, adheres to Hindutva. The connection is important to understand the flexibility that both of them enjoy and the possibilities of mobilizing public opinion in favour of the BJP.
>
> (Palshikar 2017b: 12)

Though the national narrative of RSS helped the BJP make its footprint visible in Assam, the BJP could realize well the inherent limitations of pursuing the Hindu nationalist agenda for political consolidation in a deeply diverse state. This realization pushed the BJP towards adopting a 'bottom-up' approach so that it could both project for itself an image of an insider party as well as a party that could accommodate regional and ethnic aspirations. After 2015's humiliating electoral defeat in the Bihar and Delhi Assembly elections, the BJP has shifted its electoral strategy of going it alone to forming coalitions with regional parties. The BJP has 'crafted a new social coalition as well as electoral alliance along the ethnic axis in Assam based principally upon the precedence of regional subtext' (Tripathi et al. 2018). Tripathi et al. argue,

> working a social coalition with regional players turned out to be a major concern for the BJP because it could enhance its legitimacy and acceptability in a region characterized by deep diversity along regional, religious, linguistic and ethnic lines but could also serve to contain the anti-Congress vote split.
> *(Tripathi et al. 2018: 3)*

The BJP could sense that only with the religious card and marginal support base as well as weak organizational base, they could not challenge the Congress dominance from this region. As the Congress Party became the dominant player in Assam with its politics of institutional accommodation through creating many autonomous councils for different ethnic communities as well as electoral representation, which cut across diverse ethnic and linguistic groups. Tripathi et al. argue that the institutional mechanism of co-opting tribal groups through creation of autonomous councils that received patronage of the successive Congress governments was a potent factor in establishing local dominance as well as ensuring co-option of the regional and ethnic agenda in favour of the Congress (Tripathi et al. 2018: 3). This compelled the BJP to engage electorally the autonomous councils in an unprecedented manner as a part of its 'bottom-up' strategy in Assam. For this purpose the BJP forged a new social coalition with diverse ethnic groups like Rabha, Tiwa and Karbi and electoral alliances with political parties like Asom Gana Parisad (AGP), Bodoland People's Front (BPF) and the Ganashakti Party. This bore dividends for the BJP in Assembly elections.

This electoral alliance as well as social coalition helped the BJP make inroads to the tribal areas and portrayed them as the insider party. This alliance showed the BJP as being accommodative of the ethnic and regional aspirations and consequently enhanced the legitimacy and acceptability of BJP in Assam as an insider party. Misra argues:

> Apart from its understanding with the AGP, the BJP leadership made another master move in bringing within the fold of the BJP alliance the Tiwa and Rabha organisations. This gave the party a tribal friendly face and helped its fortunes not only in Tiwa and Rabha areas but also in the hill constituencies of Karbi Anglong and Dima Hasao. Here it virtually replaced the Congress that had held power for decades.
> *(Misra 2016: 21)*

BJP's understanding with Bodo and Rabha in Lower Assam and Tiwa, Kachari and Mishing in Upper Assam led to an unprecedented consolidation of the BJP across regions (Tripathi et al. 2018). Consequently, the BJP-led NDA coalition won 75% seats in Upper Assam, 64% seats in Lower Assam and 60% seats in the Barak Valley. The BJP's dominance is quite distinct from other parties in the sense that it is one party that made local issues and local politics quite central to this electoral plank. After the 2014 Lok Sabha election, as part of the strategy to expand its social base, the BJP became unusually involved in local politics so that it could easily capture the local dominance from the Congress Party (Tripathi et al. 2018: 8). The BJP first contested in the Autonomous Council as well as the Sixth Schedule Councils, which helped them to expand their social base towards tribal communities through alliance and understanding with tribal leaders. The BJP in Urban Local Bodies election won 39 out of 74 municipal boards and committees in Assam (*Assam Tribune* 2015a). In both BTAD and North Cachar Hills Autonomous Councils, the BJP also contested against the Congress Party (*Assam Tribune* 2015b).

An analysis of the Assembly election results region-wise since the mid-1980s points to the BJP's expansion into all the three regions for the first time since the 2014 Lok Sabha elections. The BJP won total 33 seats out of 56 in Upper Assam in 2016. On the other hand, during the previous Assembly elections, the BJP hardly won two to five seats in this region (Figure 4.2 and Table 4.3). In Lower Assam also, the BJP became an active player by capturing 15 seats out of 50. Traditionally the Lower Assam region had been dominated by the Bodoland People's Front (BPF) in Kokrajhar and Mangaldoi districts and the All India United Democratic Front (AIUDF) and Congress in Dhubri, Barpeta, Goalpara and so forth. The BJP's performance over the Lower Assam seats could be attributed to its alliance with the BPF

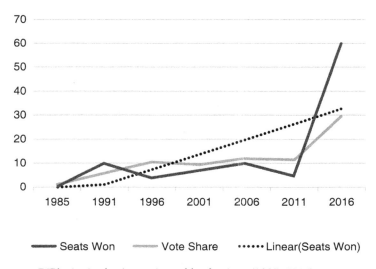

FIGURE 4.2 BJP's rise in the Assam Assembly elections (1985–2016)

TABLE 4.3 Political performance of BJP in Assam Assembly elections region-wise (1985–2016)

Region	Years						
	2016	2011	2006	2001	1996	1991	1985
Upper Assam (56)	33	2	5	3	0	0	0
Lower Assam (50)	15	3	0	1	0	1	0
Barak Valley (20)	12	0	5	4	4	9	0
Total seats (126)	60	5	10	8	4	10	0

Source: Author's own calculation based on Election Commission of India's statistical report on State Assembly elections of Assam from 1985–2016, available at https://eci.gov.in/statistical-report/statistical-reports/.

that withheld the dispersion of anti-Congress votes and consolidated the position of the BJP-led alliance. The Barak Valley can be considered a BJP's stronghold of support, where out of 20 seats including Autonomous District, the BJP was able to win a significant number of seats compared to other regions. In the three Bengali-dominated districts (Cachar, Hailakandi and Karimganj in the Barak Valley), where the BJP has strong dominance for a long time in constituencies such as Silchar, Dholai, Katigora, Patharkandi and Ratabari, the BJP won 8 seats out of 15. For the first time in Autonomous District also, the BJP won four seats out of five. In Upper Assam constituencies such as Behali, Rangapara, Lumding, Dibrugarh and Duliajan, and in Lower Assam constituencies such as Golokganj and Sorbhog, the BJP could uphold its dominance in Assembly elections. Previously, during the Lok Sabha elections, the BJP could capture all the Assembly segments in Lok Sabha constituencies of Dibrugarh and Tezpur. The BJP-led alliance performed most impressively in Scheduled Tribes (ST) reserved constituencies where out of 16 such reserved ST seats BJP could win 14. BJP's alliance partner BPF won six seats whereas BJP itself won a total of eight seats. BJP's consolidation in tea tribe–dominated areas remains unprecedented. The decision by the Union government led by Narendra Modi giving support for granting Scheduled Tribe (ST) status to six communities including tea tribes, Tai-Ahom, Koch-Rajbongshi, Moran, Mattak and Chutia communities helped the BJP to obtain support from these communities during the 2016 Assam election (Tripathi et al. 2018). The BJP has not only established its dominance in both Lok Sabha and Assembly elections, but the BJP also became the largest party in the Assam panchayat election held in December 2018 (India Today 2018). From the 2014 Lok Sabha election to the 2018 panchayat election in Assam, the BJP has emerged as the dominant national player that has replaced Congress not only at the national level but also in the grassroots-level elections (Table 4.4).

Religion as a factor

In Assam's diverse society, where issues of illegal migration, militancy and tribal separatism have dominated politics in recent decades, parties having bases cutting

TABLE 4.4 BJP and other parties' performance in Assam panchayat election (2018)

Party-Post	GPM (21,990)	GPP (2,199)	APM (2,199)	ZPM (420)
BJP	9,025	991	1,020	212
INC	7,239	760	772	147
AGP	1,676	137	117	19
AIUDF	1,023	130	138	26

Source: Assam State Election Commission press release, 2018.

Note: GPM: Gaon Panchayat Member; GPP: Gaon Panchayat President; APM: Anchalik Panchayat Member; ZPM: Zila Parishad Member.

across ethnic/religious cleavages have a good chance of garnering widespread support (Sharma 2014a). Against the backdrop of contentious issues of religious identity occupying centre stage at the national level, the State Assembly polls expectedly witnessed sharpened ethnic-religious polarization, especially on the long-standing issue of illegal migration from Bangladesh. After the 2014 polls, the Congress broke its alliance with the BPF that had been seen as patronizing tribal militants in their anti-Muslim pogroms. However, Congress' efforts to build up an alliance of 'secular' parties emulating the Bihar model did not materialize. Moreover, the defection of its main dissident leader, who had been its star campaigner and strategist since the late 1990s, along with his followers including nine Congress MLAs into BJP in 2015 led to a sea change in the political scenario.

The victories of both the AIUDF and the BJP in 2014 point to a polarization of votes along religious lines. Given the high turnouts across the state, an unprecedented Hindu consolidation backed by Narendra Modi's popularity in the state may have impacted the outcome. Modi's extensive campaigns in the state in the run-up to the elections drew spectacularly huge audiences. He specifically raised the issue of migrants from Bangladesh, drawing a distinction between those who he said were being brought for 'vote bank' politics and the Hindu migrants who he said were being harassed in the neighbouring country and hence needed to be accommodated (*Times of India* 2014). On the other side of the religious divide, the Muslims, constituting about 35% of the population, did not seem to have voted for the Congress with the same intensity as the Hindus voted for the BJP, with the AIUDF scoring heavily in constituencies dominated by Muslims of East Bengal origin. A consolidated Hindu vote and a divided Muslim vote could be one of the key reasons for the BJP's victories in constituencies with substantial Muslim populations, like Nagaon. Nagaon is significant because despite all its nine assembly constituencies being represented by other parties including Congress, AIUDF and AGP, the BJP in 2014 was able to retain the Lok Sabha seat that it had held since 1999. Overall, out of the six Lok Sabha seats with a Muslim population in the range of 20% to 40%, the BJP won three and AIUDF one. There are two seats – Karimganj and Dhubri – where Muslims constitute over 40% of the total population, and both were won by the AIUDF (Sharma 2014a).

In 2016, the BJP managed to patch up a 'rainbow alliance' with regionalist and tribal parties in a move to consolidate votes on the issue of protection of indigenous identity from 'illegal Bangladeshi Muslim infiltrators'. The census figures showing a steady rise in the percentage of Muslim population (from 24.6% in 1971 to 34.22% in 2011) became handy in this campaign, raising fears among non-Muslims that the state was gradually becoming Muslim-majority due to continuous illegal migration, allegedly with Congress' patronage. The BJP's projection of a charismatic ex-All Assam Student Union (AASU)and ex-AGP tribal leader known for his 'Assamese-nationalist' and anti-immigrant views as its chief ministerial candidate and the tie-up with regional and tribal parties enabled the party to change its 'Hindi-speaking' and 'Hindu-nationalist' image to that of a national party with regional orientation. The BJP-led central government's September 2015 decision to allow minority refugees from Bangladesh and Pakistan to stay in India even after the expiry of their visas on humanitarian grounds also helped in drawing the substantial Bengali Hindu votes towards the party (The Indian Express 2015).

The alliance forged between the BJP and the AGP in March 2016 just a month ahead of the State Assembly polls further consolidated the Hindu votes. In terms of issues, the main issue for AGP and the BJP in Assam had always been the same, that of illegal migrants, with one important difference: while the AGP was against all illegal migrants irrespective of religion, the BJP targeted only the Muslim migrants (Sharma 2014a). The BJP gained ethnic and regional projection through its ability to craft a coalition with AGP and BPF. This ethnic-regionalist coalition enhanced the BJP's legitimacy and acceptability while also absorbing the anti-incumbency vote against Congress. The BJP's strategy of seeking alliances with 'like-minded parties' to keep the Congress out of power, while keeping up its rhetoric against the AIUDF which it portrayed as the 'protector of illegal migrants', clearly helped in consolidating the Hindu voters and played a decisive role in ensuring the BJP alliance's landslide victory, even as the Muslim votes remained largely divided between the Congress and AIUDF.

In a situation where voters' literacy/educational levels are low and large sections of rural population lack access to various forms of media, the impact of political mobilization through internet/SMS becomes minimal, while local channels of TV and radio and local newspapers may have only a limited influence. Here political mobilization through public meetings as well as through informal channels including social and religious gatherings makes a considerable impact. Mobilization by local religious clerics and open use of religious symbolism by the AIUDF supremo Maulana Badruddin Ajmal, himself a noted cleric as well as business magnate, may have effectively mobilized mass support: his party, founded in 2005, draws strength from the fear among migrant Muslims settled in central and western Assam of being persecuted on suspicion of being Bangladeshi infiltrators. The AIUDF and the BJP, with opposing political and ideological positions, cater to different communities and their support bases do not overlap; religious polarization thus works in favour of both, though such polarization may not hold for long in the backdrop of linguistic and ethnic tensions (Sharma 2014a).

Conclusion

In an ethnically divided milieu, the rise of religious polarization and the consolidation of religious identities may be transient. In case of Assam, the dominant social cleavages run more along ethnic-linguistic than along religious lines. Among the many streams of migrants pouring into the sparsely populated province during British rule and thereafter, the Bengali migrants including Hindus who came mostly as government functionaries and small traders, and Muslims who were mostly peasants constituted the most numerous groups. A large number of Hindu refugees from East Pakistan also had to be accommodated in the wake of partition. Demographic changes occurring as a result of immigration became a cause of concern for native populations, including the non-tribal Assamese and tribal groups with less numerous populations.

Historically, Assamese identity aspirations since the pre-independence days centred around the preponderance of Bengali speakers in the government offices and educational institutions of the state, fearing that the numerical strength of Bengali speakers and their perceived unity enabled them to dominate over other language groups. To counter this, the Assamese sought to construct a larger Assamese society encompassing the smaller tribal groups. With India's independence and partition, Assam's demographic structure changed substantially, as Sylhet district became separated, taking away the Bengali majority component of the province's population. Leaders from the Brahmaputra Valley – the traditional Assamese homeland – now dominated in the state legislature, and the Assamese language gained importance in government offices and educational institutions. The responses to the gradual 'Assamization' policy differed among ethnic groups, varying from total resentment in the case of the Bengali Hindus and the hill tribes to open acquiescence in that of the tea and ex-tea garden workers and migrant Bengali Muslim peasants (Sharma 2002: 142). As Myron Weiner puts it, Assamese anti-outsider sentiments were directed mainly against Bengali Hindus who dominated in the bureaucracy and educational institutions and Marwari traders who controlled the economy (Weiner 1978: 91).

The separation of a few major hill districts from the state by the early 1970s left the population of hill tribes in Assam much reduced and resulted in a sharper division between the two major linguistic communities concentrated in the two valleys of the state – the Assamese in the Brahmaputra Valley and the Bengalis in the Barak Valley. The Assamese now sought to consolidate their numbers by actively seeking the inclusion of tea workers, immigrant Muslim peasants and other marginalized groups within the Assamese identity. The Assam Sahitya Sabha, the main literary body championing the cause of Assamese language, lent support to these trends among the *Na-Asamiya* (literally 'New Assamese'), including the tea community and the immigrant Muslims, whom it held as the model for other settler groups to follow (Sharma 2002: 144).

The tumultuous Assam Movement against 'illegal immigrants' that captured nationwide attention in early 1980s embittered relations between natives and migrant settlers, and brought issues of ethnic-religious identity to the fore. Anti-migrant sentiments now shifted focus to the growth in numbers of migrant Muslim peasants from Eastern Bengal and their descendants. The argument of the movement leaders was that migration of both Hindus and Muslims from what was earlier East Pakistan, and now Bangladesh had continued on a large scale after partition, and that their growing numbers were reducing the natives to a decided minority. Specifically it was the growth in percentage of Muslim population in many districts that began to be focused upon, especially in the context of the 'Foreigners' Issue' assuming communal dimensions. It was the religious angle of the immigration issue that became a handy tool for the BJP to establish roots in Assam.

The regional party, AGP – which came into existence after the Assam Movement with the avowed goal of driving out all illegal migrants irrespective of language or religion as per the terms of the Accord of 1985 – failed to live up to its expectations and lost credibility as an effective bulwark against illegal migrants. Its leadership tussles and electoral debacles in the period between 2001 and 2014 reduced it to the position of a minor party on the eve of the 2016 State Assembly elections. Such compulsions compelled it to agree on an alliance with the BJP as a subsidiary partner. The genius of the BJP lay in its ability to convert anti-outsider sentiments among Assamese and tribal populations into fear of being outnumbered by 'illegal migrants' belonging to one religious category. Specifically it raised the issue of protection of *jati, mati, bheti* ('community, land and homestead') from 'illegal Bangladeshi Muslim migrants' and managed to draw support from diverse ethnic communities with its promise of freeing the land from the foreigners' clutches. The contradiction, however, lies in the fact that religious categories overlap the insider-outsider divisions, and hence political equations in a changing situation become vulnerable to varying types of ethnic mobilization. The recent rise of popular movements led by multifarious groups based mainly among native populations in the Brahmaputra Valley including the All Assam Students' Union, as well as by organizations based mainly among Muslims against the Citizenship (Amendment) Bill that seeks to bestow citizenship upon certain categories of non-Muslim migrants escaping religious persecution in neighbouring Muslim-majority countries (including Bangladesh) appears to have put the BJP on the defensive on the eve of the 2019 Lok Sabha elections, with the AGP withdrawing support from the BJP-led government on the sensitive issue (The Assam Tribune 2019: 1). The future of the saffron party in the state, and indeed in the entire region, depends on its ability to accommodate regional aspirations within its larger framework of religious nationalism.

References

ACMS (2000). *Memorandum presented to Sonia Gandhi, President, All India Congress* Committee by Tea Tribes' MLAs led by P.S. Ghatowar, President, Assam Chah Mazdoor Sangh (ACMS), Dibrugarh.

The Assam Tribune. (2015a, February 10). '72 Pc Turnout in State Civic Polls'. Retrieved June 18, 2016, from www.assamtribune.com/scripts/mdetails.asp?id=feb1015/at050.

The Assam Tribune. (2015b, October 11). 'Cong: Reduced to Minority in NCHAC'. Retrieved June 18, 2016, from www.assamtribune.com/scripts/detailsnew.asp?id=oct1115/at053.

The Assam Tribune. (2019, January 14). 'Citizenship Bill: Centre Ignored Warnings from Security Agencies'. Retrieved January 15, 2019, from http://www.assamtribune.com/scripts/mdetails.asp?id=jan1419.

Bhattacharjee, Malini (2016). 'Tracing the Emergence and Consolidation of Hindutva in Assam', *Economic and Political Weekly*, 51(16), pp. 80–7.

Bijukumar, V. (2019). *Parties and Electoral Politics in North East India*, New Delhi: Kalpaz.

Borpujari, H.K. (1995). 'The Politics of Migration in Assam', *The Assam Tribune*, January 4.

Census of India. (2011). 'Population by Religion Community – 2011', *The Registrar General & Census Commissioner*, India. Archived from the original on 25 August 2015.

Deka, K.M., M.N. Das, A.N.S. Ahmed, N.L. Dutta and T. Lahon (1987). *Election Politics in Assam*, Guwahati: Bani Prokash.

Firstpost. (2017, April 21). 'Rise of Hindutva in North East: RSS, BJP Score in Assam, Manipur But Still Untested in Arunachal'. Retrieved January 6, 2019, from www.firstpost.com/politics/rise-of-hindutva-in-north-east-rss-bjp-make-a-mark-in-assam-manipur-but-poll-waters-still-untested-in-arunachal-3391504.html.

Gohain, H. (2003). 'Sangh Politics in Assam', *Communalism Combat*, No. 88. Retrieved January 6, 2019, from www.sabrang.com/cc/archive/2003/july03/spreport3.html.

Goswami, Sandhya and Vikas Tripathi (2015). 'Understanding the Political Shift in Assam: Withering Congress Dominance', *Economic and Political Weekly*, 50(39), pp. 67–71.

Guwahati Plus. (2018, January 22). 'Hindutva and Bharat Are Inseparable: RSS Chief Mohan Bhagwat'. Retrieved January 6, 2019, from www.guwahatiplus.com/daily-news/hindutva-and-bharat-are-inseparable-rss-chief-mohan-bhagwat.

The Hindu. (2016, March 31). 'AASU Cut Up with BJP, Congress and AIUDF'. Retrieved April 12, 2016, from https://www.thehindu.com/elections/assam2016/aasu-cut-up-with-bjp-congress-and-aiudf/article8418901.ece.

India Today. (2018, December 18). 'Relief to BJP as Party Wins 50% Seats in Assam Panchayat Elections'. Retrieved January 6, 2019, from www.indiatoday.in/elections/story/bjp-assam-panchayat-polls-rural-elections-results-seats-win-1412280-2018-12-18.

The Indian Express. (2015, September 7). 'India to Allow Minorities from Pakistan, Bangladesh to Stay Without Papers'. Retrieved April 12, 2016, from https://indianexpress.com/article/india/india-others/india-to-allow-minorities-from-pakistan-bangladesh.

The Indian Express. (2016, April 8). 'The Politics Around the Two Ends of Assam's Complex Muslim Spectrum'. Retrieved April 12, 2016.

Jaffrelot, Christophe (2016). 'BJP's Assam Win Is Proof Hindutva Has Reached Areas Where It Was Marginal', *Indian Express*. Retrieved February 11, 2017, from http://indianexpress.com/article/opinion/columns/bjp-sarbananda-sonowal-assam-assemblyelections-tarun-gogoi-congress-the-enigma-of-arrival-2846193/.

Mahanta, Nani Gopal (2014). 'Lok Sabha Elections in Assam', *Economic and Political Weekly*, 49(35), pp. 19–22.

Mehta, Pratap Bhanu (2016). 'A BJP-Dominant System', *Indian Express*. Retrieved February 11, 2017, from https://indianexpress.com/article/opinion/columns/bjp-assam-electionssarbananda-sonowal-tarun-gogoi-kerala-elections-2809631/.

Misra, Udayon (2016). 'Victory for Identity Politics, Not Hindutva in Assam', *Economic and Political Weekly*, 51(22), pp. 20–3.

News18. (2018, March 4). 'North East Elections: Rise, Reach and Outreach of the Sangh'. Retrieved January 6, 2019, from www.news18.com/news/politics/north-east-elections-the-rise-reach-and-outreach-of-the-rss-1677851.html.

Palshikar, Suhas (2014). 'India's 2014 Lok Sabha Elections: Critical Shifts in the Long Term, Caution in the Short Term', *Economic and Political Weekly*, XLIX(39), pp. 39–49.

Palshikar, Suhas (2017a). 'India's Second Dominant Party System', *Economic and Political Weekly*, 52(12), pp. 12–15.

Palshikar, Suhas (2017b). 'What Makes BJP Really Different', *Economic and Political Weekly*, 52(19), pp. 12–13.

Palshikar, Suhas (2018). 'Towards Hegemony: BJP Beyond Electoral Dominance', *Economic and Political Weekly*, 53(33), pp. 36–42.

Sharma, Dhruba Pratim (2002). *Labour and the Politics of Identity: A Study of Tea Garden Workers in the Brahmaputra Valley (1985–2001)*, PhD Thesis, Centre for Political Studies, Jawaharlal Nehru University, New Delhi.

Sharma, Dhruba Pratim (2014a). 'Assam: BJP's Entry in North East', *The Hindu* (website), June 26. Retrieved August 28, 2018, from www.thehindu.com/opinion/op-ed/assam-bjps-entry-in-north-east/article6151572.ece.

Sharma, Dhruba Pratim (2014b). 'Saffron Surge in Assam', *Research Journal Social Sciences*, Department of Political Science, Panjab University, Chandigarh, 22(2), pp. 224–33.

Srikanth, H. (1999). 'Communalising Assam: AGP's Loss is BJP's Gain', *Economic and Political Weekly*, 34(49), pp. 3412–14.

Thapa, Rudraman (2002, February 20). 'Samprati Asamat Chah Janagosthir Rajnoitik Bhumika', *Dainik Janambhumi (Assamese Daily)*, p. 4.

Times of India. (2014, February 22). 'We Must Accommodate Hindu Bangladeshi Migrants: Modi in Assam'. Retrieved April 12, 2016, from https://timesofindia.indiatimes.com/india/We-must-accommodate-Hindu-Bangladeshi-migrants-Modi-in-Assam/articleshow/30856540.cms.

Tripathi, V., T. Das and S. Goswami (2018). 'National Narrative and Regional Subtext: Understanding the Rise of BJP in Assam', *Studies in Indian Politics*, 6(1), pp. 1–11.

Weiner, Myron (1978). *Sons of the Soil: Migration and Ethnic Conflict in India*, Princeton: Princeton University Press.

5
CHURCH AND POLITICAL ACTION IN MIZORAM

V. Bijukumar

The conventional wisdom regarding political action is that it always relates to the state and its institutions, and it is often legitimized and assumed to have predominance because it is based on reason and public good. However, apart from the state, other institutions have also plunged into political action, especially in democracy. For instance, religious institutions resort to political action and thereby facilitate or undermine the democratic process. Religious institutions' resorting to political action is often related to applying values involved in the religion. The religious mission of the church motivates political activity infusing ecclesial ethics or Christian values and morality in political action. In other words, religious cultures, values and privileges also influence the political action of the church. Since people are extending their obligation to the church and the religious principles, religion smoothes political action. Political action in this context is based on morality which includes principles of action and personal ethics. When the state resorts to political action, political morality is considered to be the basis of a political action. To Aristotle, the hallmark of human action including politics is the pursuit of moral virtue, which ultimately ensures common happiness for the individual and society at large.

The role of religious values and institutions in liberal democracy was recognized by many scholars. Max Weber, for instance, recognized the role of Protestant ethics in the flourishing democracies in Europe. It is often argued that evangelism often promotes moralism and associational life conducive to democratization. Fukuyama also establishes a link between religion and democratization, highlighting religious institutions and religious values. Religion's relevance in political life is recognized by Tocqueville, who argues that religion as a unifying social force to maintain democratic life. According to him, Christianity is responsible for the rise of political freedom in America, and a free society necessarily requires religious foundation. Religion is the most important source of common beliefs for citizens and as the preservation of a decent political order. He also recognized contribution of religion to sustain public morality and that religion can bring morality in public life. Moral convictions rooted in religious belief can be used to solve the malaise of politics. According to him, almost all human actions 'arise from a very general idea men have conceived of God, or his relations with the human race, of the nature of their souls, and of their duties towards those like them' (Tocqueville 1969: 12). Democratic citizens need a shared understanding of religion. Tocqueville uses Christian morality for political action in a democracy. Democracy can be saved from authoritarianism invoking religious morality, sensitizing and teaching the people.

The conventional wisdom regarding the state and church relationship is that when the church interferes in politics, it denigrates governmental autonomy. When the state interferes in religion, it erodes religious authority. Secular reason is the basis of political action. It is argued that

> a secular reason for an action (or a belief) is roughly one whose status as a justifier of action (or belief) does not evidently depend on (but also does not deny) the existence of God; nor does it depend on theological considerations, or on the pronouncement of a person or institution as a religious authority.
> *(Audi 2011: 67)*

Secular reason is based on governmental neutrality in religious matters. Secular reason may not be put in a watertight compartment as it sometimes involves religious matters for the common cause.

In a secular democracy, churches have a prima facie obligation to abstain from supporting candidates for public office overtly. Such obligation of neutrality would be good, as it confines its commitment to its own religious mission. It is argued that 'political involvement is often highly preoccupying, and competent political action requires time and energy that could instead be devoted to the internal needs of the church and its members' (Audi 2011: 5). Church is not only an institutional character but also a way of life setting certain values, as its identity and faith are premised in Christ. Moltmann sees the identity of the church primarily as a missionary identity and while spreading the gospel, it creates certain consciousness among the believers. Rationalization and modernization of the world do not deter the spirit of church in society (Moltmann 1965).

In religious authority, legitimacy is derived from the religious obligation of individuals. In most cases, religious legitimacy surpasses political legitimacy enjoyed by the state and thereby undermines its political action. Religion organizes people for political action by involving its religious obligation and legitimacy. In other words, the political action of the church can distort state authority and power. The legitimacy enjoyed by the church in society influences political action. However, the political action of religion raised the question of political neutrality of religion. Religious citizens should be guided by religious morality, not political morality. However, others argue that since liberal democracy is morally guided, the absence of political morality leads other forms of morality, including religious morality.

Advent of the church in political action

The genesis of political action of the church can be traced back to the advent of the Christianity in Mizoram, when the Christian missionaries arrived in the Lushai Hills for proselytization work. The pioneer missionaries, Rev. J.H. Lorrain and Rev. F.W. Savidge, arrived in Mizoram on 11 January 1894. The church missionaries promoted evangelicalism through education, health and so forth, and the tribals embraced evangelical Christianity and thereby became influenced by evangelical ethics. In Mizoram, one of the largely Christian inhabited states in Northeast India, the church plays a vital role not only in social and religious life but also in the political life of the people. The church exercises social control and goes beyond the boundaries of sacred space. The social and political life revolves around the church, making the inseparability of religion and politics difficult. The church is not merely a religious institution but is also a social institution where many social activities are coordinated and performed. Its contribution to the social development of the state is well-known, especially in the areas of literacy, education and health, and making people awareness of social issues such as drug abuse and alcoholism. The church is attached to a web of institutions such as schools, hospitals, training centres and associations and youth organizations, thereby exercising its social control and public legitimacy. On many occasions, the church resorts to political action that is aimed at influencing the everyday life of the people in the state. The church mission is not confined only to propagating the Gospel in Mizo society and to focus on philanthropic responsibilities but also to engage in political activities.

The church was instrumental in enacting the Mizoram Liquor Total Prohibition and Control Act, and as result prohibition was imposed in 1997. The Mizo National Front's defeat in the Assembly election in 1989, among other things, was considered as the consequence of the church's political action due to government's reluctant to impose a ban on liquor sale in the state. In fact, the church complied with the demand of Yound Mizo Association (YMA) on prohibition. In July 2014, prohibition was lifted in spite of stiff opposition by the Presbyterian Church. Confrontation between state and church over lifting prohibition in the state can be seen as confrontation over two obligations enjoyed by church and state. However, the government adopted a tactical position that the move was to curb illegal, spurious liquor and thereby able to reduce the church's grudge against the government's decision. Thus the government was able to neutralize the political action of the church against lifting ban on liquor in a positive way.

The church not only engages in religious activities but also exercises its ethnic role. The church imposes moral values and norms among the Mizos and at the same creates an ethnic consciousness among them. Church beliefs and doctrines are deeply rooted in Mizo society and the church's role is evident in creating identity consciousness and erecting identity boundaries among the Mizos. Rising ethnic conscious and sentiments through its political action was considered to be an effort to indigenize the churches and win back the support of the ethnic communities. The church through its political action initially raised the ethnic conscious of the tribals and fused it with the Christian theological consciousness. Often the ethnic identity of the Mizos combined with religious values propagated by the church. Even the self-identity of the Mizos is defined in terms of Christian religious values. It also stands for protecting ethnic identity and culture. The church offers incentives for the ethnic communities to encourage couples to have more babies. The church also imposes a dress code on women, as they should not wear see-through dresses or clothes that expose the breasts or show too much skin. The church on many occasion insists on people to wear tradition Mizo *puan* – a piece of cloth woman wrap around their waists reaching their ankles.

The political action of the church was explicated in its role in conflict resolution when it emerged as the broker of peace in the insurgency that hit Mizoram. During the insurgency, the Presbyterian Church initiated a peace process and dialogue and played a vital role in the signing of the Mizo Accord in 1986. It negotiated peace talks between the church and MNF leaders. The Presbyterian Church condemned the violent activities of the MNF. At the beginning of 1982, peace talks were initiated by the church against insurgency and gruesome killings. On 30 July 1982, 24 representatives of various denominations formed a committee called the Zoram Kohharan Hruaitute Committee (ZKHC) – Christian Peace Committee – Mizoram Churches Leaders Committee to bring peace in the state. The church committees brought the insurgent groups to dialogue with the Government of India. The political action of the church, especially its role in peace negotiations in the late 1960s, was criticized by the MNF, which accused the church of interfering politics. In 1966, the conflict between the church leaders and MNF surfaced when the Church leaders condemned the violence unleashed by the Mizo movement. The MNF claimed that church should not interfere in politics. The political action of church was criticized by the insurgents.

The church as an election watchdog

The church in Mizoram normally does not overtly support any political party in polls and never calls for the people to vote for particular party candidates. Unlike other societies, the church does not anchor on any particular candidates sponsored by any political parties or issue statements to particular parties for power. The church is not proposing but pushing for a candidate on the basis of his/her merit and cleanness in public life. However, it sets new morality in political life which enables ensuring peaceful, free and fair elections, public and institutional morality and religious duty. Often posters appear in the form of 'vote for Christ' manifesting exercising franchise as a religious duty. The electoral politics in Mizoram is centred around the state, YMA and the church. Political parties use Sunday mass to connect the electorate. In 1993, a state level coordination committee on election was set up to monitor the process of elections in the state. In 2004, the Mizoram Presbyterian Church in its synod agreed to take electoral reforms to clean up the electoral system. As Fernandes asserts, the

> church does not mention names of particular political candidate but highlights what kind of people are trustworthy and can have a government

relationship with church and society. Church in Mizoram therefore gives Mizo citizen a guide to elect responsible leaders.

(Fernandes 2009: 141)

The more overt form of church's political action in Mizoram was the formation of Mizo Peoples Forum (MPF), a conglomeration of major churches and non-governmental organizations to 'cleanse' electoral politics, in 20 June 2006. The major churches include Presbyterian Church of Mizoram, Catholic Church of Mizoram, Evangelical Free Church of India, Wesleyan Methodist Church, Evangelical Church of Maraland and Lairam Jesus Christ Baptist Church. Apart from major church organizations, the MPF constitutes the ethnic organizations such as YMA, Mizo Hmeichhe Insuihkhawn Pawl (Women's Federation), Mizo Upa Pawl (Elders' Association) and Mizo Zirlai Pawl (Students Association). Though MPF involves diverse stakeholders, it is controlled by the Presbyterian Church, the largest church in Mizoram to which 85% of Christians belong, and it has a local wing in various localities and decentralized units across the state.

In the 27-point Memorandum of Undertaking (MoU) signed with major political parties in the state, the MPF enforced certain 'dos' and 'don'ts' to political parties during the electioneering. Accordingly, parties were requested to refrain from organizing grand feasting on the eve of election, distribution of money during election, prohibiting parties from dropping the voters at their polling station by means of vehicles, restricting number of flags, posters and banners, allocation of designated places for political speeches and rallies and so forth. It also bans door-to-door campaigning ten days prior to the polling day, which they felt would encourage bribes. It also ensures no political campaigning on Sundays. It also insists that political parties should only make an election manifesto which they can implement. The MPF volunteers distribute pamphlets of political parties to people, distribute voter identification slips to people and monitor seating arrangements outside the polling stations for those waiting for casting their votes. It also sensitizes people and political parties to respect the integrity of candidates by each other.

The 'Election Guidelines', often described as 'Moral Code of Conduct' enforced by the MPF on par with the 'Model Code of Conduct' issued by the Election Commission of India, among other things stressed the need for ensuring peaceful election by monitoring the selection of candidates by the parties, taking into account of their hard work and integrity. It urges desisting from selecting candidates having corrupt and criminal backgrounds. According to the MoU, any party violating the Moral Code of Conduct will lead to invalidation of the party. Further, the church ensures peaceful elections, selection of party candidates, monitors the election campaign and sensitizes people. It also plays an important role in educating the public on political matters and issues guidelines on election campaigns. It monitors spending by parties and candidates, imposes restrictions on the use of microphones and littering public places with pamphlets and posters. The campaign should not be a disturbance to the public and the church prohibits any use of force. Political parties in the state have to acquire the prior permission of the MPF to organize political rallies. The guidelines are often read out at churches to sensitize the believers under its denominational jurisdiction. While the church's Moral Code of Conduct was abided by all people, it also warns of 'exemplary punishment' for the violation of guidelines both by the parties and voters. For the first time, in Assembly election in 2018, each constituency in the state had one polling booth set up exclusively for women voters, manned by women polling and security personnel. These booths, pink polling stations, have been named after the flower called 'Dingdi'. In addition to this, voters were provided with benches to sit instead of standing for long hours in a queue to cast their vote.

The church's political action as the 'election watchdog' was appreciated and even endorsed by the Election Commission of India. The Election Commission of India meets ethnic organizations along with parties in discussing the electoral preparedness. The former chief election commissioner of India, S.Y. Quraishi, appreciated the role of the church in the Seventh Regional Consultation of Electoral Reforms in Guwhati in 2011, stating that 'this is wonderful idea. Electoral corruption creeps in from door-to-door campaigning. So banning such campaigns is one of the most effective ways of stopping corruption in poll process' (*Mizoram Post*, 17 June 2011).

Church and ecclesial citizenship

The church assumes its legitimacy in enforcing the 'Moral Code of Conduct' derived from the ecclesial citizenship of the Ecclesial Authority (EA). The EA, in the footsteps of Jesus, creates a form of ecclesial citizenship where everyone belongs to an ecclesial community. As against political citizenship, where citizens are considered to be members of a political community, membership in an ecclesial community is based on theological morality and emotional values attached to religion. In most cases, ecclesial citizenship conflicts with values of political citizenship, since membership in an ecclesial community does not accommodate others and thereby denies others political freedom. The moral principles invoked by the EA contradict the values of other religious communities and thereby lead to systematic exclusion of certain sections of society. The EC enforced by the church derives from religious norms. While political citizenship grounded in the principles of equality believes that self-realization is possible in the political community, the ecclesial citizenship believes that self-realization is possible only through its adherence to religious values. EC guarantees a citizen's rights and responsibilities towards church authority. Political citizenship also recognizes the importance of guaranteeing religious freedom to its citizens. The state recognizes the religious groups and ensures religious freedom and is not guided by any religious values. Political citizenship involves legitimate political action that people have to act the rules set by the state, establishing legitimacy between the state and citizenship. The ethics of good citizenship have certain moral principles. When democracy moves away from morality, religious morality steps in.

Second, obeying the 'Moral Code of Conduct' gains legitimacy from the idea of obligation enjoyed by the EA. The EA establishes a kind of obligation of people which is parallel to the political obligation of the state. Religious citizenship brings rights and duties of individuals to the EA. The political action of the church gets legitimacy through ecclesial citizenship. Religious obligation is not only pious but also physical. Obeying the EA is equated with obeying God. The ecclesiastical obligation often forces the believer to pay tax to the church. It is to remind that under the Sixth Schedule of the Constitution, tribals in Mizoram are exempted from paying income tax to the Government of India, but they have to contribute one-tenth of their income to the church in the name of God for the welfare of the people. As William Singh argues:

> Reverence towards the church remains strong in Mizoram and the church's authority has never been questioned in Mizoram since the evangelization of Mizo society in 1903. Indeed, so revered is its role that the church functions like a state within a state. Not surprisingly, the church, which should remain confined to matters pertaining to religion, often intrudes into Mizoram's institutional and political sphere. So while criticism of the church is absent in Mizoram, the state government is criticized on issues like corruption, price rise, rising in equality between rich and poor, etc.
>
> *(Singh 2012: 24)*

The church without political authority

The political actions of the church often take on the political authority in ransom where the state in most cases is unable to exercise its will on the people. The church through its action ensures that no political activity take place in Sundays. Political parties and people also ensure no political encroachment is taking place in the state on Sunday, a day devoted to sacred purposes, cessation from worldly labours and employment. During the day, worldly occupations are forbidden. It is based on the obligation to God. Detracting from temporal affairs, it focuses on spiritual concerns. Six days are for promotion of temporal interests and the seventh day for spiritual life. In October 2008, the major political parties in Mizoram submitted a memorandum to the Chief Election Commissioner of India asking him to change the date of State Assembly polls as the poll day (29 November) falls on the Sabbath (Saturday), a sacred day for some churches and the Mizo Jewish community. Sabbath is observed as a holy day by other smaller church denominations and also by the Jewish community in the state, who believe that they are the lost tribe of Israel. The Seventh-Day Adventist Church even asked for the extension of polling time, if the change of date is not possible. It appealed the ECI that church members could exercise their franchise after 6 p.m. on polling day, when the sacred day is over. In the 2013 State Assembly election, the Mizoram Kohhran Hruaitute Committee, a conglomerate of leaders of 13 major churches, pressured the ECI to change the dates of polling (4 December) and counting of votes (8 December) to accommodate the Presbyterian Church's five-day synod. The polling and counting days fell on Sundays, which is confined to prayer. The

ECI later preponed the poll day to 25 November and postponed counting to 9 December to suit their convenience.

In the exercising its political action, the church always seek the help of the ethnic organizations such as the Young Mizo Association (YMA), a quasi-church youth organization with over 40,000 members, to promote good Christian life in the state. YMA exercises its social control and political control in the state, and many times acts as an arm of the church. Community life is cemented by the agency of the church. The office bearers of YMA have direct line with the church. On many occasions such critical dependence perverts the stated goals of its political actions. The YMA terrorise the non-Mizo communities during electioneering, checking their electoral identity cards. Many times, the church is unable to discipline the YMA, as the former critically depends on the latter in its political action. The church for its political action empowers YMA and makes it difficult to comply with political authority. Many actions of the YMA in the past contributed to the erosion of community relations between the Mizos and non-Mizos. It weakened even the bridging capital between various communities in the state and failed to create an inter-ethnic networking (Bijukumar 2008, 2014).

The church-led MPF's political action in electioneering in the state undermines the autonomy of the political institutions and functioning of democracy, though the church through its political action makes the state accountable to the people. In other words, the political action of the church and ethnic organization overshadow the institutions of the state. The subservience of political and constitutional institutions to a religious institution, even for a good cause, can dampen the institutional values and its independent functioning. In exercising political action in electioneering the church and other ethnic organizations emerge as the parallel institutions to public institutions. It is argued that 'the style of electioneering in Mizoram where the church acts like an authority and supervises the electoral process is simply the manifestation of religious politics in Mizo society which can also be called as "desecularization of politics"' (Shyamkishor 2014: 144). The MPF's demand that only genuine citizens of India should have the right to vote often creates a political mess in the state. It gives leverage to the ethnic organizations to tease the non-Mizos and small ethnic communities in the state, such as the Reagnas.

Putting religious morality over political morality

The church's political action based on religious morality overshadows the principles of political morality. Election in a democracy as a secular activity has assumed the image of divine activity. The religious morality employed in the electioneering proves that political morality does not yield much results. Election is demeaned as a divine activity infused with religious morality. Invoking religious morality in a secular political action has much repercussions on democracy itself. Often questions raised whether religious moral principles can apply to a political action of the state. Even the political action of the church in electioneering was legitimized to cleanse politics and to bring new political culture in the state, it has devastating effect on the politics. The church is invoking its morality to cleanse electoral politics in the states.

Religious obligation violates political obligation leading to chaos in society. Obeying EA is part of religious obligation. The active engagement of church in the electoral process of Mizoram turns out to be critical of the principles of ecclesiastical political neutrality as it interferes imposing reasonable restriction on candidates during electioneering. It violates the very idea of ecclesiastical political neutrality. Religious institutions such as the church should ensure neutrality. Church involvement in political action triggers a debate on the principles of ecclesiastical political neutrality. The ecclesiastical political neutrality is justified on the ground that 'political involvement is often highly preoccupying, and competent political action requires time and energy that could instead be devoted to the internal needs of the church and its members' (Audi 2011: 95). Neutrality ensures the institutional sustainability and the welfare of the church itself. The ecclesiastical political neutrality principle is justified from the point of view of institutional ethics. When it enters into political action, the role of church tends to be compromised by political activity. The opposite view is that neutrality will not work when political morality is declining in democracy. So the principle of political neutrality should be modified.

Church 'selective' political action

Though the church engages in political action which gained wider acceptability in the Mizo society, it was not able to extend its political action in many other areas. While the church pushes for candidates having integrity and hard work, it is always silent on ensuring women representation in the selection of candidates by various political parties. It should be mentioned that in Mizoram, female voters outnumber male voters. In 2011 the women voters outnumbered their male counterparts by 16,573. The total number of female voters was 388,046 and the total number of male voters was 371,473. The representation of women in the Assembly is meagre, though Mizoram is outwardly projected as a woman-friendly state where most of the women run shops and markets. Though the church was successful in bringing peace to the insurgency-hit areas and achieving high social development, it failed to ensure the 'second democratic upsurge' – the representation of women in the government and Assembly. Since 1972, when Mizoram became a Union Territory and full-fledged state in 1987, only three women – Thanmawi (1978), K. Thansiami (1979) and Lalhlimpui (1987) – won seats in the State Legislature and Lalhlimpui was the only woman minister in 1987 in the MNF government.

Second, the church was also silent on giving representation to both smaller tribal communities. For instance, the church took a lackadaisical attitude towards the problems faced by the Hindu Reangs, commonly described as Brus. The Reangs faced ethnic cleansing and displacement in Mizoram from the dominant Mizo community forced to settle in the refugee camps in neighbouring Tripura. Though a tripartite agreement was arrived at by the Government of India and the governments of Mizoram and Tripura on the repatriation of displaced Brus, they declined to back them in Mizoram, fearing further ethnic cleansing. It should be remembered that in 1997, the ethnic organizations such as YMA and MZP, with the connivance of the church, went on rampant ethnic cleansing in the aftermath of the killing of a Mizo forest guard allegedly by the Brus. The political deprivation of the Brus reached its height when their demand for a separate Autonomous District Council (ADC) for the Brus-inhabited areas of Mizoram was rejected by the Mizoram government under pressure from ethnic organizations. In political retaliation and the pressure from ethnic organization, around 17,000 names of Brus were deleted from the voters' rolls. The move was seen as an attempt to reduce the political voice of the minority Brus in the state politics. The church's selective political action also visible when the Election Commission of India conducted voting in Brus settlement areas in Tripura for the Mizoram Assembly election in 2013 under the direction of the Supreme Court. When the ethnic organizations critical of the government's move to extend right to franchise beyond its state jurisdiction to ensure the political rights of the Brus, the church – which is considered as the watchdog in the election and torchbearer of clean politics in the state – remained a mute spectator.

Conclusion

The political action of the church in the name of cleansing electoral politics in the state has serious repercussions not only for democracy but also peace and stability. The church warns of exemplary punishment for the violation of election guidelines by people and political parties, showing that political obligation is more physical than moral or ethical. The critiques often see that since the EA promotes an ecclesial citizenship, it exhibits certain exclusionary tendencies. The church's critical dependence on ethnic organization for monitoring electioneering in the state leads to further ethnic animosity among other communities in the state. In most cases, the social elite which controls the church uses political action to ignite ethnic polarization in the state. It should be remembered that with the class formation in Mizo society, the church augmented its role as an ethnic organization. It fails to control bandhs, blockades and even atrocities against non-tribal communities. The church had no voice in the issue of Myanmar refugees along the border, especially in Lawngtlai district. Often it became an instrument in the hands of the ethnic organizations to legitimize their actions against other ethnic communities.

The elusive peace achieved by the state is often hampered by the activities of the YMA when it unleashes atrocities against non-Mizos. Sometimes, the government often comes under undue pressure of the ethnic organizations. In many cases, the church was not successful in cleaning electoral politics in the state. Sometimes, the ethnic-based organizations are a liability for the church itself. The church's political action in some other levels leads to the inciting ethnic identity consciousness. Fernandes argues that 'in some extreme cases, church leaders even play a role in fanning communal tensions and ethnic rivalries by resurrecting age-old myths about tribal difference and the wrongs done to one tribe by another' (Fernandes 2009: 144).

The invocation of religious identity for political action has implications for democracy. The Christian identity is not only used by the church in its political action but also by extremist groups to gain legitimacy for their activities. In the 1960s, the Mizo National Front (MNF) legitimized its action, claiming that they are the true defenders of Christianity. The Mizo movement claimed that the impoverishment of Mizos in the Lushai Hills of Assam is of their stigmatized Christianized identity and it was used to legitimize its radical political action. There was a competitive use of Christian identity in political action by both church and extremist organizations to legitimize its action. As Fernandes argues,

> insurgency groups, terrorist organizations, and separatist movements taking the idiom of Christianity as a way of defining their political project have at times come up against the church, which tends to be more moderate politically and more conciliatory towards the Indian government and the Indian security forces.
>
> *(Fernandes 2009: 144)*

The National Socialist Council of Nagalim (NSCN) legitimized its demand for Nagalim – integration of all Naga-inhabited areas – invoking 'Nagaland for Christ'. In such situations, differentiating a political action of the church for a good or bad cause is a really cumbersome task, as invoking religious morality for a political action for a good cause, such as election watchdog and cleansing electoral politics, can be used for the most virulent forms of ethnic segregation and assertion in democracy.

References

Audi, Robert (2011). *Democratic Authority and the Separation of Church and State*, Oxford: Oxford University Press.
Bijukumar, V. (2008). 'Civil Society and Social Capital in Mizoram: Changing Dimensions and Emerging Trends', *Man and Society (A Journal of North-East Studies)*, V, pp. 57–80, Spring.
Bijukumar, V. (2014). 'Ethnicising Social Capital in Mizoram: The Role of Young Mizo Association', *Eastern Quarterly*, 10(3–4), pp. 111–23, Autumn–Winter.
'EC Pat for Mizo Church Ban on Door-to-Door Campaigning', *The Mizoram Post*, June 17, 2011, p. 3.
Fernandes, Sujatha (2009). 'Ethnicity, Civil Society, and the Church: The Politics of Evangelical Christianity in Northeast India', in (ed.), David Halloran Lumsdaine, *Evangelical Christianity and Democracy in Asia*, Oxford: Oxford University Press, pp. 131–51.
Moltmann, Jurgen (1965). *Theology of Hope: On the Ground and the Implications of a Christian Eschatology*, New York: Harper & Row Publishers.
Shyamkishor, Ayangbam (2014). 'Church as Election Watch Dog: The Mizoram Model', *Eastern Quarterly*, 10(3–4), Autumn and Winter, pp. 133–46.
Singh, N. William (2012, December 29). 'Politics of Divine Edict and Reverse Secularism', *Economic and Political Weekly*, 47(52), pp. 23–4.
Tocqueville, Alexis de (1969). *Democracy in America*, New York: Doubleday & Company.

6

IDENTITY, RELIGION AND DEVELOPMENT

The changing nature of political mobilization of Muslims in post-Sachar West Bengal

Abdul Matin

The Sachar Committee Report (SCR)[1] has generated heated public debates on the question of development deficit, social citizenship, inclusion and redistribution of India's largest Muslim minority community. This official document has not only broken the post-colonial myth of 'minority appeasement' but also broadened the horizon of 'Muslim politics' which were centred around the question of Urdu, Aligarh and personal laws by opening up the debates of everyday Muslim lives, such as myriad forms of social exclusion, socio-economic marginalization, security and educational disempowerment (Jaffrelot 2006; Hasan 2013). Zoya Hasan and Mushirul Hasan have argued that one of the biggest gains of the Sachar Committee was its reconstruction of the Muslim community as 'developmental subjects' of the state rather than primarily as a cultural and religious community (Hasan 2013: 242). Surinder Jodhka also argues that, in analyzing the issue of Muslim exclusion, the Sachar report foregrounded the question of citizenship, relegated issues of identity or cultural distinctiveness, and treated 'the Muslim question' as a question of social justice, human rights and the development of the marginalized and excluded (Jodhka 2007).

In the context of West Bengal, the Muslim population constitutes around 27% of the total population of the state, and the Sachar Committee Report (SCR) categorically pointed to the dismal socio-economic and educational marginalization of the Muslim community despite the 34-year rule of the Left Front Government (LFG from 1977–2011) led by the Communist Party of India (Marxist). Therefore the pro-poor and minority credentials of LFG came under serious scrutiny by community leaders, academics, social activists and needless to say the opposition party in the state, particularly the Trinamool Congress. While explaining the reasons behind the downfall of the left rule in West Bengal, Psephologists, including many social scientists, have argued that the impact of the SCR is one of the crucial issues which helped community organizations and later the Trinamool Congress to build a massive campaign for the mobilization of Muslims and resulted the erosion of the traditional rural Bengali Muslim social base of the left parties (Chakrabarty 2011; Bhattacharya 2014; Bose 2013).

This chapter addresses three important questions: What was the role of the Sachar Committee Report in changing the political discourse and the landscape of contemporary West Bengal? How are the religious minority organizations (here Muslim) able to form a 'political society' in the state of West Bengal where the left parties have ruled the state for more than three decades with a pro-minority image? And what are the changing natures of religious mobilizations in post-Sachar West Bengal?

Locating the 'Muslim minority' in post-colonial West Bengal

Muslims constitute the second-largest religious community and single largest minority community in West Bengal, constituting around 27% of the total population of the state as per the 2011 Census of India. The Muslim population is scattered almost all over West Bengal but is thickly concentrated in the districts of Murshidabad (63.67%), Maldah (49.72%), North Dinajpur (48.18%), Birbhum (35.18%), South 24 Parganas (34.07%), South Dinanpur (28.02%), Nadia (25.41%), Howrah (24.44%), Cooch Behar (24.24%), North 24 Parganas (24.22%), Kolkata (20.27%), Burdwan (19.18%), Hooghly (25.14%), East Medinipur (13.19%) and five more districts with Muslim populations between 5% and 10%. Twelve out of the 19 districts in West Bengal are recognized as Minority Concentrated Districts (MCDs) through a baseline survey by the Government of India based on the socio-economic backwardness (Census 2011).

Muslims are overwhelmingly concentrated in rural West Bengal and a large majority of them is engaged in agrarian activities and informal sectors. In the post-economic reform era, significant numbers of Muslims have been migrating out of West Bengal for employment as day labourers, particularly in the informal sectors including the construction industry, goldsmithing, the garment sector, and maidservants in the major cities like Delhi, Mumbai, Hyderabad, Trivandrum, Ahmedabad, Jaipur and so on.

Politically, Muslims in post-independent West Bengal have always remained with the mainstream 'secular' political parties. In the first three decades after independence till the late 1980s, Muslims in Bengal accepted the 'secular policies' of the Indian National Congress by rejecting the politics of the Muslim League. The election results of 1952 demonstrated that the large numbers of Muslims did support Congress, and as a result candidates of the Congress Party won in most Muslim-concentrated constituencies in West Bengal (Dasgupta 2011). From the late 1980s onwards till 2011, the great majority of the rural Muslims had supported the left parties, which undisputedly played a crucial role in continued the world's longest elected government in West Bengal. Christophe Jaffrelot argued that the inconsistent emphasis of left parties on secular politics and its principled opposition to the wave of Hindu nationalist, chauvinist and anti-Muslim politics that affected large parts of India from 1980s onwards attracted Muslims towards left politics (Jaffrelot 1999). It is a fact that, due to secular politics, the state of West Bengal has largely remained free from communal violence as well as the politics of Hindutva. Therefore the 'physical security' of the lives of minorities continues to remain safe and unthreatened (though large numbers of individuals in marginalized communities continue to lose their lives in routine electoral violence in West Bengal, and Muslims constitute significant numbers of these).

The Sachar Committee Report and various other studies and reports through different research institutes such as the Indian Council of Social Science Research, CSSSC[2] and the latest socio-economic study of Muslims in West Bengal conducted by Association SNAP[3] and the Pratichi Trust clearly revealed the dismal socio-economic condition of Muslims by using various parameters of measuring underdevelopment and backwardness. The rates of poverty (both urban and rural), unemployment, malnutrition, child mortality, illiteracy, gender discrimination, school drop-out rates and so forth are extremely high among the Muslims of West Bengal. The representation of Muslims in government employment, education, bureaucracy, the judiciary, the executive and the legislature is very low and grossly out of proportion with the community's population figures in the state (Government of India 2006, 2007; ICSSR Report 2008; Alam 2009; SNAP Report 2016).

The SCR categorically pointed out the miserable socio-economic and educational backwardness of Muslims in India, with state-wise breakup data on various parameters such as poverty, unemployment, illiteracy, school dropouts, malnutrition and so forth. According to the SCR, the socio-economic and educational condition of Muslim community in West Bengal is absolutely dismal and abject compared to many other states in India. The literacy rate of the Muslims in West Bengal is 57.47% (2001 census), which is lower than the other Hindu backward castes and Dalits. The representation of Muslims in the state government employment is 2.1% (lowest among the Indian states); the rural poverty rate among Muslims is 33% and the rural poverty of SC/ST is 27%. These data are just the tip of the iceberg, but they give an impression of the state of the Muslim minority in West Bengal.

In the post-Sachar scenario, West Bengal has witnessed a massive mobilization of Muslims against the incumbent Left Front Government (LFG) by different Muslim organizations and groups, particularly Furfura Sharif (popular and influential Sufi shrine-cum-religious network based in the Hooghly district of West Bengal) and Jamiat-e-Ulama-e-Hind (JUH, one of the largest pan-Indian nationalist Muslim organizations in post-independent India), based on the issues related to the development of the Muslim community, such as reservation for backward Muslims in jobs and educational institutions, forceful acquisition of agricultural lands, better health and educational facilities and so on.

Kenneth Bo Neilsen argued that in order to overcome the 'development deficit', Muslim organizations in West Bengal have successfully mobilized large numbers of the Muslim electorate (as Partha Chatterjee called it, 'political society') and put significant pressure on all political parties in the state, especially on the eve of the 2011

Assembly election, when the political parties were engaged in an intense political competition that culminated with the ouster of the incumbent LFG (Neilsen 2013).

Sachar Committee Report and the new language of mobilization

The SCR has not only provided sufficient empirical evidence of socio-economic marginalization and exclusion of Muslims but has also given sufficient moral ground to the Muslim community to put forward the collective demand of social justice and inclusion. In post-partition West Bengal, in the complete absence of Muslim middle-class intelligentsia the discourse of 'collective and public identity of Bengali Muslim community' was under serious continuous threat. Whatever minor Muslim identity was present, it was mainly dominated by the Calcutta-based urban *Ashraf* Urdu Muslim identity. The identity of the Bengali Muslim community (who constitute more than 95% of the total Muslim population in West Bengal) faced triple marginalization based on religion, caste and language (Chatterji 1998; Dasgupta 2009).

The Congress era in Bengal (post-independence to the late 1980s) was the era of acute security and identity crisis in the Muslim community due to partition trauma and a moral burden on Muslim community. Left politics has given the confidence of physical security among the Muslim community, as a result West Bengal was largely free from communal or religious violence, which was not the case in many parts of north and western India. During the early days of the LFG, the much acclaimed policy of 'land distribution' and 'local decentralized government' had attracted marginalized communities (Dalits, Muslims and Adivasi) towards left parties. Therefore these marginalized communities become the social base of the left parties in West Bengal. On the other hand, due to the dominant discourse of left politics, the politics of social justice, caste, and backward class (Mandal politics) did not emerge in West Bengal, unlike Uttar Pradesh and even the immediate neighbouring state of Bihar.

The 'socio-cultural and political space' in West Bengal has been completely hegemonized by the Bengali Brahminical political forces (including Left Parties) due to the absence of Mandal politics or the politics of social justice; as a result, communities such as Dalits, Muslims, and Adivasis remain at the margins. This has had serious implications for the question of social justice; for example, the category of Other Backward Caste (OBC) which constitutes a majority of the population of Muslims, was grossly neglected by the LFG due to non-recognition of caste, and rethinking is a necessary condition the redistribution. Hence Muslim representation in public employment is 2.1% where the Muslim population is 27% in West Bengal. This shocking figure is not only the lowest in comparison to other Indian states, including the so-called BIMARU states of Uttar Pradesh, Bihar and Jharkhand, but it also tells us the saga of systematic exclusion of the Muslim community in West Bengal.

The SCR has provided a new language of mobilization (bargaining and social justice) to the Muslim community, The SCR has brought three broad general perspectives regarding Muslims of India. First, Muslims as a socio-economically marginalized community compared to other religious groups, which refuted the idea of Muslim appeasement generally put forward by the right-wing political parties. Second, the Sachar Committee generated new debates on public policy discourse and affirmative actions toward Muslims not as a homogeneous religious community but as heterogeneous religious groups based on caste, class and deprivation (Hasan 2009). Third, SCR has broadened the horizon of Muslims politics, which was basically limited to identity politics such as pushing the cause of Urdu, Aligarh and personal laws in the Hindi heartland. Noted sociologist Surinder Jodhka argues that, in analyzing the issue of Muslim exclusion, the SCR foregrounded the question of citizenship, relegated the issue of identity or cultural distinctiveness and treated 'the Muslim question' as a question of social justice, human rights and the development of the marginalized and excluded (Jodhka 2007).

Therefore, Muslim/Islamic organizations (Jamiat-e-Ulama-e-Hind, Furfura Sharif, Minority Youth Federation, All India Minority Association, JIH, SDPI, etc.) in the aftermath of SCR mobilized large numbers of Muslims adopting the new language of representation, social justice and development. In doing so, these Muslim organizations have generated new debates on social justice in the political discourse of West Bengal using their power to influence electoral outcome and intervention among the rural Bengali Muslim community. For example, due to electoral defeat and disenchantment of Muslim social base and mammoth anti-left Muslim mobilization, the then LFG led by Chief Minister Buddadeb Bhattacharya was compelled to introduce OBC reservation for backward caste Muslims in the year 2010, two decades after the Mandal Commission.

Mobilization for 'Sonkhaloghu Unnayon' (minority development): Pirs of Furfura Sharif

Furfura Sharif is a popular and influential Muslim religious shrine of the great Sufi saint and socio-religious reformer of 19th-century undivided Bengal, Pir Maulana Shah Abu Bakar Siddique (Allama Ruhul Amin, 1347 Bengali year), who died in 1939. Pir Abu Bakar is popularly known as Dada-Huzur. The shrine is based in the Hooghly district of present West Bengal and has a massive following in rural Bengal among the vernacular Bengali-speaking Muslims. The important striking features and uniqueness about Furfura Sharif is that it is a well-networked living Sufi order (*Silsila*), and still the descendants of Pir Abu Bakar are connected with their *Mureeds* (disciples) through regular visits, establishing and maintaining hundreds of mosques, madrashas, and organizing thousands of *waz-mahfil*[4] or *Isalesawab* (religious gatherings) in the countryside of Bengal. At present 30 grandsons and more than around 80 great-grandsons of Pir Abu Bakar are completely engaged and associated with religious activities and well connected with their millions of disciples in the Bengal region, which includes West Bengal, Assam and Bangladesh (Bahauddin 2009; Matin 2018).

In the aftermath of the Sachar Committee there has been large-scale mobilization of Muslims by different Muslim organizations against the incumbent LFG, who had been ruling the state for than three decades. Kenneth Bo Neilsen has rightly put forward his argument that, in the period 2007–11, West Bengal witnessed an increasing mobilization of Muslim organizations and groups seeking to address and overcome the 'development deficit'. As part of this mobilization in search of development, these organizations have used the Muslim electorate, whose vote determines the outcome of somewhere around 80 of the state's 294 Assembly constituencies (Nielsen 2011, 2012).

In the entire process of mobilization and campaigning for the inclusion of Muslims in the mainstream development agenda, Furfura Sharif has played a key role in South Bengal, especially in the districts of South 24 Parganas, North 24 Parganas, Howrah, Hooghly, Medinipur, Bankura, Nadia and Burdwan districts of West Bengal. Muslims organizations have adopted different mechanisms and methods to put pressure not only on the incumbent LFG but also on various political parties, especially *Trinamool* Congress (the main opposition party in West Bengal) and the Indian National Congress.

The organizations under the banner of *Pir Saheb* of Furfura Sharif have extensively used the traditional method of *waz-mahfil* (religious gathering) in different remote villages as well as published and distributed numerous cheap vernacular tracts, leaflets and handbills amongst the Muslims on different issues related to Muslims deprivations and their rights. Apart from these, *Pir Sahebs* of Furfura Sharif have organized hundreds of *Prokashho Somabesh* (open rallies and meetings), convention, press conferences, symposium and so forth, both in the city of Kolkata as well as different towns of West Bengal on the issue of *Sonkhaloghu Unnoyon* (minority development), which attracted large numbers of Muslims and cut across political affiliations. While addressing the series of *waz-mahfil* in the Chamkaitala in West Medinipur district, Arambagh in Hooghly district, Bhangore in South 24 Parganas district, Basirhat in North 24 Parganas district and Bagnan in Howrah district in West Bengal in 2009–10, Maulana Toha Siddique, an influential Pirzada of Furfura Sharif, explained:

> For the sake of argument I accept that Muslims do not have education that is why they do not get employment as doctor, engineers, teachers etc. but don't even deserve unskilled job such as clerk, peon, security guard, sweeper in government office where high education is not necessary. This government (CPM) is biased against Muslims which is properly highlighted by Sachar committee report. It is true that in spite of highly educated Muslim youths they do not get government employment simply because of Muslim identity.

Pirzada Toyeb Siddique, an another young Pirzada of Furfura said:

> our *waz-mahfil* are basically to impart religious knowledge among the poor illiterate masses regarding the day to day religious affairs such as *Namaz* (five

time prayer in a day for Muslims), *Roza* (one month fasting in a year), *Zakat* (Islamic alms), *Kalma* (Muslim attestation of faith) etc. Another important feature of our *waz-mahfil* is to aware Muslims masses about their rights and socio-economic status of community. The Sachar committee report clearly pointed out the discrimination of Muslims in India where the situation of Bengali Muslims is extremely dismal in every aspect of life. Therefore it is our moral responsibility and duty to look after the pain and sorrow of our people in the state. It is our duty to inform and aware the Muslim community about their conditions.

(Pirzada Toyeb Siddique, personal interview, 2014)

The leaders of different political parties, mainly the Trinamool Congress led by Mamata Banerjee and the Indian National Congress used to attend and confirm their solidarity with Pir Sahebs of Furfura Sharif. The daily Bengali newspapers such as *Sangbad Pratidin* and *Bortaman* as well as Muslim-owned community-centric newspapers, mainly *Kalom*,[5] *Notun Gati* and *Akhbar-e-Mashriq*[6] used to give wider coverage regarding these rallies and meetings.

These mobilizations, demonstrations, newspaper coverages and symposia have not only helped to create public awareness among Muslims but have also forced different political parties (both ruling and oppositions) in the state to consider the issue of the 'development deficit' of Muslims with seriousness. The close analysis of the election manifesto of the 2011 Assembly election of West Bengal, both the ruling Communist Party of India (Marxists) and then the main opposition Trinamool Congress gave sufficient importance to Muslim-specific issues in the manifesto by promising reservations in jobs and employments, proper development package, development of Furfura Sharif into national pilgrimage centre, opening more educational centres and so forth (AITMC 2011; CPIM 2011).

In search of equality and dignity: role of West Bengal state *Jamiat-e-Ulama-e-Hind*

Jamiat-e-Ulama-e-Hind (JUH, Association of Islamic Scholars in India) is one the influential Muslim organizations in India. JUH was officially formed in the year 1919 under the leadership of Shaikhul Hind Maulana Mahmood Hasan on the occasion of the Khilafat Conference held at Delhi, and it resolved to constitute a new organization for carrying on a non-violent freedom struggle as well as anti-colonial and anti-imperial movement in cooperation with fellow countrymen (JUH Annual Report 2007). In post-independent India, JUH has been actively involved in preserving secularism, minority rights, communitarian identity, personal laws and different welfare activities in the fields of social, educational and economic development of Muslims in general.

The West Bengal state JUH is an active well networked Muslim organization. According to the annual report of JUH West Bengal state committee 2010–12, JUH has more than 14 lakhs primary members, 19 district committees and 650 branch committees. JUH has been working under the leadership of Maulana Siddiqullah Chowdhury (General Secretary of JUH, West Bengal) and Maulana Husamuddin (president of JUH, West Bengal). The state head office of JUH is located at 81, Rabindra Sarani, old city of north Kolkata (JUH Reports 2007–10).

The West Bengal unit of JUH caught the public imagination in the state when Buddadheb Bhattacharya led the LFG to aggressively move to acquire agricultural land for *Shilpayon* (industrialization). The issue of land acquisition and the Sachar Committee report (SCR) were the two major issues of JUH's Muslim mobilization in West Bengal. Muslims in West Bengal live in a rural agrarian community as well as socio-economically marginalized community, both these issues helped JUH to mobilize large Muslim masses in the rural Bengal. JUH has played an important role in the *jomi-bachaoandolon* (Save Land Movement) throughout West Bengal, and in the recent past it is the first organization which was involved in the anti-land grab movement in different parts of the state, especially in Bhangore, Singur and Nandigram. JUH was also the principal force behind the Nandigram movement under the local Jamiat leadership (Maulana Muslim 2011).

Apart from leading the aggressive anti-land grab movement, the JUH was also actively involved in massive Muslim mobilization for inclusion, equal opportunities, reservations and development. JUH organized its first large mass rally at Kolkata on 28 January 2010, demanding 20% reservation for Muslims. The rally attracted thousands of Muslims from different districts of West Bengal. JUH loudly demanded reservation for Muslims by repeatedly citing the reference of Sachar Committee and Ranganath Mishra Commission. While speaking at the huge rally Maulana Siddiqullah Chowdhury said:

> Ten percent reservation will not be enough to solve the West Bengal Muslim problems. Therefore, we demand 20 percent reservation because currently only 2.5 percent Muslims are in government job while they comprise 30 percent of the total population of the state. We gave ultimatum to the government to take the decision on the matter on earliest because we cannot wait any more. We have fed up of promises since last 30 years now government has to step in practically.

JUH's demands for reservation had huge support not only from Muslim community but also from different political parties, intellectuals, activists and many other right-based organizations. Maulana Siddiqullah Chowdhury requested different Muslim organizations and political parties to form a larger unity to carry forward the struggle for social justice and democratic rights (Maulana Muslim 2010). Responding to the growing demands of reservation for Muslims, on 8 February 2010, then Chief Minister of West Bengal Buddhadeb Bhattacharya announced a 10% reservation in the field of job for the socio-economically backward Muslims under the OBC (Other Backward Classes) quota (BCWD, Government of West Bengal 2010).

These massive mobilizations of Muslim organizations in West Bengal not only generated sufficient 'minority discourse' in the state politics but also contributed immensely to the overthrow of three and half decades of the Left Front Government in the 2011 Assembly election.

Mamata, Muslim and Hindutva: the politics of 'co-option'

The 2011 Assembly election witnessed watershed changes in the contemporary political history of West Bengal by overthrowing 34 years of communist/left regime by the Trinamool Congress under the charismatic leadership of Mamata Banerjee. The Trinamool Congress (TMC) got a thumping majority in the 2011 and 2016 State Assembly elections. In the post-TMC West Bengal has been witnessing rapid change in the socio-political spheres. The new forms of political and religious mobilization have been taking place in contemporary West Bengal. (This requires further research to understand the changing political culture in the state where left political culture dominated for more than three decades.)

TMC after 2011 have co-opted large numbers of Muslim community leaders, politicians, religious organizations and community newspapers through various means and methods such as providing election tickets, allocating grants for shrine development and through various other state patronages. Examples include Maulana Siddiqullah Chowdhury (state president of Muslim mass organization *Jamiat-e-Ulama-e-Hind* and present minister in Mamata Banerjee's cabinet), Mr. Idris Ali (Member of Parliament representing the Basirhat parliamentary constituency from Trinamool Congress in 2014 and founder of All India Minority Forum) and Mr. Ahmed Hassan Imran (Rajya Saha MP from TMC and editor of *Bengali Muslim Daily*).

The Mamata Banerjee government started co-opting major religious temples and shrines. For example, she formed the Tarapit Temple Development Authority, Furfura Sharif Development Authority, Kalighat Temple development and so forth, and these kinds of direct state interventions have developed new religious patronage. Instead of implementing the recommendations of the Sachar Committee Report, the TMC government is more interested to implement polarizing schemes such as the introduction of monthly honorariums to *imams* and *moazzins* (those who leads prayer in mosques). Though the honoraria for *imams* and *moazzins* are given from the Waqf Fund, which is the exclusive charity fund of the Muslim community, around 38,446 imams and 25,486 moazzins have benefited from this scheme (Board of Wakfs, West Bengal 2017).

On the other hand, in the post-TMC era there has been rampant growth of Hindutva forces in the state, the numbers of RSS sakhas have grown multiple times over, and the most interesting development is that a rise in Hindu Samhati (a breakout of RSS, a more radical form of vernacular Hindutva organization) emerged and penetrated in rural West Bengal. The Hindu Samhati was established in the year 2008 but it has flourished in the last few years under the leadership of Mr. Tapan Ghosh. This organization recently attracted the attention of the national media by publicly organizing a *ghar wapsi* program of 14 Muslims in the heart of Kolkata.

The Hindu Samhati aggressively take up issues of so-called love jihad, arms training to Hindus and many other venomous activities against Muslims throughout West Bengal but mostly active in the South Bengal region, especially in the districts of South 24 Parganas, North 24 Parganas, Nadia, Howrah, Hooghly and other Indo-Bangladesh bordering districts of West Bengal.

The Hindu Samhati has published its monthly mouthpiece called *Swadesh Sanhati Sangbad* since its inception, and this publication contains venomous, blatant anti-Muslim writings full of hatred and propaganda. The violent celebration of Ram Navami and Hanuman Jayanti (these festivals are new to the Hindus of West Bengal) in different parts of West Bengal including the district towns in the last three to four years has not only increased the appeal of Hindutva among a large section of vernacular Hindu society but has also set up the political discourse of the 'Muslim question' in the form of love jihad, *ghar wapsi*, minority appeasement and many other traditional stereotypes centred around the Muslim community in post-colonial India. The ruling TMC party itself patronized large number of Hindu festivals including the celebration of Ram Navami across the state of West Bengal.

Conclusion

The Sachar Committee Report has generated new debates on the 'Muslim question' in India and more particularly in contemporary West Bengal based on the issues of social justice, citizenship, inclusion and socio-economic marginalization. In the early post-Sachar phase (2006–12) the debates on the 'Muslim question' were mostly centred around the SCR, but in later years there has been major shift towards the issues posed by Hindutva politics, and Muslim community organizations in West Bengal have also fallen into the trap of the communal-secular binary, eroding the question of social justice.

Notes

1 Government of India (2006). *Social, Economic and Educational Status of Muslim Community of India*, The Prime Minister's High Level Committee, Cabinet Secretariat, New Delhi (popularly known as the Sachar Committee Report because the committee was headed by Retired Chief Justice of Delhi High Court, Mr. Rajinder Singh Sachar).
2 CSSSC is the Centre for the Study of Social Science Calcutta located in Kolkata. A reputed research institute, which undertook the baseline survey research to ten Minority concentrated districts of West Bengal between 2007 and 2010, sponsored by the Ministry of Minority Affairs, Government of India
3 Association SNAP (Social Network Assistance to People) is an independent Muslim civil society organization established in 2008 by group of educated Muslim professional. The formation of this type of civil society association with an objective of social and human development of Muslim citizens of West Bengal is basically the post-Sachar phenomenon. (Series of Interview with Munshi Amirul Alam, Jahangir Hossian, the office bearer of Association SNAP between 2014 and 2017).
4 *Waz-mahfil* is typical religious Muslim gathering. *Waz* means religious discussions or sermon and *mahfil* means gathering. *Waz-mahfils* are very popular among Muslims in rural Bengal. The *waz-mahfil* nowadays take place round the year except in the monsoon season. *Waz-mahfils* also symbolize the rural religious public sphere.

5 *Kalom* has for years been the leading Muslim weekly newspaper in Bengali. Recently in 2012 it converted to a daily and the editor of this paper is Mr. Ahmad Hasan Imran, who is also the Member of Parliament (Rajya Sabha) from Trinamool Congress.
6 *Akhbar-e-Mashriq* is of the leading Muslim Urdu newspaper based in Kolkata. The editor of *Akhbar-e-Mashriq*, Mr. Nadimul Haque, is also the Member of Parliament (Rajya Sabha) from Trinamool Congress. This newspaper largely attracts Urdu-speaking Muslims, which are around 3% to 4% of the total population in West Bengal.

References

Alam, Mohd Sanjeer (2009). 'Is Relative Size of Minority Population Linked to Underdevelopment?' *Economic and Political Weekly*, 46(24), pp. 10–13.
Bahauddin, Sayed (2009). *Banglar Srestha Ulamader Jiban o Karma: 100 Bachharer Itihas 1901–2002*, Furfura Sharif: Pir Abu Bakr Research Centre.
Bhattacharya, Dwaipayan (2010). 'Left in the Lurch: The Demise of the World's Longest Elected Regime?' *Economic and Political Weekly*, 45(3), pp. 51–9.
Bhattacharya, Dwaipayan (2014). 'Left in the Lurch: The Demise of the World's Longest Elected Regime', in (ed.), Sudha Pai, *Handbook of Politics in Indian State*, New Delhi: Routledge, pp. 211–26.
Bose, Sumantra (2013). *Transforming India: Challenges to the World's Largest Democracy*, Picador-India, Pan Macmillan.
Chakrabarty, Bidyut (2011). 'The 2011 State Assembly Election in West Bengal: The Left Front Washed Out!' *Journal of South Asian Development*, 6(14), pp. 143–67.
Chatterji, Joya (1998). 'The Bengali Muslims: A Contradiction in Terms? An Overview of the Debate on Bengali Muslim Identity', in (ed.), Mushirul Hasan, *Islam: Communities and the Nation: Muslim Identities in South Asia and Beyond*, New Delhi: Manohar Publication.
Dasgupta, Avhijit (2009). 'On the Margins: Muslims in West Bengal', *Economic and Political Weekly*, 44(16), pp. 91–6.
Dasgupta, Abhijit (2011). 'On the Margins: Muslims in West Bengal', in (eds.), Masahiko Togawa, Abhijit Dasgupta and Abul Barkat, *Minorities and the State: Changing Social and Political Landscape of Bengal*, New Delhi: Sage Publications, pp. 18–38.
Hasan, Zoya (2009). *Politics of Inclusion: Castes, Minorities and Affirmative Action*, New Delhi: Oxford University Press.
Hasan, Zoya (2013). 'Assessing UPA Government's Response to Muslim Deprivation', in (eds.), Zoya Hasan and Mushirul Hasan, *India: Social Development Report 2012: Minorities at the Margins*, New Delhi: Oxford University Press, pp. 242–9.
Jaffrelot, Christophe (1999). *Hindu Nationalist Movement and Indian Politics: 1925 to the 1990s*, New Delhi: Penguin.
Jaffrelot, Christophe (2006). 'The Muslims of India: Towards Marginalisation?' in (ed.), Christophe Jaffrelot, *India: Since 1950, Society, Politics, Economy and Culture*, New Delhi: Foundation Books and Yatra Book, pp. 564–79.
Jodhka, Surinder Singh (2007). 'Perceptions and Receptions: Sachar Committee and the Secular Left', *Economic and Political Weekly*, 42(29), pp. 2996–9.
Matin, Abdul (2018). 'Socio-Religious Reform and Sufism in 20th Century Bengal: A Study of the Role of Pir Abu Bakr of Furfura Sharif, India', *South Asian Cultural Studies*, Special issue, pp. 25–33.
Maulana, Md. Muslim (2010). *Songrokkhon Juddhe Jamiat-e-Ulama-e-Hind*, Burdwan: Noorani.
Maulana, Md. Muslim (2011). *Bhangore, Singur, Nandigram: Jomi-Juddhe Jamiat-e-Ulama-Hind*, Kolkata: West Bengal State Jamiat-e-Ulama-e-Hind.
Nielsen, Kenneth Bo (2011). 'In Search of Development: Muslims and Electoral Politics in Indian State', *Forum for Development Studies*, 38(3), pp. 345–70.

Nielsen, Kenneth Bo (2012). 'Campaigning for Inclusion: Muslims and Social Exclusion in Contemporary West Bengal', in (eds.), V. Rama Krishna, R. Shashidhar and M. Muniraju, *Social Exclusion – Inclusion Continuum: A Paradigm Shift*, New Delhi: Niruta Publications, pp. 119–35.

Neilsen, Kenneth Bo (2013). 'In Search of Development: Muslims and Electoral Politics in an Indian State', in (eds.), Kenneth Bo Nielsen, Uwe Skoda and Marianne Qvortrup Fibiger, *Navigating Social Exclusion and Inclusion in Contemporary India and Beyond: Structures, Agents, Practices*, New York: Anthem Press, pp. 73–96.

Reports and documents

Census of India. (2011). Published by Registrar General of India, New Delhi.

Communist Party of India (Marxist) Review of the 15th Lok Sabha Elections Adopted by the Central Committee Meeting Held on June 20 and 21, 2009, New Delhi.

CPI (M)'s Review Report of 2004 Lok Sabha Election, Adopted by the Central Committee Held on 30th July and 1st August, 2004, New Delhi.

CPI (M)'s Campaign Material for West Bengal Assembly Election 2011, on 'Left Front Government and Development of Muslim Minority in West Bengal'.

CPI (M)'s Charter of Advancement of Muslim Community on the Basis of Finding by the Justice Sachar Committee Report, March 5, 2007.

CPI (M)'s Document 'On the Reservation of Backward Muslims in West Bengal' published in 2010.

Election Manifesto Cum Vision Document of All India Trinamool Congress for 15th West Bengal Assembly Election, 2011 Titled *'West Bengal: A Change for Better and Brighter Tomorrow'*.

Government of India. (2006). *Social, Economic and Educational Status of Muslim Community of India*, The Prime Minister's High Level Committee, Cabinet Secretariat, New Delhi (popularly known as Sachar Committee report).

Government of India. (2007). *Report of the National Commission for Religious and Linguistic Minorities*, Ministry of Minority Affairs, New Delhi, 2007 (generally known as Ranganath Mishra Commission report).

Government of West Bengal, Backward Classes Welfare Department's order no 6320-BCW/MR-84/10, September 24, 2010.

ICSSR (Indian Council for Social Science Research) Base Line Survey Reports. (2008). 'Minority Concentrated District Project, Murshidabad, Nadia, North 24 Parganas, Birbhum', sponsored by Ministry of Minority Affairs, GoI, conducted by Centre for Studies in Social Sciences Calcutta.

Jamiat-e-Ulama-e-Hind (JUH), West Bengal State Committee (2007–2010). *Poschimbongo Rajjo Jamiat-e-Ulama-e-Hind er Sonkhipto karjo bibirini*, a brief annual activities in the form of annual reports from 2007–2010, Kolkata.

SNAP. (2016). 'Living Reality of Muslims in West Bengal: A Report', Association SNAP and Guidance Guild in Association with Pratichi Institute, Kolkata.

Interviews and websites accessed

All India Trinamool Congress for West Bengal Assembly Election 2011. Retrieved February 12, 2014, from www.aitmc.org/manifesto_english_2011.pdf.

Interviewed Pirzada Mohammad Toyeb Siddique on 25 June 2016 at Furfura Sharif, Hooghly.

Interviewed Pirzada Toha Siddique on 26 June 2016 at Furfura Sharif, Hooghly.

Official Website of Ministry of Minority Affairs, Government of India, List of MCDs (Minority Concentrated Districts). Retrieved February 13, 2014, from http://minorityaffairss.gov.in/schemesperformance/multi-sectoral-development-programme/list-90-mcds338-towns-and-1228-cd-blocks.

Official Website of Board of Auqaf, West Bengal. Retrieved December 20, 2017, from http://auqafboard.org/welfare-scheme/.

West Bengal 15th Assembly Election Manifesto, Left-Front Committee, West Bengal 2011. Retrieved February 13, 2014, from www.cpim.org/documents/2011-WB-manifestol.pdf.

7
HINDUTVA AS A 'SACRED FORM'
A case study of Karnataka

Malini Bhattacharjee

Perhaps one of the most spectacular phenomena in Indian politics since the past decade has been the meteoric rise of the Bharatiya Janata Party. After its successful win in the 2014 Lok Sabha elections, the party now has managed to form governments either individually or in partnership with a regional party in 21 states across the country. Hindutva's advancement from periphery to the centre of Indian politics explains its remarkable adaptability to the changing socio-political landscape of India. Apart from the political outfit, the Sangh Parivar now has its presence in almost every possible region in the country. This is an interesting fact, considering the Sangh Parivar's rigid adherence to the idea of building a corporate and unified 'Hindu Rashtra' as envisaged by Savarkar, Hedgewar, Golwalkar and the other builders of the Rashtriya Swayamsevak Sangh (RSS). K.B. Hedgewar, the founder of the RSS, claimed that India is a Hindu Rashtra. Savarkar's Hindu Mahasabha pleaded that Hindustan is one homogeneous country and states are mere administrative units. Golwalkar also clearly spelt out: 'We are one country, one society, and one nation...; and hence, it is natural that the affairs of the nation are governed through a single state of the unitary type' (Golwalkar 1980[1966]: 224). Deendayal Upadhyaya also favours an 'integrated Bharat' which is based on his idea of 'national soul' (*chiti*) that has to be 'awakened' to its destiny and its *virat* ('life force') (Bhatt 2001: 158). The Bharatiya Jana Sangh (BJS), Hindutva's first affiliate, in its first election manifesto in 1951 stated: 'The whole of Bharatvarsha, from Himalayas to Kanyakumari, is and has been, through the ages, a living organic whole – geographically, culturally and historically' (Bhartiya Jana Sangh 1973).

The BJS, soon after its formation in 1951, echoing Golwalkar's enunciation, adopted 'One Country, One People, One Culture, One Nation and One Ideal' as its fundamentals. Hindutva's uncompromising agenda of a unitary India also logically compelled it to search for an all-encompassing national language in the post-independence period. As language constituted an integral part of Hindutva's concept of nationhood, it propagated rhetoric like 'Hindi, Hindu, Hindusthan'. In Hindutva's understanding, political unity could be maintained only by making Hindi as the lingua franca, not only between the centre and the states but between one state and another as well. Rigid adherence to the concept of an organic state, however, has not stopped Hindutva from making a dent in regional politics.

In a country like India with innumerable diversities, myriad combinations of language, religion, caste, tribe and class often juxtapose themselves into interesting combinations within its different regions. The Parivar realizes this and therefore intelligently and strategically expands itself by embarking upon certain region specific mobilization campaigns. Political compulsions have also necessitated Hindutva to change its stance on regions. Regionalization of Indian politics became a permanent feature since 1996, when regional parties and few independent candidates captured 171 seats in the 11th Lok Sabha elections. The failure of the BJP to garner support from regional parties to win a confidence vote and formation of the United Front Ministry called for an introspection. Still the BJP was not prepared to come to terms with this new political reality; the 1998 Election Manifesto echoed the old Jana Sangh commitment to 'one nation, one people and one culture'. However, the BJP quickly corrected course by shrewdly forging an alliance with regional parties to control New Delhi in 1998. Besides ensuring power at the Centre, this alliance provided Hindutva a great opportunity to transcend geographical barriers in spreading its social and political tentacles into the vast tracts of the nation. This chapter is focused on the ways in which Hindutva has negotiated regional specificities in Karnataka while subscribing to its core ideology of building a strong organic 'Hindu Rashtra'. This analysis becomes pertinent especially after the emergence of the Bharatiya Janata Party (BJP) as the single-largest party in the Assembly elections of Karnataka in 2018, despite its inability to form the government. The immediate triggers for the success of the party can obviously be located in the political strategies deployed by the central and the state-level BJP functionaries, the consolidation of dominant castes against the Congress and the failure of the Congress to weave together a winning social coalition ahead of the polls. The popularity of the BJP in this region, however, requires an analysis that deploys the lens of a longer time frame and its entrenchment outside the electoral realm. This is especially important because in most regions of the country, the Sangh Parivar operates as an ecosystem that pervades every conceivable sphere of society, and a comprehensive understanding of the political outfit necessitates an unpacking of this ecosystem.

Karnataka: brief overview of the state and demography

The territory of Karnataka (originally known as the state of Mysore) was formed in 1956 when the Kannada-speaking districts of the states of Bombay, Andhra, Madras, Hyderabad and Coorg were integrated. The state of Mysore was officially christened as Karnataka on 1 November 1973, which is celebrated as Kannada

Rajyotsava day. Currently the state consists of 30 districts which are spread across four administrative divisions: Belagavi, Bengaluru, Kalburagi and Mysuru.

In terms of its religious demography, as per the Census of 2011, Hindus constitute 84%, Muslims constitute 12.92% and Christians constitute 1.87% of the state's population. Sikhs, Buddhists and Jains each constitute less than 1% of the population.

Amongst the southern states in India, Karnataka has the second-largest population of Muslims after Kerala. While Muslims are spread across all districts of the state, the northern districts of Bidar, Gulbarga and Bijapur, the central districts of Dharwad and Haveri and the coastal districts of Dakshin Kannada and Kodagu have considerably large concentrations of Muslim population. The presence of Muslims is particularly high in the towns of Gargeshwari (Mysore district), Allipura (Chikkaballapura), Manjanady (Dakshin Kannada) and Bhatkal (Uttar Kannada).

Christians are mostly concentrated in the coastal districts of Dakshin Kannada, Udupi and Bengaluru Urban.

Major religious traditions

It is interesting to note that while Hindus constitute an overwhelming majority in the state, they are far from being a homogeneous community. Since ancient times, this region has been a confluence of myriad Hindu sects such as Saivism, Saktism and Vaisnavism.

Saivism assumed its most popular form in the Virasaiva/Lingayat movement led by Basaveshwara in the 12th century (Aerthayil 1989). Virasaivism, which became immensely popular in the region now identified as Karnataka, was essentially a reformist movement which sought to oppose ritualism and casteism in Hinduism. The followers of this movement popularly known as Lingayats became an important political power in subsequent years. Vaisnavism, more precisely the Vishisthadvaita branch of Vedanta Hinduism, was popularized by Ramanuja Acharya around the 11th and 12th centuries. Ramanuja, who hailed from Tamil Nadu, was given patronage by the Hoysala King Vishnuvardhana, who enabled him to propagate Vaisnavism in the region that now comprises Karnataka. The Dvaita philosophy advocated by Madhavacharya also helped in popularizing Vaisnavism during the 13th century in Karnataka. Saktism is represented in the Chamundeshwari temple in Mysore.

Both the Mahayana and Theravada sects of Buddhism also flourished in the region since the first millennium. Jainism gained popularity in the medieval period in this region, and its most popular shrine in Shravanabelagola continues to attract large numbers of people from across the country.

Islam entered the region through Arab traders who visited coastal Karnataka from the 8th century onward, and several Muslim communities such as the Moplahs, Byaris and Navayaths in coastal Karnataka are mostly descendants of these traders. Islam, however, found a solid footing in the region only from the 14th century onward after dynasties such as the Bahamani and Adilshahi established the sultanates of Bidar and Bijapur, respectively. It was further consolidated after the entry of the Mughal rule through Aurangzeb in the 17th century and the installation of Hyder Ali and his son Tipu Sultan subsequently in Mysore.

Christianity entered the region through the Portuguese in the 16th and 17th centuries and found a substantive following amongst the local people.

Political scenario

The Congress held sway in Karnataka from 1956 to 1983. Even after the imposition of the Emergency in 1975, the party did not lose its popularity, and contrary to its fate in several other states, it was returned to power after the Emergency. However, the party lost power in 1983 to the Janata Party which formed the government under the leadership of Ramakrishna Hegde with the support of the BJP, which had won 18 seats. The Congress, however, regained power in the 1989 State Assembly elections. After the Janata Party started disintegrating from the end of 1980s, Janata Dal started gaining ground, especially since the 1994 elections. The BJP also made strident progress from the 1994 elections onward when it managed to capture 40 seats, and it has since been a major force in the state. The BJP's first major breakthrough occurred in the 2004 elections when it emerged as the single largest party by winning 79 of the 224 seats. However, it could not immediately form the government because the Congress Party, which had secured 65 seats and the Janata Dal (S) (JD(S)), which won 58 seats entered into a coalition and formed the government. This alliance did not last for long, however; in early 2006, JD(S) withdrew its support from the coalition and entered into a new alliance with the BJP. H.D. Kumaraswamy from JD(S) became the chief minister and B.S. Yedyurappa became the deputy chief minister with an understanding that after 20 months, the former would relinquish his position to the latter. However, this arrangement did not last long due to disagreements regarding power sharing between the two parties. Fresh elections were called for in 2008 when the BJP again emerged as the single largest party, winning 110 out of 224 seats. BJP was able to form the government with the support of six independent MLAs and Yedyurappa became the chief minister. In 2013, Congress again returned to power, winning 122 seats, and formed the government under Chief Minister Siddaramaiah, while BJP won only 40 seats.

Evolution of Hindutva in Karnataka

The origin of Hindutva in Karnataka can be traced to pre-independence times when the first RSS shakha was started by Dadarao Paramarth, a Sangh pracharak, in Chikkodi, a small town in Belgavi district of Karnataka in 1935. Dadarao Paramarth was one of the three pracharaks handpicked by Hedgewar to initiate Sangh work in Karnataka. The other two pracharaks were Bhavoo Rao Deoras and Yadav Rao Joshi. Two years later, on 16 January 1937, Sarsanghchalak Hedgewar visited Chikkodi.[1] It was however the relentless efforts of Yadav Rao Joshi that led to the strengthening of Sangh activities in Karnataka. He began working in this region as a Prant Pracharak from 1941 and organized the work of the RSS in the region by dividing Karnataka prant (province) into four Vibhags and appointed Vibhag Pracharaks for each Vibhag.[2] He also took the lead in starting publications such as *Jagarana Prakashan* (1971), *Pungava Jagarana* newspaper (1979), and *Balgokulam of Kerala* (1974) amongst others. In 1949, Sarasanghchalak Golwalkar visited Bangalore and Hubli in 1949 along with Yadav Rao Joshi after the ban on RSS was lifted.

Yadav Rao Joshi also became instrumental in establishing several Sangh affiliates dedicated to *seva* (service) and cultural activities such as the Rashtrotthana Parishat (1965), Hindu Seva Pratishthana (1980), Jana Seva Vidya Kendra (1972) and Hindu Munnani (1980) and Hindu Samajotsavas. Seva activities of the Sangh Parivar continue to be carried out by these organizations even today. According to a report[3] published by the Rashtriya Sewa Bharati, in 2014, there were 7,646 *seva* projects operational in Karnataka that consisted of welfare activities in the realm of health, education, 'samajik' (social) and economics.

Apart from the work of the RSS, other affiliates simultaneously acquired footing in this region. In 1944, V.D. Savarkar, accompanied by Nathuram Godse, visited Shimoga to address a state-level Hindu Mahasabha conference which was organized to instil 'love' and 'pride' amongst Hindus (Mellegatti 2004). Savarkar appealed to the people to continue organizing the Ganesha festival every year under the banner of the Veer Savarkar Hindu Sanghatan Mahamandali. Shimoga was deliberately chosen as the venue for the conference as it was considered favourable to the Hindutva cause (Mellegatti 2004). The conference was considered a big success and was attended by 50,000 people. Meanwhile the political affiliate of the Sangh Parivar also started building base from the early 1960s onward. In 1968, Bharatiya Jan Sangh won the civic body elections in Udupi – apparently the first occasion when the party came to power in an elected body in South India (Rao 2008). Several leaders like Kesari Jagannatha Rao Joshi, A.K. Subbaiah, Dr. K.S. Dattaatri, Varadaraja Shetty, Mallikarjunaiah, Karmaballi Sanjeeva Shetty, Dr. V.S. Acharya, and D.H. Shakaramurthy played an important role in popularizing the ideology of Bharatiya Jana Sangh.

When Vishwa Hindu Parishad was formed in 1964, Dadasaheb Apte found an ally in Mysore Maharaja Sri Jayachamaraja Wadeyar, who agreed to lead the Parishad as one of its conveners.[4] The VHP held its third national executive meeting on 27–28 May 1965 in the royal palace of the Mysore maharaja. The head of the Pejavar matha in Udupi, Teertha Swami, a disciple of the second RSS Sarsanghchalak Golwalkar, was another founder member of the VHP from this region who had an influential role to play in promoting Hindutva in coastal Karnataka in the early years (Mondal 2015). Teertha Swami was associated with the Ram Janmabhoomi movement right from the beginning. In 1969, Teertha Swami also organized the first state-level conference of the VHP and invited Golwalkar to be the chief guest in the event. According to RSS veteran leader M.G. Vaidya, the approval for allowing re-conversion (popularly known as *ghar wapsi*) in Hinduism was first given in Sri Krishna Math, Udupi, Karnataka in 1969, when shankaracharyas, mahants and several Hindu saints held a gathering.[5] Teertha Swami was particularly strong in his advocacy for *ghar wapsi* and he questioned those leaders who had kept silent when large-scale conversions of Hindus into other religions had taken place.[6]

As an ardent supporter of the VHP, his matha collaborated on several social welfare activities with the VHP, especially in the realm of education and health for poor tribals. However, the most important activity towards which the VHP directed itself was the prevention of cow slaughter. Police records in this region from the 1960s onward reveal that several Muslim cattle traders were attacked (Mondal 2015). The VHP grew in popularity during the years of the Emergency; it attracted several Congress and even left-wing leaders within its fold and gradually expanded to other regions of the state such as such as Hubli, Dharwad, Raichur and Bagalkot (Mondal 2015). From the end of the 1970s, however, more extremist and militant groups such as the Hindu Yuva Sene, and at a later stage (in the 1990s), the Hindu Jagarana Vedike and the Bajrang Dal (particularly after the Godhra riots in 2002), took on the task of cow protection and unleashed a more virulent form of Hindutva in the state (Mondal 2015). Over a period of time, these groups started attacking churches, forming vigilante groups that sought to enforce dress codes and 'appropriate behaviour' for women and condemning and attacking young couples who were engaged in inter-religious relationships under the pretext of countering 'love jihad'. Another fringe group to join this club was the emergence of Sri Rama Sene under the leadership of Pramod Muthalik in the mid-2000s, following a split in the Bajrang Dal in Karnataka. Sri Rama Sene drew enormous negative attention when its members attacked young men and women in a Mangalore pub in January 2009, on the pretext of 'teaching them a lesson' for inappropriate behaviour.

Hindutva in coastal Karnataka

The ideology of Hindutva found popular support in the state, especially the coastal districts, even before the BJP captured state power in the year 2008 for the first time. Assadi (2002) notes that Hindutva had established its presence in several districts of coastal Karnataka by adopting a multipronged strategy. He draws attention to the ways in which Hindutva forces benefited from the changing socio-economic conditions in this region from the 1970s onward following the breakdown of erstwhile feudal structures such as the 'Guttenar system' (through land reforms), the Gulf boom and the sense of displacement that the dominant castes suffered from. While one section of the dominant castes migrated to Mumbai and other metropolitan cities, a small percentage who stayed back entered into the banking and education sectors. The former group tried to overcome their sense of loss of identity by reproducing local festivals such as 'Nagamandala', 'Bhoot Kolas' or 'Kambalas'. The latter group were disgruntled to see that they now had to contend with hitherto marginalized groups such as the Baerys (Muslims) in small businesses and jobs.

Hindutva forces saw in this an opportunity to bring the disgruntled Hindu groups into their fold. Organization of 'Hindu Samajotsavas' (large assemblies of Hindus), apart from the usual Ganesha festivals, by leaders of VHP and other members of the Sangh Parivar has been another useful strategy to mobilize the Hindu masses in this region. Hindus of all denominations, castes and class groups along with leaders of their respective mathas are invited to participate in these spectacles, thus enabling a coalition of support base amongst dominant castes such as 'bunts', backward castes/classes such as 'billavas, kulalas, devadiagas' and the upper castes such as 'konkanis' and brahmins. Other groups that were subsequently brought into their fold were the mogaveeras, kulalas and devadigas who were becoming insecure after Muslims started entering their traditional occupations of fishing and canning. Assadi also draws attention to the fact that in constructing this social coalition, the Sangh Parivar has deployed 'new narratives' and 'new discourses' while building the 'other' than the usual stereotypical discourses. It typically uses an economic argument here to demonise two categories of Muslims: the Baerys and the Navayaths. It is easy to construct these communities as the 'enemy' as they benefited immensely from their trade ventures in West Asia during the Gulf boom and pumped back their profits in the textile, hotel, timber and canning industries in coastal Karnataka.

A case in point is Bhatkal, a town in Uttar Kannada which comprises an overwhelming population of Navayaths and a small percentage of Namdharis (toddy tappers) who are Hindus. Navayaths were traditionally, land owners and Namdharis were the caretakers. In a place where Hindus were numerically outnumbered and less dominant economically, the Hindutva rhetoric found an easy entry. Moreover, this small town became an epicentre for a radical form of Islam from the early 1990s onward under the influence of rich Muslim youth who returned with an enormous amount of wealth made in the Gulf countries. This community invested their money in establishing educational and religious institutions and over a period of time also became instrumental in encouraging young men and women to join extremist organizations such as the Student's Islamic Movement of India (SIMI), Indian Mujahideen (IM) and the Islamic State (IS) (Ullekh 2015). Several intelligence reports have also periodically drawn attention to the fact that Pakistan's Inter-Services Intelligence (ISI) has been operating in India through its agents in Bhatkal (Subramanya 2006). All of these factors have led to Bhatkal becoming a fertile territory for communal polarization and several riots from the 1990s onward.

The spread of Hindutva in coastal Karnataka however, did not go uncontested. After the communal riots at Surathkal near Mangalore in 1998, an Islamic organization named the Karnataka Forum for Dignity (KFD) made an entry into this region (Mondal 2015). The group later merged with another extremist, Kerala-based political outfit named National Development Front and was rechristened as the Popular Front of India (PFI) in 2006. The PFI and its political affiliate, the Social Democratic Party, have been opposing the Sangh Parivar and has also been allegedly involved in forced religious conversions and attacking those who are viewed as opponents of Islam.

Mathas

Several scholars and media articles have also drawn attention to the 'mathas' as being important allies of Hindutva in the state of Karnataka. Parvathy Menon has pointed out that though mathas are legally defined as religious establishments headed by a leader, in reality their role extends much beyond the religious (Menon 2004). She further adds that the mathas are sharply divided along caste lines and play an important role in political outcomes by offering either direct or indirect support to certain political parties. The Pejavar and the Adamar mathas in particular have been champions in espousing Hindutva. Menon mentions that the eight Madhwa mathas in the coastal belt, who are the joint custodians of the Krishna temple in Udupi, have been very instrumental in spreading Hindutva, both ideologically and as an electoral force. The Pejavar matha, she mentions, has actively promoted the institution of the samavesha, which has been the most popular avenue for advocating unification of all Hindus. These samaveshas and samajotsavas serve as platforms for political mobilization, where leaders like Togadia are periodically invited to deliver speeches. Menon provides evidence to argue that erstwhile religious functions like paryaya (which marks the transfer of authority from one leader to the other) have now become 'state level' functions and a source of status for mathas.

Menon also argues that despite their affiliations to distinct caste groups, mathas are increasingly trying to advocate for Hindutva across caste lines and have toned down Brahminism at least in their rhetoric to make themselves popular amongst the lower castes. Thus hitherto marginalized groups such as cobblers, weavers, fishermen and carpenters are actively welcomed into rallies and other public functions organized by the mathas. The mathas have also realized that unless they build political relationships with groups affiliated to the Sangh Parivar, their outreach and scale would be limited. They also run a series of social welfare projects in the realm of health and education.

It is well know that Lingayats and Vokkaligas are the two dominant communities in Karnataka that exercise significant influence during elections. While the Veerashaiva mathas have been successful in mobilizing Lingayats for electoral purposes, the Adichunchungiri matha is seen as the religious authority of the Vokkaliga community. The Siddaganga matha in Tumkur district is another matha that is seen as wielding enormous political power and politicians ranging from Congress to the BJP are seen vying for the pontiff Shivakumar Swamy's support, though the latter is primarily seen as an important ally for the BJP.

Communal riots

A news report in a national daily in October 2015 mentions that Karnataka features among the top five states in the country for communal violence (Kumar 2015).[7] The article elaborates that the state recorded 321 incidents of communal violence between January 2011 and June 2015 which injured 930 people and killed 16. Another report of August 2016 mentions that according to the National Crime Records Bureau, Karnataka recorded the second highest number of communal riots across the country in 2015 (Rao and Narayanan 2016).[8] This report also adds that of the 6,603 riots reported, 163 incidents were labelled communal riots. Needless to say, these riots have deepened the wedge between religious communities and have helped the consolidation of the saffron brigade in the state.

Though the number of communal riots have spiked in number since 2015 onward, it is important to bear in mind that Karnataka has been prone to communal conflagrations since the 1970s. One of the first major riots in this region took place in the town of Bhatkal in 1978 during state elections. Mysore witnessed its first communal conflagration in December 1986, after riots broke out in Bangalore following the publication of a story in Deccan herald titled 'Mohammed the Idiot'. It has been alleged that the riots were provoked by the display of thousands of saffron flags that were planted by VHP on vehicles, streets and housetops on the pretext of celebrating the upcoming Sankranti festival. The Ram Janmabhoomi movement had a considerable impact in Karnataka as in several other places in the country. Communal riots broke out in Dharwad, Shimoga, Arsikere and Hubli, soon after the laying of the foundation stone for the building of a Ram temple in Ayodhya in 1989.

This was followed by a subsequent riot in 1991 in Bhatkal, when the BJP used a loudspeaker of the local mosque to deliver an election speech. As mentioned previously, Bhatkal has been a communal hotspot due to the animosity between Muslims and Hindus catalyzed by forces of Hindutva. Large-scale riots broke out in 1993 and lasted for around six months in which 17 people were killed. Following this, the state government of Karnataka set up an enquiry commission under Justice Jagannatha Shetty. Even before the Commission had submitted its report, in April 1996, the sitting Bharatiya Janata Party MLA, Dr. U. Chittaranjan, made the situation further tensed and increased the polarization between Hindus and Muslims.

Another communally sensitive spot that has been exploited by the Sangh Parivar to its advantage is Hubli. Hubli has been prone to communal violence since 1972 and has witnessed over 30 communal incidents since then. In August 1994, the Sangh Parivar tried to invoke communal violence when Uma Bharati and her colleagues tried to hoist the national flag at the controversial Idgah maidan in Hubli, even though the ownership of the property was sub judice and a curfew had been imposed a day before. In 2001 again, riots broke out after the erstwhile VHP leader celebrated his birthday in Hubli and led a rally where provocative speeches were delivered against Muslims and Pakistan.

Apart from overt communal riots, the Sangh Parivar has been consistently working towards building communal consciousness by promoting the public celebration of Hindu festivals. In 1984, for instance, the RSS and BJP decided to organize the Ganesha festival in a grand manner in Kolar, doing away with all mohalla-based celebrations of the event.[9] A Sarvajanika Ganesh Samiti was formed with the cooperation of the JP MLA K.R. Srinivasiah, and authorized to collect funds from the public. This samiti managed to collect enormous amounts of funds and all preparations done by Sangh sympathizers, thus leading to a consolidation of the Hindus in the town.

Another strategy that has worked with the Sangh in popularizing Hindutva in the state is that of conflating linguistic chauvinism with that of religious nationalism.

It is a well-known fact that owing to the mass exodus of 'non-Kannadigas' from outside the state of Karnataka, especially after the IT boom in the 1990s, has led to a heightened sense of insecurity amongst local people about a presumed loss of identity. Though a pro-Kannada movement had acquired momentum from the 1970s onward with the celebration of Rayotsava festivals, it was in the mid-1950s, soon after the 'unification' of the state of Karnataka, that language activists advocated for the institutional predominance of Kannada in the state. Lingappa, a member of the Socialist Party, established the Kannada Yuvajana Sabha (KYS) in Mysore, which spearheaded this initiative (Gowda 2010). Over a period of time a plethora of pro-Kannada organizations have emerged such as the Kannada Shakti Kendra, the Rajkumar fans' associations or the Kannada Chaluvaligar movement, Karnataka Rakshana Vedike amongst others. Sangh-affiliated organizations are often seen joining hands with these groups in order to garner some political mileage. A case in point is the language riots that occurred in Bengaluru in October 1994 due to the introduction of a ten-minute Urdu bulletin on Doordarshan during the prime time slot, soon after the Kannada language newscast. The BJP wasted no time in joining hands with pro-Kannada organizations like Mico Kannada Sangha, the Channakeshavapura Kannada Sangha and the SKF Sangha, who were organizing protest marches and dharnas in various parts of the city and alleged that the telecast had been started by the Congress government to garner the votes of Muslims in the upcoming State Assembly elections (Engineer 1994). The riots that ensued from these events led to the death of 25 persons and left 350 people injured. There was also massive loss and damage of property in South Bangalore.

Similarly in Kolar, on the lines of the festivities of Kannada Rajyotsava day, where several local deities are brought out in a procession, the RSS started organizing Hindu samajotsavas. In these samajotsavas, all the deities in Kolar are gathered in one place and a procession is taken out. Slogans like 'Bharatiyaru Hindugalu' (All Indians are Hindus), 'Namma Desha Hindu Desha' (My country is Hindu), 'Namma Rakta Hindu Rakta' (My blood is Hindu blood) and 'Navalla Vondu Hindu' (We are all Hindus) are common in such rallies and obviously create a sense of insecurity amongst the minority communities.

As demonstrated previously, Hindutva forces have been active in the state much before its political outfit, the BJP, acquired power in the state. However, the thrust of its activities became more intensive after the BJP formed the government for the first time in 2008. Apart from a rise in the number of communal riots, there was a series of church attacks in coastal Karnataka allegedly by Bajrang Dal activists. The state government appointed an inquiry commission under Justice B.K. Somashekara to investigate these attacks, which in an interim report submitted to the government in September 2009 highlighted the involvement of Bajrang Dal in the attacks. However, in its final report submitted in 2011, the commission changed its stance and exonerated the Sangh Parivar of any role in the church attacks. It also stated that an impression of the Parivar's involvement was deliberately created to taint the image of the BJP government (The Indian Express 2014).

Politicization of Tipu Sultan and Baba Budangiri

The polemic surrounding Tipu Sultan's birthday celebrations in Karnataka is a classic illustration of how contentious historical accounts and perceptions about different communities regarding certain historical figures can aid political parties to meet their goals. It is common knowledge that Tipu Sultan ruled the kingdom of Mysore in the last decades of the 18th century. While several historians have celebrated Tipu as a brave warrior who fought the British, many communities in Mangalore and Kodagu view him as a religious bigot who forcibly converted many people to Islam. In what is often perceived as a gesture of winning over Muslim vote banks, the Congress government under Siddaramaiah initiated the annual practice of celebrating Tipu's birthday from 2015 onward. Hindutva-affiliated groups, which had been opposing the government's plan to mark the 266th anniversary of Tipu Sultan's birth, protested against this and several clashes broke out between Hindus and Muslims in places like Kodagu and Hubli, which also led to the death of a VHP activist (India Today 2015).[10]

The controversy surrounding the ownership of the Baba Budangiri shrine in Chikmaglur district of Karnataka has provided the Sangh Parivar with an opportunity to communalize the issue and consolidate Hindus in the state. This shrine, which is known as 'Sree Dattatreya Bababudan Swamy Dargah', has long been a place of pilgrimage for both Hindus and Muslims as it is believed that Dada Hayath Meer Khalandar (popularly known as Baba Budan), a companion of the Prophet Muhammad, arrived here in the 7th century BC. The seat of his meditation is also believed to be the seat of Dattatreya Swamy, a reincarnation of Vishnu (Asia Research Institute 2012: 17). In 1978, a controversy broke out after a government order directed the transfer of the shrine to the Wakf Board which had already issued a gazette notification that declared the property as *wakf* (Asia Research Institute 2012: 17). The Hindu groups pleaded against the decision and the matter went to court. The courts (at the district and state levels and the Supreme Court dismissed the petitions of the Wakf Board on the grounds that the shrine was a unique place of worship where both Hindus and Muslims offered prayers. From the 1980s onward, Sangh Parivar affiliates such as the VHP launched an initiative to 'liberate' the Dattatreya shrine from 'Muslim control'. They also started performing 'Vedic poojas' outside the shrine and took out rath yatras and jeep yatras to reclaim the site as a Hindu place of pilgrimage. The issue has been deliberately incited over the past few months with an eye on the upcoming elections.

Congress toeing a soft Hindutva line?

It is often argued that the success of Hindutva cannot be measured in electoral terms alone. The electoral gains of the BJP are just one of the many parameters of understanding the influence of Hindu nationalism today because the Sangh Parivar has managed to build its presence in every conceivable sphere of civil society. What is even more interesting to observe is the rising popularity of the idea of

Hindutva in the public realm, to the extent that even those political parties which are opposed to the ideology of Hindutva are now seen to be appropriating it. Chief Minister Siddaramaiah drew the attention of the media just before the 2018 elections when he made public statements such as the following: 'I am practicing Hindutva with humanity'; 'I am also a Hindu. In my name also Rama is there'; 'My name is Siddaramaiah. My family deity is Siddarameshwara. There is Ram Temple in my village' (Vattam 2017).[11]

These statements have come as a surprise to many especially since the chief minister has always stood by the stance that he is proud to be a 'Ahinda' leader (the acronym in Kannada for 'Alpa sankhyatara' or minorities, Hindulida, or backward castes and Dalits). Several analysts see this as a strategy to woo the Hindu voters in the upcoming elections ever since the BJP has accused the Congress of being anti-Hindu. Similar attempts were also made by the Congress chief Rahul Gandhi in Gujarat before the State Assembly elections in December 2017, when he was seen visiting several temples in the state and asserting his Hindu identity in several fora. However, what also needs to be acknowledged here is the appropriation of a certain discourse that is gradually seen as being legitimate and even essential to win elections.

Conclusion

This chapter has argued that any analysis about the meteoric rise of the BJP in specific contexts today needs to acknowledge the larger role of the Sangh Parivar in legitimizing and popularizing the discourse of Hindutva in that environment. In Karnataka, as in other states and regions of India, Hindutva operates as a holistic ecology that encapsulates a variety of organizations that work in different realms of society, ranging from the social and the cultural to the political. What unites these institutions is a certain ideological commitment to idea of building what is believed to be a strong 'Hindu rashtra'. Since its formal beginning in this region, with the establishment of a *shakha* in the year 1935, Hindutva has been able to make considerable forays in various realms of society including the political. In the concluding section of this chapter I spend some time reflecting on the cultural appeal of Hindutva and why I think it is gaining ground as an ideology.

Studies on the expansion of the Sangh Parivar in different regions of India[12] have raised interesting insights on the reasons for its rise as a political power. However, none of these studies provides a macro explanation for the phenomenal rise of Hindutva as a political ideology in the pan-Indian context. This chapter begins with the proposition that the theory of secularization seems to have failed, in India too as elsewhere, as religion has made a convincing comeback in the public sphere. Here, I try to expand on this idea a little further by examining if the phenomenon of Hindutva is symptomatic of a resurgence of 'religion' or something else.

Drawing from the theoretical framework offered by Gordon Lynch (2012), I find it more appropriate to use the term 'sacred form' to understand contemporary Hindutva. Building on the works of several other scholars such as Durkheim,

Edward Shils, Robert Bellah and Jeffrey C. Alexander, Lynch (2012: 29) defines the 'sacred' as follows:

> The sacred is defined by what people collectively experience as absolute, non-contingent realities which present normative claims over the meanings and conduct of social life. Sacred forms are specific, historically contingent, instances of the sacred. Sacred forms are constituted by constellations of specific symbols, thought/discourse, emotions and actions grounded in the body. . . . The normative reality represented by a sacred form simultaneously constructs the evils which profane it, and the pollution of this sacred reality is experienced by its adherents as a painful wound for which some form of restitution is necessary.

Lynch (ibid.: 133) further adds that the sacred is a 'communicative structure', imbued with power, that 'constructs the idea of human society as a meaningful, moral collective'. What is of particular relevance to the contemporary Indian context is Lynch's discussion on the concept of the sacred in modern societies. Lynch says that although the form and significance of sacred forms are contingent and contextual, there are some general traits about the nature of the sacred in late modern societies. Contrary to more homogeneous societies, he argues, which are organized in relation to an omnibus sacred form, 'late modern societies are characterized by the simultaneous presence of multiple sacred forms that exert complementary and conflicting fields of influence' (ibid.: 135).

If one were to analyze the Hindu nationalist movement through the aforementioned framework, in Karnataka, as elsewhere, it would become evident that it indeed functions as a 'sacred form' that though connected to Hinduism is also different from it. Though this ideology laid a footing in the region as early as 1935, it could not create a significant impact in the beginning, perhaps owing to its unpopularity after the assassination of Gandhi in 1948 by one of its previous members. Over a period of over 60 years, however, the Sangh Parivar had managed to establish a strong foothold in civil society by expanding its activities in the domains of service, religion and politics. These activities were nurtured through the efforts of a variety of affiliates of the Sangh Parivar. Finally, the electoral success of the BJP, especially after the 2004 state elections when it emerged as the single largest party, provided a solid footing for the ideology to consolidate itself politically.

The various activities of the different wings of Parivar have facilitated the construction of a discourse and a communicative structure that upholds the sacred form of Hindutva. This has been achieved through the help of symbols and discourses relating to issues of 'liberating' Hindu places of worship from the 'other', prohibition of cow slaughter, promotion of yoga, protection of Hindu culture from the onslaught of the 'others', rejuvenation of Hindu institutions such as *seva* and so forth. In this regard it is important to note that even though the RSS's goal of protecting the Hindu Dharma (religion), the ideology of building a robust Hindu Rashtra (Hindu nation) and the use of specific symbols of worship impart to it a 'Hindu' character' (Religions and Development Research Program 2009),[13] it has always maintained that it is a 'cultural' group. The concept of the Hindu Rashtra is constructed around the idea of Hindu culture which is identified as the national culture. This recourse to culture, which is a seemingly apolitical category when compared to religion, is advantageous as it encompasses practically everything ranging from customs, rituals and festivals to political behaviour. The political project, which lies at the heart of Hindutva, makes a back-door entry through culture. In this scheme of things, the religious dimension, to the extent that it exists, is only instrumental and is appropriated from certain outward forms of the Hindu religion.

Notes

1 'RSS Karnataka Celebrates 75th Year of Dr. Hedgewar's Visit to Chikkodi of Jan 16, 1937', January 15, 2012. Retrieved 26 December 2017 from http://samvada.org/2012/news/rss-karnataka-celebrates-75th-year-of-dr-hedgewars-visit-to-chikkodi-of-jan161937/.
2 'Images That Inspires: Life Sketch of Yadav Rao Joshi, the Sangh Pioneer of Karnataka', 7 July 2014. Retrieved form http://samvada.org/2014/news/images-life-sketch-of-yadav-rao-joshi-sangh-pioneer-of-karnataka/.
3 'Seva Disha', Rashtriya Sewa Bharati, New Delhi, 2014.
4 Champat Rai. 'VHP at a Glance', *Hindu Vivek Kendra*. Retrieved from http://www.hvk.org/2014/0914/39.html.
5 'Re-Conversion to Hinduism Was Approved by Acharyas in Udupi in 1964–65', 24 December 2014. Retrieved from https://bharatabharati.wordpress.com/2014/12/24/re-conversion-to-hinduism-was-approved-by-acharyas-in-udupi-in-1964-65-daijiworld-media/.
6 Ibid.
7 Chetan Kumar (2015). 'In South, Karnataka Tops in Communal Violence', *Times of India*, 9 October. Retrieved 24 February 2016.
8 Mohit M. Rao and Vivek Narayanan (2016). 'Communal Riot Cases Second Highest in State: NCRB, Bengaluru', *Hindu*, 31 August.
9 'Communalism in Karnataka' (n.d.). Retrieved 26 December 2017 from http://altlawforum.org/wiki/communalism-in-karnataka/.
10 'What Is the Ongoing Controversy Around Tipu Sultan Jayanti? Here's All You Need to Know', *India Today*, New Delhi, 12 November 2015.
11 Shyam Sundar Vattam (2017). 'Siddaramaiah, from Ahinda Neta to Soft Hindutva Proponent?' *Deccan Chronicle*, 2 December.
12 See for instance Gerald A. Heeger (1972). 'Discipline Versus Mobilization: Party Building and the Punjab Jana Sangh', *Asian Survey*, 12(10), October; K. Jayaprasad (1991). *RSS and Hindu Nationalism: Inroads in a Leftist Stronghold*, New Delhi: Deep & Deep; Thomas Blom Hansen (1999). *The Saffron Wave: Democracy and Hindu Nationalism in Modern India*, New Delhi: Princeton University Press; Christophe Jaffrelot (1996). *The Hindu Nationalist Movement and Indian Politics 1925 to 1990s*, New Delhi: Viking Penguin; Pralay Kanungo (2003). *RSS's Tryst With Politics: From Hedgewar To Sudarshan*, New Delhi: Manohar; Sud Nikita (2005). *Liberalization, Hindu Nationalism and the State*, New Delhi: Oxford University Press; Tariq Thachil (2011). 'Embedded Mobilization: Nonstate Service Provision as Electoral Strategy in India', *World Politics*, 63, pp. 434–69; Malini Bhattacharjee (2016). 'Tracing the Emergence and Consolidation of Hindutva in Assam', *Economic and Political Weekly*, 51(16), pp. 80–7, 16 April, for an account of the rise of Hindutva in Punjab, Kerala, Maharashtra, Odisha, Gujarat, Chhattisgarh and Assam, respectively.
13 Padmaja Nair (2009). *Religious Political Parties and Their Welfare Work: Relations Between the RSS, the Bharatiya Janata Party and the Vidya Bharati Schools in India*. Religions and Development Research Program (Working Paper 37). Retrieved 12 May 2012 from http://www.religionsanddevelopment.org/files/resourcesmodule/@random454f80f60b3f4/1256735869_working_paper_37.pdf.

References

Aerthayil, James (1989, January–March). 'Virasaivism – A Saivite Revolution in Karnataka', *Journal of Dharma: Dharmaram Journal of Religions and Philosophies*, 14(1), pp. 93–106.

Asia Research Institute. (2012, July). *The Difficulties of Religious Pluralism in India: Analysing the Place of Worship as a Legal Category in the Ayodhya and Bababudangiri Disputes* (Working Paper Series No. 187). Geetanjali Srikantan.

Assadi, Muzaffar (2002). 'Hindutva Policies in Coastal Region: Towards a Social Coalition', *Economic and Political Weekly*, 37(23), pp. 2211–13.

Bharatiya Jana Sangh (1973). *Bharatiya Jana Sangh: Party Documents, Vol. I, Principles, Manifestos, Constitutions*, New Delhi: BJS Publications, p. 48.

Bhatt, Chetan (2001). *Hindu Nationalism: Origins, Ideologies and Modern Myths*, Oxford: Berg.

Bhattacharjee, Malini (2016). 'Tracing the Emergence and Consolidation of Hindutva in Assam', *Economic and Political Weekly*, 51(16), pp. 8–87.

Engineer, Asghar Ali (1994). 'Bangalore Violence: Linguistic or Communal?' *Economic and Political Weekly*, 29(44), pp. 2854–8.

Golwalkar, M.S. (1980). *Bunch of Thoughts*, Bangalore: Jagarana Prakashana.

Gowda, Chandan (2010). 'Many Lohias? Appropriations of Lohia in Karnataka', *Economic and Political Weekly*, 45(40), pp. 78–84.

Hansen, Thomas Blom (1999). *The Saffron Wave: Democracy and Hindu Nationalism in Modern India*, New Delhi: Princeton University Press.

Heeger, Gerald A. (1972). 'Discipline Versus Mobilization: Party Building and the Punjab Jana Sangh', *Asian Survey*, 12(10), pp. 864–78.

India Today. (2015, November 12). 'What Is the Ongoing Controversy Around Tipu Sultan Jayanti? Here's All You Need to Know'. Retrieved from https://www.indiatoday.in/fyi/story/what-is-the-ongoing-controversy-around-tipu-sultan-heres-all-you-need-to-know-272459-2015-11-12 (Accessed January 12, 2018).

The Indian Express (2014, October 17). 'Karnataka Govt Rejects Commission Report on Church Attacks', Bengaluru. Retrieved from https://indianexpress.com/article/india/india-others/karnataka-govt-rejects-commission-report-on-church-attacks/ (Accessed January 14, 2018).

Jaffrelot, Christophe (1996). *The Hindu Nationalist Movement and Indian Politics 1925 to 1990s*, New Delhi: Viking Penguin.

Jayaprasad, K. (1991). *RSS and Hindu Nationalism. Inroads in a Leftist Stronghold*, New Delhi: Deep & Deep.

Kanungo, Pralay (2003). *RSS's Tryst with Politics: From Hedgewar to Sudarshan*, New Delhi: Manohar.

Kumar, Chetan (2015, October 9). 'In South, Karnataka Tops in Communal Violence', *The Times of India*. Retrieved from https://timesofindia.indiatimes.com/india/In-South-Karnataka-tops-in-communal-violence/articleshow/49280129.cms (Accessed January 12, 2018).

Lynch, Gordon (2012). *The Sacred in the Modern World: A Cultural Sociological Approach*, Oxford: Oxford University Press.

Mellegatti, Pramod (2004, September 22). 'Godse Accompanied Savarkar to Shimoga in 1944', *The Hindu*. Retrieved from www.thehindu.com/2004/09/22/stories/2004092205650400.htm.

Menon, Parvathi (2004, March). 'Hindutva at Work: The Spread in the South', *Frontline*, 21(6).

Mondal, Sudipta (2015, September 9). 'In Coastal Karnataka, History of Communalism Is Yet to Be Written', *Hindustan Times*. Retrieved from https://www.hindustantimes.

com/india/in-coastal-karnataka-history-of-communalism-is-yet-to-be-written/story-a4JoMe06mhAw3sPjMzt7AJ.html (Accesed January 14, 2018).
Rao, Mohit M. and Vivek Narayanan (2016, August 31). 'Communal Riot Cases Second Highest in State: NCRB, Bengaluru', *The Hindu*. Retrieved from https://www.thehindu.com/todays-paper/Communal-riot-cases-second-highest-in-State-NCRB/article14599075.ece (Accessed January 14, 2018).
Rao, Venkatsubba K.N. (2008, May 31). 'Sangh Parivar Has a Strong Presence', *The Hindu*. Retrieved from www.thehindu.com/todays-paper/tp-national/tp-karnataka/Sangh-Parivar-has-a-strong-presence/article15232324.ece (Accessed January 12, 2018).
Religions and Development Research Program. (2009). *Religious Political Parties and Their Welfare Work: Relations Between the RSS, the Bharatiya Janata Party and the Vidya Bharati Schools in India* (Working Paper 37). Padmaja Nair. Retrieved May 12, 2012, from www.religionsanddevelopment.org/files/resourcesmodule/@random454f80f60b3f4/1256735869_working_paper_37.pdf
Subramanya, K.V. (2006, January 12). 'Karnataka Ignored Report on ISI Activities in Bhatkal, Karnataka', *The Hindu*. Retrieved from https://www.thehindu.com/todays-paper/report-on-isi-activities-ignored/article3238959.ece (Accessed January 13, 2018).
Sud, Nikita (2005). *Liberalization, Hindu Nationalism and the State*, New Delhi: Oxford University Press.
Thachil, Tariq (2011). 'Embedded Mobilization: Nonstate Service Provision as Electoral Strategy in India', *World Politics*, 63, pp. 434–69.
Ullekh, N.P. (2015, April 3). 'Bhatkal and Its Struggle with History and Radical Islam', *Open Magazine*. Retrieved March 1, 2018, from www.huffingtonpost.in/open-magazine/a-place-called-bhatkal_b_6888512.html.
Vattam, Shyam Sundar (2017, December 2). 'Siddaramaiah, from Ahinda Neta to Soft Hindutva Proponent?' *Deccan Chronicle*. Retrieved from https://www.deccanchronicle.com/nation/current-affairs/031217/siddaramaiah-from-ahinda-neta-to-soft-hindutva-proponent.html (Accessed Janury 15, 2018).

8
NATURE AND DYNAMICS OF RELIGION-ORIENTED POLITICS IN KERALA

Josukutty C. A.

Politics in Kerala has been unique in many respects. Caste and communal organizations were sites for political and social mobilization even before the formation of the state. Social reform movements in the late 19th and early 20th centuries, such as the Malayalai Memorial in 1891, Nivarthan Movement in the 1930s and Vaikom and Guruvayoor Satyagrahas in 1931–32 were led by community organizations (Kumar 2014: 321). The Sree Narayana Dharma Paripalana Yogam Sangham, Sadhujana Paripalana Sangham and the Yogas Kshema Sabha and Nair Samajam formed in the wake of the social reform movements catered to the interests of their own communities and became sectarian in outlook and practice (Pillai 1999). At one stage the Nairs and Ezhavas came together under 'Hindu Mandalam' to face the challenge of Christians. The social reform movements that fought social, economic and political discrimination never shunned religious and caste identities. The formation of governments in the states of Travancore and Kochi between 1948 and 1954 had been tussle for power among different castes and communal groups. Tickets to the legislature and cabinets posts including that of the chief minister were allocated on communal lines. On account of the power struggle among castes and religious groups, there were six cabinets under five chief ministers in a span of six years in Travancore and Kochi (Kumar 1986: 18).

Demographic composition and communal politics

Kerala inherited a highly differentiated caste and religious structure and unique demographic composition. Demographically, Kerala has one of the least percentages of Hindus among the states of India. The minority Muslims (26.6%) and Christians (18.6%) together constitute 45% of the population (see Tables 8.1 and 8.4). It is the only major state in India where two religious minorities each constitute more than

15% of the population. The Nairs, Ezhavas, Christians and Muslims that together constitute 78.2% (Table 8.1) of the population have been major political players in Kerala since 1956.

The Nair Service Society (NSS) and Sree Narayana Dharma Paripalana Yogam (SNDP) –the community organizations of the Nairs and Ezhavas, respectively – were formed to take care of their own interests. The Indian Union Muslim League (IUML) and Kerala Congress (KC) were political parties predominantly of Muslims and Christians, respectively. These caste and political organizations with the support of a number of feeder organizations own and manage a substantial number of educational and charitable institutions, media houses and property in prime locations. 'In fact they were the pillars of politics in Kerala, and the slight shift in their voting pattern greatly influenced the fortunes of political parties' (Victor 1970: 6).

Most of the political parties have their support base among different castes and religious groups with a combination of class and secular make-up. The Congress traditionally had the support of Hindu Nairs, the communist parties of Ezhavas, SCs and STs, the Kerala Congress of the Christians and the Muslim League of the Muslims (Table 8.2). Apart from their specific support base, Congress and the communists have marginal influence in all sections of Hindus and minorities.

The demographic composition and its geographic concentration is key to electoral politics, as a few districts in Kerala are dominated by the minorities. Muslims constitute about 70% and 40% of the population in Malapuram and Kozhokode-Kasargod districts, respectively (Office of the Registrar General and Census Commissioner, India). Most of the seats won by the IUML in the Kerala Assembly have been from these districts. In the 2016 Assembly election, of the total 16 seats in Malappuram, all except one have been won by Muslims and of these 14 by the IUML. Both the United Democratic Front (UDF) and Left Democratic Front (LDF)[1] on most of the occasions fielded Muslim candidates in the district (Office of the Registrar General and Census Commissioner, India). The electoral achievements of Kerala Congress have been mainly from the districts of Kottaym, Idduki,

TABLE 8.1 Population of Kerala by major caste/religious communities (2011)

	Percent	Cumulative
Nairs	11.6	11.6
Ezhava	21.6	33.2
Christians	18.4	51.6
Muslims	26.6	78.2
SC and ST	9.6	87.8
Other Hindu sects	12.2	100
Total	100	100

Source: Zacharia, K.C., April 2016, Working on Religious denomination in Kerala, Working Paper 468, Kerala Migration Surveys, http://cds.edu/wp-content/uploads/2016/05/WP468.pdf, and Census of India data.

TABLE 8.2 Caste and religious base of political parties in Kerala

Sr. no.	Party	Religious-caste support base
1.	Congress	Upper-caste Hindu Nairs, some Christians, Muslims, Ezhavas
2.	Communist Parties: CPM and CPI	Backward castes, mainly Ezhavas, SCs and STs, and some upper-caste Nairs
3.	Kerala (KC)	Majority of Syrian Christians, other upper-caste Christians and a small minority of Nairs
4.	Indian Union Muslim League (IUML)	Muslims, predominantly in the Malabar region
5	Bharatiya Janata Party (BJP)	Hindus, mostly upper-caste Nairs and some lower castes across the spectrum
6	Bharat Dharma Jana Sena (BDJS).	Lower-caste Hindus, Ezhavas

Source: Compiled from the Kerala, Chief Electoral Officer, available at www.ceo.kerala.gov.in/; Census of India Reports, available at http://censusindia.gov.in/; Manorama Election Guide, 2011.

TABLE 8.3 District-religious profile of Kerala

District	Hindus	Muslims	Christians
Thiruvananthapuram	66.94%	13.72%	19.10%
Kollam	64.42%	19.29%	15.99%
Pathanamthitta	56.93%	4.59%	38.12%
Alapuzha	68.64%	10.55%	20.45%
Kottayam	49.81%	6.41%	43.48%
Idukki (2001)	48.86%	7.41%	43.42%
Ernakulam (2001)	45.99%	15.67%	38.03%
Thrissur (2001)	58.42%	17.07%	24.27%
Palakkad (2001)	66.76%	28.93%	4.07%
Malappuram (2001)	27.60%	70.24%	1.98%
Kozhikode (2001)	56.21%	39.24%	4.26%
Wayanad (2001)	49.48%	28.65%	21.34%
Kannur (2001)	59.83%	29.43%	10.41%
Kasargod (2001)	55.83%	37.24%	6.68%

Source: Census of India Reports, available at http://censusindia.gov.in/.

Ernakulam and Pathanamthitta, where Christians constitute around 40% of the population (Office of the Registrar General and Census Commissioner, India).

The concentration of the minority populace in a few districts is shown in Table 8.3, and electoral success has helped them to protect their political and economic interests better than the majority Hindu groups. The increase in the percentage of population of the minorities over the years, depicted in Table 8.4, has correspondingly increased their political clout as well.

TABLE 8.4 Kerala population religion-wise (1911–2011)

Year	Hindus	Muslims	Christians	Others
1911	66.63%	17.68%	15.41%	0.28%
1921	64.75%	17.43%	17.64%	0.18%
1931	63.34%	17.08%	19.54%	0.64%
1941	60.73%	17.08%	20.52%	1.67%
1951	61.59%	17.53%	20.85%	0.03%
1961	60.83%	17.91%	21.22%	0.04%
1971	59.41%	19.30%	21.25%	0.04%
1981	58.15%	21.50%	20.56%	0.04%
1991	57.28%	23.33%	19.32%	0.07%
2001	56.20%	24.70%	19.00%	1.10%
2011	54.73%	26.86%	18.38%	0.71%

Source: Census of India Reports, available at http://censusindia.gov.in/.

Coalition governments and communal politics

The unique demographic composition and caste-based politics in Kerala rendered coalition governments inevitable. The making and breaking of coalition governments was the salient feature of Kerala politics from 1956 to 1981. Different alliance formations were tried by the Congress and the Communists led UDF and LDF fronts, but none could provide stability. Only one government completed its full term during the period. Splits in major parties and the emergence of communal and religious parties furthered political instability. Since 1981, the coalition pattern assumed stability with governments being formed alternatively by the UDF and LDF with a critical role for the minority and caste-based parties and organizations such as the KC, IUML, SNDP and NSS.

There was a general aversion to the role and influence of minority parties and caste organizations in the early years. The major parties were reluctant to ally with them. Between 1957 and 1979 the key portfolios in governments were dominated by the major parties (Manorama Election Guide 2011). In 1960, Congress was reluctant to include the IUML in the ministry. Since no major parties could muster enough strength to form the government on their own, they compromised with religion-oriented minority parties and caste groups. The IUML was a constituent of the left ministry in 1967 with two cabinet berths. Subsequent ministries included the IUML and KC as partners without any hesitation. Thus, since 1960 both the communists and Congress aligned with the IUML and KC to form governments on different occasions.[2]

Having the minority religion parties in the alliances was a guarantee for electoral victory. The communal and religion-oriented parties have routinely secured more than 20% of the votes polled (and sometimes up to 28%), and more than a fifth of the total seats and sometimes up to a half of the cabinet portfolios since the late 1970s (Mannathukkaren 2017). This cemented the political significance of Muslim

League and Kerala Congress in the body politic of Kerala. The electoral utility of minority parties enabled them to derive great political mileage from both the fronts. The Muslim-majority district of Malappuram and the University of Calicut were created by the left ministry under pressure from the IUML. The IUML gained permission to start many private schools, got Muslim festivals declared as holidays in educational institutions, secured important positions in bureaucracy, created employment opportunities for mullahs (Muslim clergy) and made Arabic compulsory in all Muslim-run schools, thus opening up thousands of jobs for Arabic teachers with madrasa educations (Kumar 2014: 331). The clout of small communal parties even led to an installation of a government led by the Muslim League in 1979 – an unprecedented event in independent India (Mannathukkaren 2017). Similarly, minority politics played by the Kerala Congress helped the Christian churches run a number of educational and medical institutions.

With the consolidation of bipolar coalition politics since 1980, the clout of the religious minorities increased manifold. The IUML and KC successfully gained control of major portfolios like finance, education, Public Works Department, industry, revenue and local administration (which constitute 70% of state revenue) irrigation, transport, pocketed appointments to key posts in boards, corporations and universities and obtained permission for self-financing educational institutions and title deeds for government lands (Kumar 2014: 331). The NSS and SNDP also could pocket some benefits through pressure politics. National parties had to adjust with less important ministries. In the fragmented party system, the small parties determine the kind of role the major parties are supposed to perform (Kumar 1980). The success of the minority parties prompted the NSS and SNDP to form their own caste-based parties in the 1970s but had only limited success.[3] In 2015 the SNDP launched a new political outfit: Bharat Dharma Jana Sena (BDJS), aligned with the NDA. In the UDF ministry (2011–16), the minority parties together had more ministerial berths in the cabinet than the majority community (The Economic Times 2012).[4] Similarly in 2018, the Congress succumbed to the pressure of KC and IUML and allocated its Rajya Sabha seat to Kerala Congress. It provided a good opportunity for the RSS to whip up majority religious passions on minority appeasement.

The CPM has openly courted and appeased both minority and minority communal and caste-oriented parties. The steps taken by the LDF (during 2006–11) to control unaided educational institutions had to be withdrawn under pressure from caste and religious groups (Kumar 2014: 399). The decision by the LDF government to recruit Dalit and backward communities as temple priests, a 10% reservation for economically backward upper-caste Hindus and increase in the quota for OBC and SC and ST in five public-run Devaswom boards were aimed at appeasing the majority community. The competition between the CPM and BJP to conduct temple and Hindu festivals is another version of majority endearment. In an attempt to keep the Hindu sects with them, there is competition among major parties, with majority community support base, to celebrate Hindu festivals like Sree Krisha Jayanti, Durga Puja and Ganesh Chaturvedi separately.

Politics in Kerala has been marked by compromise and adjustment among different religious castes and secular and class entities. Most political parties including the left have played religious and communal politics to win elections and maintain power under compulsion of coalition governments. This, to some extent, deradicalized and diluted the secular and class credential politics of the left parties and Congress. The minority parties through pressure tactics have derived immense political mileage under coalition governments, to the dissatisfaction and anger of a section of the majority Hindu communities. According to the study conducted by the Survey Research Centre, 52% of people in Kerala are of the view that minority parties and caste and community leaders have high influence in governments (Survey Research Centre 2016). Very often the major parties with support base among Hindus had to succumb to the demands of the minority parties, as governments survived on wafer-thin majorities. For minority parties, religion-oriented politics has been more a strategy to secure political power and to protect their own specific interests than a means to promote religious interests or believes. Despite intense competition among the various caste and religious groups for political and economic privileges, inter-religious and caste relationships have been strong and peaceful in Kerala. However, there is a perceptible change in this situation with the assertion of Hindutva politics.

Communal tensions and polarizing politics

Despite being a peaceful and tolerant state in inter-religious relationships, sporadic violence and religiously divisive controversies with political overtones have occurred between Muslims, Christians and Hindus. According to the Union Home Ministry statistics (NCRB 2016), Kerala has been witnessing an increase in communal incidents over the last few years, with 10 in 2007, 22 in 2008, 36 in 2009, 24 in 2010, 30 in 2011, 56 in 2012 and 41 in 2013, and a 100% rise in the number of communal incidents in 2017 as compared to the previous year (The News Minute 2018). The Nilakkal Church dispute between the Christians and Hindus, the Marrad and Nadapuram communal violence involving Hindus and Muslims, political clashes between CPM and RSS, controversies over issues of religious conversion, love jihad, ISIS recruitment and activities of right-wing organizations of all religious groups and growing religiosity have subtly prepared the ground for religious polarization and consequent consolidation of religion-oriented politics in Kerala.

The Nilakkal Church dispute in 1983 was over the demand of Christians for the construction of a church at Nilakkal near the Lord Ayyappa Temple in Sabarimala. The Hindus opposed it on the ground that the site falls in the garden of Lord Ayyappa. Though the issue was settled by giving permission to construct a church away from the temple, it led to unprecedented Hindu-Christian tensions and religious polarization. Hindus were supported by the RSS and Christians by the church. The RSS decried the Nilakkal church as a symbol of government-sponsored communalism. The dispute provided great political mileage to the Hindutva movement, as it enabled the Hindu Munnani candidate to secure second place (21% of votes) in Thiruvananthapuram Lok Sabha election in 1984 and impressive performance in a few other places in subsequent elections.

Political clashes in Nadapuram in Kozhikode district started in 2000 when one each CPM and IUML sympathizers were killed. According to police, nearly 600 rioting cases and five political killings have been officially recorded in this small area since 2001 (Hindustan Times 2016). Though the clash was between the CPM and IUML, eventually it turned out to be a fight between Ezhavas (Hindu sub-castes) and Muslims where these secular parties turned communal and religious to protect their vote bank. Gradually, religion-oriented radical groups like Popular Front of India (PFI) and the RSS penetrated the region. The massacre of eight Hindu fishermen at Marad in Kozhikode on 2 May 2003 was the worst communal violence in the history of Kerala. It started as a minor altercation between Hindu and Muslim fishermen at Marad beach in January 2002 that ended in the death of three Hindus and two Muslims. Subsequent developments brought the Hindus in the village under the influence of the RSS. In its report, the judicial commission that probed the incident concluded that IUML was directly involved in both the conspiracy and execution of the massacre (The Indian Express 2006). Even after 15 years, the situation in the region continues to be tense, and about 500 Muslim families that fled the site could not return to their residence due to opposition from the Hindu outfits. The incident polarized Hindus and Muslims of the coastal village on religious lines. Similarly, political clashes between the RSS and the CPM gradually become a fight between the Hindus and atheist communists.

The controversy over love jihad in Kerala is based on the notion of Hindu women being forcefully converted to Islam and radicalized through marriages to Muslim men. The issue assumed political dimensions as both pro-Hindu and pro-Muslim organizations adopted religiously radical positions. The perception propagated by the RSS is that conversion is an organized activity by radical Muslim entities.[5] There is a deep-rooted perception that the decrease in the Hindu populace in Kerala from 66.63% in 1911 to 54.73% in 2011 and the increase in minority numbers (Table 8.4) from 33.09% in 1911 to 45.24% 2011 (Office of the Registrar General and Census Commissioner, India 2018) has been on account of conversions to Islam and Christianity from Hinduism through unethical preaching methods and tactics (Hindu Aikavedi 2018). But according to a study by Media Research and Development Foundation, during the period January 2011 to December 2017, 60% converts in Kerala chose to embrace Hinduism (Manorama Online 2018).[6] Over the years the Muslim population have grown at a higher rate compared to Christians and Hindus. A Study by the Centre for Development Studies, Thiruvananthapuram shows that the population growth of all communities, including that of Muslims, has been declining over the decades (Zacharia 2016). The recruitment of youth from Kerala to ISIS fits well with the Sangh Parivar narrative of Islamophobia. It is estimated that over a hundred people have joined ISIS from Kerala (India Today 2017), and of these 21 had already left for ISIS-controlled territories in Afghanistan and some were killed (Jacob 2017).

Concomitant to these developments, Kerala has witnessed a spurt in the activities of right-wing Muslim and Hindu organizations. Radical Muslim organizations like the Social Democratic Party of India (SDPI), National Development Front, PFI and Jamaat-e-Islami are active in Kerala. These organizations have been linked to recruitment of people to ISIS, moral policing, killing and attack on political and religious rivals and prescription of regimental adherence to medieval/primordial Islamic life practices. It is reported that these organizations have infiltrated mainstream political parties, as some of the arrested in connection with the observance of an anonymous hartal to protest against the rape of a minor girl in Kathua were members simultaneously of either CPM, Congress or IUML and separatist organizations such as PFI and SDPI (Nair 2018). There are 56 active Sagh parivar organizations working in Kerala (Malayala Manorama 2018). The RSS has a base of 6,845 shakas, with four lakh members, two lakh active members, 84,000 daily attendance in Sakhas in Kerala (compared with BJP core states like Gujarat with 1,000 shakhas) and a 7% increase in RSS membership in the state in 2017 (Rajeev 2018).

Concurrently, there is a revival of religiosity in Kerala. In the second half of the 20th century, people were reluctant to display religious symbols or speak about their religion or caste in public. It was a secular repression of caste and religious identity (Lukose 2016). But now everything connected to religion is loud, public and well-funded (Latha 2016). People readily and proudly identify themselves as Hindus, Muslims and Christian rather than citizens of India (Panicker 2011). The growing adherence to religious dress and symbols across religions, renewed emphasis on obscure religious rituals and practices, a spurt in spirituality centres and pilgrimages, the growing influence of god persons, the construction of grander churches, mosques and temples and controversy over everything that breaks with traditional customary religious practices – be it entry into places of worship (controversy over women's entry into Sabarimal Ayyappa Temple) or more roles for women in churches (no to the papal proposal to wash the feet of women on Maundy Thursday by Syro-Malabar and Syro-Malankara Churches) reflect the return of rigid religiosity into Kerala's public sphere. Sangh Parivar uses all sorts of religious and cultural symbols to reach out to the people. The growing religiosity has an economic dimension where the reference point of comparison, particularly for poor Hindus, is the affluent sections of minorities. The narrative of the Sangh Parivar is that Hindus have been sidelined and discriminated by the bipolar politics of the state while the Christians and the Muslims have been pampered with economic and political privileges. It becomes an easy emotional justification for the economic hardships faced by Hindus.

The cumulative outcome of these incidents of communal violence, religiously sensitive controversies, activities of the extremists outfits and growing religiosity is the circulation of assertive religious propositions in the public leading to the crystallization of religious identities and the consequent emergence of religion-oriented politics. The pitching of the Sangh Parivar on Hindu hegemony, Muslim fringe elements on puritanical Islam and Pentecostal rhetoric on evangelism challenge the secular fabric. It strengthens the Sangh Parivar demand for political and religious unity among Hindus. Though the communal tensions in Marad and Nadapuram and the Nilakkal church dispute were over local issues, it had resonance all over Kerala. All the local issues and controversies with religious overtones are modulated to give a homogeneous explanation for the threats faced by Hindus. Consequently, the majority and minority communities are lining up on religious basis on the opposite sides of the political spectrum.

Electoral performance and religion-oriented politics

Minority religious and communal parties have been influential in Kerala since the formation of the state. On average the IUML secured 7% of popular votes and 20% of seats in the Assembly elections since 1960 (Chief Electoral Officer, Kerala). In terms of ministerial berths in the state cabinet, its share varied from 12.5% to 23% between 1982 and 2011 (Manorama Election Guide 2011). Similarly the share of ministerial berths of Kerala Congress ranged between 15 and 22 over the same period (Manorama Election Guide 2011). Technically, members of the majority community on an average had more than 50% of the ministerial births in both UDF- and LDF-led governments. But the Congress and the communists never propounded the cause of majority communities as minority parties did for the minorities. This is where the Sangh Parivar outfits could carve out a space for majority Hindutva politics. The BJP and its feeder organizations have been contesting elections since the 1980s but with negligible success till 2011. Between 1982 and 2011, the vote share of the BJP was in the range of 2% to 6% and it could never win a seat either in the Assembly or Parliament (Chief Electoral Officer, Kerala). The vote share of the BJP/NDA suddenly jumped to 14.62% and won its first-ever seat in the Assembly in 2016. A similar gain was visible in the Lok Sabha election in 2014 and in the local body election in 2015 with 11% and 15.63% of votes, respectively (Chief Electoral Officer, Kerala).[7] Overall there is 9% increase in the vote share of BJP/NDA in a span of five years (2011 to 2016). During this period, ending its political untouchability in Kerala, BJP expanded the alliance with the inclusion of Bharat Dharma Jana Sena (BDJS) and the Janadhipathya Rashtriya Sabha (JRS) (representing the Ezhavas and Adivasis, respectively), Janathipathiya Samrakshana Samithy led by Rajan Babu, Kerala Congress led by P.C. Thomas, Kerala Vikas Party, Lok Janshakti Party, Praja Socialist Party and Pravasi Nivasi Party.

The 2016 Assembly verdict was politically significant in many respects. BJP won an assembly seat for the first time in Kerala, and emerged second in seven constituencies (Chief Electoral Officer, Kerala 2016) and secured more than 20% of the vote in 31 constituencies – an improvement from just three in 2011 (Majumdar 2016). Previously the BJP was strong only in the districts of Thiruvanathapuram and Kasargod, but in 2016 it secured more than 10% of the votes in 11 of the 14 districts (Sadandan 2016). The BJP has mustered enough critical mass and demolished the myth that NDA could not be a viable alternative in the bipolar politics of Kerala. The BJP/NDA vote share is increasing, especially in Lok Sabha elections as compared with the Assembly election, as shown in Table 8.5 and Figure 8.1.

Religion-oriented politics in Kerala   133

TABLE 8.5 Vote share of BJP/NDA in Lok Sabha elections in Kerala (1982–2016)

Year	1984	1989	1991	1996	1998	1999	2004	2009	2014
% of votes	1.75	4.51	4.61	6.22	8.02	6.56	12.09	7.31	11

Source: Chief Electoral Officer Kerala, Lok Sabha elections, available at www.ceo.kerala.gov.in/election history.html.

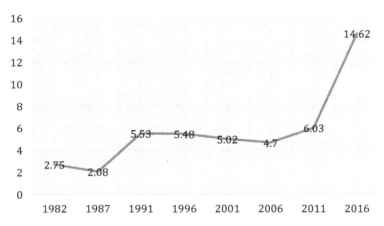

FIGURE 8.1 Vote share of BJP/NDA in Lok Sabha elections in Kerala (1982–2016)

Source: Chief Electoral Officer, Kerala, Legislative Assembly Election Kerala, available at www.ceo.kerala.gov.in/electionhistory.html.

Further, the pattern of caste and religion-wise voting in the 2011 and 2016 Assembly elections underlines the growth of religion politics in Kerala. The vote share of the BJP has increased dramatically among the Hindu caste groups between 2011 and 2016 – from 11.3% to 33.5% among the Nairs and 6.8% to 17.9% among the Ezhavas (see Table 8.6). Among the other OBCs and the SCs also, the support for BJP/NDA increased substantially (Table 8.6). The major loser in this shifting of vote was the UDF, followed by the LDF.

The LDF won the Assembly election in 2016 with a convincing margin of 91 seats (out of 140), but its vote share was lower by 1.53% and that of the UDF by 7% (Kerala, Chief Electoral Officer, 2016). Out of the of 47 seats won by the UDF 27 (out of total of 39 from the districts) are from the predominantly minority districts of Malappuram, Ernakulam and Kottayam (of these 18 was won by IUML and six by KC) and the remaining 20 (out of 101) are from 11 districts (see Table 8.7).

Evidently in the Hindu majority districts, the UDF, especially the Congress, is losing its support base to both the BJP/NDA and LDF. On the one hand, BJP has succeed in carving out a portion of the erstwhile Hindu votes from the Congress and the CPM, and on the other a portion of the erstwhile UDF minority votes got

TABLE 8.6 Caste/religion and voting behaviour, 2011 and 2016 Assembly elections

Caste/Religion Party/Alliance Preferred (%)

	LDF		UDF		BJP/NDA		Others	
	2011	2016	2011	2016	2011	2016	2011	2016
Nairs	42.4	44.7	43.2	19.9	11.3	33.5	3.1	1.9
Other upper castes	29.7	36.1	39.1	52.8	28.1	11.1	3.1	–
Ezhavas	64.2	49.4	26.4	27.8	6.8	17.9	2.6	4.8
Other OBCs	59.3	49	30.4	26.5	7.5	19.4	2.8	5.1
Scheduled castes	63.8	51	26.3	22	7.6	23	2.2	4
Scheduled tribes	42.6	71.4	44.4	23.8	9.3	4.8	3.7	–
Muslims	31	35.1	64.6	57.6	1.4	3.3	3.1	4
Christians	26.7	35.3	67.4	50.6	0.6	9.6	5.3	4.5
Others	51.4	48.4	33.9	28	11.3	16.1	3.4	7.5
Total	44.9	42.6	45.7	38.7	6	14.6	3.3	4.2

Source: CSDS New Delhi Survey, 2011 and 2016.

TABLE 8.7 District-wise performance of fronts: Kerala elections 2016

No.	District	Total seats	LDF	UDF	NDA/BJP	Others
1	Thiruvananthapuram	14	9	4	1	–
2	Kollam	11	11	0	0	–
3	Pathanamthitta	5	4	1	0	–
4	Alapuzha	9	8	1	0	–
5	Kottayam	9	2	6	0	1
6	Idukki	5	3	2	0	–
7	Ernakulam	14	5	9	0	–
8	Thrissur	13	12	1	0	–
9	Palakkad	12	9	3	0	–
10	Malappuram	16	4	12	0	–
11	Kozhikode	13	11	2	0	–
12	Wayanad	3	2	1	0	–
13	Kannur	11	8	3	0	–
14	Kasargod	5	3	2	0	–
	Total	140	91	47	1	1

Source: Chief electoral officer, Kerala Legislative Assembly election 2016, available at www.ceo.kerala.gov.in/electionhistory.html.

shifted to the LDF in an attempt to counter the threat from resurgent Hindutva (Menon 2016). There is a tendency among the minority communities to vote for the LDF in areas where they are sparsely populated on the perception that the left is better equipped to deal with the threats posed by BJP to the minorities (Josukutty 2016). The religion oriented politics asserted by the Sangh Parivar outfit is politically significant at two levels, one it has created a new Hindu consciousness that emphasizes the need for unity among different Hindu castes across the spectrum. Two, it has created a kind of fear/anxiety among the minorities. Both these developments have accrued electoral dividends for the BJP/NDA by attracting more votes from the Hindus and distracting a small portion of minorities' votes from the UDF to the LDF. This has been the result of the simultaneous growth of religious identity politics both among the minorities and majority communities.

Conclusion

Communal and caste politics with subtle religious connotations has been a feature of politics in Kerala. The concentration of minority population in certain districts and the dynamics of coalition governments gave minority parties a decisive advantage in electoral politics to the envy of the majority community. The caste and religious support base of political parties, sporadic incidents of communal violence, religiously divisive narratives on conversion and love jihad, the politics of cow slaughter, cultural confusion and growing religiosity, compromise politics played by the liberal and left parties, religiously divisive political clashes and the resurgence of Hindutva at the national level have shrunken the secular and class spaces and broadened the spaces of religion-oriented politics. BJP has skilfully exploited the communal and caste-oriented political frame of Kerala to practice its version of religion-oriented politics. The growth of religion-oriented politics is manifested in the impressive electoral performance of the BJP in Kerala since 2011. This has enabled the party not only to increase its vote share to critical mass but also to overcome its political 'untouchability'[8] in Kerala by attracting more alliance partners. The BJP has emerged as a viable political alternative capable of changing the decades old bipolar front politics in Kerala into tripolarity or to a new format of coalition. In a real tripolar contest the BJP could win a number of seats, particularly in constituencies where it has come second or third with substantial share of votes.

In the past, politics particularly among various Hindus sects had been caste-based and inclination towards religion-oriented politics was modulated by class and secular political parties. Now the mainstream political parties in Kerala with a support base among the Hindus increasingly compromise with religious politics. Religiously assertive politics practiced by the Sangh Parivar by highlighting issues of empowerment of Hindus, temple administration, perceived threats posed by minorities and emphasis on the economic and political clout of the minorities have succeeded in creating a common Hindu identity. The economic hardships of the majority Hindus are explained in terms of the political and economic clout of the affluent sections of minorities. Strong inter-religious civic engagement, a unique feature of Kerala society, is on the decline. Politics of hate, intimidation, violence and religious polarization are on the increase. Kerala is witnessing a direct crystallization of religion-oriented politics under the influence of religiously assertive politics played by the Sangh Parivar outfits and fringe elements among the minorities in the backdrop of the communal and caste politics already prevalent. However,

Hindutva politics practiced by the BJP in Kerala is not as virulent as in other parts of the country on account of the electoral and demographic significance of the minorities.

Notes

1 Since 1980, politics in Kerala have been dominated by the Congress and communist-led alliances – the UDF and the LDF, respectively. Power alternated between these fronts with none of them getting consecutive terms.
2 The formation of Kerala Congress in 1964 due to split in Congress was partly in protest against the lower-caste Chief Minister R. Shankar.
3 The National Democratic Party (NDP) formed by the Nair community in 1974 and the Socialist Republican Party (SRP) by the Ezhavas in 1976 were part of the coalition governments for an interlude but lost relevance towards the end of 1980s.
4 In 2011, the UDF government yielded to the pressure of IUML for a fifth minister in the 21-member council of ministers and with the induction of one more minister from the Kerala Congress (J), the UDF government had more ministers from the minority communities.
5 The idea of love jihad took root in public imagination in Kerala in 2016, when a Christian woman named Merin and a Hindu woman named Nimisha married a pair of siblings, Bestin and Bexen; the four of them then converted to Islam and left for Afghanistan to join the Islamic terror network ISIS. The most prominent case of this genre was that of Hadiya. In 2016, 25-year-old college student Hadiya, who was born Hindu – converted to Islam and left her home. The narrative was that she was a victim of love jihad and that she was converted so she could fight for ISIS in Syria.
6 It is estimated that from January 2011 to December 2017, a total of 8,334 people chose to convert to a different religion. A total of 4,756 Christians and 212 Muslims converted to Hinduism during the seven years. Christianity attracted 1,424 Hindus and 72 Muslims. The period saw 1,864 conversions to Islam and 1,496 to Christianity. Conversions to Islam numbered at 1,864, of which 1,472 converts were Hindus and 390 were Christians. (Manorama Online 2018)
7 In the 2004 Lok Sabh election, the BJP alliance secured a vote share of 12.09% and one of its partners, the Indian Federal Democratic Party, won a parliamentary seat. But it was mainly a vote against the leadership of the Kerala Congress. Technically it was the first parliamentary election victory for the NDA in Kerala. But in the next Lok Sabha election in 2009, the vote share of the BJP dwindled to 7.31%.
8 There was a time in Kerala when it was considered taboo for political parties to align with the BJP on account of its extreme communal and religious politics.

References

Chief Electoral Officer, Kerala. (2016). 'Legislative Assembly Election Kerala 2016', Government of Kerala. Retrieved August 12, 2018, from www.ceo.kerala.gov.in/generalelection2016.html.
The Economic Times. (2012, April 13). 'In Kerala Council Ministers the Minorities Are Majority'. Retrieved July 14, 2018, from https://economictimes.indiatimes.com/news/politics-and-nation/in-kerala-council-of-ministers-the-minorities-are-majority/articleshow/12643324.cms?from=mdr.
Hindu Aikavedi. (2018). Retrieved from www.hinduaikyavedi.org/p/about.html.
Hindustan Times. (2016, September 11). 'Violence Leaves North Kerala Bloody as Political Equations Change'. Retrieved September 6, 2018, from www.hindustantimes.com/

india-news/violence-leaves-north-kerala-bloody-as-political-equations-change/story-PmvnXLtkX97ST57NJX8a2H.html.
India Today (2017, November 11). 'About 100 People from Kerala Joined ISIS Over the Years: Police'. Retrieved from September 5, 2018, from www.indiatoday.in/india/story/about-100-keralites-suspected-to-have-joined-isis-police-1084495
The Indian Express (2006, September 27). 'Marad Report Slams Muslim League'. Retrieved from http://archive.indianexpress.com/news/marad-report-slams-muslim-league/13497/
Jacob, Jeemon (2017, September 2). 'The Jehadis of the South: Why Kerala Became Fertile Ground for New ISIS Recruits', *India Today*. Retrieved September 5, 2018, from www.indiatoday.in/magazine/nation/story/20170911-omar-al-hindi-isis-module-kerala-jihad-simi-operation-pigeon-1034806.
Josukutty, C.A. (2016, June 4). 'Nyuna Paksha Vottukal Ozhukiyethi' (Malayalam), *Kerala Kaumudi*, p. 8.
Kumar, G. Gopa (1980). *Regional Political Parties and State Politics*, New Delhi: Deep & Deep Publications.
Kumar, G. Gopa (1986). *Political Parties and State Politics*, New Delhi: Deep & Deep Publications.
Kumar, G. Gopa (2014). 'Changing Dimensions of Coalition Politics in Kerala', in (ed.), E. Sreedharan, *Coalition Politics in India: Selected Issues at the Centre and States*, New Delhi: Academic Foundation.
Latha, Jishnu (2016, May18). 'BJP Won't Capture Kerala Yet but RSS Culture Is Sweeping the State', *The Wire*. Retrieved August 7, 2018, from https://thewire.in/communalism/bjp-wont-capture-kerala-yet-but-rss-culture-is-sweeping-the-state.
Lukose, Ritty (2016). 'Re(casting) the Secular: Religion and Education in Kerala, India, Social Analysis', *The International Journal of Social and Cultural Practice*, 50(3), pp. 38–60. Retrieved from http://utsynergyjournal.org/2018/04/20/navigating-caste-inequality-in-kerala-caste-as-present-hidden-and-denied/
Majumdar, Sayan (2016, June 6). 'What Do Kerala Elections Tell Us About State's Political Equations', *Swarajya*. Retrieved August 13, 2018, from http://swarajyamag.com/politics/what-does-the-recent-kerala-elections-tell-about-the-political-equations-in-the-state.
Malayala Manorama. (2018). 'Kalamorrukkan RSS Samunyaya Bitak' (Malayalam), p. 8.
Mannathukkaren, Nissim (2017). 'Communalism Sans Violence: A Keralan Exceptionalism?' Retrieved from www.tandfonline.com/doi/abs/10.1080/17448727.2017.1289680.
Manorama Election Guide. (2011). 'Malayla Manorama, Kottayam'.
Manorama Online. (2018, March 7). '60% Kerala Converts Chose Hinduism, Shows Study'. Retrieved from https://english.manoramaonline.com/news/kerala/2018/03/07/60-per-cent-kerala-converts-chose-hinduism-shows-study.html.
Menon, Girish (2016, May 20). 'Congress Debacle May Echo Nationally', *The Hindu*. Retrieved from www.thehindu.com/news/cities/Thiruvananthapuram/cong-debacle-may-echo-nationally/article8623415.ece.
Nair, Naveen (2018, April 21). 'Communal Heat in Kerala: Extremist Political Outfits Use Kathua Rape to Spread Radicalism, Fish in Troubled Waters', *First Post*. Retrieved August 6, 2018, from www.firstpost.com/politics/communal-heat-in-kerala-extremist-political-outfits-use-kathua-rape-to-spread-radicalism-fish-in-troubled-waters-4440073.html.
NCRB (2016). *Crime in India 2015: Compendium*, New Delhi: Ministry of Home Affairs, Government of India. Retrieved from http://ncrb.nic.in/StatPublications/CII/CII2015/FILES/Compendium-15.11.16.pdf.
The News Minute. (2018, March 3). '100 Percent Rise in Communal Incidents in Kerala in 2017; Home Ministry Report'. Retrieved July 6, 2018, from www.thenewsminute.

com/article/100-cent-rise-communal-incidents-kerala-2017-ministry-home-affairs-report-77329.
Office of the Registrar General and Census Commissioner, India. Retrieved from http://censusindia.gov.in/2018.
Panicker, K.N. (2011). 'Matalmakathayil Ninnu Vargiyathayileke', in (ed.), K.N. Panicker, *Oru Chunvanna Suryante Orma* (Malayalam), Trivandrum: Chinta Publications, pp. 19–22.
Pillai, Raman K. (1999). 'Coalition Politics: The Kerala Experience', in (ed.), M.A. Ommen, *Rethinking Development: Kerala's Development Experience*, Vol. 1, Institute of Social Science, New Delhi: Concept Publishing Company, p. 100.
Rajeev, P.K. (2018, March 16). 'RSS Added 8000 New Members in Kerala Last Year: State Chief', *Times of India*. Retrieved from http://timesofindia.indiatimes.com/articleshow/63322319.cms?utm_source=contentofinterest&utm_medium=text&utm_campaign=cppstshakhas.
Sadandan, Anoop (2016, May 27). 'The BJP's Electoral Triumph in Kerala Could Reshape Politics in the State and Beyond', *The Wire*. Retrieved September 4, 2018, from https://thewire.in/politics/the-bjps-electoral-triumph-in-kerala-could-reshape-politics-in-the-state-and-beyond.
Survey Research Centre. (2016). *State of Polity in Kerala: A Study*, Department of Political Science, University of Kerala.
Victor, M. Fic (1970). *Kerala Yenan of India*, Bombay: Nachiketa Publications.
Zacharia, K.C. (2016). *Working on Religious Denomination in Kerala* (Working Paper 468), Kerala Migration Surveys. Retrieved May 6, 2018, from http://cds.edu/wp-content/uploads/2016/05/WP468.pdf.

9
POLITICS OF HINDUTVA IN MAHARASHTRA

Actors, causes and political effects

Parimal Maya Sudhakar

Maharashtra, electorally, is the second-largest state in India with 48 Lok Sabha constituencies. In the elections for the 16th Lok Sabha held in April–May 2014, the Hindutvavadee[1] (proponents of Hindutva) alliance won 42 seats in the state. The Bharatiya Janata Party and Shiv Sena were major partners in this alliance along with a few minor political parties in the state. The rout of the Indian National Congress (INC) and the Nationalist Congress Party (NCP) alliance in Maharashtra, with victories in only two and four Lok Sabha constituencies, respectively, was a milestone event in the electoral history of the state. A few months after the 16th Lok Sabha election, Maharashtra underwent an Assembly election in October–November 2014. The Hindutvavadee alliance broke on the issue of seat sharing, and the BJP and Shiv Sena contested against each other on almost all the Assembly seats in the state. Similarly, the INC–NCP alliance did not take place for the 2014 Assembly election as both parties decided to test their own strength throughout Maharashtra. In this election, the BJP emerged as the largest party in the assembly with 122 seats, falling short of a majority in the house of 288. Its erstwhile ally Shiv Sena won 63 seats, while INC and NCP won 41 and 40 seats, respectively. Even when the BJP and Shiv Sena contested separately, each of them polled more votes than either the Congress or NCP. In the Assembly election of 2014 in the state, the vote share of the BJP on the seats contested was 31.15% while Shiv Sena was a distant second with a 19.80% vote share on the contested seats. The vote shares of Congress and NCP were 18.10% and 17.96%, respectively. Thus, the Lok Sabha and Assembly elections of 2014 shifted the political balance decisively towards Hindutvavadee parties in the state (Birmal 2014; Verniers 2015).

The year 2014 shifted political balance away from the INC-led alliance, which was the stable political force in the state since 1998. From the Lok Sabha election of 1998 till the Assembly election and local bodies elections of 2012–13 in the state, the INC–NCP alliance had managed to halt the forward march of the Shiv

Sena-BJP alliance. Prior to it, elections from 1989 onwards witnessed a consistent growth in the electoral strength of Shiv Sena and BJP in the state. The Lok Sabha election of 1989 and the Assembly election of 1990, for the first time in the state's history, brought to the fore the Hindutvavadee parties, with Shiv Sena leading the charge and BJP being the junior partner. Noteworthy is the fact that Hindutvavadee parties were a marginal, if not negligible, force in state politics since independence till the late 1980s.

Thus we can see four distinct phases of Hindutvavadee parties' influence in the politics of Maharashtra. In the first phase of 1947 to 1985, Hindutvavadee parties were on the margins of electoral politics. The second phase of 1989 to 1996 saw a remarkable ascendency of Shiv Sena-BJP in state politics. The third phase from 1998 till 2009 witnessed a tough contest between two alliances in the state (i.e. Shiv Sena-BJP versus INC-NCP with an electoral advantage to the latter). The fourth phase began in 2014, where BJP-Shiv Sena emerged as the number one and number two parties in Maharashtra, relegating INC and NCP to distant 3rd and 4th positions respectively, as shown in Table 9.1. In this context, this chapter attempts to assess the factors and situations that led to emergence of Hindutvavadee parties as dominant force in the politics of Maharashtra.

Historical context

The state of Maharashtra came into existence on 1 May 1960. Prior to it, particularly during British rule, today's Maharashtra was spread into three different entities: the Bombay province, Central Provinces and Berar and the Nizam rule. The Bombay province was one of the leading regions during the British rule in terms of the establishment of colonial institutions including the spread of education. At the same time, the Bombay province was also in the lead in articulating discontent against British rule in India. While leading figures of late 19th century such as Dadabhai Nauroji, Justice Mahadev Ranade and Gopal Krishna Gokhale brought to the fore economic exploitation occurring during the colonial rule, Bal Gangadhar Tilak, popularly known as Lokmanya Tilak, began to mobilize people against colonial exploitation using religious and historical symbols. The third stream was generated by the leadership of Jyotirao Phule and Gopal Ganesh Agarkar, who were the crusaders for social reforms. This stream had welcomed establishment of British rule in the backdrop of Peshawa rule in the Bombay province. They had seen the British rule as an opportunity for oppressed and marginalized to get education and employment opportunities in the colonial institutions (Guha 2010).[2] At the same time, Jyotirao Phule had cautioned that the Brahmins in India had co-opted British rule, thus making it difficult for the oppressed to make further progress (Deshpande 2012).[3] It is important to understand intertwined positions of these three groups on political and social reforms. The first group, led by Gopal Krishna Gokhle, was advocating political reforms to represent the will of the Indian people in the British administration. This group was not averse to the social reforms but was advocating either an incremental approach or preferred political reforms to social reforms

TABLE 9.1 Party-wise Lok Sabha seats in Maharashtra (1952–54)

Party-wise Lok Sabha seats in Maharashtra: 1952–2014

Lok Sabha election year	Total seats	Congress	Jan Sangh/ BJP	Shiv Sena	Socialist Parties/ BLD/ Janata Dal	NCP	Communist Parties (CPI/ CPM/ Peasants and workers' party, forward block)	Others
1962	44	41	0	–	1		0	2*
1967	45	37	0	–	3		4	1*
1971	45	42	0	–	1		1	1**
1977	48	21		0	19@		8	1**
1980	48	39	0	0	8@@		0	1***
1984	48	43	0	0	2@@	2+	1	0
1989	48	36	6	2	3@@@		1	0
1991	48	38	5	4	0		1	0
1996	48	15	18	15	0		0	0
1998	48	33	4	6	0		1	4**
1999	48	10	15	13	1@@@	6	1	2**
2004	48	13	13	12	0	9		1**
2009	48	17	9	11	0	9		2##
2014	48	2	23	18	0	4		1$

Source: Statistical reports on general election to Lok Sabha as available on website of Election Commission of India (www.eci.gov.in).

*   Independents
** Republican Party of India
@   BLD (Bharatiya Lok Dal)
@@ Janata Party
*** Congress (U)
+   Congress (Socialist)
@@@ Janata Dal
1 Bahujan Vikas Aghadi and 1 Swabhimani Shetakari Paksha
$ Swabhimani Shetakari Paksha

in their approach and actions. The third group, led by Jyotirao Phule, was firmly rooted for continuation of British rule, as they feared the exit of British people would bring back the orthodox social rule of which Peshwai was the symbol. The second group, led by Tilak, was demanding maximum political reforms but was averse to social reforms. It was this differentiation that led to Tilak adopting aggressive religious and historic symbols in mobilizing people for his political demands. Tilak's propagation of public celebration of birth anniversaries of Lord Ganesha as *Ganeshotsav* and King Shivaji as *Shiv-Jayanti* was aimed at political mobilization of Hindus against the British rulers. Through this tactic, Tilak aimed to achieve two objectives: first, to relegate Muslims to margins in anti-colonial struggle; and second, to undermine social reformers' attempts to mobilize lower-caste and women

Hindus against the upper-caste Hindu hegemony in Indian society. This dynamics was replayed in its best form in the year 2018 during the conflicts that happened in Maharashtra in the first week of January on the Bhima-Koregaon issue.[4]

While Tilak used religious and historic symbols in mobilizing Hindus, his vision about the future of India or Indian society had been influenced by a mixture of colonial and liberal ideas of early 20th century. Like his contemporaries, Tilak could not envision an independent and sovereign India, but wanted a dominion status to India with the idea of home rule, which was a radical idea for his time. However, he realized that under a dominion status, not only Hindus would be invited to administer the country. Rather, Tilak's realization that without Hindus and Muslims jointly demanding a dominion status, the colonial power would not give any concessions that led to his leading role in the Lucknow Pact of 1916 between Congress and the Muslim League (Chandra et al. 2016). Nonetheless, Tilak's legacy of considering Hindus and Muslims as separate from each other even while fighting against the British rule and his use of religious and historic symbols to mobilize people had a lasting impact on political memories of people in the state.

After Tilak's demise, the decade of 1920s witnessed a re-emergence of three contesting streams of ideas in what today constitutes the state of Maharashtra. The first stream was led by Congress under the leadership of M.K. Gandhi, which was a radically refined version of a group led by Dadabhai Nauroji and G.K. Gokhale in the late 19th and early 20th centuries. Congress under Gandhi's influence rapidly transformed itself into a mass organization through mass movements and began to propagate an idea of India with equal status and representation to all communities and people through democratic means. A great deal of effort was made to forge unity between Hindus and Muslims as well as to win over lower caste and the then untouchable people in Hindu social hierarchy. The second stream was represented by two distinctly similar yet different groups: Hindu Maha Sabha under the leadership of V.D. Savarkar and Rashtriya Swayamsevak Sangh (RSS) established by K.B. Hedgewar at Nagpur, which was the capital of the then Central Provinces and Berar. In the year 1923, V.D. Savarkar proposed his thesis of Hindutva under the 'two nations' theory. Accordingly, his Hindu Maha Sabha was to ensure administrative control of Hindus over India relegating Muslims and Christians to 'second-class citizens'. Savarkar openly denounced the caste system and untouchability amongst Hindus, yet Hindu Maha Sabha could not attract more than a section of Hindu Brahmins. The RSS, on the other hand, was established with the stated objective of organizing Hindus and strengthening their physical and cultural capacities. Savarkar's Hindu Maha Sabha actively participated in the electoral process under British rule, but the RSS did not participate in the elections in British India. While Savarkar and RSS ideologues K.B. Hedgewar and M.S. Golwalkar exhorted glorification of ancient India, they differed on the caste system, role of women in society and promotion of modern scientific outlook. Savarkar enthusiastically promoted modernity and scientific outlook through his writings and literature. He was vocal against inequality in Hindu society. The RSS defended caste-based and gender inequality in Hindu society while denouncing modernity and scientific outlook as foreign or Western in origin. Savarkar also was a proud enthusiast about the Marathi language, literature and culture, which was in contrast with the then RSS ideologues. Savarkar's following in Maharashtra was based on his passionate love for the Marathi language, his Muslim hatred or both. On the other hand, workers with RSS were more passionate about preserving and strengthening conservative Hindu society. While Savarkar's Hindu Maha Sabha saw an opportunity for united Hindus to establish their rule through the electoral process, the RSS had disgusted democratic process and institutions. In a nutshell, Savarkar propagated Hindutva as a political tool while RSS wanted to establish Hindu Rashtra with social and cultural mobilization of Hindus through its organization. Dr. B.R. Ambedkar led the third stream. He believed in organizing the untouchables against caste oppression and working with the British administration to ensure legal avenues for Scheduled Castes and Scheduled Tribes to get guaranteed representation in the administration. He argued, like Phule, that oppressed sections within society had to fight against their social oppressors. If the social oppressors also become political rulers, the lower caste and untouchables along with women in Hindu society would not be able to experience freedom. This was the main thesis of Phule and Ambedkar during the British period (Guha 2010).

The first stream, led by Gandhi, became a dominant narrative in Maharashtra. The Congress under Gandhi actively engaged with the politics of Savarkar and RSS on the one hand and with Dr. Ambedkar on the other hand. This engagement along with its anti-colonial mass movements helped in keeping the Hindu Maha Sabha and RSS at bay while co-opting Ambedkar's agenda against untouchability and for political representation for Scheduled Castes and Scheduled Tribes. The Congress propagated soft, reformist, inclusive narration of Hindu religion, which is being called as *Hinduism*, and which can coexist with other faiths and religions in modern India. Gandhi called it *Ram Rajya*. Savarkar envisioned all Hindus – male and female – as modern political entities standing up against cruelty and rigidity of other religions, mainly Islam. He called it Hindutva. The RSS preached and practiced conservation of orthodox Hindu religious practices. It also believed that India is for Hindus and hence should be ruled by the prescriptions of Hindu texts for materialization of Hindu Rashtra. Similarity in the positions of Savarkar and RSS was that both of them conceptualized their narration of a country for Hindus from the Western discourse of 'nation'. Dr. Ambedkar provided a detailed yet sharp critique of Hindu religious texts and practices and proclaimed that without denouncing those texts and practices, India cannot be a modern and egalitarian country.[5]

Post-independence developments

Independence accompanied with the partition of British India into India and Pakistan provided an opportunity to Hindu Maha Sabha and RSS to take advantage of communally divided and charged society. Division of the sub-continent into India and Pakistan along with Nizam of Hyderabad's refusal to merge with the Indian Union was a fertile ground to mobilize Hindu sentiments. Against this backdrop, both the organizations did their best to rake up religious sentiments amongst Hindus. However, the assassination of Gandhi on 30 January 1948 at the hands of an alleged aide of Savarkar who used to attend RSS shakha in the past had turned the public sentiments against Hindu Maha Sabha and RSS. Both organizations could not recover from it for long. In fact, the Hindu Maha Sabha's electoral influence kept diminishing even though Savarkar acquired an iconic status with a section of Hindus in Maharashtra. Meantime, the RSS decided to float a political wing named Bharatiya Jana Sangh (BJS) to contest elections (Graham 1990). However, BJS remained a marginal political force in the state for the following reasons.

First, non-participation in popular movements against colonial rule kept the RSS and Hindu Maha Sabha away from the masses. People were more connected with Congress and socialist leaders fighting against British rule. On the top of it, the alleged involvement of RSS and Hindu Maha Sabha in Gandhi's killing had severed their public relations for many years.

Second, other organizations, parties and leaders were more eloquent in talking about issues that were close to people's sentiments. For example, on integration of the state of Nizam (Hyderabad) in India, on the creation of Marathi linguistic state and liberation of Goa, the socialists, communists and rank and file of Congress were actively participating in the movements. Even though the BJS and Hindu Maha Sabha were part of joint struggles on these issues, they could not establish their separate identities based on religious sentiments. It happened because Congress, socialist parties and the Communist Party of India led the joint struggles on these issues. These leaders succeeded in keeping the nature of the struggles secular to a great extent in its form and content.

Third, in the 1950s, B.R. Ambedkar campaigned and convinced thousands of Scheduled Caste people to denounce the Hindu religion and embrace Buddhism. It became difficult for Hindu Maha Sabha and the RSS to cope with this situation. Even though Savarkar himself welcomed Ambedkar and his followers' conversion to Buddhism and the RSS called Buddhism a branch of the Hindu religion, these positions could not enthuse their own rank and file.

Fourth, the domination of Gandhian ideas of society, politics and economy till the late 1970s was a major hindrance in expansion of religion-based organizations and political parties in the state. Several Gandhian organizations and institutions as well as leaders such as Vinoba Bhave had greater influence over public discourse in the state, including on the minds of the youngsters. Gandhi's constructive programme, chalked out in the 1930s, and organizations established for its implementation had more active followers in the state in the post-independent years than the cadre of RSS or Hindu Maha Sabha. These organizations not only attracted idealist youth of the time for offering voluntary services but also propagated Gandhian teachings of peace, harmony, tolerance and non-violence amongst them. While some aspects of Gandhian ideology as preached by the Gandhian organizations were in tandem with the social conservative ideas of RSS, its approach was not directed against other religions, nor were their methods vicious and venomous.[6]

Fifth, the Marxist movement was on the rise in Maharashtra, in consonance with the global trend, through which the public discourse was focused on issues of class rather than religion. Concerted efforts by Marxist organizations to organize people at the workplaces based on economic demands had contributed in relegating the issues of religion and religious identities to the margin. The freedom movement and philosophy of Marxism had also influenced the women's movement in the state. Most importantly, like the Dalit emancipatory movement, the women's movement also came out with a sharp critic of inequality enshrined in religious texts and practices. Thus, religion-based political discourse, which could have dominated public sphere in the aftermath of partition, had failed to cut much ice with the general populace in the state of Maharashtra.[7]

The only instance of both, Hindu Maha Sabha and BJS, cutting some ice with a section of populace in the state was during the debate on the Hindu Code Bill. Both the organizations openly denounced it. The opposition to the Hindu Code Bill was on two counts: first, terming it against Hindu religious practices; and second, for the Hindu-specific nature of the Bill. During this period, the BJS in particular was able to attract attention of orthodox and patriarchal men from Hindu society towards its agenda. Yet it was overshadowed by three factors: first, the skilful negotiations by Jawaharlal Nehru on the Hindu Code Bill within and outside Parliament; second, the social conservative leadership within Congress hogged more limelight in the public discourse than BJS leaders; third, the radical positions on this issue by Dr. B.R. Ambedkar as well as the women's movement in India overpowered BJS opposition to the Hindu Code Bill. Nonetheless, BJS was more able to articulate its position in terms of appeasement of minorities by the Congress, which found resonance to some extent beyond its core voters. More important was its ability to develop ambiguity in its position and continuous propagation of the ambiguity amongst the general public in the future. On one hand, the BJS articulated its own position by calling the bill provisions as going against Hindu traditions and religious sanctions. It had catered to the conservative and orthodox sections of Hindu society. On the other hand, it demanded inclusion of minorities – particularly Muslim – under the jurisdiction of the bill. It had catered to the not so much conservative sections within Hindu society, in particular the newly growing middle class in urban and semi-urban areas. Both positions had an obvious contradiction. How could provisions against Hindu traditions and religious sanctions be nullified if minorities were brought under the domain of the bill? Over the years, BJS folded its position on provisions of the Hindu Code Bill and its implications on Hindu society in ambiguity. It articulated its opposition to the bill for exclusion of minorities. It was a regressive stance painted in universalism and uniformity. This articulate ambiguity has become the hallmark of BJS and then BJP's politics on crucial issues in the future. Equally noteworthy is the fact that RSS began to combine its own social conservative positions with Savarkar's positions on social reforms through the BJS politics. It was an attempt to preserve the conservative base of the RSS while signalling to women and lower-caste people that the BJS was not against their interests. Ironically, Savarkar's followers within and outside Hindu Maha Sabha never championed his positions on social reforms, resulting in failures in building organization across the state as well as failures in successive elections. Yet, Savarkar remained their hero for his rhetoric against the Muslims and his contribution to refinement of Marathi language. It had profound implications for the politics in Maharashtra after Savarkar's death in 1966.

Rise of Shiv Sena

Shiv Sena came into existence in 1966. It was against the backdrop of intense linguistic state movement and inclusion of Mumbai in Maharashtra that Shiv Sena was established by Bal Thackeray Eckert (2002b). He had too little a role in the movement for formation of Maharashtra state to be remembered by the public. In fact, parochialism and jingoism were remarkably absent from the state formation movement. Naturally, Shiv Sena was able to attract only a small number of unemployed youth in the cities of Mumbai and Thane in its campaign against South Indians working in Maharashtra. It was rather a strange selection of the 'other' and 'outsider' by Shiv Sena. The South Indian migrants were mostly self-employed, particularly the set of people targeted by Shiv Sena. There had been no evidence that only the South Indian migrants were encroaching on jobs in formal or semi-formal sectors. In fact, the narrative of 'we' against 'they' during the state formation movement was directed against the Gujarati business and industrialist lobby in Mumbai. However, they were not at the receiving end of Shiv Sena's ire. There is plenty of literature available now which focuses on how Shiv Sena was prompted to break working-class unions in Mumbai and to raise the proxy unions. This literature strongly suggests that Shiv Sena acted at the behest of ruling classes and under the protection provided by the state government. In the process, the business–industrialist lobby of Gujarati-speaking people was benefited, whose dominance was feared during the Sanyukt Maharashtra Movement that became a basis for the demand of Mumbai's inclusion in Maharashtra. Shiv Sena and this industrialist lobby were never against each other (Dhawale 2000). Apart from it, there are other significant issues that require attention while discussing Shiv Sena and its role in religious politics in Maharashtra.

First, Bal Thackeray had taken over from Savarkar the role of promoting Marathi literature and culture. However, he did it without inciting religious feelings, and even without any grand design to change the nature and character of Indian state and its constitution. As a result, he was more appealing to the Marathi middle class (i.e. the employed population of Mumbai in formal and semi-formal sectors). The same class had great respect for Savarkar without politically supporting his Hindu Maha Sabha (Heuze 1995).

Second, Bal Thackeray's father, Prabodhankar Thackeray, was a radical social reformer. He had severely criticized superstitions prevalent in Hindu society and held the Brahminical mindset responsible for it. Bal Thackeray neither carried forward nor denounced his father's legacy. However, the legacy helped him in appealing to a larger section of society. While Savarkar and RSS leadership was always viewed as Brahminical, Bal Thackeray was not. His leadership had an appeal for a section of urban Hindu youth that was uncomfortable with any type of Brahminical leadership. This, however, did not mean either Shiv Sena or its young followers were craving for social change.

Third, Shiv Sena was not a force in electoral arena even with all of its above characteristics. Initially, it did not contest any election. Even when it began to contest elections, its arena was limited to Mumbai and Thane. These attempts were without success and it could never win assembly seats in double digits till 1990. Thus, Shiv Sena was electorally irrelevant till mid-1980s. However, its semi-fascist worldview took shape during this period (Eckert 2002a).

As stated earlier, Shiv Sena did not have any known designs to constitute a particular type of government or a system. What became evident with the passage of time was its disdain for the rule of law, a liking for authoritarianism and a tendency to take the law into its own hands. First, it was the violent attacks against South Indians as well as against the trade unionists from communist movement in Mumbai. Second, it was a support to emergency and subsequent support to Congress during 1977 general election. Third, it was leading of mobs in Marathwada region to attack Dalit settlements to oppose the demand for change in nomenclature of Marathawada University after Dr. B.R. Ambedkar (Dhawale 2000). These instances made it clear that development of ideological outlook of Shiv Sena was neither progressive nor democratic in nature. Yet, minority bashing, charges against Congress of appeasement of Muslims and glorification of the Hindu religion was not the part of Shiv Sena's agenda till the early 1980s. This is not to suggest that Shiv Sena's character was secular. In fact, some of the literature suggest that Shiv Sena workers actively participated in local conflicts and riots between Hindu and Muslim communities in parts of Mumbai and its suburbs (Hansen 1996). However, their participation was more as an active members of Hindu community rather than as Shiv Sena workers. Neither were there any concerted attempts to capitalize on these riots to expand organizational base of Shiv Sena. It all mysteriously changed in the 1980s.

Mainstreaming of the fringe: BJS to BJP

All this while, Bharatiya Jana Sangh was struggling to increase its organizational base and legislative presence in the state of Maharashtra. The BJS, lacking its own organizational network, created healthy bonds with non-Congress parties in the state in the decade of 1960s. In the next decade, many of the BJS members shot to fame in their localized areas as they were arrested during the Emergency. BJS members' arrest and subsequent release from jail resulted in legitimizing its role in India's democratic process. The process had also created bonhomie amongst BJS members on the one hand and activists of other non-Congress parties on the other hand. Amongst the arrested people during the emergency in Maharashtra, the BJS and RSS members formed the majority group within the jails followed by the socialists, Gandhians and communists, respectively. This situation resulted in the BJS and the RSS members enforcing a long-term political relationship with the non-Congress leadership in the state. Shiv Sena was not part of this process as it was in support of the Emergency.

Post-Emergency, the BJS became part of the Janata Party and thus got into the corridors of power at the Centre. In Maharashtra too, the Janata Party became part of the coalition government formed by rebel Congress leader Sharad Pawar in 1978. This has further helped the BJS members to access government machinery and spread its organizational network. The most important development of this period was realization by the RSS and the BJS of a vacant socio-political space in the state, which no other political party in the state realized. The RSS astutely decided to stitch caste equations in the state for reaping political benefits. The Hindu religion identity has been used as a glue to bring together different castes vying for political space in the state. It simultaneously propagated the caste and religious identity of different social communities under the umbrella of Hindu religion. The strategy worked perfectly to dilute the anti-caste movements in the state, while strengthening the monolithic Hindu religious identity across different caste groups. However, the cobbling of the social equation of different caste groups was full of contradictions, and keeping them together merely with the Hindu religious identity tag was difficult. It was an alliance of caste groups aspiring for greater political representation and social identity, which itself would have created conflict of interest amongst the constituents. Conscious of this contradiction, the RSS created a bogey of Muslim dominance in Indian socio-political life. It was a strategy of dual use of religion in politics – glorification of Hindu religion and vilification of Islam (Jaffrelot 1996). Meantime, with the breakup of the Janata Party, the BJS faction formed a Bharatiya Janata Party (BJP) at a rally in Mumbai.

Reincarnation of Shiv Sena

Shiv Sena was not able to create political impact and gain electoral dividend on the basis of its *Marathi Manus* agenda (i.e. upholding the interest of the Marathi population, particularly in metropolitan regions). The demography of Mumbai and its suburbs also changed rapidly and percentage of Marathi population diluted in the region. While the tirade against non-Maharashtrians was still able to rally around significant sentiment, its electoral limitations became evident (Gupta 1981). Instead of Maharashtrians against 'outsiders', religion as a polarizing issue looked lucrative from an electoral point of view. Shiv Sena used a couple of riots in Mumbai region, particularly the riot of Bhiwandi, for its reincarnation as an organization of Hindus (Hansen 1996).

From 1986 onwards, Shiv Sena began to address its supremo Bal Thackeray as *Hindu Hridaysamrat* (Heartthrob of Hindus). This title remained with him even after his death. It was Bal Thackeray who made the term Hindutva popular and acceptable to wider sections of people in the state than anyone else. *Garv Se Kaho Ham Hindu Hai* ('Say with Pride that We Are Hindu') became a tag line of Shiv Sena, which appeared on autos, taxis, private vehicles, shops and even the entrances of homes of all those pledging their loyalty to Shiv Sena. It was not only the rebirth of Shiv Sena but a reincarnation of Hindu Mahasabha's Hindutva politics of pre-independence era. Bal Thackeray quite often publicly ridiculed the Gandhian ways of non-violence and glorified Hitler and Nathhuram Godse (Eckert 2002a). This has delighted members, followers and admirers of the defunct Hindu Mahasabha. As a result, everyone sympathetic to V.D. Savarkar began to follow Bal Thackeray and Shiv Sena flourished in the space ploughed by Hindu Mahasabha in the past.

Minority bashing mixed with Marathi chauvinism was a potent explosive to incite thousands of unemployed youth to join Shiv Sena's rank in the decade of 1980s. This also suggests that the political financier lobby in Maharashtra, in particular of Mumbai, helped Shiv Sena in resurrecting itself in the state politics in 1980s. Hindutva was 'inclusive', hence convenient, from the point of view of this financier lobby than the 'parochial' *Marathi Manus* agenda (Lele 1995). In its new avatar, Shiv Sena supremo Bal Thackeray began to attract much larger audience including the unemployed youth beyond the city of Mumbai. It was ably supported by wealthy industrialists in Mumbai, realizing its potential to distract people in general and youth in particular from taking up class issues of employment and inflation. In the early years of 1980s, Mumbai was rocked by strike of thousands of mill workers, which was led by trade unionist Datta Sawant. Once again, the industrialists in Mumbai deployed the Shiv Sena to disrupt the strike through its hooliganism. This, accompanied by Datta Sawant's own adventurist positions, resulted in collapse of the mass movement by workers (Dhawale 2000). Failure of the strike in meeting its objectives broke the backbone of trade unions in Mumbai and created a huge political vacuum. Shiv Sena quickly filled the space with its Hindutva agenda.

Issues, tactics and strategy of Hindutva politics

Even though Hindutva politics and its agenda was always there in public discourse in Maharashtra since the time of independence, response to it by the common people was of neglect at best. From the time of independence till the early 1980s, the Hindutva agenda was concentrated around three issues: the Uniform Civil Code, the abrogation of Article 370 of the Indian Constitution and a ban on cow slaughter. People's response to Hindutva agenda suddenly changed in the 1980s. The three issues that changed the political landscape in favour of Hindutva politics were the Shah Bano case, demand for construction of Ram Mandir at a disputed site in Ayodhya and political disturbances in the state of Jammu and Kashmir with sudden spurt of terrorist violence in the Kashmir Valley. The Shah Bano case fitted into the discourse of creating a Uniform Civil Code, while the terrorism in Kashmir fuelled the demand of nullifying article 370 of the constitution. The Ram Mandir issue supplanted the cow slaughter ban. Each of these issues was coloured in Hindu versus Muslim dichotomy. The underlying emphasis was on the then ruling Congress party's alleged appeasement of Muslim sentiments to harvest a minority vote bank. The tactic of creating an analogy of Congress' appeasement of Muslims appealed to a large section of the urban population, even though they hadn't immediately turned into members or voters of either Shiv Sena or BJP. The issue of the Congress government overruling the Supreme Court decision in Shah Bano case came against the backdrop of the Congress-led state government allowing all the mosques in Maharashtra to use loudspeakers for daily *namaz*. Another issue of government subsidy to the Hajj (pilgrimage) was also consistently raked up by Shiv Sena and BJP (Jaffrelot 2007). These issues galvanized the then moribund Hindutva sympathizers in the state. Apart from these issues, three factors proved helpful in making the Hindutva politics attractive to different sections of society.

First, the Congress-led state government did not adequately address demands of the massive farmers' movement led by Sharad Joshi. These were early days of upcoming agricultural crisis in the state. The social democratic group led the farmers' movement, while its leader Sharad Joshi was a neo-liberal. The movement captured the vast opposition space in the rural areas of the state; however, its leadership was unwilling to create a political alternative to the Congress Party. Its inability to create a political front for almost a decade and a half provided opportunity to Shiv Sena and BJP to capitalize on farmers' disenchantment against the Congress government. For the first time, voters in rural areas (i.e. farmers) considered the option to vote out the then ruling Congress party from power. While the objective conditions, to a large extent, were created by the farmers' movement, political benefits were reaped by Shiv Sena and BJP. In all the mass agitations led by Sharad Joshi, Shiv Sena and BJP workers actively participated. They were successful in linking themselves to the rural agricultural network, which was till then the monopoly of the Congress Party.

Second, the decision of V.P. Singh government to implement 27% reservation for Other Backward Classes (OBCs) in government jobs created social fragmentation in Maharashtra. It resulted in the consolidation of Brahmin, Jain and Vaishya (Bania) communities behind Shiv Sena and BJP. While BJP's central leadership did not openly oppose the decision of V.P. Singh government, a large section of its members and workers from upper-caste communities played active role on the ground in polarizing the social opinion in the state. On the other hand, Shiv Sena supremo Bal Thackeray openly opposed caste-based reservations. The tactic of having divergent positions at official level but opposing the OBC reservation on the ground helped Shiv Sena and BJP in different ways, and the net result was increased electoral base for the combine. Many of the upper-caste voters in Maharashtra's urban and semi-urban areas are wealthy non-Marathi communities such as Banias from Uttar Pradesh, Marwadis from Rajasthan and Jains from Gujarat. All of them forgot Shiv Sena's rhetoric against 'outsiders' and started supporting alliance of Shiv Sena and BJP in an unprecedented way. Congress had a significant support amongst the state's Brahmin voters, who are numerically less but socially influential and have been influential opinion makers in the society. Almost all of them switched to support the Shiv Sena-BJP alliance in the state. In its anti-reservation rhetoric, Shiv Sena openly stated that 'Being a Hindu is not a crime; being a *savarna* is not a sin; being a dalit is not a merit' (Palshikar 1999: 11).

BJP's official support to OBC reservation also helped the party continue to win over the backward caste communities who were disenchanted with Congress leadership, organization and policies. It was a glaring failure of Congress and other pro-Mandal parties in the state to bring to focus the contradiction in BJP's official position and its campaigns amongst upper-caste Hindus on OBC reservation. Many amongst the middle-class voters in Maharashtra, who had not shifted their allegiance even after vitriolic campaign on the Shah Bano case, began to support Shiv Sena and BJP due to the OBC reservation. The Congress in the state dithered on capitalizing over its support to OBC reservation because its leadership from top to bottom level was dominated by the Maratha community, which is the largest non-Dalit, non-tribal, non-OBC group in the state. The Marathas, the non-Brahmin upper-caste community, donned the hat of progressivism for a long time and it became difficult for this group to take a position against OBC reservation. However, Congress Party championing the cause of OBCs would have been resented by the Marathas. Thus, Congress tried to balance its position on OBC reservation by supporting it but not championing it. This situation turned favourable for the Shiv Sena-BJP alliance. The upper-caste consolidation behind the alliance was followed by a large number of OBC and ST groups supporting the Hindutva alliance. These groups had developed antipathy towards the Congress Party because of two factors: first, dominance of Marathas in the overall structure of the Congress Party; and second, only few sub-castes from the OBCs and only few tribal groups from the STs were beneficiaries in terms of political representation and taking advantage of reservation system. The others amongst OBCs and STs felt excluded and jumped into the emerging political power in the state (the Shiv Sena-BJP alliance). Over the years, affiliate organizations of RSS have brought various OBCs and non-neo Buddhist castes into the fold of Brahminical traditions, while creating Hindu identity for various tribal groups. Glorification of certain deities such as Ganesha and Rama, as well as standardization of certain festivals such as *Diwali* and *Dussera*, were tactfully utilized to create Hindutva amongst these groups (Jaffrelot 2007).

Third, Maharashtra was on the path of urbanization with relatively better educational and health facilities that became available in major cities and even at some of the district headquarters. The network of roads and availability of transport facilities were also the reasons behind the impetus to migration to urban areas. The most fundamental reason for growing urbanization was the limitation to agriculture-based development in the state. Urbanization in the state has been much higher in proportion to the industrialization process. The looming agricultural crisis and the rising level of education accompanied with unemployment made the urbanization a process of contestation to utilize the available opportunities for oneself and one's community members. As there were fewer opportunities, each of the opportunities availed by other communities was looked down upon by the rest in the society. The Hindutva groups were quick to react to the situation in each town and each city by creating a notion of 'us' amongst Hindus against 'them' as Muslims. 'They' were the ones who were portrayed as sucking up all the opportunities, particularly in the informal sector, in the growing urban areas. This was the space keenly contested by OBC youth, who were migrants from rural areas, and some of the Dalit youth. These youth in large numbers began to look at the Muslims as their rivals. The

Hindutva politics made these youth to believe that Muslims are not only their rivals in urban spaces but also the country's enemy (Hansen 1996).

These factors created a fertile ground for penetration of Hindutva ideology and electoral growth of Shiv Sena-BJP in Maharashtra since the mid-1980s. The period since 1985 onwards has seen a rise in small and big communal riots throughout the state. Often, the immediate causes for the riots were India-Pakistan cricket matches and *Ganeshotsav* or *Shivjayanti* or *Ramnavami* processions. The Muslims were attacked for their alleged celebration of Pakistan's victory in a cricket match. The processions of Hindu festivities would be deliberately organized to pass through the Muslim-populated areas, wherein the procession would linger upon raising communally provocative slogans. In the decade of 1990, Shiv Sena supremo Bal Thackeray ordered organization of *Maha-aratis* in Mumbai to counter the Friday *namaz* by Muslims. As a result, the city experienced huge shows of *Maha-aratis* being organized on main roads by Shiv Sena's local branches. It was a fit case of direct use of religious practices for political mobilization. The state administration, in particular the police, would always be in a fix over organization of such programmes by Shiv Sena. If it denied permission, the issue would take a violent turn, but if it gave permission, the programme would preach hatred and violence in the name of protecting Hindus and Hindu interests (Lokshahi 1992). In majority of the cases, the administration succumbed and allowed the *maha-aratis* on public roads and granted permission for procession of Hindu festivities to pass through Muslim-populated areas. All of this ultimately culminated in one of the most brutal riots of 1992–93 in Mumbai and in many other parts of the state, in which the police administration was complicit in an unprecedented way (Dalwai 2017).

The communal polarization accompanied by unproven charges of the then ruling party's leadership protecting Muslim smugglers and criminals created widespread public opinion against the Congress Party. In the Assembly election of 1995, the Congress suffered its first-ever defeat in the state and pre-poll alliance of Shiv Sena-BJP emerged as a single largest group in the assembly. The alliance, or *Yuti* as popularly known, was still short of a majority. Along with the Hindutva offensive, the Congress Party's prospects in the election were marred by internal factionalism resulting into subterfuge of its own candidates as well as rebel Congress leaders emerging victorious as an independent MLA. In 1995 Assembly election as many as 40 rebel Congressmen became independent MLAs and most of them extended outside support to Shiv Sena-BJP alliance. The end result of a decade-long communal campaign in the state was the formation of a saffron government with support from the independent MLAs. This has also proved the stretch and limits of communal polarization and campaigns of hatred in the state. Since then till the Assembly election of 2014, Shiv Sena remained confined to the heights it reached in 1995 and could not break new ground in the state. On the other hand, BJP has not only grown electorally but also been able to perpetuate the RSS agenda in the society (Palshikar 2018).

Ever since the shocking defeat of the Shiv Sena-BJP government in the Assembly election of 1999, the RSS and its affiliates concentrated more on spreading the ideology of Hindutva through public spaces such as public parks, temples and religious gatherings for celebration of Hindu festivals. Youth groups received encouragement to organize religious festivities on a mass scale to consolidate Hindu identity of the involved people. During this period (i.e. since 1999 onwards), the state has witnessed proliferation of Patanjali's branches, the Yoga organization of Baba Ramdev, which often worked in tandem with RSS local networks. Its disciples inundated the public parks by organizing Yoga classes in the morning and evening hours. The Yoga classes have been organized in many of the housing societies in urban centres of the state. Some of the private educational institutes offered a regular weekly platform to Patanjali to teach Yoga to their students. These Yoga classes do not remained confined to physical exercises but often preached about the Golden Era of ancient India when all the important discoveries and inventions took place. The preaching in such classes helped developing an inferiority complex amongst the middle class in general and the students, youth, and women in particular. The mass psychological complex is about losing out the status of being the 'superpower' in the world at some unknown time in the past and not doing enough in the recent past to regain that status. This would be accompanied with vilification of 'Muslim rulers' since the medieval period who were blamed for 'looting' India as well as causing social evil practices in Hindu society. In particular, the status of women including the *Parda* system and stratified caste system are considered to be due to the 'Muslim rule' over India, as Hindus were struggling to defend their lives and honour. Thus, the discourse has swiftly been shifted from Hindu religious scriptures sanctioning caste system and lower status of women in the family to that of such practices evolved during 'Muslim rule'. There would be no mention of British rule over India or the colonial loot of Indian resources that happened systematically for over 150 years in recent history. Subsequently, the foundation of modern India (i.e. India's freedom movement along with movement for social equality) would be misrepresented and often misinterpreted. Apart from Patanjali's branches, there is a battery of public speakers and writers who would keep on expressing the same opinions, as mentioned previously, through different platforms such as all types of media, public lectures as well as workshops for journalists, activists of non-governmental organizations and so forth. All of this has created the hegemony of idea about need for Hindutva to overcome the subjugation of centuries (Heath 2015). It was in such an atmosphere of overwhelming opinion in favour of Hindutva, particularly amongst the middle and lower middle income category families in the state, that the Shiv Sena-BJP swept the Lok Sabha election of 2014 under the leadership of Narendra Modi. The Shiv Sena-BJP alliance that also included few smaller parties won 42 Lok Sabha seats out of 48. In the subsequent Assembly election same year, BJP broke away from Shiv Sena and both the parties contested separately. In this election BJP emerged as the single largest party with 122 seats and Shiv Sena as the second largest party with 63 seats. The Lok Sabha and Assembly elections of 2014 had established the dominance of Hindutva parties in state's politics (Rasam 2014; Verniers 2015).

Conclusion

The political influence of Hindutva parties grew gradually in the state of Maharashtra. First of all, trajectory of Hindutva politics in Maharashtra is not much different from its national growth path. Rather, Maharashtra has a central place in the arrest and ascendency of Hindutva politics in India. Hindutva politics can be categorized in four segments in the state. The first segment is that of ideological development of contours of Hindutva that had taken place from early years of freedom movement till early 1970s. The second segment is that of organizational growth of Hindutvavadee parties such as BJP and Shiv Sena, which took place in the 1970s and 1980s. The third segment is that of political outreach of Hindutvavadee parties, which took place from the 1970s till the 1990s. The fourth segment is that of complete dominance, which happened in 2014.

It was Hindu Mahasabha that invented the politics of Hindutva, but could not sustain it. Shiv Sena took up the baton only in the mid-1980s, even though Shiv Sena was active in the state from the 1960s. The Shiv Sena could not become a political force with its *Marathi Manus* agenda, but it emerged as a powerful player with Hindutva agenda. Meantime, it was RSS that ploughed the ground for Hindutva in the state. It had adopted a twin approach: to go along with any political combination against the Congress Party and to keep on sanskritizing different Hindu caste groups to bring them closure to Hindutva agenda. It was a combination of the crude Hindutva of Shiv Sena and the subtle but assertive Hindutva of RSS that was not countered effectively by the 'secular' parties and organizations. Rather, there had hardly been attempts by opponents of Hindutva politics to dissect the strategies and tactics of Hindutva parties. As a result, the secular opposition could never come up with a long-term strategy to counter Hindutva politics.

It was decay of different ideological alternatives in the state that had helped Shiv Sena and BJP to capture the political space against the then dominant Congress Party. In the process, Shiv Sena and the BJP, particularly the latter, initially aligned with many non-Congress parties. However, at a later phase, the BJP was successful in painting all non-Hindutvavadee parties as pseudo-secular or appeasers of religious minorities. Its main thrust in its political strategy was to ensure continuous organizational outreach while tactically shifting or hiding its ideological positions. It was a glaring shortcoming of opponents of Hindutva to realize the political cost of organizational outreach undertaken by Shiv Sena and RSS, and a gross failure in exposing the 'clever by half' ideological positions and convenient shifts in those positions in front of the common people. Even today, opponents of Hindutva politics lack imagination, ideas, vision, strategy and tactics, except for forming electoral alliances. It is a guarantee of a continuation of a Hindutva spell in Maharashtra's politics, which has a potential to turn into the political epoch of 21st century.

Notes

1 The term 'Hindutva' was used by V.D. Savarkar for the first time in 1923. It broadly refers to sensitize people belonging to Hindu religion for a political consciousness of unity against the 'others' active in political field. 'Hindutvavadee' is a term usually referred to

person(s) or organization(s) working with the political consciousness of unity of Hindus as defined by V.D. Savarkar.
2 Ramachandra Guha discusses the scuttle differences amongst the reformists, freedom fighters and revolutionaries in his book *Makers of Modern India*.
3 G.P. Deshpande elaborated in his introduction to the translated writings of Jotirao Phule that the 19th-century reformer was not merely advocating social reforms but was contextualizing the British Raj and its social alliances in India.
4 In the year 1818, Peshawa's forces were defeated by the *Mahar* regiment of British Army on 1 January at the battle of Bhima-Koregaon near Pune, Maharashtra. Dalit groups have been celebrating this event each year as a day of victory of Dalit masses over the socially oppressive Peshawa regime. In the run-up to 1 January 2018, a few Hindutvavadee groups have taken position against celebration by Dalit groups that led to violent clashes in and around Bhima-Koregaon.
5 Several writings of Dr. B.R. Ambedkar explained the inherent inequality and exploitation in the caste system and reached to the conclusion that the caste system is the soul of the Hindu religion and all attempts to reform the caste system were exhaustive.
6 The Constructive Programme of M.K. Gandhi since 1930s, the *Bhoodan* movement by Vinoba Bhave in the 1950s and 1960s and the *Sampurna Kranti* movement by Jai Prakash Narayan witnessed participation of youth of Maharashtra in good numbers. RSS-affiliated youth also participated in such programmes but could not dominate them.
7 From organizing the working class in the city of Mumbai to organizing tribal in remote areas of the state to organizing employees in the state and quasi-state sectors, the Marxist organizations played an important role in creating a class narrative in the state against the religious or religion-based narrative.

References

Birmal, Nitin and Rajeshwari Deshpande (2014). 'Maharashtra: The End of a Congress System?' *Research Journal Social Sciences*, 22(2), pp. 152–61.
Chandra, Bipin et al. (2016). *India's Struggle for Independence*, New Delhi: Penguin Random House.
Dalwai, Sameena (2017). *Babri Masjid 25 Years On*, New Delhi: Kalpaz Publications.
Deshpande, G.P. (2012). *Selected Writings of Jotirao Phule*, New Delhi: Leftword Books.
Dhawale, Ashok (2000, April–June). 'The Shiv Sena: Semi-Fascism in Action', *The Marxist*, 16(2). Retrieved from www.cpim.org/marxist/200002_marxist_sena_dhawle.htm
Eckert, Julia (2002a). 'The Charisma of Autocracy: Bal Thackeray's Dictatorship in Shiv Sena', *Manushi* (130). Retrieved from www.indiatogether.org/manushi/issue130/shivsena.htm
Eckert, Julia (2002b). 'Shivshahi in the Mohalla: How Shiv Sena Entrenched Itself in Bombay', *Manushi* (129). Retrieved from www.indiatogether.org/manushi/issue129/shivshahi.htm
Graham, B. (1990). *Hindu Nationalism and Indian Politics: The Origin of Bharatiya Jana Sangh*, New York: Cambridge University Press.
Guha, Ramchandra (2010). *Makers of Modern India*, New Delhi: Viking.
Gupta, Dipankar (1981). *Nativism in a Metropolis: The Shiv Sena in Bombay*, New Delhi: Manohar.
Hansen, Thomas B. (1996). 'Recuperating Masculinity: Hindu Nationalism, Violence and the Exorcism of the Muslim "Other"', *Critique of Social Anthropology*, 16(2), pp. 137–72.
Heath, Oliver (2015). 'The BJP's Return to Power: Mobilisation, Conversion and Vote Swing in the 2014 Indian Elections', *Contemporary South Asia*, 23(2), pp. 123–35.
Heuze, Gerard (1995). 'Cultural Populism: The Appeal of the Shiv Sena', in (eds.), Sujata Patel and Alice Thorner, *Bombay: Metaphor of Modern India*, Bombay: Oxford University Press, pp. 213–47.

Jaffrelot, Christophe (1996). *The Hindu Nationalist Movement and Indian Politics, 1925 to the 1990s*, London: Hurst and Co.

Jaffrelot, Christophe (2007). *Hindu Nationalism A Reader*, New Delhi: Permanent Black.

Lele, Jayant (1995). 'Saffronisation of the Shiv Sena: The Political Economy of City, State and Nation', in (eds.), Sujata Patel and Alice Thorner, *Bombay: Metaphor for Modern India*, Bombay: Oxford University Press, pp. 185–212.

Lokshahi Hakk Sanghatana and Committee for the Protection of Democratic Rights. (1992). *The Myth and Reality of the Bombay Riots*, Fact Finding Report.

Palshikar, Suhas (1999). *Shiv Sena: An Assessment, Occasional Paper Series*, Pune: Department of Politics and Public Administration, University of Pune.

Palshikar, Suhas (2018, October 18). 'Farewell to Maratha Politics? Assembly Elections in Maharashtra', *Economic and Political Weekly*, 49(42), ISSN (Online) 2349–8846.

Rasam, Vasanti (2014). 'Changing Politics of Maharashtra – An Analysis of Maharashtra Assembly Elections 2014'. Retrieved from www.researchgate.net/publication/299514684_Changing_Politics_of_Maharashtra_-_an_Analysis_of_Maharashtra_Assembly_Elections_-_2014.

Siddiqi, Kalim (2016). 'A Critical Study of Hindu Nationalism in India', *Journal of Business and Economic Policy*, 3(2), pp. 9–28.

Verniers, Gilles (2015). 'The BJP and State Politics in India: A Crashing Wave? Analyzing the BJP Performance in Five State Elections', *Asia. Visions 80*. Centre for Asian Studies. Retrieved from www.ifri.org/en/publications/enotes/asie-visions/bjp-and-state-politics-india-crashing-wave.

10
RELIGION-POLITY INTERFACE IN JAMMU AND KASHMIR

An analysis

Muhammad Tajuddin

The founder of Jammu and Kashmir polity, Gulab Singh, started his career in Lahore state as a soldier in 1809. By dint of his prowess and loyalty, he and his two younger brothers ascended to become notables of the state. In addition to his distinguished role in several military expeditions, he had stabilized the rule of Lahore in the hill territory of the Shivalik Ranges across the river Ravi (i.e., his own homeland territory) by neutralizing rebellions from his own kinsmen. All the neighbouring principalities beyond Shivalik in the Peer Panjal Ranges had been annexed by him before 1822 (Panikkar 1992: 19–33). He was assigned *rajgi*: the authority to govern Jammu as part of Lahore state in 1822 by his master Maharaja Ranjit Singh after deposing the then Rajah of Jammu Jit Singh. Jammu Raj in 1822 included roughly the present Jammu Division of the state including its Pakistan Occupied Kashmir (PoK) areas but excluding Poonch jagir where his brother had been made Rajah. As Rajah of Jammu, his forces marched and added Ladakh and Baltistan in 1841 with the consent of Lahore and the company.

The present polity of Jammu and Kashmir was imagined in the Treaty of Amritsar signed between the British government (i.e. the East India Company) and Rajah Gulab Singh of Jammu on 16 March 1846. The rationale of this treaty was based on Articles 4 and 12 of the Treaty of Lahore signed between the company and Lahore state on 9 March 1846. The British government in the Amritsar Treaty added Kashmir, Gilgit, Hunza and Nagar to Jammu Raj and recognized Gulab Singh as independent Maharaja of his territories. Since the treaty did not define the name of the new state, from its birth it has been identified by at least three names: Kashmir, Jammu and Kashmir, and Jammu. The imagined polity of Jammu and Kashmir became a reality after six months on 9 November 1846 when Gulab Singh entered Srinagar after neutralizing the rebellion of the governor of Lahore state with the assistance of the company and Lahore state on 23 October (Sufi 2015: 792).

The polity not only suffers from confusion in its name but also in the name of the pre-accession ruling dynasty.[1] As per the treaty, the British government recognized Gulab Singh the designated Maharaja and after him 'the heirs male of his body' as the hereditary rulers of the state. The ruling family is called the Dogra dynasty, and their ethnic community is also identified as Dogra. Undoubtedly Gulab Singh and his progeny were the most notable members of the Dogra ethno-linguistic community of Shivalik Hills, but the whole Dogra community is not his descendants. The ruling lineage of Gulab Singh from the 14th century in recorded history is an established fact. The self-identity of the clan is Jamwal Rajput, most superior even among the aristocratic *Mian* Rajputs of the Dogra Rajput caste. The term 'Dogra dynasty' has been uncritically derived from the term 'Dogra Brothers' or 'Dogra Rajahs', particularly used for Gulab Singh and his two brothers in Lahore state (Charak 2017: 203–5).

In search of legitimacy through lineage according to the spirit of his age after the foundation of his kingdom, the Machiavellian prince Gulab Singh, the new Maharaja, commissioned Ganesh Das Badera, the author of the *Chirag-i-Panjab*, to write his family history. Badera connected the pedigree of Gulab Singh with the Puranic genealogy of Suryavanshi Rajputs in his work *Rajdarshani*, completed in 1847 (Charak 2017: 1–6). Contrary to the imperial historiographic tradition of the Asiatic Society, Major G. Carmichael Smyth's work *A History of the Reigning Family of Lahore, with Some Account of the Jummoo Rajahs, the Seik Soldiers and their Sirdars* published in the same year also stated the same genealogy in the legendary tradition of James Tod. Smyth 'discovered' a common lineage of Gulab Singh and the reigning families of Jodhpur and Jaipur. In 19th-century colonial historiography, establishing Rajput lineage was the most 'natural' source of legitimacy for the Hindu rulers of the independent principalities that emerged in later Mughal era in Rajputana and Punjab Hills (Rai 2004: 68–73). Kripa Ram, the official biographer of Gulab Singh in *Gulabnama*, had written chapters on the 'angelic pedigree', 'medieval genealogy' and 'modern ancestors' of the Maharaja on the basis of *Rajdarshani* (Translation of the Persian biography of Gulab Singh by Diwan Kripa Ram; Charak and Billawaria 2013: 3–12). One's identity as Dogra Rajput in general, as Mian Rajput in particular and among them as Jamwal Rajput specifically was the most important credential to be inducted in civil and military government services. After opening of the civil services for well-educated Punjabis, Pratap Singh protected their privileged position through the Pratap Code introduced in 1894. It identified Dogra Rajput as 'brethren' of the ruler and entitled them with greater privileges in land, education, possession of firearms and exempted them from *begar* (forced unpaid labour), cattle tax and capital punishment.

Religion has been the universal common source of legitimacy in every pre-modern polity. It has been the substance of sovereignty, remained intertwined with politics and an important claimant of the state patronage. According to tradition, the ritual of *rajyabhisheka* of Gulab Singh as Jammu Rajah in 1822 established him as a temporal subordinate sovereign 'under the shelter of Sikh authority' with the dual role of 'mediator between God and his subjects' and 'the chief worshipper and sacrificer (*yajnaman*) on behalf of his subjects'. On the advice of H. M. Lawrence, the British signatory of the Amritsar Treaty 'to make no difference between... [his] subjects of different religions and sects', Gulab Singh replied that 'there would be no active interference in the religious beliefs of the Muslims, as a Hindu ruler he would have to give priority to the religion of the Hindus' (Rai 2004: 82, 93). He was conscious to have an image of a devout Hindu ruler through his personal religiosity and state observance. He had made an endowment for Hindu religious purposes in 1826 which was made a department after his elevation as Maharaja in 1846. Following the tradition of Lahore state, he made the Hindu religious *Vikrami* era as the official calendar of the state. Pratap Singh introduced the Common Era as a substitute secondary date in all official documents. The practice continued even in the post-accession regimes, probably up to the presidential rule in the state in 1990s when the national norm of dating primarily in Common Era and secondarily in the *Saka* era was introduced in the state.

His successor Ranbir Singh consciously transformed the polity into a Hindu polity. He introduced Ranbir Dand Bidhi on the pattern of the Indian Penal Code of 1861 (IPC) (Bamzai 2016: 781). It was renamed the Ranbir Penal Code (RPC) by his successor. It contains the same chapters and sections with minor additions or deletions in the definition of some crimes and/or degree of punishments of some crimes. The most notable added feature which gives RPC a Hindu character is the criminalization of 'slaughtering of cow or the like animals' (Section 298A), 'keeping in possession flesh of killed or slaughtered animals as mentioned above' (Section 298B), and even 'slaughtering of he or she buffalo' (Section 298C), 'sale of having possession of untanned hide, or meat or flesh of a Gond' (Section 298D) in its chapter XV common with IPC dealing with the 'Offences Relating to Religion'. Slaughtering of buffalo is not criminal anywhere in India other than Jammu and Kashmir (the only Muslim majority state) and Chattisgarh, with the highest percentage of tribal population excluding northeast states (*Indian Express*, 20 January 2019).[2]

Two other rules framed during his regime, *Dastur-al-Amal* and *Ain-i-Dharmarth*, strengthened the Hindu character of the polity. The *Dastur* defined the role of direct descendance, Hindu religion and family tradition in succession and governance in the polity. The *Ain* strengthened, systematized and made permanent arrangement for the administration of the *Dharmarth* Fund. Gulab Singh had created the fund in 1826 on the pattern of Ranjit Singh or the medieval Delhi sultans and Mughal emperors. It constituted a council for its independent regulation with 'a view solely to ensure the advancement of the sacred religion of the Hindus' and defined the duties of the council members as regular courtiers. The trust was assigned duty to maintain all existing temples and to construct new temples throughout the state. The priest of the mufassil temples were duty-bound to give monthly reports through the police to the Dharmarth office about the happenings in their localities. The sobriquet for Jammu as 'city of temples' is a legacy of Ranbir Singh, who aspired to build Jammu into a 'second Benares'. The *Ain* made it mandatory to seek permission of the state to build a temple which would be named after the monarch and to perform *prayog* ('the ritual of meditation and penance performed on behalf of others'). By associating loyalty to the monarch and public expression of Hindu religiosity, he territorialized the Hindu religious space (Rai 2004: 114–20). The successors of Ranbir Singh maintained and asserted whenever required each of the three elements of the dynasty identity: Hindu-Jamwal-Rajput in isolation or in combination of any two or all three together as per the demand of the situation as sources of their legitimacy.

Commonality of faith between rulers and the Kashmiri Pandits despite difference in rites, rituals and customs became the basis for the rulers to give patronage and seek legitimacy among the powerful minority in the valley and for Pandits to justify any favour sought from the state. Though Kashmiri Pandits were the followers of Tantric Shaivism-Shaktism and the dynasty derived its legitimacy from Vaishnavism with Ram as the chief deity, the monarch patronized the Tantric Shaivism of Kashmir and extended Vaishnavism by building its temples. Recognizing the political utility the local custom of worship and important Hindu shrines in Kashmir-Khir Bhavani, Shri Jawalaji and Sharkaji were patronized by the state. Relaxing the Vaishnavite tradition, the Ain sanctioned the serving of 'zarda and mutton' at the Sharkaji shrine. Measures were taken to bring together Kashmiri and Jammu traditions of Hinduism closer. The *Ain* mandated the priests of the Sharkaji shrine to perform *parkarma* (circumambulation on behalf of the ruler). The monarch commissioned the composition of *mahatmya* (sacred text narrating the myth and legend of a deity and explaining the importance of pilgrimage of the deity, and rituals of the pilgrimage) of goddess Khir Bhavani and built her island temple. In the *mahatmya*, the deity was depicted as 'one who grants *Ramrajya* . . . and who had made *Satidesa* her abode'. The process to build Jammu and Kashmir as a Hindu polity was completed during the regime of Pratap Singh and one single Hindu religious community was constructed by removing the barriers between the Hinduism of Jammu and Kashmir, which emerged as the source of legitimacy of the monarchical state (Rai 2004: 121–7).

Religion, struggle for responsible government and accession

The colonial power imposed the British Resident, a liaison institution in every princely state on Pratap Singh, the successor of Ranbir Singh, in 1885 and forced him to observe 'the good of his people' of all regions as a new source of legitimacy in addition to caste and religion. The requirement of 'monarch with obligations' towards 'subjects with rights' to be monitored by the British Resident was a challenging task for the new ruler. The colonial-induced reforms in administration brought changes in governance without bringing any noticeable change in the character of caste and religion of the ruling class and the 'separate and unequal subject' policies of the ruler. The most important reform undertaken was the land settlement completed in Kashmir in 1895 and in Jammu after. This gave relief to the tenant by reducing the land revenue and controlling the corruption of the intermediaries between the monarch and the tenant and chain of revenue officials. *The Valley of Kashmir*, the book published by settlement officer Walter Lawrence on the basis of his survey and investigation in course of his work, made the country aware about the sufferings of the Kashmiri peasantry in detail.

With the privileged position given to the Hindu religious community and the Rajput caste in the public affairs, it was logical that Muslim subjects had to suffer denial and discrimination on the basis of religion, particularly in the valley where their population was 94%. The Archaeological and Research Department founded by the state in 1904 gave patronage only to Hindu archaeological sites; Muslim shrines were kept out of its patronage. The stated objective of the research branch was to restore Kashmir as a centre of Sanskrit/Hindu learning. Kashmir had to suffer provincial administrative discrimination vis-à-vis Jammu which increased during the regime of Hari Singh. A portion of the Dharmarth Fund came from land revenue collected from 'all the people irrespective of religion'. Different types of taxes,[3] in addition to land revenue, *rasum* (illegal levies) of the officials and interests of the money lenders kept the masses appallingly poor. Sir Albion Bannerji, a Bengali Christian civil servant employed by Hari Singh as foreign and political minister, feeling disgusted over the insensitivity of the rulers to bring necessary changes, resigned after two years of service in 1929. In Lahore he narrated the situation in Kashmir before the Associated Press on 15 March 1929, which became an issue for the educated people in the country and agitated the Kashmiri (Bazaz 2003: 135).

Religion and caste as sources of legitimacy for the regime made it also legitimate for the subjects to organise themselves if they desired into caste and religious organizations for social reform and to compete for symbolic political and economic benefits available through petitioning. It resulted in multiple fragmented, competitive and contradictory casteist and religionist public spaces instead of one unified common public space for all subjects – an unhealthy legacy of the era considered normal and effective in the contemporary era in the state. The presence of the Resident in Srinagar as a watchdog gave confidence, and the increasing number of educated youths enabled the Kashmiri Muslims to express their grievances and assert their rights as a religious community from the last decade of 19th century with increasing frequency, tone and number in the succeeding decades. The issues of denial and discrimination in employment, incentive and support given by the government for entrepreneurship, exclusion of non-Dogra and non-Punjabi from defence service, discrimination in criminal justice system and the practice of *beggar* (forced labour) were creating mass disaffection among the youths. Under the Arms Act, only Rajputs and Dogras were allowed own and use firearms, which still has not been annulled. The growing resentment resulted in mass protest in Srinagar on the issue of stopping of the imam in between the mandatory sermon in Eid prayer on 29 April 1931, followed by another incident of disrespect of the Qur'an by a police constable in Central Jail Jammu (Ahmad 2017: 102–3). It culminated in violent suppression on 13 July 1931 in Srinagar, which is considered as the beginning of freedom struggle in Kashmir. Despite all repressive measures, when the revolt could not be suppressed the ruler announced general amnesty and proclaimed consideration of reasonable demands (Anand 2011: 26–7). Representations were submitted pointing out the grievances and expected measures for resolution. People were also demanding an impartial enquiry into their grievances, which got wide support of Muslim organizations of Punjab and rest of India to control the situation the British felt pressured for it.

The government appointed an enquiry committee headed by Bertrand J. Glancy, a senior official of the Indian Political Service, on 20 October 1931. The committee in its report submitted in March 1932 recognized the problem of denial, discrimination and under-representation of Muslims and recommended for their redressal. Accepting most of the recommendations the government issued a notification in April 1932. As a follow-up action, a Reform Conference was constituted which recommended the establishment of a legislative assembly which was enacted in April 1934 (Anand 2011: 29–30). Two of the most important civic liberties granted by the monarch were freedom of press and freedom of political association. The All Jammu and Kashmir Muslim Conference was founded in October 1932 and the first issue of the Kashmir *Daily Vitasha* newspaper was also launched at the same time (Bazaz 2003: 158). The foundation of the organization is considered in Kashmir historiography as the beginning of its freedom struggle. Though the Muslim Conference demanded a joint electorate, the enacted Praja Sabha was to consist of 75 members – 15 official and 60 non-official, of which 27 were nominated and 33 were elected by a limited male religious electorate of 21 Muslims, 10 Hindus and 2 Sikhs.

The nature and power and functioning of assembly did not satisfy the Muslim Conference, which demanded the establishment of responsible government and observed 8 May 1936 as Responsible Government Day (Bazaz 2011: 191). To achieve the goal of responsible government, it was essential to get support of the Hindus and Sikhs: two powerful minorities. Nehru and Gandhi also advised the progressive sections of the minorities and Sheikh Abdullah and others in the Muslim Conference for united struggle. The Working Committee of the Muslim Conference in June 1938 decided to change the name of the organization to the National Conference and opened its membership to non-Muslims. A majority of the Hindu population, both the elite and the masses, perceived responsible government with constitutional monarchy as a threat to their interests and favoured continuation of an autocratic monarchy as a guarantee of their interests. The progressive section which joined the National Conference worked for the protection of their community interest and to bring it closer to Congress. In response to the popular demand the Maharaja first improved the rule of law regime through a constitutional proclamation in February 1939 followed by a constitutional act in September 1939. Without compromising sovereignty or its religionist character and subordinated status with the chosen council of ministers, he changed the composition of the assembly.

Modern mass education under state patronage was launched in the state in the late 19th century and gained momentum in the first and second decades of the 20th century. Sanskrit and Persian were taught to Hindu and Muslim students separately.

The government decided in 1911 to give compulsory religious instruction in every class by respective priests simultaneously in separate rooms after segregating the students into religious groups. Religion was taught to Muslims and Hindus in their 'respective vernaculars – Urdu and Hindi'. The education policy was aiming to produce 'good Muslims', 'good Hindus' and so on instead of making them loyal and patriotic subjects (Tajuddin and Sharma 2012: 324–5). The official language (Urdu) was neither a compulsory nor an optional paper for any recruitment examination to be conducted by the Civil Service Recruitment Board formed in 1930. The government constituted an Education Reorganisation Committee in 1938 to recommend ways and means to make Devnagari and Nastalique both scripts as medium of instruction. With the objective of winning Hindu support the National Conference in its December 1939 Working Committee meeting passed a resolution to include Hindustani as a compulsory paper with option to write in either of the scripts. The committee unanimously rejected the dual script proposal, which was supported by the education minister. The government ousted the minister and issued an order on 21 October 1940 to make 'simple Urdu' with dual script as the medium of instruction. When the order was opposed by Muslims under the leadership of Mirwaiz Yusuf Shah, the National Conference, contradicting its resolution, opposed the order in January 1941 and its eight members resigned from their assembly membership. In response to the growing Hindu pressure, for the third time he changed his position on the language issue in January 1942 and stated that he would favour the stand of Congress on national language, whether it would be Sanskrit or Persian (Ahmad 2018: 186–94).

The National Conference joined the Congress-affiliated All India State People's Conference in 1941, which annoyed the pro-Muslim Conference faction in the party to revive it. Two rival organizations supported by rival Congress and Muslim League divided and weakened the goal of responsible government. The rivalry often resulted in violence between the supporters of the two organizations. To maintain his legitimacy in Muslim masses vis-à-vis Mirwaiz Yusuf Shah of Muslim Conference, he aligned with the rival Mirwaiz, used religious metaphor in his public speeches, founded the All Jammu and Kashmir Auqaf Trust with himself as founder and president for the development and management of Muslim shrines and other endowments in the state in 1940 and used its resources for his politics, delivered *Khutba* (sermon) in the weekly congregational Friday prayer in the Hazartbal mosque, organized functions on religious days and used them for political propagation (Zutshi 2003: 267–8). The minority communities either actively or passively gave support to the National Conference. The stands of the National Conference on public issues were generally based on appeasement of Muslims or Hindus because its leaders usually took a stand on a religious line in the Working Committee meetings (Bazaz 2003: 168). The Hindu nationalist organizations became dormant onlookers.

In response to the separate campaigns of the two conferences, the Maharaja appointed a commission for further constitutional reforms in July 1943 which gave its report in October 1944. To associate subjects in administration he appointed two ministers one of them was a nominee of National Conference. The National Conference approved its blueprint of the state constitution, Naya Kashmir, in its annual session held in September 1944. In response to the 12 May Cabinet Mission declaration of post-colonial return of paramountcy, Sheikh Abdullah launched a mass movement to achieve responsible government, calling it the 'Quit Kashmir' Movement in an illogical imitation of the Quit India movement of Congress. He and other leaders of his party were jailed on charges of treason followed by the arrest of the leaders of the Muslim Conference.

Most of the leaders of both the popular parties were in jail on 15 August 1947. Among the three available options – accession to India, accession to Pakistan and independence – the Maharaja preferred the third option and adopted delaying tactic. He wanted to achieve his goal through the supernatural powers of an ascetic Sant Dev (Singh 1984: 37). The Muslim Conference had stated in September 1946 in its document 'Azad Kashmir' to achieve independence with the Maharaja as the constitutional head of responsible government, which was reaffirmed in May 1947 but demanded accession with Pakistan with maximum autonomy to accommodate its Kashmiri leadership (Zutshi 2003: 302–3; Puri 2010: 19). The Hindu majoritarianist organizations supported independence except a section's support for accession with India. Sheikh Abdullah after his release demanded 'freedom before accession', which meant complete responsible government including nationalization of army and semi-independent status recognized by India and Pakistan (Noorani 2010: 94).

Rebellion broke out in Poonch, a district bordering Pakistan, in the second week of August. The formation of Azad Kashmir in reaction to the state forces created three-mile-deep depopulated zones by evacuating Hindus and massacring Muslims (Zutshi 2003: 306). Hindu and Sikh refugees migrated into the state from bordering areas of Pakistan which enflamed the Muslim massacre in Dogra-dominated districts in which the regime and its forces directly or indirectly participated (Ahmad 2018: 56–100). Sheikh Abdullah was released on 29 September in lieu of 'a qualified letter of apology'. The sequence of violence and disorder culminated into the Pashtun tribe's invasion from the frontier region into Kashmir on 22 October, which was supported by Pakistan. The State Forces and Militia Force formed by the volunteers of the National Conference unsuccessfully tried to hold the march of the raiders to Srinagar. Viewing imminent danger to his life, the Maharaja left Srinagar in the night of 25 September, signed the Instrument of Accession on 26 October after reaching Jammu, which was accepted by the government of India on 27 October and was followed by arrival of Indian forces to defend the state. According to the memoir of the then prime minister of the state who was negotiating with Nehru, Sheikh was present in the house and persuaded Nehru by a note for signing the instrument (Mahajan 1963: 152).

However, both leadership and public in Kashmir were either divided or undecided between India and Pakistan. After accession, Yusuf Shah left for the Azad Kashmir.[4] The confusion is depicted in these lines of a poem of the most celebrated Kashmiri poet Mahjoor, written in October 1947: 'though I would like to sacrifice my life and body for India, yet my heart is in Pakistan' (Bazaz 2003). Even in the post-accession early years, it was normal to see photographs of Sheikh, Jinnah and Iqbal in the shops and homes of Kashmiris irrespective of party affiliation (Zutshi 2003: 303). Sheikh was made chief emergency administrator by the Maharaja on 30 October 1947. On 5 March 1948 through a proclamation the ruler made him prime minister of a popular responsible government. Despite the conscious efforts of the ruler to maintain the polity as an independent polity after decolonization sequence of events after partition forced him to access with India in his existential optionlessness. The logic of events also decided the destiny of the divided and confused subjects and forced them to accept it willingly or unwillingly.

Religion in the era of constitutional governance

The accession decided the future of the polity but could not eradicate the socio-economic overlapping divisions which created serious contradictions between the logical course of republican democratic politics of India and the course of politics in which the outgoing polity had socialized them. The first unavoidable tangible variable of democratic politics in the polity was its demographic profile, a legacy of centrality of Hindu religion in the self-image of the monarchical polity and its discriminatory policy towards its majority subjects. The comparative economic, educational and social backwardness of Muslims of all ethnicities other than the Hindus, Sikhs and even Buddhist minorities was an obvious legacy of the past regime. The majoritarian organizations and national public sentiment in favour of minority Hindus would pressure Delhi to act as protector and promoter of their interests. The second unavoidable tangible variable of state politics has been the irredentist claim of bordering Pakistan – the occupant of almost half of the polity and its people. Non-redressal of the historical grievances of the majority community was bound to create disaffection among majority to be exploited by Islamabad.

The double overlapping (1) of weak and backward socio-economic status of numerical majority on the one side and (2) strong and comparatively developed socio-economic status of numerical minority on the other side was a dangerous cocktail for the stability of Jammu and Kashmir polity.[5] In employment the majority has still not achieved its due share (Fayaz, 23 January 2017). The egalitarian decisions were essential to make the power structure republican and democratic. This demanded strict observance of republican and democratic ethics (i.e. taking decision through consensus or at least by majority vote in appropriate forum). This was a prerequisite to avoid any mass feeling of grievance among the erstwhile ruling class. To bring minorities overboard if needed, the good offices of the central government would have been useful. It was equally necessary to persuade the majority to accept democratic method and peaceful means for amelioration of their grievances instead to musing over independence or Pakistan as panacea. For all this, it was obvious that the leadership had extraordinary vision, patience, persuasiveness and resilience.

The immediate tangible variables which determined the constitutional framework of internal governance in the polity and its relation with Union government were the schedule of the Instrument of Accession; the commitment of the governor general in his reply to the Maharaja to settle the 'the question of accession' by 'a reference to the people' soon after restoring order and clearing the soil from invader; ongoing war in the territory; and peace to be established on terms and conditions of the Security Council. The instrument signed by the Maharaja was also on the pattern defined in the Government of India Act 1935. Most of the states had signed the instrument before 15 August 1947. These states signed instruments of merger in 1948, accepted the Indian Constitution as their constitution and surrendered their sovereignty to frame their own constitutions for internal governance (Hingurani 2017: 123). Jammu and Kashmir did not sign the Instrument of Merger. The four nominees of the state who joined the Indian Constituent Assembly as members in June 1949 stated that relationship of the state with the Union would be governed by the terms of the accession and internal governance would be according to its Constitution Act 1939 till framing of its constitution. Article 370 was incorporated in the Indian Constitution as an instrument of applicability of the constitutional provisions and Union laws in the state (Sharma 2011: 13).

As Prime Minister Sheikh Abdullah began land reform in 1948 by abolishing all types of state grants – jagir, muafi and mukarrari – postponing realization of all debts for one year and stopping eviction of tillers without court procedure. There were 6,250 acres of state land freely distributed among landless labourers. The former omnipotent ruler could not adapt to function as 'constitutional head' under his appointed responsible government. Due to disagreement with Sheikh on policy issues and on Nehru's acquiescence to avoid antagonizing Sheikh, the Maharaja appointed his son Karan Singh as regent on 20 June 1949 and left the state (Mullik 1971: 10–11). War ended on 1 January 1949 and Jammu and Kashmir was divided between the two warring countries through the ceasefire line formalized through the Karachi Agreement signed on 27 July 1949. On 26 January 1950, the provisions of the Indian Constitution specified in the Instrument of Accession were applied in the state through a presidential order. To give further relief to indebted peasants, the Distressed Debtors Relief Act 1950 was enacted and to generate surplus land for distribution among the tillers a ceiling of 22.75 acres was enacted on land holdings excluding orchard, grass farms and fuel and fodder reserves Big Estates Abolition Act 1950 (Rai 2004: 282). The Act placed a ceiling on land ownership at 186 kanals (about 22 acres) and rest of the land of a landlord was redistributed without any compensation to the landlord.

The 75-member Constituent Assembly elected on the basis of universal adult suffrage was convened on 31 October 1951. Major decisions of the assembly in its first phase were not to give compensation for the expropriated surplus land, to abolish hereditary monarchy and to have a state flag. For concurrence of the Union on these and other important issues, the representatives of the two governments negotiated in July 1952 in Delhi and mutually decided; this is known as the Delhi Agreement. These decisions were approved by the respective assembly and the parliament. As a follow-up action the assembly abolished the monarchy on 12 November 1952 and the Regent was appointed Sadar i-Riyasat (Hingurani 2017: 167).

Sheikh was dismissed and arrested on 8 August 1953 when Nehru, Abul Kam Azad and Rafi Ahmad Kidwai failed to convince him to ratify accession in the Constituent Assembly.[6] In its second phase the assembly ratified the accession on 17 February 1954. The next presidential order was issued on 14 May 1954, which superseded the parent order of 1950. The order applied most of the provisions of the Indian Constitution with exceptions and modification wherever required maintaining the internal autonomy of the state (Anand 2011: 129). The draft constitution was approved and adopted on 17 November 1956 and came into force on 26 January 1957.

The constitution like any constitution is the basis of internal order in the state but it has failed in its function because it does not fulfil the Comtean prerequisites of order 'consensus on principles' and 'stability of principles'. 'We, the people of Jammu and Kashmir' on the one side and the 'Union of India' of which the state 'is an integral part' (Constitution of Jammu and Kashmir 2003: 1) on the other side must have to maintain the Comtean prerequisites for prevalence of order in the state. If the logic events made accession rational for the parties despite their competitive and contradictory religionist rationality, achievement of immediate objectives in the logic of circumstance prevailed over them to make the constitution setting aside differences in the 'dangerous decade'. But they failed to construct a commonwealth political community of Jammu and Kashmir and an ordered progressive polity for its citizens. The constitution has a stillbirth which made the polity dysfunctional.

The competitive majoritarian assimilationist Hindu nationalism and separatist Muslim nationalism resolved the contradiction of India and Pakistan by partitioning their common homeland and forcing out or subordinating their respective religious minorities. In Jammu and Kashmir, the accession with India took away both these majoritarianist strategies of resolving contradictions of religious communities in the framework of republican-democratic polity. The internal presence of Hindu nationalist organizations and external presence of the Islamic Republic of Pakistan in the neighbourhood has kept valid the currency of religion in the politics of the Indian Republic since its birth. Confused, irrational and autocratic decisions taken in an undemocratic authoritarian manner, executed by inefficient and corrupt bureaucracy resulted in disaffection, resentment and organized protests in the state (Lamb 1991: 196–7). Anti-government protests began in 1949 onward against violations of civil democratic rights in Srinagar, Jammu and Leh. In Srinagar it was led by dissident leaders of National Conference. The All Jammu and Kashmir Praja Parishad, an RSS-affiliated party, led the protests in Jammu, and in Leh they were led by the Ladakh Buddhist Association (LBA). Willingly or unwillingly, the people of Jammu and Kashmir lost their agency, became the object of rival Indian and Pakistani nationalisms and their homeland became the most conducive space for religionist politics.

The state constitution begins in the name of 'we, the people of Jammu and Kashmir' but the government has not endeavoured through its 'ideological state apparatuses' and 'repressive state apparatus' to construct an all-inclusive state political community of Jammu and Kashmiris (Carnoy 1984: 95–7). The state's language policy, pedagogical content in the school textbooks, multiple separate school sessions, multiple separate examination schedules, content of the curricular and co-curricular activities is not inculcating the values of a modern republican democratic political community.[7] The state operated 'Educational Ideological Apparatus' does not produce Jammu and Kashmir Indian citizens but produces Kashmiri Muslim, Kashmiri Hindu, Kashmir Sikh, Dogra Hindu, Gujar Muslim, Pahari Muslim, Ladakhi Muslim and Ladakhi Buddhist individuals. Conventional politics to protect and promote rights of peasants, workers, women, students, marginal identities or issues of governance, human rights or environment of all the people of state are conspicuously absent in the state. Unlike other states, the universe of politics in Jammu and Kashmir is not state but region. Three regions in the state have been imagined and constructed as hegemonic universes of Kashmiri Muslims, Dogra Hindus and Ladakhi Buddhists. The semantics of the parochial-xenophobic politics is ethnicity and region, but its semiotics, syntactics and pragmatics is religion.

None of the three divisions/regions – Kashmir, Jammu or Ladakh – is homogeneous space inhabited only by Kashmiri Muslims, Dogra Hindus or Vjrayan Buddhists. Due to the LoC both area and population of the state has shrunk. According to 1941 census the population of Muslims, Hindus and Sikhs, Buddhists and Others was 77.11%, 20.12% and 2.77%, respectively (Sharma 2011: 1). The percentage of Muslim population in the three administrative units of the state – Kashmir, Jammu and Frontier Region (Ladakh Gilgit) in 1941 was 93.45%, 61.63% and 86.7%, respectively. According to 2011 census the overall population percentage of Muslims, Hindus, Sikhs and Buddhists in the state was 68.31%, 28.43%, 1.87% and 0.89%, respectively. The percentage of Muslim population in Kashmir is 96.40% and that of Hindus is 2.45%. Muslims in the valley are largely Kashmiris, but there is also a sizable number of Gujar and Pahari. Six out of the total ten districts of Jammu division located in Middle Himalaya/Peer Panjal Ranges are Muslim majority. The overall percentage of Muslim population in the division was 33.45% in 2011. Ladakh as a Buddhist majority region is a state-supported myth.[8] According to the 2011 census, the regional percentage of Muslim, Buddhist and migrant Hindu populations was 46.40%, 39.65% and 12.11%, respectively. The religious rivalry and contestation has converted the politics of the state into a binary of Kashmir/Muslim on the one side and Jammu/Hindu and Ladakh/Buddhist on the other side. The state's Sikh population of 1.87% is more than double the 0.89% Buddhist population, but in absence of a 'homeland' it is not a notable party.

Whereas in the rhetoric of region 'Kashmir' maximally means the whole state and minimally means valley and the Muslim majority districts of Jammu Division, and 'Jammu' means the whole Jammu division, but 'Kashmiris' means only Kashmiri ethnic community of Valley and 'Dogra' means only Dogra or all Hindus. In this religionist politics articulated through the clichés of 'regional imbalance', 'regional discrimination', 'Kashmir-centric policy' and 'Jammu-centric policy', the unrepresented and unarticulated geographical zone is the Middle Himalayan districts rhetorically included in both but shunned by both. Almost all the civil society organizations (i.e. chambers of commerce, chambers of industry, bar associations) are separate and region specific. The state does not have a bar council. All the state autonomous bodies have two divisional structures with autonomous functions and state secretariat shuttles every six months between Srinagar and Jammu. In their statutory powers the governor as ex-officio chairman of the two Hindu shrine boards – Vaishno Devi and Amarnath and chief minister as the ex-officio chairman of the Muslim Waqf board are the guardians of the religious affairs of their respective communities. The association of offices of head of state and head of government in their ex officio capacities to religious bodies is violation of the constitutional values observed throughout India. Second, it indirectly associates religious qualification to these offices (Bi 2014: 29, 45, 48).

The failure of Nehru's experiment in composite nation building in Jammu and Kashmir through Sheikh changed his perception. Jammu and Kashmir as a Muslim majority state was an asset for Indian nationalism till 1953; henceforth it became a liability to be contained and managed for national security. He acquiesced Machiavellian practices of Sheikh in governance for the sake of national interest. During post-Sheikh regimes both in internal governance and centre state relations Machiavellianism has either coexisted or even subordinated constitutionalism in the governance of the state. It has been generally accepted as a fact even by constitutionally created independent and autonomous institutions (Rawat 2018: 8). This includes use and abuse of religion against one another and propping up Jammu and Ladakh in alliance against valley. Post-1953 regimes have remained in office, not on the will of the people but on the will of the centre.[9] To manage the 'threat' of the Muslim majority population, presidential orders have been issued with the concurrence of the state governments under Article 370 of the Indian Constitution, and the state constitution has been amended to dilute or remove the special provisions of the state.

Religion inspired violence, governance and way out

Authoritarianism, corrupt and inefficient governance, erosion of the special status and undemocratic attitude of state and central governments perceived under the religionist dynamics has transformed the peaceful protest in the valley into armed struggle with Pakistan's support in 1989. The only objective these armed groups and Pakistan share is secession from India because justice cannot be expected from Hindu India. There is division and confusion among them and between them and Pakistan on the post-secession goal (Bose 1997: 55–67; Swami 2003: 55–88). In case of constitutional breakdown in the state, for the first six months governor rule is imposed under Section 92 of the state constitution, to be followed by president rule. Under governor rule, the governor has both executive and legislative powers, which was publicly stated by the present governor (Malik 2019). During the breakdown of law and order after the outbreak of terrorism in 1989, a presidential proclamation was issued in July 1990 under president rule which authorized the Parliament under Article 356 of the Indian Constitution to legislate for Jammu and Kashmir. The Parliament enacted Armed Forces (Jammu and Kashmir) Special Power Act 1990 under this provision. In July 1992, Parliament enacted the Jammu and Kashmir State (Delegation of Powers) Act to delegate this legislative power to the president (Jaleel, 17 December 2018, *Greater Kashmir*, 16 February 2019). Many presidents' acts were enacted, including the Jammu and Kashmir Disturbed Areas Act 1992, during the long span of president rule.

In the religious binary of politics, governor rule is supported in Jammu and Ladakh. Ladakh has achieved scheduled tribe status for its natives except the Sunni Muslims of Leh, the autonomous development council and divisional status all in governor rules. The ultimate goal of the Buddhist religionist politics in Ladakh is to get separation from state as a union territory. In the context of violence and instability in valley there has been fast development in Jammu. Most of the headquarters of the central government offices in state have been shifted to Jammu. When each state gets one all institution normally to be located outside capital this state gets two to be located in the two capitals. Jammu is persistently striving to end Article 35A and Article 370 of the Indian Constitution or trifurcation of the state into separate states of Jammu, Kashmir and a union territory of Ladakh (Chadha 2007: 115–43). Panun Kashmir, an organization of the displaced Kashmiri Pandits, demands division of the valley to create their homeland 'Panun Kashmir' (panunkashmir.org).

Religion or any other primordial identity, due to its exclusivist nature, cannot be basis of ordered and stable modern republican democratic polity. In the Indian constitutional scheme, both the sovereign national polity and its constituents' autonomous state polities have been imagined as universal and inclusive of all its citizens irrespective of their primordial identities. Accession of Jammu and Kashmir into the union was a challenge and opportunity to delegitimize religion as a variable in politics. It demanded dereligionization of politics both in its internal governance and state centre relations. On the contrary, the course of post-accession politics has made the state one of the most religionized polities. The first step to resolve the problem is dereligionized routine governance under a freely and fairly elected government which has to be loyal only to the constitutions and accountable to people of Jammu and Kashmir not to the central government. This will strengthen human values end human debasement in the state.[10] The second step is to deconstruct the religionist concepts, assumptions and paradigms of politics in the state and reconstruct them according to republican democratic values and their mass inculcation among the citizens. In the next step, the central government, the state government, opposition parties and other stakeholders in the state should resolve issues of internal governance and centre state relations in letter and spirit of the Instrument of Accession and Article 370 of the Indian Constitution. The problem in the state is primarily internal Pakistan disaffection and alienation in the valley provides Islamabad chance 'to fish in the troubled water'. If the state and central governments ensure to resolve all troubles in democratic spirit Pakistan will become irrelevant beyond LoC. Settlement of borders and making it meaningless for the divided people will be the only issue to be settled with Pakistan in the perspective of human security and human development.

Notes

1 The Amritsar Treaty, which created the polity, is signed between 'British government and Maharaja Gulab Singh of Jammu'. The treaty recognized the new position of the Raja of Jammu as the Maharaja of Jammu which practically meant the new polity which it designed by seceding Kashmir from Lahore Empire and integrating it with Jammu Raj which included at that time Ladakh and Baltistan also but it did not identify the polity by any name. In the second commercial treaty signed between the two polities in 1870, the ruler was addressed as 'Maharaja of Kashmir' and in all subsequent formal and informal expressions the colonial paramount power addressed the rulers as 'Maharajah of Kashmir' (Frederic 2009: 1–2, 406–7). The rulers formally identified them as Maharaja of Jammu and Kashmir and Ladakh and Balistantan and other territories. The formal name of the present state both in Indian and the state constitutions is Jammu and Kashmir or J&K or JK. It is usually called 'Kashmir' both in formal and informal expressions. In the instrument of Accession the monarch identified himself simultaneously as 'Jammu and Kashmir Naresh' and also as 'Ruler of Jammu and Kashmir' (Sharma 2011: 503).
2 Since 2011 beef (buffalo) export from India since 2011 has increased at an average rate of 14% as result of government policy of the pink revolution. India is one of the four largest beef exporting country in the world. It became the largest beef exporting country in 2012 and remained so in 2015, 2016. According to projection its rank may become second after Brazil in 2018. https://times of india.indiatimes.com, Chennai, 1 April 2013, https://www.thehindu.com/news/national, New Delhi, 10 August 2015. Retrieved 25 January 2019.
3 Everything and everybody was taxed and taxes were very heavy, particularly before posting of the British Resident. It was a common proverb to explain the taxation system in Kashmir the statement that 'each and everything except water and air was taxed in Kashmir'. The peasantry had to pay 75% of the agricultural produce as revenue. The artisans – the second important occupation – were also heavily taxed. There were taxes even on social activities like marriage (Wani 2015: 21–30).
4 Opinions of scholars are divided on the sequence of events and the role of important players before and after the accession. The conspicuous absence of archival materials of this period in the state archive makes the examination difficult. According to the dominant opinion in contemporary Kashmir, Sheikh Abdullah deceived his people for power. He was released from jail on the intervention of Nehru on his consent for accession with India but befooled people by the slogan of 'freedom before accession'. He was a personal guest of Nehru before the tribal raid and signing of Instrument of Accession by India.
5 The situation has improved in the seven decades after accession. The overall gap in the socio-economic indicators between Muslims on one side and upper-caste Hindus, Sikhs and Buddhists on the other has shrunk and their proportion in government jobs has increased but it is still far below their proportionate share (Ahmad 2017: 304–6). The universal basis of worldly achievements both in public and private sectors is education. Literacy rate is a litmus test of education and the best indicator to observe the potentiality of material achievements of a society. According to the Sachar Committee assessment, based on the 2001 census the literacy rates in Jammu and Kashmir of different communities in percentage was Muslims (47.3%), upper-caste Hindus (71.2%), SCs and STs (46.5%) (Sachar Committee 2006: 287). According to the 2011 census, the 1st and 2nd position in literacy rate is of Jammu and Samba (both Hindu majority districts) and Leh (the only Buddhist majority district) is at 3rd rank. The summer capital of the state (Srinagar) is at 6th rank below Kathua (Hindu majority) and Kargil (Muslim majority in Ladakh). Except Kargil and Srinagar the remaining 15 Muslim majority districts out of the 22 districts are consecutively placed from 8th to 22nd below the 7th rank Udhampur, the lowest literacy rate Hindu majority district of the state (https://www.census2011.co.in).
6 He hoped to create a 'reversal of the Dogra empire' (Lamb 1991: 187). On this issue he lost majority support in his cabinet. In the words of Balraj Madhok, the Government of

India treated him as 'de facto Sultan of the whole state'. Nehru gave 'him such a long rope as would have prompted even a better man to hang himself with it' (Madhok n.d.: 100).

7   The language policy adopted in 2006 has made English the first language and medium of instruction from class one. The second language is Urdu (state official language) practically for Muslims only or Hindi for Hindus and others. As a third language, schools in Kashmir teach Kashmiri to Kashmiris and Punjabi to Sikhs. Private schools in Kashmir teach Arabic as fourth language. In Dogra-dominated areas of Jammu, some schools teach Dogri and some Sanskrit. In Ladakh, the third language is Arabic for Muslims and Tibetan (Bhoti) for Buddhists (Sharma 2011). Kashmir and Ladakh has one academic session; Jammu has two for summer and winter zones. The examination schedule of Kashmir is one, summer region of Jammu is one and winter region of Jammu another. Examinations in Kargil have been conducted till 2018 along with Kashmir and in Leh along with the winter zone of Jammu.

8   According to C.S. Sapru, Director Census Operation J&K, 'we should not look at the population of Ladakh together as a region but population of the two districts needs to be looked into separately'. *Rising Kashmir*, 17 April 2016. Retrieved 15 February 2019, from jammu-kashmir.com/archives/archives2016/kashmir20160417a.html.

9   In reply to a question on 6 January 1968 by a reporter whether he would like to be chief minister again, he replied in the negative and further stated that 'only a person who enjoys the confidence of the government of India can be the chief minister of Kashmir'. He became chief minister in 1975 when he achieved it (Noorani, 12 February 2019: 90).

10 The debasement can be understood in this Kashmiri poem of Ghulam Nabi Gowhar. Its translation is: 'Tell me how much you will pay, should I sell you Kashmir? Will sell life, will sell voice, will sell soul. Thousand times I sold it to lakh of customers, Will sell it for penny, should you buy brick by brick', Haroon Mirani (2018). 'G N Gowhar: The Judge Who Delivered Verdict in Poetry, Stories', Jammu, *Greater Kashmir*, 6 July.

References

Ahmad, Khalid Bashir (2017). *Kashmir: Exposing the Myth Behind the Narrative*, New Delhi: Sage.
Ahmad, Khalid Bashir (2018). *Kashmir: A Walk Through History*, Srinagar: Gulshan.
Anand, A.S. (2011). *The Constitution of Jammu & Kashmir: Its Development & Comments*, New Delhi: Universal.
Bamzai, P.N.K. (2016). *A History of Kashmir: Political-Social-Cultural from the Earliest Times to Present Day*, Srinagar: Gulshan.
Bazaz, Prem Nath (2003). *The History of Struggle for Freedom: Cultural and Political from Earliest Time to Present Day*, Srinagar: Gulshan.
Bazaz, Prem Nath (2011). *Inside Kashmir*, Srinagar: Gulshan.
Bi, Fatima (2014). *Interface of Government and Religious Institutions in Jammu and Kashmir Polity: A Critical Analysis*, Jammu: Political Science, University of Jammu.
Bose, Sumantra (1997). *The Challenges in Kashmir: Democracy, Self Determination and Just Peace*, New Delhi: Sage.
Carnoy, Martin (1984). *The State and Political Theory*, Princeton: Princeton University Press.
Chadha, Navnita Behera (2007). *Demystifying Kashmir*, New Delhi: Pearson.
Charak, S.D.S. (2017). *Ganesdas Badera's Rajdarshani: A Persian History of North Western India: From Earliest Times to 1847 AD*, Jammu: Jay Kay.
Charak, Sukhdev Singh and Anita Charak Billawaria (2013). *Gulabnama: A History of Maharaja Gulab Singh of Jammu & Kashmir*, Srinagar: Gulshan.
Drew, Frederic (2009). *Jammu and Kashmir Territories: A Geographical Account*, Srinagar: Gulshan.
Fayyaz, Ahmed Ali (2017, January 23). 'Jammu Beating Valley in All PSC Selections Since 1995', Jammu, *State Times*, Greater *Kashmir*, February 16, 2019, Jammu.

Government of India. (2006, November). *Social, Economic and Educational Status of the Muslim Community of India: A Report*, Prime Minister's High Level Committee, Cabinet Secretariat, New Delhi, p. 287.
Hingurani, Aman M. (2017). *Unravelling the Kashmir Knot*, New Delhi: Sage. http://panunkashmir.org. Retrieved November 20, 2018. www.census2011.co.in. Retrieved February 9, 2019.
Jaleel, Muzamil (2018, December 17). 'How Governor's Rule and President's Rule Set J&K Apart from Other States', *Indian Express*. https://indianexpress.com/article/explained/how-governors-rule-and-presidents-rule-set-jk-apart-from-other-states-satya-pal-malik-5492730/. Retrieved March 21, 2019.
Lamb, Alstar (1991). *Kashmir: A Disputed Legacy: 1846–1990*, Hertingfordbury: Roxford Books.
Madhok, Balraj (n.d.). *A Story of Bungling in Kashmir*, New Delhi: Young Asia.
Mahajan, Mehr Chand (1963). *Looking Back: The Autobiography of Mehr Chand Mahajan*, New Delhi: Asia Publishing House.
Malik, Satya Pal (2019, February 11). 'I am Not Only Governor; I am Chief Minister as Well: Governor', Jammu, *State Times*.
Mirani, Haroon (2018, July 6). 'G N Gowhar: The Judge Who Delivered Verdict in Poetry, Stories', *Greater Kashmir*, Jammu.
Mullik, B.N. (1971). *My Years with Nehru: Kashmir*, Bombay: Allied.
Noorani, A.G. (2010, February 12). 'Myth and Reality', *Frontline*, pp. 89–93.
Noorani, A.G. (2010, September 10). 'Kak and Sheikh', *Frontline*, pp. 91–7.
Panikkar, K.M. (1992). *Gulab Singh (1792–1888): Founder of Kashmir*, Jammu: Vinod.
Puri, Luv (2010). *Across the LoC: Inside Pakistan Administered Jammu and Kashmir*, New Delhi: Penguin.
Rai, Mridula (2004). *Hindu Rulers and Muslim Subjects: Islam, Rights, and the History of Kashmir*, New Delhi: Permanent Black.
Rawat, O.P. (2018, December 2). 'Idea Exchange', *Indian Express*, p. 8.
Sharma, S.K. (2011). *The Constitution of Jammu & Kashmir: A Perspective with Reference to the Constitution of India*, New Delhi: Universal.
Singh, Karan (1984). *Heir Apparent: An Autobiography*, New Delhi: Oxford University Press.
Sufi, G.D.M. (2015). *Kashir: Being a History of Kashmir: From the Earliest Times to Our Own*, Srinagar: Gulshan.
Swami, Praveen (2003). 'Terrorism in Jammu and Kashmir in Theory and Practice', in (ed.), Sumit Ganguly, *The Kashmir Question: Retrospect and Prospect*, London: Frank Cass.
Tajuddin, Muhammad and Vandana Sharma (2012). 'Review of J&K Language Policy in the Perspective of the Nehruvian Language Policy', *South Asian Survey*, 19(2), pp. 324–6.
Wani, Showkat Ahmad (2015). 'Taxation and Economy of Kashmir Under Dogra Rule (1846–1930)', *Asia Pacific Journal of Marketing & Management*, 5(4), pp. 21–30.
Zutshi, Chitralekha (2003). *Languages of Belonging: Islam, Regional Identity, and the Making of Kashmir*, New Delhi: Permanent Black.

11
RELIGION AS A TOOL FOR POLITICAL MOBILIZATION IN BIHAR

Umakant

> A caste has no feeling that it is affiliated to other castes except when there is a Hindu-Muslim riot. On all other occasions each caste endeavours to segregate itself and to distinguish itself from other castes. Each caste not only dines among itself and marries among itself but each caste prescribes its own distinctive dress.[1]
>
> In India, the majority is not a political majority. In India the majority is born; it is not made. That is the difference between a communal majority and a political majority. A political majority is not a fixed or a permanent majority. It is a majority which is always made, unmade and remade. A communal majority is a permanent majority fixed in its attitude. One can destroy it, but one cannot transform it.[2]

In the light of the preceding two quotations from B.R. Ambedkar, one could infer that social and religious factors do play an important role in political mobilization at several levels. Religion has been and continues to be utilized by different political organization in the country as a handy tool not only to mobilize people for electoral benefits but also in the process to seek legitimacy for its politics. From the ancient times till the present it has been evident that society and religion have been guiding the formation of political regimes. Whichever socio-religious group(s) have played a dominant role at different points of time in history, it is very clear that religion has played an important role for administering the small as well as the vast tracts of geographical boundaries and also for devising different sets of codes for publics and subjects to follow in their day-to-day life.

Thus it is not a surprise to note here that at the time of independence in 1947, and even prior to that, from the British colonial rule, religion again played a crucial role in the birth of two new countries: India and Pakistan. This is also to state the fact that ever since the political consciousness among different social and religious groups arose, religious mobilization has been a hallmark of Bihar politics too. Reported incidents of communal violence during the partition time and also afterwards extending into decades have paid rich dividends to different political parties at the helms of power and also in opposition in Bihar and elsewhere too. The focus of this chapter is to examine the role of religion as a handy and useful tool for garnering support during elections from 1980s onwards till the present. There may have been several causes, be it economic, social or religious hatred, for communal riots happening in the state of Bihar, but political dimensions of communal riots have overshadowed all other factors.

Sanjay Kumar and others (2008: 5) have clearly stated that

> although Hindus constitute the dominant religious group in Bihar, Muslims with 17 percent of the total population of the state also constitute a significant part of society. While they are not uniformly distributed, there are certain pockets where they are in majority or constitute a number that could be critically important for electoral outcomes. Based on CSDS estimates, there are about 26 assembly constituencies where the Muslim population exceeds 30 percent. There are another 20 assembly constituencies where the Muslim population ranges between 20 and 30 percent.

Whether Muslims vote en bloc as a community is a reality or based merely on perception of being so remains to be proved with hard facts. But what is clear is that Muslims have not formed any political party of their own and have remained largely with non-Muslim political parties. They have at best been seen to be creating a space for peaceful coexistence with other caste and communities. On the other hand it is clearly visible that BJP, RSS, VHP, Bajrang Dal and their other frontal organizations have used religion as a tool for political mobilization. It is also being observed over the years that the Hindu-Muslim communal divide that existed at the time of partition of the country in 1947 has remained alive and still plays its sinister role, culminating in a polarized politics in a state like Bihar and as elsewhere in the country.

Electoral democracy, minority groups and politics of the dominant castes and communities

For participation in electoral democracy on an equal footing or to play second fiddle by aligning with the dominant caste and communities has been a constant dilemma that minority groups face. Tactical moves in the absence of large numbers that could safeguard their political and other interests becomes the guiding principles for any minority groups in the democratic political set up. It is no wonder then that without following any isolationist approach, they always tend to remain relevant politically and in the process also bargain for their personal security and over all socio-economic and political development for their community. Harry W. Blair made an observation in this regard, saying that

> the practice of electoral democracy places a hard dilemma before minority groups. If the members of the minority want to participate as fully

equal members of the polity, they must integrate themselves into the larger group and play the games of politics according to the majority's rules, but they do so at the risk of seeing their minority identity and culture disappear.

(Blair 1973: 1275)

It has been a pattern widely observed that different political parties resort to mobilize minority groups by either putting up candidates from the respective groups or by promising beneficiary schemes for the groups of religious and linguistic community once they are voted into power. In the areas where these groups are in a position to influence the electoral outcomes, it has a been a regular practice for political parties to target these groups support either by playing up their vulnerabilities of being a minority in an otherwise situation surrounded by people from dominant/majority community or on the other hand by criticizing the minority's so-called appeasement and thereby catering to the majority community's desire of putting the minorities in a situation wherein they should not look for unwarranted special treatment from the state.

Imtiaz Ahmad opined that

> political parties often seek to mobilize whole communities in favour of particular candidates and the process of elections serves to reinforce and accentuate communal consciousness farther than eliminate it. The consolidation of whole communities in favour of particular candidates or political parties is not an entirely independent phenomenon; it depends upon the nature of the electoral contest, the composition of the population and the issues raised by different parties at the time of election.
>
> (Ahmad 1972: 84)

From the first general election held in 1952 to the latest that is in progress, what is very clearly visible is that all political parties in their attempt to reach out to a wider sections of the electorate resort to several tactics which may or may not bring larger number of victories for their respective parties. All kinds of valid as well as not so valid considerations play their role in ticket distribution to probable candidates on the grounds of the ability to win, which may include factors like caste, community, religion, region, language, ethnicity and so forth.

It is clear from Table 11.1, depicting candidates who contested and also candidates who got elected in the Assembly and Parliamentary elections, that the number of Muslims has not been very high. Starting from 22 MLAs in 1952 and going up to 25 MLAs in 1972 has remained a kind of trend that Muslim representation in political establishment in Bihar has been maintained over the years. It was not the areas with sizable Muslim population that elected its Muslim candidates but also in areas where Muslims do not account for large numbers they got elected. On the basis of these hard facts it would be very difficult to surmise that Muslims vote en bloc or Muslims indulge in communally polarized politics.

TABLE 11.1 Muslim candidates in Bihar: votes polled, candidates and winners (1952–72)

Legislative Assembly (MLAs)	1952	1957	1962	1967	1969	1972
% of valid votes polled by Muslims	4.53	5.84	7.88	6.80	6.27	7.45
Muslims as % of candidates (number of Muslim candidates)	4.70 (72)	6.73 (90)	7.19 (110)	8.00 (162)	6.18 (133)	8.17 (162)
Muslims as % of winners (number of Muslims elected)	7.01 (22)	7.86 (25)	6.60 (21)	5.66 (18)	5.97 (19)	7.86 (25)
Member of Parliament (MPs)	**1952**	**1957**	**1962**	**1967**	**1971**	
% of valid votes polled by Muslims	2.35	4.39	6.31	4.20	3.37	
Muslims as % of candidates (number of Muslim candidates)	2.03 (4)	5.29 (10)	8.15 (19)	5.08 (16)	6.41 (27)	
Muslims as % of winners (number of Muslims elected)	5.66 (3)	5.66 (3)	3.77 (2)	3.77 (2)	5.66 (3)	

Source: Harry W. Blair, 'Minority Electoral Politics in a North Indian State: Aggregate Data Analysis and the Muslim Community in Bihar, 1952–1972', *American Political Science Review*, Vol. 67, No. 4 (December 1973), pp. 1280.

In the absence of any proportionate representation system in the country, the aforementioned data analysis also reveals that Muslim community political representation at its best has been quite mixed and perhaps reflected the community's urge to be part of the national mainstream political arrangements. One could very well infer that Muslim leadership, whether in the Congress Party or in the opposition parties, was always trying to create a space within the existing political space and did not indulge in any kinds of political bargaining for an exclusionary or even special treatment demand driven politics.

In the early years the Jan Sangh too did not fare well in the state elections. This is visible from the number of seats they were able to win and the vote percentage that they acquired in these elections.

> Performance of the Jana Sangh in Bihar Legislative Assembly Elections from 1952 to 1972 were as follows: 0 seats (1.18% vote share) in 1952; 0 seats (1.19% vote share) in 1957; 3 seats (2.77% vote share) in 1962; 26 seats (10.42% vote share) in 1967; 34 seats (15.63% vote share) in 1968–69; and 26 seats (11.37% vote share) in 1972.
>
> *(Jaffrelot 1996: 555)*

A new turning point: politics of communal polarizations since 1980s onwards

With the assassination of Indira Gandhi in 1984, the Congress Party under Rajiv Gandhi steamrolled to power, riding a sympathy wave. Large-scale communal genocide like killings of Sikhs, another religious minority group, further established religious bigotry's role in vitiating the political atmosphere in the country. It was also marked by changes, which saw the emergence of Hindu right-wing politics in an unprecedented new way. This decade also marked the beginning of a belligerent Hindu mass, which perceived minority appeasement, as an extra-constitutional dole that should be banished and every attempt should be made to establish a Hindu nation.

Christophe Jaffrelot, while analyzing the changing contours of Indian politics, thus remarked that

> in the second half of the 1980s, the central Congress government showed an increasing willingness to take sides in disputes within and between religious communities. Earlier in the decade it had been accused of supporting extremist groups in the Punjab, but it now appeared to be granting favours or privileges to certain groups with the result that the state no longer seemed to be above the religious divisions in society.
> *(Jaffrelot 1996: 369–70)*

There has been a general feeling among the Hindu majority community that minorities were being pampered by the ruling Congress government over the years, thereby resulting in political isolation as well as downgrading of their cultural or ideological power through lack of dominance in country's polity. These kinds of sentiments as perceived by the Hindu majority community started the communal polarization through RSS, VHP and BJP in a much more pronounced way from the 1980s onwards. These kinds of perceived grievances held and nurtured by the Hindu organizations and their followers have wreaked havoc on the secular fabric of the country to the extent that communal riots have become a handy tool for political mobilization in several states in India with more vigour from the middle of the 1980s and continues even in present times. Branding Muslims and other minorities as anti-national and hurling abusive slogans on them has become a common and regular practice as part their mobilization tactics.

Jaffrelot (1996: 388) further commented that

> as applied in the 1989 election campaign, the Hindu nationalist strategy of mobilization involved not only the continued use of traditional religious symbols but also the introduction of fresh elements, such as newly invented rituals and new versions of old myths.

The mass mobilization on religious lines that became a hallmark of BJP across several states in northern India started paying rich dividends too. 'It is no wonder then that from a mere two seat that BJP had won in the Parliamentary election in 1984 that it jumped to 85 seats in the 1989 election' (Jaffrelot 1996: 524). The success of the BJP in the 1989 Parliamentary election was also made possible due to it being part of the National Front led by Janata Dal and other non-Congress opposition parties. This happened mainly due to the compulsion of not dividing the non-Congress votes. Tactical understanding between Janata Dal and the BJP proved to be a boon for the BJP in a much wider sense that it not only helped in spreading its areas of influence across the north Indian states but also helped it in gaining further political legitimacy. It was for the second time in a span of 12 years that BJP was accorded such kind of political legitimacy by the non-Congress political formation after 1977 when for the first time Bharatiya Jana Sangh, the previous avatar of BJP, was accommodated in the grand non-Congress alliance called Janata Party.

In the context of Bihar, wherein BJP was also part of alliance with the Janata Dal-led National Front, it would be worthwhile to look at the religious polarization that happened prior to the 1989 Parliamentary and State Assembly elections. Indu Bharti writing about communal riot and killings of Muslims narrated the horrific event thus:

> Bhagalpur which has a history of communal riots was gripped by tension as a result of the Ram Shila Puja plan of the VHP. The killing of alleged dacoits belonging to the Muslim community in encounters after S.K. Dwivedi had taken over as SP of Bhagalpur had also contributed to the tension.
> *(Bharti 1989: 2643)*

She further noted that

> as the Ram Shila procession entered Tatarpur, provocative slogans denouncing Muslims, their religion and their suspect patriotism – such as 'Hindi, Hindu, Hindustan, Mullah Bhago Pakistan' ('India is for Hindi-speaking Hindus; Muslims must go to Pakistan') – were rending the air. It was at this point that a bomb was hurled at the procession by some miscreants and this set off the violence. Another bomb was hurled at the heavily armed police party and it went on a rampage, killing four in the indiscriminate firing, and looting and burning Muslim localities in the area.
> *(Bharti 1989: 2644)*

The State's complicity in escalation of the violence leading to riot, looting, killing and destruction of properties was clearly visible through callous manner in which the local administration and also the State government handled the situation. According to PUDR,

> the majority of those killed or those whose means of livelihood were destroyed were agricultural labourers, rickshaw-pullers, bangle sellers and weavers. Ninety-three percent of those killed were Muslims. A total of

595 incidents of rioting, arson, loot and killing were recorded in FIRs by the Police.

(PUDR 1996: 2)

The biggest beneficiary of the Bhagalpur riot and the Ramshila Pujan movement of RSS/VHP was the Bharatiya Janata Party. It heralded a new era of religious polarization, which catapulted the BJP onto the centre stage of national politics.

Not surprisingly from 16 seats (7.5% votes) in 1984 the BJP jumped to 39 seats (11% votes) in 1989 and further in 1993 to 41 seats (13.1% votes) in Bihar Legislative Assembly. In the Parliamentary elections in Bihar from zero seat (6.9% votes) in 1984 it won 8 seats (11.7% votes) in 1989 and 5 seats (15.9% votes) in 1991.

(Jaffrelot 1996: 555)

'It continued its onward march in the Parliamentary elections with 18 seats (20.5% votes) in 1996, 23 seats (23.1% votes) in 1999 and 5 seats (14.6% votes) in 2004' (Sanjay Kumar et al. 2008: 16). Thus started an era in which it became a top priority for BJP to resort to any trick that could pay it rich dividends in terms of votes in the elections. It also helped in creating a new tactic of direct confrontation on issues related to religious differences.

Seemanchal: is it a laboratory for religious mobilization?

Seemanchal has four districts – Kishanganj, Katihar, Araria and Purnea – each having a fairly large Muslim population. While Kishanganj has 67.97% Muslim population – the highest in the country after Kashmir – Katihar has 44.46%, Araria 42.94% and Purnea 38.46% Muslim population. The percentage of Muslim population in the entire Seemanchal region is 45.93%.

With numbers on their side, it may have been expected that Muslims would always win from the Seemanchal without any hiccup. The electoral data tell a different story altogether. Out of 24 Assembly seats, Muslims have never won more than eight seats – the number Muslim candidates have won only three times so far. The lowest performance was in 1995 when only five Muslim candidates could win. Among political parties, it is only the BJP, which has registered constant growth since its entry in the region. In the 1990 Assembly polls, the party won just two seats but in the next election in 1995, it more than tripled its tally and won seven seats. It maintained strength in 2000 and grew to nine in 2005. The 2010 Assembly polls were the most successful for the party in the region when it won 13 out of 24 seats. The average victory of Congress party since 1990 has been just 3.2 seats. The best performance of Rashtriya Janata Dal (RJD) was in 2000 when it won six seats but the last assembly polls of 2010 was the worst for it when the party won only one seat (IndiaTomorrow.net 2015). The spectacular victory of BJP in Seemanchal districts goes on to prove the fact that it has been able to communally polarize the Hindu voters against the visibly large population of Muslims.

Manindra Nath Thakur (2015: 91) is of the view that despite internal heterogeneity among Muslims in Seemanchal areas of Bihar, Muslims at times do cast their votes en bloc to defeat BJP.

> The evidence of the en bloc voting of the Muslim voters can also be adduced from data about the vote margin in the 2009 and 2014 elections. In the Purnea constituency in 2009 the BJP defeated the independent candidate by the margin of 1,86,227 votes, whereas in 2014 elections the BJP candidate was defeated by JD(U) by the margin of 1,16,669 votes. In the Katihar constituency BJP won the 2009 elections by 14,015 votes by defeating NCP and in 2014 NCP defeated BJP by 1,14,740 votes.

The author has cited other reasons as well to prove his point on the question of Muslim en-bloc voting patterns as visible in the election results from Seemanchal areas.

However, this views held by Manindra Nath Thakur may not be true to explain why some times BJP wins in a remarkable fashion and why at other times non-BJP parties score spectacular victories. In the absence of a clear pattern of voting amongst the Muslims, Hindus and people belonging to different castes it may not be possible to jump to a conclusion that Muslims always vote en bloc to defeat BJP candidates.

While critically examining Manindra Nath Thakur's hypothesis about en bloc voting behaviour of Muslims in the Seemanchal areas of Bihar, Hilal Ahmed, who has been writing on the issues for a long time observed that

> nevertheless, the Muslims voters, like other social groups, participated in the election process primarily at the constituency level. There is no evidence that suggests that Muslim voters actually vote strategically or en bloc at the regional level in favour of any one particular party. BJP's defeat in these constituencies, in this sense, cannot entirely be attributed to Muslim political response. Since the author is only concerned with Hindu-Muslim binary, he fails to notice the other local political configurations that could have played more decisive role.
>
> *(Ahmed 2015: 301)*

As per the Election Commission Report in the 2015 Assembly election in Bihar, from the 24 Assembly Constituencies in the Seemanchal Districts comprising of Araria, Kishanganj, Katihar and Purnea, the Mahagathbandhan (RJD-JD(U)-INC) bagged 17 seats whereas the BJP got only six seats and one seat went to CPI(ML) (Election Commission Report 2015). Though Muslims consists of about 45.93% of the total population, all the elected candidates were not Muslims. This should settle the question of Muslims voting en bloc or not but on the contrary it has remained alive and allegations and counter allegation rule the roost.

The number of Muslim legislators in Bihar's new 243-member assembly in 2015 has gone up, 24 now from 19 in 2010. All the Muslim members are from the grand alliance, which routed the BJP-led NDA, except one who was elected on a CPI-ML ticket. The RJD has 12 MLAs from the minority community, Congress six, JD(U) five and CPI-ML one. Four of them were elected from seats in Muslim-dominated Kishanganj district, three each from East Champaran and Purnea, two each from Araria, Darbhanga and Katihar and one each from Sheohar, Madhubani, Saharsa, Gopalganj, Samastipur, Bhojpur, Rohtas and West Champaran districts (Nezami 2015). It only goes on to prove the fact that Muslim legislators have been elected mainly from constituencies where Muslim population comprises 20% or more but not necessarily from the Seemanchal districts.

In the by-election for Araria Parliamentary seat on 11 March 2018 (Election Commission 2018), the RJD candidate Sarfaraz Alam defeated the BJP candidate Pradeep Kumar Singh by a margin of 61,798 votes. The RJD candidate bagged 509,344 votes whereas the BJP candidate bagged 447,546 votes as per the results declared by the Election Commission. The by-election was held because of the death of incumbent RJD Member of Parliament, Md. Taslimuddin. In the election campaigning prior to voting on 11 March, the BJP state president Mr. Nityanand Rai alleged that if RJD candidate wins this election, Araria would become a den of Pakistan ISI agents (New Indian Express 2018). Some other leaders of BJP even after losing the election have been found to be indulging in Muslims bashing statements and communal tension in Araria and other places in Bihar. On a closer examination one could very well claim that the RJD victory was a testimony to the fact that the Mahagathbandhan (the grand alliance), even with JD(U) once again in alliance with BJP, managed to garner support of OBC-Dalits-Muslim votes quite remarkably.

Religion as a tool for political mobilization continues

From the aforementioned electoral analysis from the state of Bihar ever since the first election held in 1952 and more so from 1980s onward it is very clear that not only the districts where for example Muslims may be residing in fairly large numbers, but even in places where Muslims may not be in large numbers, and may be politically aligned with either Congress Party, the Left Parties or even with the social justice plank of RJD, the Hindu religious groups and political parties like the Jan Sangh earlier and Bhartiya Janata Party in later years have indulged in communal politics. The Ramjanma Bhumi and Babri Masjid dispute at Ayodhya in the state of Uttar Pradesh found echo in Bihar as well. Mobilizations through 'Ramshila Pujan' across several communally sensitive districts in Bihar in late 1980s and early 1990s laid the foundation for strong support for BJP among the Caste Hindu electorates. The Bhagalpur riot of 1989 was a strong reminder to Muslims in Bihar and elsewhere that State's non-action could have devastating impact on harmony among different socio-religious groups.

The politics of 'Mandal and Kamandal' signifying the OBC's Social Justice plank of Janata Dal and Ram Temple plank of BJP as well as the emergence of Laloo

Prasad Yadav on the scene in Bihar politics all through the 1990s till the present times has made the political dynamics quite pronounced to the extent that Yadavs, other OBC castes, Dalits and Muslims have become a force to reckon with in the political domain. The arrest of L.K. Advani which literally stopped his 'Rath Yatra' in Bihar by the Laloo Prasad Yadav government, the subsequent Babri Masjid demolition in 1992 and the strict response from the state in terms of checking communal riots made Bihar peaceful for almost a decade and half.

Commenting on the state capacity on the question of controlling the outbreak of communal riots, Steven I. Wilkinson observed,

> even Bihar, which is generally agreed to have the weakest state administration in India, has been able to prevent Hindu-Muslim violence when its government has made this a priority. Administrators in Bihar — especially after the murder of a district magistrate by politicians in 1995 — may find their capacity for independent action limited, and political retribution has made many reluctant to take action against anyone they think might be politically connected. But the number of Hindu-Muslim riots in Bihar nonetheless fell sharply after Laloo Prasad Yadav took office as chief minister in 1989.
>
> *(Wilkinson 2004: 86)*

Echoing similar views, Jeffrey Witsoe said,

> Perhaps the RJD government's best performance was in protecting Muslims from the 'communal' riots that swept much of India in the 1990s (Hansen 1999). But even here it was not an effectively functioning state machinery that offered protection but, rather, Laloo's personal vigilance and intervention whenever Hindu – Muslim violence began to erupt – he would immediately travel to the sensitive area and threaten local officials with dire consequences if the violence was not quelled.
>
> *(Witsoe 2011: 624)*

In this regard it would be also useful to highlight the fact that a State administration when it is willing to control communal violence and ready to protect the vulnerable groups like Muslims from the communal disturbances whether due to its political expediency or because of its firm commitment for maintaining peace, law and order needs to be appreciated. The net result was that due to strict policing and a tight law and order situation maintained all over the state it became possible to maintain peace for a significant part of Laloo Prasad Yadav's regime in Bihar.

The proclivity of Muslim community to parties like RJD and JD(U) provided them protection from the wrath of the communal riots and at the same time also gave them a voice in the political system. The JD(U) and its previous avatar the Samata Party headed by Nitish Kumar has been in power in the state due to its alliance with BJP in the post-Laloo Prasad Yadav regime. The JD(U) too had a comfortable relationship with the Muslim community especially the lower caste

Muslims. This period marked some good initiative by the government to empower the Muslim community. But on the other hand BJP, RSS, VHP, Bajrang Dal have been found to be continuously indulging in communal polarization over the years. This gets reflected in the number of communal riots that have happened in recent times.

With the BJP sharing power in the previous and current regime of Nitish Kumar led JD (U), its approach towards communal mobilization has not been given up. Rather the stress on communal mobilization by the BJP has increased especially after the 2014 Parliamentary election and also after the 2015 Assembly election in Bihar. Santosh Singh (*Indian Express* 2018), while writing about communal pot simmering in Bihar ever since Nitish Kumar returned to its earlier alliance with BJP, 'since July 2017 there have been 200 incidents of communal tension, as many as 64 this year alone'. He further stated that this year, 'besides the Araria incident, when an allegedly fake video of three Muslim youths shouting 'anti-India slogans' went viral after the RJD's win in the by-poll there, communal incidents were reported from Bhagalpur, Munger, Aurangabad, Samastipur, Shekhpura, Nawada and Nalanda'.

Conclusion

What is clear from the aforementioned accounts of religious violence being reported from different places in Bihar is the persistent use of religion as a tool for political mobilization continues to be in operation especially by the BJP and several religious groups allied with it. The immediate provocations for any communal violence that has been reported so far may have been to teach Muslims a lesson in subservience, but its long-term objective has always been and continues to remain so to propel BJP to seats of political power in the state and also at the centre in New Delhi. What else could explain such brazen display of disregard to communal peace and harmony. The political euphemism of development is always blabbered but ultimately it is communal and caste mobilizations which drives the electoral politics and BJP seems to have mastered it better than others.

Breaking away of Nitish Kumar and Ramvilas Paswan from the Janata Dal and their subsequent alliance with the BJP few years ago has allowed them space at the helm of power in the state and also in the central government in New Delhi. But as a matter fact as it was visible in the last Assembly election in Bihar in 2015, the OBC-Dalit and Muslim combine is still a force that could halt the onward march of right wing politics. With the Nitish Kumar–led Janata Dal (United) breaking up again from the Laloo Prasad Yadav led RJD, and with the formation of JD(U)-BJP government has once again made the communal situation in Bihar quite gloomy.

It would not be out of place to ask a question whether Muslims have been actually appeased in the elections held so far or have there been return gifts bestowed upon them after the elections? This is a question that requires broad based analysis of government's programmes and policies for empowering the minority community especially the Muslims. Even the question of political representation of Muslims also needs to be looked at before making any final judgment about them being given special treatment to the extent of marginalizing the dominant Hindu community. The manner in which larger Hindu consolidation project of RSS, BJP, VHP, Bajrang Dal and other casteist groups have been operationalized and are still being carried forward, it leaves little space for Muslims or any other religious minority groups to play a reconciliatory role in Indian politics. They simply cannot afford belligerence of any kind.

A pattern that was visible in the elections in the post-independent phase is also visible now. And that pattern is about the below average political representation of Muslims in Assembly and Parliamentary elections held in Bihar so far. Bihar is one of the few state in India, which had a Muslim chief minister, Abdul Ghafoor, from 2 July 1973 to 11 April 1975. There have been other politicians too who have been playing active role in the state politics belonging to Congress Party and other non-Congress parties like Janata Dal, RJD, Samata Party and later JD(U) and even communist parties. But rarely have they posed any threat to hegemonic leadership of any of these political parties be it Congress or any other dominant OBC caste led parties. Why the communal pot remains boiling is a question defies any sound logic. The only simple answer to such question is that use of religious differences as a tool for political mobilization is an attempt to divert people's attention from real and pressing issues of development, social justice and communal harmony.

In this age of social media (Twitter, WhatsApp, Facebook, etc.), it has become that much easier to spread fake news and foment communal disturbances in the shortest possible time. Be it Ramnavami, Durga Puja and any other Hindu festival with mass participation in their celebrations are being increasingly used by RSS, Bajrang Dal, Vishwa Hindu Parishad and other smaller outfits to indulge in large scale mobilization in the name of collective Hindu pride. Cow protection vigilante groups owing allegiance to RSS and its allied organizations have sprung up all over India leading to regular harassment and even killing of Muslims, Dalits and Adivasis.

A nationalism based on Hindu religious and cultural supremacy is being superimposed which has all the possibility of breaking the country's unity and integrity. Whether it is the question of love jihad or honour killing or suspicious beef-eating or any other such excuse(s) becomes a handy tool for strengthening the larger Hindu solidarity in the name of one nation one pride. Political patronage enjoyed by the vigilante groups leading to impunity and many a times even direct or indirect complicity of the duty-bearers results in perpetrators going scot free even after committing heinous crimes. If the state and several of its agencies which are duty bound to protect and promote law, order, peace and justice are found to be lacking in their commitment then a serious question on the credibility of the state and its agencies should warrant the much-needed course correction or else the idea of India as a secular, modern and democratic nation would always remain doubtful.

In such kind of polarized situation how could the state respond and how could other responsible citizens in the country responds is a question that warrants an immediate answer. How a targeted Muslim or any other minority group would respond would also help in understanding the role that religion plays in political mobilization and government formation. Fear, hatred, violence, loss of lives, destruction of properties and consistent questioning of nationality creates an atmosphere wherein it would be near impossible for any minority to live in peace and dignity. It should be the utmost priority of the state and society at large to promote and protect all human rights for all with dignity and justice not as gift but as an inalienable right for everyone.

Whichever direction the politics takes in Bihar in coming months and years, what is evident is the clear role religion would continue playing in much of politics in Bihar and also elsewhere in the country. However, the question that remains unanswered is how the state would help in safeguarding the secular fabrics of society and polity? If the state and political parties fail in this regard then the democratic ethos and egalitarian principles of Indian Constitution would be endangered. Indian polity cannot and should not be guided by the regressive majoritarian values and norms. It is all the more important to emphasize in this connection that socio-religious-cultural diversity is the strength that drives the idea of India as a secular and modern polity.

Notes

1 B.R. Ambedkar (1979). 'Annihilation of Caste', *Babasaheb Ambedkar Writings and Speeches, Education Department*, Vol. 1, Bombay: Government of Maharashtra, p. 50.
2 B.R. Ambedkar (1979). 'Communal Deadlock and a Way to Solve It', *Babasaheb Ambedkar Writings and Speeches, Education Department*, Vol. 1, Bombay: Government of Maharashtra, p. 377.

References

Ahmad, Imtiaz (1972). 'Religion in Politics: A Comment', *Economic and Political Weekly*, 7(2), pp. 81–6.
Ahmed, Hilal (2015). 'How to (Not) Study Muslim Electoral Responses?' *Studies in Indian Politics*, 3(2), 299–304.
Bharti, Indu (1989). 'Bhagalpur Riots and Bihar Government', *Economic and Political Weekly*, 24(48), pp. 2643–4.
Blair, Harry W. (1973). 'Minority Electoral Politics in a North Indian State: Aggregate Data Analysis and the Muslim Community in Bihar, 1952–1972', *The American Political Science Review*, 67(4), pp. 1275, 1278–87.
Facts Debunk Myth About Political Dominance of Muslims in Seemanchal, India Tomorrow.net, September 18, 2015. Retrieved from www.indiatomorrow.net/eng/facts-debunk-myth-about-political-dominance-of-muslims-in-seemanchal
Jaffrelot, Christophe (1996). *The Hindu Nationalist Movement and Indian Politics, 1925 to the 1990s*, New Delhi: Viking, Penguin Books.
Kumar, Sanjay, Mohammad Sanjeer Alam and Dhananjai Joshi (2008). 'Caste Dynamics and Political Process in Bihar', *Journal of Indian School of Political Economy*, 20(1–2), pp. 1–32.
New Indian Express (2018, March 10). 'Linking Muslim LS Candidate to ISIS Exposes BJP's Communal Mindset'. Retrieved from http://www.newindianexpress.com/nation/2018/mar/10/linking-muslim-ls-candidate-to-isis-exposes-bjps-communal-mindset-rjd-1785070.html.

Nezami, Sheezan (2015, November 10). 'Bihar Election Results 2015: More Muslim Legislators This Time in Assembly', *Times of India*. Retrieved from https://timesofin dia.indiatimes.com/elections/bihar-elections-2015/news/Bihar-election-results-2015-More-Muslim-legislators-this-time-in-assembly/articleshow/49730446.cms.

Report, Election Commission, Bihar Assembly Election Results 2015. Retrieved from https://eci.gov.in/files/file/3904-bihar-2015/.

Report, Election Commission, Government of India, Parliamentary By-Election Results, 2018. Retrieved from https://eci.gov.in/files/file/2547-bihar-9-arariapc/.

Report, Recalling Bhagalpur, PUDR, 1996.

Singh, Santosh (2018, April 2). 'How Communal Pot Has Simmered Bihar Since Nitish Kumar's NDA Return', *Indian Express*. https://indianexpress.com/article/india/bihar-nitish-kumar-communal-clashes-hindu-muslim-violence-bhagalpur-aurangabad-clash-bjp-5119972/.

Thakur, Manindra Nath (2015). 'How Do Muslims Vote? Case of Seemanchal 2014 Parliamentary Election', *Studies in Indian Politics*, 3(1), pp. 81–93.

Wilkinson, Steven I. (2004). *Votes and Violence: Electoral Competition and Ethnic Riots in India*, New York: Cambridge University Press.

Witsoe, Jeffrey (2011). 'Rethinking Post-Colonial Democracy: An Examination of the Politics of Lower Caste Empowerment in North India', *American Anthropologist*, 113(4), pp. 619–33.

12
BEYOND OTHERING
A study of Hindu Political in Gujarat

Dhananjay Rai

Religion plays an important role in politics. The role has been exhibited by its 'impact' on electoral politics. In this explication, ascending (increasing role of religion) and descending (decreasing role of religion) methods become important tools for comprehending the status of religion in politics as to its profound and lesser impacts. The issue, however, is also to map out the formation of subjects which travel beyond 'electoral politics' to decide its outcome. This chapter explains the process by way of 'Hindu Political'. Besides an explanation of the contour of Hindu Political, the chapter focuses on its components like sects and dominant castes (identity as guardians; integration not by confrontation; and new identities as to new gods/goddesses), political communication ('unabashed, unhesitant and unequivocal' commitment), procedural opposition/political opposition (dominant vocabulary in place of vocabulary of political opposition) and dissenting masses/critical masses (non-conversion of dissenting masses into critical masses). In the end, the nature of the relationship between Hindu Political and electoral politics is underlined.

Anatomy of Hindu Political

The idea of Hindu Political goes beyond 'othering'. Othering is a definition for the delineation of categories. It could be an initial stage but bereft of political action. Othering itself does not provide the political action. The categorical clarity is needed to make sense of Hindutva and Political. V.D. Savarkar rejects the notion of Hinduism because of its vagueness. For Savarkar, vagueness is not what is required for Hindutva. 'By an "ism" it is generally meant a theory or a code more or less based on spiritual or religious dogma or system ... Hindutva embraces all the departments of thought and activity of the whole Being of our Hindu race' (Savarkar 1969: 4). However, for being a Hindu, the geographical significance is not only the important criteria. 'For although the first requisite of Hindutva', he points out, 'is that he be a citizen of Hindusthan either by his self or through his forefathers, yet it is not the only requisite qualification of it, as the term Hindu has come to mean much more than its geographical significance' (Savarkar 1969: 84). Those who adhere to three essentials (nation (Rashtra), race (Jati) and civilization (Sanskriti)) of Hindutva, they are Hindu. Savarkar cites the example of the Bohra and Khoja communities.

> But take the case of a patriotic Bohra or a Khoja countryman of ours. He loves our land of Hindusthan as his Fatherland which indisputably is the land of his forefathers. He possesses—in certain cases they do—pure Hindu blood; especially if he is the first convert to Mohammedanism he must be allowed to claim to inherit the blood of Hindu parents. He is an intelligent and reasonable man, loves our history and our heroes; in fact the Bohras and the Khojas as a community, worship as heroes our great ten Avatars only adding Mohammad as the eleventh. He is actually, along with his community subject to the Hindu law—the law of his forefathers. He is, so far as the three essentials of the nation (Rashtra), race (Jati) and civilization (Sanskriti) are concerned, a Hindu. He may differ as regards a few festivals or may add a few more heroes to the pantheon of his supermen or demigods. But we have repeatedly said that difference in details here or emphasis there, does not throw us outside the pale of Hindu Sanskriti. The sub-communities amongst the Hindus observe many a custom, not only contradictory but even, conflicting with the customs of other Hindu communities. Yet both of them are Hindus. So also in the above cases of patriotic Bohra or a Christian or a Khoja, who could satisfy the required qualifications of Hindutva to such a degree as that, why should he not be recognized as a Hindu?
>
> *(Savarkar, 1969: 101-102)*

In fact, this example is followed by the categorical criteria for being a Hindu: for being a Hindu, one has to consider land as *Pitribhu* (Fatherland), land of patriarchs and forefathers Hindu Dharma that is land of *Matribhu* (Motherland) and attachment to sanskriti that is *Punyabhu*. 'We have found that the first important essential qualification of a Hindu is that to him the land that extends from Sindhu to Sindhu is the Fatherland (Pitribhu), the Motherland (Matribhu) the land of his patriarchs and forefathers'.

(Savarkar 1969: 110)

> Hindu Dharma of all shades and schools, lives and grows and has its being in the atmosphere of Hindu culture, and the Dharma of a Hindu being so completely identified with the land of the Hindus, this land to him is not only a Pitribhu but a Punyabhu, not only a fatherland but a holyland.
>
> *(Savarkar 1969: 111)*

After laying down the rules, the principle of exclusions is followed. For Muslims and Christians, although the land is fatherland but cannot be holyland (sanskaras, i.e.

rites and rituals, ceremonies and sacraments, that makes a land a holyland), because their holyland is far off in Arabia or Palestine.

> That is why in the case of some of our Mohammedan or Christian countrymen who had originally been forcibly converted to a non-Hindu religion and who consequently have inherited along with Hindus, a common Fatherland and a greater part of the wealth of a common culture—language, law, customs, folklore and history—are not and cannot be recognized as Hindus. For though Hindusthan to them is Fatherland as to any other Hindu yet it is not to them a Holyland too. Their holyland is far off in Arabia or Palestine.
>
> *(Savarkar, 1969: 113)*

As per Savarkar theorization, priority to holyland over fatherland is natural.

> Their mythology and Godmen, ideas and heroes are not the children of this soil. Consequently their names and their outlook smack of a foreign origin. Their love is divided. Nay, if some of them be really believing what they profess to do, then there can be no choice—they must, to a man, set their Holy-land above their Fatherland in their love and allegiance. That is but natural.
>
> *(Savarkar, 1969: 113)*

So what is the choice? According to Savarkar,

> We are not condemning nor are we lamenting. We are simply telling facts as they stand. We have tried to determine the essentials of Hindutva and in doing so we have discovered that the Bohras and such other Mohammedan or Christian communities possess all the essential qualifications of Hindutva but one and that is that they do not look upon India as their Holyland.
>
> *(Savarkar 1969: 113)*

There the choice before Mohammedan and Christian communities is very limited that 'a choice again which must be a choice of love'.

> This is a choice which our countrymen and our old kith and kin, the Bohras, Khojas, Memons and other Mohammedan and Christian communities are free to make – a choice again which must be a choice of love. But as long as they are not minded thus, so long they cannot be recognized as Hindus.
>
> *(Savarkar 1969: 115)*

Thus the process of subordination and humiliation get finality in Hindutva. Savarkar achieves four important steps towards concretization of Hindutva, a way beyond the 'benign' category of Hindu of Hinduism. First, he establishes 'irreconcilable civilisational contradictions'. This is crucial and required act in the infrastructure of Hindutva. There could be the existence of two or more communities in the landscape but without harmony. Second, 'irreconcilable civilisational contradictions' are further reduced to subordination. This subordination is required for the distribution of resources and public offices. Third, subordination is further reduced to 'humiliation'. Humiliation is defined and practiced in terms of not only construction of hierarchized parity for beings but also constant reminding by way of creating numerous signposts. Fourth, the practice of the principle of 'differencing' is not discrimination. It is very interesting to know that Savarkar does not talk about that *differencing is not exploiting*.

Most of the scholarships on Hindutva politics in Gujarat (or India) have analysed from either of perspectives. Due to this form of theorization, 'liberal constitutionalist' standpoint has appeared which could be theorized as 'constitutionalism versus Hindutva'. In this, it is argued that constitutional standpoint is crucial, even for Hindutva due to immense legitimacy acquired from the former and due to this, later will not dilute the sanctity of the former. Therefore, 'differencing' is not exploitation is popularized because propagation of 'differentiation' is the right, whereas constitutional artefacts will take care of 'exploitation' per se. I argue that this is not a comprehensive analysis of arrival of Hindu Political which has also advanced the original postulations of Hindutva.

In the Hindu Political, the Hindu is Hindutva of Savarkar, whereas political is political action which can be explained by the idea of Carl Schmitt, who coined the term political while writing two most influential books, *The Concept of Political* and *Political Theology*, along with joining the Nazi Party in 1933. His idea of *political* is based on friend and enemy. The *political* is a category which demarcates friend and enemy. His conception of sovereignty is about making decisions along with the idea of exception. The sovereign decisions are final, having a religious miracle. In fact, there is no sovereign, but sovereign acts 'invoked' as 'existential intervention'. The demarcation is very much clear. Politics has both friend and enemy who is with you and who is against you or struggling against whom is identifiable. It is important to note that the fighting and the possibility of death are crucial to call political.

Carl Schmitt remains a bitter critique of liberal democracy where reliance on procedure causes de-politicization and dehumanization of the world. The idea of political adversaries of a clear political theory is required. For Schmitt, the friend-enemy distinction is very necessary to make ourselves clear who 'we' are and 'what is rational' for us. We and rational are defined by friend-enemy formulation. The adversary is not the only enemy, but also a disturber of the peace and thereby designated to be an outlaw of humanity. The political enemy is not necessarily a morally evil, aesthetically ugly, economic competitor. Nonetheless, he/she is a stranger, and being a stranger is enough for existentially different and alien, thereby extreme conflict is possible.

Regarding sovereign and the state of exception, no norm can be valid in an entirely abnormal condition. According to Carl Schmitt,

> To create tranquility, security, and order and thereby establish the normal situation is the prerequisite for legal norms to be valid. Every norm presupposes a normal situation, and no norm can be valid in an entirely abnormal situation.
>
> As long as the state is a political entity this requirement for internal peace compels it in critical situations to decide also upon the domestic enemy.
>
> *(Schmitt 2007: 46)*

The natural corollary of this argument is to defy the *normal* rule of law. He makes explicitly clear in following words: 'I now distinguish not two but *three* types of legal thinking; in addition to the normativist and the decisionist types there is the institutional one' (Schmitt 2005: 2). His answer is: 'All law is 'situational law" (Schmitt 2005: 13) because 'for a legal order to make sense, a normal situation must exist, and he is sovereign who definitely decides whether this normal situation actually exists' (Schmitt 2005: 13). The definition of sovereign becomes extremely important in the context of 'state of exception'. According to him,

> Sovereign is he who decides on the exception.
> Only this definition can do justice to a borderline concept. Contrary to the imprecise terminology that is found in popular literature, a borderline concept is not a vague concept, but one pertaining to the outermost sphere. This definition of sovereignty must therefore be associated with a borderline case and not with routine. It will soon become clear that the exception is to be understood to refer to a general concept in the theory of the state, and not merely to a construct applied to any emergency decree or state of siege.
> *(Schmitt 2005: 5)*

Herbert Marcuse unravels the idea and demand of sacrifice in Carl Schmitt. 'An ontological state of affairs' is 'justified by the mere existence'.

> Thinking of the 'emergency' in which sacrificing one's own life and killing other men are demanded, Carl Schmitt inquires into the reason for such sacrifice:"There is no rational end, no norm however correct, no program however exemplary, no social ideal however beautiful, and no legitimacy or legality that could justify men's killing one another". What, then, remains as a possible justification? Only this: that there is a state of affairs that through its very existence and presence is exempt from all justification, i.e. an 'existential', 'ontological' state of affairs – justification by mere existence (Marcuse, 1968: 21).[1]

Against the backdrop of the previous discussions, the Hindu Political can be defined as follows:

> The Hindu Political decides friend and enemy thereafter elevated Hindus into sovereign position. Hindus are not only sovereign, but their acts also become sovereign. Essentially, acts are sovereign. Any threat or perceived threat to the sovereign invites the state of exception.

In other words, Hindu Political is not a benign nomenclature or definitional or hermeneutic endeavour. It is not a mere segregation category. It creates absolute binary not only for everydayness delineation, but also turning 'othering' into the realms of friend and enemy. It thereafter postulates and gives the status of unquestioning power to the numerical majority that is Hindus in the form of 'sovereign'. In fact, the sovereign position is extended to Hindus. Interestingly, not only being is elevated to the sovereign position but also its acts. Since 'acts' can be defined and performed against the backdrop of binary, it ipso facto derives immunity from laws/rules in the form of the state of exception.

Hindu Political and Gujarat

What makes Gujarat the artillery of Hindu Political? For this comprehension, the political economy of Gujarat becomes extremely crucial. An analysis delinked from the political economy will be an infructuous exercise due to the role played by the former in the contemporary social formation. The initial capitalist formation, demand of cotton in the western world, role of land reform which gave land to 'caretaker' classes/castes, disappearance of communist movement for accentuating contradictions, and beneficiaries of land reform redirecting a portion of their both agricultural surplus and industrial surplus by way of creating massive temples and religious identity for stability of capital and guaranteed income led to the social formation which seeks legitimacy of both capital and social in the name of Hindus.

Since much of Hindutva per se has been widely discussed and discerned, I will be limiting my discussion to Hindu Political which is a recent development but also intertwined with previous attempts. The study of Hindu Political cannot be confined to mere the structural study of the Rashtriya Swayamsevak Sangh which is the concrete signpost of the social formation of the Hindu Political but needs inclusion of various processes through which this social formation makes it presence felt or galvanized. In fact, the RSS remains the cynosure of the Hindu Political but it has gone beyond in form unleashing processes and outcomes.

In Gujarat, the RSS acquires an indomitable position due to constant winning of elections by the Bhartiya Janata Party (BJP), powerful presence of ideological, electoral para-organizations, and absence of formidable ideological opposition. It has not become influential due to *only* organizational per se but also due to its ideological reach which concretizes the Hindu Political. In Gujarat, it has a massive presence in the form of organizing activities in numerous places (more than 550), operating shakhas (around 1,400), more than 1,000 weekly gatherings and having 1,084 mandalas. Its affiliated organizations, besides the Bharatiya Janata Party, are *Bharatiya Kisan Sangh* (it organizes Kisan Mahasammelan, Krushi Maha Pradrashan, 'Gau Seva, Organics forming'; Krushi Mahotsav, Balrama Kumbh Yatra, Sarvagyati Samuh Lagna, Vishva Kisan Kalyan Yagna, Mahila Sammelan, Krishi-Rishi Sanskruti Sangam, Krishi Mela And Parisamvad, Kisan Geeta Parayan, Raktadan Shibir, Krishi Vigyanik And Krushak Sammelan and Sanman Samarambh, Vruksharopan Abhiyan), *Bharatiya Mazdoor Sangh* (rashtra hit, udyog hit and mazdoor hit), *Seva Bharti, Rashtra Sevika Samiti, Akhil Bharatiya Vidyarthi Parishad, Shiksha Bharati, Vishwa Hindu Parishad, Swadeshi Jagaran Manch, Saraswati Shishu Mandir, Vidya Bharati, Vanavasi Kalyan Ashram, Muslim Rashtriya Manch* (Politics divide, culture unite) and *Bajrang Dal*. These are overt organizations incessantly working towards the formation of the Hindu Political. The next three sections unravel the formation of the Hindu Political aided and abetted by the corollary social formation of Gujarat.

Sects and dominant castes

The end of incarnation tradition or the possible future incarnation may have taken different routes in other parts of India. Nonetheless, in Gujarat, numerous sects have rekindled the reincarnation tradition. Hinduism provides a larger framework and sects take religion in a 'renewed' fashion to everydayness.

The success of Hindutva in Gujarat rests on three accounts. First, it convinces sects' identity as guardians of Hinduism. Second, the identities of sects do not operate in a confrontation with each other instead are integrated through the 'grand cause' of Hinduism. In fact, Hindutva does not solve the identity question of sects, but directs them towards strengthening of 'Hindu identity'.[2] In this manner, it is able to use the prosperous material base of each sect leading to the unification of the material basis of sects and identity questions. Third, most groups who are not or never have been part of Hinduism suddenly find the arrival of gods and goddesses in their everyday life world. Moreover, sociology of sects reveals the intrinsic link with Hinduism and Hindutva. Since most sects derive their ontology from Hinduism, their constituents become ipso facto a jugular vein of Hinduism. Sociology of these sects would reveal that all constituents of sects are substantially from dominant castes (Table 12.1). They control all sects on the premise of being inclusive.

Swaminarayan's[3] important sub-sects (like Swaminarayan Sampraday, Bochasanwasi Shri Akshar Purushottam Swaminarayan Sanstha (BAPS) and Shree Swaminarayan Gadi Sansthan) are being controlled by powerful Patidars (a.k.a Patels). Kadva Patels worship Shri Umiya Mataji. Jalalram Bapa is worshipped predominantly by Lohana community. Swadhyayis group focuses on subalterns.[4] ISKCON[5] has a presence among Patels and Banias. Pushtimarg aims at all Hindus and controls powerful *Dwarika*. They all trace their ontology to *Rama, Krishna, Vedic Texts* and one of the forms of *Durgas*. For the subalterns, *Dasha Mata*[6] is being perceived as an important goddess to change the condition (*dasha*) and has the support of the forces of Hindutva (Table 12.1). With huge resources, these upper castes (Patels, Banias, Lohanas and others) comport with Hindutva in the name of Hinduism. This has been done consciously over a considerable period of time in the form of spirituality in Gujarat. Herein, like elsewhere, religion, spirituality and capitalism go hand in hand.

> The miracles of spirituality and consumer capitalism lie in their capacity to mystify the social relations involved in the production, circulation, and consumption of commodities, and to create individual and group identities that secure the dominance of ruling class groups.
>
> *(Mckean 1996: 22–3)*

The powerful sects synonymise the strongest presence of Hindutva in Gujarat. This path goes on to the construction of Hindu Political.

Rhythmic political communication

The early electoral approval of a feudal party (the Swatantra Party; discussed in the coming section)[7] was not only the approval of nature of democratic representation but also eventual shaping up of corporate led discourse in Gujarat. Of late, the most successful business conglomerate takes place in Gujarat biennially known as Vibrant

TABLE 12.1 Major sects (Hindu) in Gujarat

Name	Headquarters	Annotations	Area of influence
Swaminarayan Swaminarayan Sampraday	Vadtal Gaddi and Ahmedabad Gaddi	Theoretically open to all; mainly controlled by Patidars	Originally from central Gujarat; now in nearly all districts of the state and amongst NRGs (non-resident Gujaratis)
Bochasanwasi Shri Akshar Purushottam Swaminarayan Sanstha	Bochasan, Gujarat	Theoretically open to all; mainly controlled by Patidars	
Shree Swaminarayan Gadi Sansthan	Maninagar, Ahmedabad	Theoretically open to all; mainly controlled by Patidars	
Kadva Patidar Kuldevi Shri Umiya Mataji Sansthan	Unjha, Gujarat	Mostly Kadva Patels (Kadva Patidars)	Mehsana, Rajkot, Junagadh, Jamnagar and Bhavnagar
Jalaram Bapa	Rajkot, Gujarat	Mostly Lohanas, but others in Rajkot area	Kutch, Saurashtra
Swadhyay Parivar	Mumbai, Maharashtra	Emphasis on Vedic texts; Mostly deprived sections	Gujarat, Mumbai and abroad wherever Gujarati community is residing
ISKCON	Mayapur, West Bengal	Bania, Patidars and other Upper caste Hindus; urban centric	Entire Gujarat
Pushtimarg/Shrinathji ki Haveli	Shree Nathji Haveli, Nathdwara, Rajsamand, Rajasthan;	Hindus; Dwarika temple is controlled by Pushtimarg	Ahmedabad, Baroda, Surat, Rajkot and urban areas
Gayatri Parivar	Haridwar	Youths target group	Entire Gujarat

Source: Prepared by the author.

Gujarat Global Investor Summit (VGGIS). So far, it has taken place in 2003, 2005, 2007, 2010, 2013, 2015, 2017 and 2019. This serves the much-desired goals of corporate India. The overboard eulogy of the Gujarat government during VGGIS by Indian corporate leaders has been constructed consciously to 'give and take' relationship. The 'givings' are allocation of lands to private industrialist, long terms tax waiving and 'uninterrupted culture' of favours in their business dealings. Takings are 'highest' donations and lobbying for national-international approval.

The 'takings' have also taken a different route. The increasing control over the media by corporate has left no option but to endorse 'Gujarat growth' model. The revenue generation through advertisement and direct control have resulted into maximum coverage to the political right. When the national electronic media sells the 'foreseen dreams', vernacular media in Gujarat emphasise on '*dharti na choro*' (sons of the soil). Contradictory concerns are totally omitted. Anyone questioning '*dharti na choro*' becomes an enemy of the state. 'Indigenized Capital' in Gujarat has successfully remodelled its project behind the 'sons of the soil' nationalism. Moreover, extraordinary capital support at the cost of centrist party has enabled the BJP in Gujarat to use neo-media at different scales. There are serious allegations of manipulation of data by neo-media to enhance the popularity.[8]

The combination of corporate and media has generated rhythmic political commitment. Corporate and media have had a long association. This relation has been largely complementary. However, ruptures have also been noticed, but these remain ephemeral. This election has advanced relationship at a greater level. The rhythmic political communication marks the arrival of media whose commitment to certain political class is 'unabashed, unhesitant and unequivocal'. There is no news on the capitalist – Hindutva combination, but a certain assertion of this particular aphorism. This particular aphorism asserts the need for 'stability'. In the end, corporate and media present rhythmic political communication of stability.

Procedural opposition/political opposition

The Hindu Political is furthered more in the absence of 'political opposition'. The sine qua non of the political space in Gujarat is the absence of 'political' opposition. The procedural opposition (existence by way of constitutional necessity) for fulfilling the minimum required need of liberal parliamentary democracy is present. Nonetheless, political opposition has remained absent in Gujarat since a long time.[9] There are three important issues in Gujarat, which have waited for the arrival of political opposition to confront the issues. However, so far, the emergence of political opposition remains evasive. More or less, mainstream ruling party and mainstream opposition party share similar policies and programmes. It has generated dominant vocabulary in place of the vocabulary of political opposition.

For analytical evidence, issues could broadly be divided into three categories. First, in Gujarat, the absence of land rights, an increasing number of daily wage labourers, casualization of work, contractualization and lowest minimum wages, and an eviction notice to Agariya (salt-pan workers) community are being construed as components/prerequisites of 'entrepreneurship' in dominant vocabulary. Second, dominant vocabulary perceives caste assertion, underrepresentation of the weaker sections in the public sphere, prevalent pervasive endogamy, regimentation of caste through the sectarian turn of religion and de-recognition of tribes as social harmony. Third, a decline of protest by significant weaker sections, political 'relinquishment' of minorities, the political absence of large unions in all sectors; the importance of expert and technocrat over representatives; absence of open debate on public issues, dysfunctional panchayats are 'good development' because 'politics is bad'. The presence of political opposition would have created an alternative vocabulary. In other words, the vocabulary of political opposition would perceive first, second and third category as 'lack of economic freedom', 'marginalization' and 'absenting the political' (Table 12.2).

It should be noticed that democracy must become a space whereby agonistic pluralism could be evinced. According to Ernesto Laclau and Chantal Mouffe, agonistic pluralism zeroes on the essentiality of political conflicts and channelization towards the betterment of the society (Laclau and Mauffe 2001). Relations of

TABLE 12.2 Signposts, dominant vocabulary and vocabulary of political opposition in Gujarat

Some important signposts	Dominant vocabulary	Vocabulary of political opposition
Absence of land rights, increasing number of wage labourers, informalization of workers, contractualization, lowest minimum wages, eviction notice to Agariya (salt-pan workers) community	Entrepreneurship	Lack of economic freedom
Caste assertion, underrepresentation of weaker sections in public sphere, prevalent endogamy, regimentation of caste through sectarian turn of religion, de-recognition of tribes	Social harmony	Marginalization
The decline of protest by significant weaker sections; political 'relinquishment' of minorities; political absence of large unions in all sectors; the importance of expert and technocrat over representatives; absence of open debate on public issues; dysfunctional panchayats.	Politics is bad	Absenting political

Source: Prepared by the author.

power and antagonisms are erased and we are left with the typical liberal illusion of a 'pluralism without antagonism' (Mauffe 2000: 20). 'The status quo has become naturalized and made into the way "things really are"' (Mauffe 2000: 5). The real purpose the political can be recapitulated as 'there comes a time when one needs to decide on which side to stand in their agonistic confrontation' (Mauffe 2000: 15). Therefore, absence or presence of political opposition decides the fate of democracy.

Dissenting masses/critical masses

The explanation of non-conversion of dissenting masses into critical masses lies in the political history of the Gujarat landscape. Industrialization and spreading of cotton mills in and around Ahmedabad led to the massive demand of the working class in the early 20th century. The formation of critical masses could be attributed to the militant labour movement. In Gujarat, Gandhi attempted to link the labour issue to the national movement on two accounts: direct engagement and politics of boycott. His most important intervention in Ahmadabad Labour Strike (1918) and formation of *the Majoor Mahajan Sangh* (TLA) (1920) would impact the eventual protest culture in Gujarat. Gandhi's siding with labour made them powerful in the Ahmedabad Labour Strike, but it had a price as well.

The Majoor Mahajan Sangh had, unlike Gandhi, reduced the protest culture to the culture of collaboration, reconciliation and peaceful coexistence, snatching away the criticality which is intrinsic to protest culture. In fact, 'the TLA almost never used the strike as a weapon in a labour dispute' (Spodek 2010: 143). Second, TLA reduced labour issues as a local issue, delinking with national and international concern. Thereafter, protests have seen primarily 'welfarist' measure rather than political. With the decline of Gandhi's influence and the disappearance of Gandhism, the space was occupied by the political right. Therefore, the dissenting masses could not convert into critical masses.

In Gujarat, presence of dissenting masses is exhibited in the form of protest against land allocation to NIRMA cement factory, acquiring land for tourism near 'Statue of Unity', Adani SEZ (Special Economic Zone), Maruti Plant, Mandal-Becharaji project/Dholera Special Investment Region (DSIR), MithiVirdi Nuclear Project to Adivasi Movement (land rights, implementation of Forest Rights Act 2006, Statue of Unity, UKAI Dam (Tapi District), Narmada Dam) in Gujarat. These dissenting masses could change the political plateau of the state. However, due to collaboration, reconciliation and peaceful coexistence aphorism, these dissent masses could not become critical masses (Table 12.3 and Figure 12.1).

Hindu Political and electoral politics

The combination of the trio (Hinduism, sects and Hindutva) has constructed 'Hindu Political' which has decisively voted on identitarian line. Gujarat has had apathy towards electing minority, particularly Muslim representative right after the 1962 Lok Sabha elections. The nationalist discourse's recourse to referring particular

TABLE 12.3 Dissenting masses in Gujarat

Protest against	Area of protest	Involvement
Land allocation to NIRMA Cement Factory	Mahuva, Bhavnagar	12 villages
Acquiring land for tourism near Statue of Unity	Narmada District	76 Villages
Adani SEZ (Special Economic Zone)	Kachchh	Four main and numerous villages
Maruti Plant	Ahmedabad and Mehasana	44 villages
Mandal-Becharaji project/ Dholera Special Investment Region (DSIR)	Ahmedabad, Bhavnagar and Kutch districts	Affected 22 villages; support from 36 villages
Mithi Virdi Nuclear Project	Affected villages: Jaspara, Mandva, Khadpar and Mithivirdi	30 villages (Bhavnagar)
Adivasi Movement in Gujarat (Land rights, Implementation of Forest Rights Act 2006, Statue of Unity, UKAI Dam (Tapi District), Narmada Dam)	Surat, Bharuch, Dangs, Valasad, Panchmahal, Vadodara	All-important Adivasi Organizations
Atrocities against Dalits	Entire Gujarat	All progressive organizations

Source: Prepared by the author.

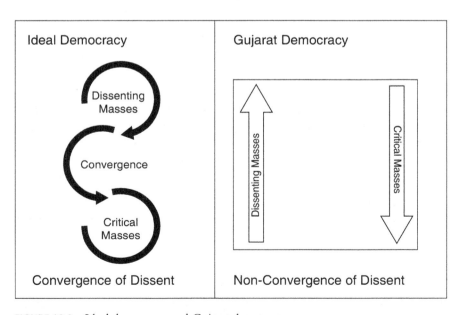

FIGURE 12.1 Ideal democracy and Gujarat democracy

religion had created binaries, which has been reflecting until contemporary time. It is inaccurate to suggest that Muslim winnability has suddenly dried up. The long process of constructing Hindu Political has caused the marginalization of minorities, especially in the electoral arena.

Conservative and official feudal political party, the Swatantra Party (1959–74), though headed by C. Rajagopalachari, had a strong footing in the state of Gujarat. K.M. Munshi, Minoo Masani and Piloo Mody were important signatures of the Swatantra Party from Gujarat. The party had four (total 18 seats), 11 (total 44 seats) and two Lok Sabha seats in the Third (1962), Fourth (1967) and Fifth (1971) Lok Sabhas. The Swatantra Party remained the second largest party in the 1962 (26 out of 154 seats with 24% votes) and in the 1967 (66 seats out of 168 seats; 38.19%) State Assembly elections in Gujarat. In fact, before the emergence of the BJP, Swatantra Party and Bhartiya Jana Sangh had a large presence. This was the early phase of constructing Hindu Political in Gujarat.

Since feudalism and Hindutva constitute an inseparable link, their presence has always rejected the even benign presence of 'significant others'. The early conservatism and massive use of religious signposts have ensured the disappearance of Muslim representation. Muslim representation in the Lok Sabha from Gujarat has always been dismal. Muslims constitute approximately 10% of the total population of Gujarat.

In so far, there have been three individuals (Joharaben Akabarbhai Chavada, 1962, Banaskantha Constituency; Patel Ahmedbhai Mohmadbhai aka Ahmed Patel, 1977 (Broach), 1980 (Broach) and 1984 (Broach); Ehsan Jafri,[10] 1977 (Ahmadabad)) who have been elected a total of five times. In Gujarat, total 356 Lok Sabha MPs have been elected right from the Third Lok Sabha till the 16th Lok Sabha. MPs from reserved constituencies have been 80. Excluding reserved constituencies, Muslim MPs' percentage has been 1.81% (of total percent of general seats). Against total seats, their percentage comes down further that is 1.40% (Table 12.4).

The Hindu Political is directly linked with the state power. The idea of the state of exception cannot be executable sans 'governmental power'. The Hindutva per se despite all definitional demarcation and creation of hierarchies remains silence on how to utilise the state power and what is to be done with 'binaries'. The Hindu Political fills the deficit and create infrastructure for the state power towards galvanization of 'state of exception' and sovereign position. In democracy, this has been done through the creation of representation deficit. This representation deficit is an outcome of the combination of the trio ('homogenized Hinduism', sects and castes, and Hindutva) which has constructed 'Hindu Political' which decisively votes on an identitarian line.[11]

Conclusion

This chapter emphasizes the need to delineate the difference between Hindutva and the Hindu Political. The Hindutva per se does not outline the concrete of infrastructure of it and also remains a cultural category which is celebrated as to 'differentiation' is an innocuous exercise. The Hindu Political is linked with the state power while

TABLE 12.4 Muslim representation in Lok Sabha from Gujarat

Year/s	Total constituencies	Reserved constituencies	General constituencies	Muslim representation in Lok Sabha	Muslim population and representation in Lok Sabha		
					Population	Percentage (only general seats)	Percentage (all seats)
1962	22	4 (2SC, 2ST)	18	1 (1962)	9.5%	5.55%	4.54%
1967, 1971	24	5 (2SC, 3ST)	19	0 (1967) and 0 (1971)	9.5%	0%	0%
1977–2014	26	6 (2SC, 4ST)	20	2 (1977), 1 (1980), 1 (1984), 0 (1989), 0 (1991), 0 (1996), 0 (1998), 0 (1999), 0 (2004), 0 (2009), 0 (2014)	10%	1.81%	1.74%
Total	356 (22+48 (24 × 2) + 286 (26 × 11)	80 (4+10 (5 × 2) + 66 (6 × 11)	276 (18+38 (19 × 2) + 220 (20 × 11)	5	10%	1.81%	1.40%

Source: Prepared by the author.

creating the political category of friend and enemy. In Gujarat, this has been achieved by organized Hindutva groups by way of sects and dominant castes, rhythmic political communication, absenting political opposition and non-convergence of critical masses into dissenting masses. This has significantly reduced, inter alia, the political power of Muslims around which the Hindu Political has been conceptualized and concretized.

Notes

1 This was also discussed by Tracy B. Strong in his foreword to *The Concept of the Political*. See (Strong 2007: xvii).
2 On this point, Sharda Sugirtharajah suggests that 'these various organizations are a disparate group, competing with each other and at times even contradicting each other. They come out of different cultural, political, social, and hermeneutical contexts, but the undergirding principle which binds them together is the desire to project an acceptable face of Hinduism' (Sugirtharajah 2003: 134).
3 According to Raymond Brady Williams, 'Swaminarayan Hinduism is on the move. In India it is developing new temples, structures, and institutions in its home state of Gujarat and expanding into urban areas where Gujarati residents provide a secure base from which it expands among other ethnic groups' (2001: 235).
4 Pandurang Shastri Athavale's, founder of Swadhyaya (literally meaning self-study) 'source of inspiration... [were] the Vedas, the smritis and the Bhagwad Gita' (Srivastava 1998: 20).
5 According to the ISKCON website, ISKCON belongs to the *Gaudiya-Vaishnava sampradaya*, a monotheistic tradition within the Vedic and Hindu cultural traditions (Source: iskcon.org; retrieved 29 May 2014).
6 The immersion of the idol of the 'mata' has become a public display involving fanfare and beating of drums only in the 21st century; usually, the immersion of the idol takes place in the wee hours when the upper castes are 'asleep', and without much display of noise. There is a distinct caste/class divide.
7 Surprisingly, the Swatantra Party was popularized as a liberal party fighting for liberal rights and freedom.
8 Google is being accused by manipulating search ranking to affect the undecided voters by Robert Epstein of the American Institute for Behavioural Research and Technology, California; http://aibrt.org/POS-real_time_display/rt_detail.php.
9 The BJP came to power in 1996.
10 Ehsan Jafri was assassinated on 28 February 2002, in what became infamously known as Gulbarg Society massacre. This cannot be explained only through focusing on the absence of 'civic life' (Varshney 2003) or 'riot-production' by the political system (Brass 2003) responsible for such a pogrom. Besides combining both factors, any explanation must focus on the creation of identity through a religious system which is not a benign realm.
11 In a similar vein, Martha Nussbaum's differentiation between 'living with equal respect' and 'living with homogeneity' becomes crucial to comprehend the process of othering. According to her, "... the real clash is not a civilizational one between "Islam" and "the West," but instead a clash within virtually all modern nations – between people who are prepared to live with others who are different, on terms of equal respect, and those who seek the protection of homogeneity, achieved through the domination of a single religious and ethnic tradition" (Nussbaum 2007: ix).

References

Brass, P.R. (2003). *The Production of Hindu-Muslim Violence in Contemporary India*, New Delhi: Oxford University Press.
Laclau, E. and C. Mauffe (2001). *Hegemony and Socialist Strategy Towards a Radical Democratic Politics*, London: Verso.

Marcuse, H. (1968). *Negations: Essays in Critical Theory*, Translations from the German by Jeremy J. Shapiro, London: Allen Lane, Penguin Press.
Mauffe, C. (2000). *The Democratic Paradox*, London: Verso.
Mckean, L. (1996). *Divine Enterprise: Gurus and the Hindu Nationalist Movement*, London: University of Chicago Press.
Nussbaum, M.C. (2007). *The Clash Within: Democracy, Religious Violence and India's Future*, Cambridge, MA: The Belknap Press of Harvard University Press.
Savarkar, V.D. (1969). *Hindutva: Who Is a Hindu?* Bombay: Veer Savarkar Prakashan. Retrieved from https://archive.org/details/hindutva-vinayak-damodar-savarkar-pdf/page/n1
Schmitt, C. (2005). *Political Theology: Four Chapters on the Concept of Sovereignty*, Translation by George Schwab; Foreword by Tracy B. Strong, Chicago: University of Chicago Press.
Schmitt, C. (2007). *The Concept of the Political*, Translation, Introduction, and Notes by George Schwab; Foreword by Tracy B. Strong, Chicago: University of Chicago Press.
Spodek, H. (2010). 'From Gandhi to Modi: Ahmedabad', in (eds.), Edward Simpson and A. Kapadia, *The Idea of Gujarat: History, Ethnography and Text*, New Delhi: Orient BlackSwan.
Srivastava, R.K. (1998). 'Introduction', in (ed.), R.K. Srivastava, *Vital Connections, Self, Society, God: Perspectives on Swadhyaya*, New York: Weatherhill, Inc.
Strong, T.B. (2007). 'Foreword: Dimensions of the New Debate Around Carl Schmitt', in *Carl Schmitt: The Concept of the Political*, Translation, Introduction, and Notes by George Schwab; Foreword by Tracy B. Strong, Chicago: University of Chicago Press.
Sugirtharajah, S. (2003). *Imagining Hinduism: A Postcolonial Perspective*, London: Routledge.
Varshney, A. (2003). *Ethnic Conflict and Civic Life: Hindus and Muslims in India*, New Haven, CT: Yale University Press.
Williams, R.B. (2001). *An Introduction to Swaminarayan Hinduism*, Cambridge: Cambridge University Press.

13
INDIAN POLITICAL SPACE AND RELIGION

Perspectives and exploring alternatives

Y. S. Alone

The objective of this chapter is to understand the nature of Indian politics as being practiced and the ways it operates as part of the political principles. I would like to state that I am not a political scientist but wish to unfold certain phenomenon of functioning as part of public and political perceptions. Understanding a phenomenon is a constant process and at the same time, is not a static process. It keeps changing, constantly moving all the time. I propose to unfold the very logic of politicality of perception and its resultant discourse of understanding through the aspects of politicality that goes into the making of political democracy through the philosophical doctrine called *pratityasamvutpāda*, which means theory of dependent origination/co-dependent origination (Digha Nikāya). It has been explained in terms of cause and effect theory. It is a Buddhist philosophical tool developed by the Buddha to explain the phenomenon, which has been extensively applied and elaborated to interrogate various aspects of life including philosophy. The *pratityasamvudpāda* also came to be known as the doctrine of the *shunyata* (i.e. idea of nothingness) – that nothing is permanent and everything undergoes constant change. In the historical past, it emerged as an important marker for understanding of the Buddhist theories, and in this case as a tool of analysis through my own conceptual formulation of 'protected ignorance'. 'Protected ignorance' is aimed at interrogating the knowledge formation process where the intention and purpose of such an exercise is needed to be judged whether the knowledge produced by various means is aimed at killing ignorance or to maintain ignorance and hence, consequently, such an act and its outcome becomes 'protected ignorance'. While explaining the *pratityasamvutpada*, the Buddha explains the nature of characteristics that gets conveyed through words, for example,

> As there is birth, therefore there are *jatis* (different types), and each have different characteristics, i.e. of *Devas* – *devatva* (*devas* to the *deva* state), *Gandharva*

– *gandhartva* (of *Gandharvas* to the state of *Gandharvas*), *yakśas-yakśatva* (of *yakśas* to the *yakśa* state), *bhutas-bhutatva* (of ghost to state of ghost), *manuśya-manuśatvata* (of humans to the human state), *pakśis-pakshitva* (of birds to the bird state), of reptiles to the reptile state, etc.

(Walshe 1987: 224–5 [Digha Nikāya, trans.])

Though they are linguistic connotations but are evolved and dependent on the types of characteristics. Types are defined on the lines of peculiarities. Peculiarities are explained certain linguistic connotations which we try to understand the nature of properties a particular signifier carries. They are interdependent. They have become part of our everyday usages and therefore, the idea of word carries meaning only at an accepted level, which operates largely at mutual collective. It also carries consciousness. In the Buddhist philosophy there is a greater emphasis on the *chetanā* (consciousness) as mentioned in the *mahaparinibbānsutta* in the *Digha Nikāya* (Walshe 1987: 231–78 [*Mahaprinibbāna sutta, Digha Nikāya, English* trans.]). Consciousness becomes key to understand functioning of mind. There are only two forms of knowledge (*pramāṇas*): perception (*pratyakṣa*) and inference (*anumāna*). The object of *pratyakṣa* is a unique particular and the object of *anumāna* is a universal. Such a critical framework is proposed to examine the ways in which political consciousness governs in the contemporary times of modern democracies.

There are numerous formulations in which the Indian political sphere is understood and analyzed only to touch upon the events that have emerged in the political democracy. There are many who would like trace the history of political democracy in multiple terms such as class struggles, caste struggle, gender struggle, power struggle, environmental struggle, economic struggle, consumerism, cultural capitalism and so forth. Dimensions of political manifestations are many. Considering the fact that there has been an attempt to see political development in India as mere power of party politics and the nature of shifts that have taken place. However, while I do not agree to such structured knowledge formulations, politics in India has to be located in the various aspects of consciousness and how political sphere also maintains and generates certain kind of consciousness. Many pre- and post-independent personas are read like a methodological exercise to claim rooted in the land or nativeness to certain thought process, and at the same time, such personas are even taught as 'great political thinkers of India'. With the coming of the Indian Constitution, participatory and representative democracy became possible. The constitution being a collective document, a role of Dr. B.R. Ambedkar and his imprint in its making is visible in many ways. It may be observed that Ambedkar was in favour of making voting a fundamental right, whereas the claimed iron-man of India, Mr. Sardar Patel, was completely opposed to it (Vundru 2017: 139–40). When Ambedkar introduced the Hindu Code Bill, only a few were in favour whereas many were opposed to it, including Sarojini Naidu, Sardar Patel, Pandit Madan Mohan Malviya and so forth (Ambedkar 1995: 791–1312). Therefore, the political sphere and politicality has to be seen from the Ambedkar and anti-Ambedkar perspective. It would mean that how consciousness is operative to the logic of Ambedkar and anti-Ambedkar. One has to understand the conscious nature of political domain and hence it becomes pertinent to examine the nature of consciousness that shapes the political sphere and political public. Ambedkar and anti-Ambedkar does not mean political parties, but a critical tool where 'representation for transformation' and 'towards transformation' as an enabling process is a key to political consciousness that constitutes as Ambedkar political consciousness whereas representation to maintain structures of exploitation as well as that of normative as sacred and divine which does not create a transformation is anti-Ambedkar. Thus, it is this political sphere which empowers to unfold the creepy nature of political consciousness.

Dr. Ambedkar was the first to present a critic of imperial discourses, Brahmanical discourses and socialist discourses which may be understood as Marxist discourses (Alone 2007: 263–4). His opposition and critic has emerged from cardinal principles of philosophical doctrine, therefore, Dr. Ambedkar viewed the very importance of philosophy. For him 'the purpose of philosophy is to reconstruct the world' (Ambedkar 1987a: 286), therefore, one observes very different understandings in his writings where it is aimed at creating an enabling process the ways in which Buddhist logic had. Ambedkar writes in 'Annihilation of Caste' that 'there is nothing fixed, nothing eternal, nothing *sanatan*; that everything is changing, that change is the law of life for individuals as well as for society' (Ambedkar 1979: 79). Later when he writes 'Buddha and Karl Marx', he says, 'Nothing is permanent or *sanatan*. Everything is subject to change. Being is always Becoming' (Ambedkar 1987a: 442). It clearly shows as to how he followed the Buddhist understanding of the law of impermanence. For a political scientist, it becomes difficult to grapple with the idea of 'consciousness of being' as he/she is directed by the normative his/her discipline/sphere of thinking has produced over a period of time. Though the post-modern philosophy claims to dismantle the presuppositions but many times the writers legitimize those presuppositions. It is very daunting task to understand presuppositions in the political domain of functioning as well as that of political memory. Presuppositions are operative means of concealing ignorance of realization of power to change as well as make the structure works for eradication of sufferings and bring in structural changes accordingly. In the democratic political elections, presuppositions are determining factors towards getting power without going into its consequences. While Foucault and others have analyzed as to how our consciousness is evolved as a part of historical reconstruction and truth is constructed, he discusses latent structure of knowledge as 'episteme' (i.e. a group of assumptions, prejudices, and mind-set) that structured thought of any particular epoch. Foucault observes,

> It seems to me that one might also carry out an analysis of the same type on political knowledge. One would try to show whether the political behaviour of a society, a group, or a class is not shot through with a particular, describable discursive practice. This positivity would obviously not coincide either with the political theories of the period or with economic determinations: it would define the element in politics that can become an object

of enunciation, the forms that this enunciation may take, the concepts that are employed in it, and the strategic choices that are made in it. Instead of analysing this knowledge – which is always possible – in the direction of the episteme that it can give rise to, one would analyse it in the direction of behaviour, struggles, conflicts, decisions, and tactics.

(Foucault 1972: 194)

Lourdunathan (2017) explains an importance of episteme and its relation within Indian situation. Thus, it is evident that episteme is embedded within. It becomes inseparable entity. However, it becomes part of problematic as to how do we subscribe to such a phenomenon. Nevertheless, I would prefer to use the term 'normative' instead of episteme as embedded within is associated with one's consciousness. Consequently a fundamental question of importance of how do we evolve our consciousness? Our consciousness is dependent on the sensory perception/organs. Hence it is also equally inter-dependent/co-dependent.

At the same time, analyzing our own 'normative' becomes equally important to understand as to how our sensorial world as well as sphere of political world get constructed, which comes through consciousness. In the colonial India, political mobilization tool had distinct religious practices and consequently, public sphere in India has also acquired religious practices as part of cultural identity, thus a meta-narrative of Hinduness become part of identity and gets propagated by the Brahmanical polity and gets established as 'normative'. Pertinent question that may be raised in this context would be how 'idea of homogeneity' gets advocated as religious expression of the cultural tradition' consequently becoming political too of mobilization. Secularism as means of modern democracies in dealing with religious ethos and political group along with their structured realities have been part of political analysis in understanding nature of 'secularism' as practice of the democratic nation state. Societal practices based on religious 'principles and rules' have been existing simultaneously despite the fact that constitutional principles are in conflict with the religious principles and rules. Consequently, claimed project of enlightenment reducing into the mere desired objectives without paying attention to the structures of ideology and their physical manifestations. Structural societal problems remained in isolation. While Ambedkar viewed caste as a deep-rooted problem of the Indian masses, Gandhi viewed caste as a problem only in terms of untouchability. While summing up the debate between Gandhi and Ambedkar as has been offered by likes of Partha Chatterjee, Aakash Singh Rathore observes that

> Chatterjee's problem is not the inability to resolve the contradictions between Gandhi and Ambedkar, but to attempt to resolve them through univocal or homogenizing discourses, pegging their lives and work to some fixed conception or narrative that plays into the dominant political theoretical paradigms and its accompanying categories, such as 'civil society' and 'citizenship' and so on. Chatterjee's approach clearly supersedes that of Guha's historical reconciliation, in so far as the latter attempts precisely to forge a

univocity out of heterogeneity under the development of an encompassing historical narrative.

(Rathore 2017: 179)

Similarly, those who claimed to be political thinkers of that time and later also had developed similar lenses. Their perception is governed by the normative in which they grew and self-reflexivity could never become critical framework to understand the structures of inequality. Dr. Ambedkar in 'Annihilation of Caste' mentions the root cause of Hindu philosophical doctrine that affected the Indian masses and therefore, his logical use of idea of impermanence could not be understood to the analysis of the Indian society. By envisaging state as an agency of change, Dr. Ambedkar addressed eradication of sufferings that are structural in nature. As politicality is centred on mere quest for power, political means as a systemic tool of transformation remained the most undesired pursuit. It is in this context one has to unfold the normative. There are several normative that are being practiced in the Indian society hate, anger, and structured idea of superiority along with belief in divine and sacred is integral part of normative. Exercising vote gradually turned out to be a practice of normative without applying choice for and reflect the idea of 'being'. Being' is a very conscious choice of righteousness towards reasoning. The very idea of 'being is becoming' is embedded in the consciousness of being righteous at moral and ethical level, therefore, the observation of Ashis Nandy becomes a problem as religion and political are intertwined.

Ashis Nandy positions himself as anti-secular, proclaims secularism as a failed project and considered religious affiliations as part of the problem. While making his stand, he writes that 'western meaning of secularism – is a hidden political hierarchy . . . this hierarchy makes a fourfold classification of the political actors in the subcontinent'. He observed 'three different hierarchies', they are '(1) those who are believers neither in public nor in private. (2) those who choose not to appear as believers in public despite being devout believing in private. (3) who are believers in public but do not believe in private' (Nandy 2004: 328–9). He cited examples of politician in all the three categories. Interestingly, public display of political leaders going to Godmans or Babas and *Kumbha melas* (religious ritualistic gathering for taking deep in river water to wash off their evil deeds and gain merit on specific days of gatherings at Allahabad, Nasik and Ujjain), gathering did not become part of the examples. According to him, 'when Bhimrao Ambedkar converted to Buddhism, he probably entered in the third category from the first' (Nandy 2004: 328–9). For the first category, he cited the example of Jawaharlal Nehru, but also add that he came to know recently that Nehru too was believer in many ritualistic practices. It is also a well-established fact that scientific communities and establishments follow rituals and belief system in their scientific institutions, therefore claims of being scientific becomes a dubious claim in India. Thus, Ashis Nandy demonstrates that going or expressing religious affiliations become part of anti-secularism. Such an understanding also poses considerable problems to create a dialogue among the groups of religious communities. The moral principles attached to behavioural practices perhaps indicate religious behaviour, which will be lacking no morality towards the self in the public sphere. Political parties have been engaged in granting generously to organize a *Kumbha* as well as endowment grants to temple institutions, however, study of such a phenomenon does not become part of understanding the nature of self that is deeply involved in diverting state money towards such incompetent projects in the realm of rationality. Dr. Ambedkar considered Dhamma to be a Saddhamma as social and not personal (Ambedkar 1992: 316) and hence, when social is evoked it becomes very important to see what religious communities follow as principles and rules. The nature of behaviours is paramount. Deepak Kumar observes that:

> An imperial rationalist discourse showed the Indians how rationalism could be turned against the European themselves. Rationalism was seen as something inherent in human nature rather than a European 'specialty' and was taken as a mark of progress independent from Europeanization. Gradually rational explanations of the physical phenomena and the new concepts of democracy and secularism were slowly assimilated. But this process was not linear or smooth; it had its own inherent disabilities which came into open during partition of the country and continued to similar thereafter.
>
> (Kumar 2016: 164)

Deepak Kumar traces the historical conflict of the religious communities in dealing with the scientific knowledge and its amalgamation with the tradition. Nevertheless, how the idea of homogeneity of tradition as a part of unification project to maintain a hold over every social and scientific establishment somehow are silently missed in the analysis and therefore, the non-Brahmanical thinkers and politician's opposition to the claimed tradition of Dharma does not become part of 'knowledge'. One good example is sufficient to prove that though Railways was brought to India and imperial and Anglo-Indian community constituted engineering key maintenance staff, but with gradual coming of the Indians mainly form the upper caste and working caste communities, the Railway workshops began to celebrate Vishvakarma day or started performing '*pooja*' in those places. Thus tradition gets rooted in the workplaces which claimed to be away from religious domain were no more so and public display of faith and tradition became integral part of the social space. Many social codes also get followed in integral work places. Therefore, Ambedkar makes specific distinction of social and personal into formulations of 'rules and principles'. For Ambedkar, 'morality is *dhamma* and *dhamma* is morality' (Ambedkar 1992: 322), consequently, moral-self becomes a basis to initiate a dialogue that will always have collective consciousness towards morality and ethicality.

As has been mentioned earlier that the political sphere in India can be understood by singular formulation of Ambedkar and anti-Ambedkar, how do we understand and analyze this particular phenomenon through the critical framework of protected ignorance based of the Buddhist logic of 'dependent origination'? 'Protected ignorance' is an everyday phenomenon but it also becomes intentional phenomenon as for the fact that any production of knowledge has to be analyzed from the point of view of 'killing ignorance'. More than often, process of knowledge formations as well as generating righteous consciousness becomes problematic as the very process is intended not to unfold the oppressions as well as mental sphere of slavery and a belief in the existence of being given by the divinity as well as fate.

Display of faith and right to profess ones religion is granted under the constitution, which would indicate the nature pluralistic society India has and every citizen gets protected under this clause. Public becomes a centre of attention as it involves beyond individuals. While observing nature of transformation and the public sphere, it appears that the globalization is also pushing the display of public visuality towards certain forms of anarchy.

> The transformation of public sphere has been breath taking and fundamental- wherein the values of the constitution have prevail over any other considerations. However, transformation of the public sphere remains majorly constrained and farce unless there is also a transformation within the private sphere – the sphere which governs the day to day affairs of the people and the national citizens in their daily lives.
>
> (Jambulkar 2017: 242)

Though the preceding observation has been made in the context of the common civil code, but as one can make out that the issue as being deeply related to the religious injunctions, there is a conflict between the private and public. Public being part of politicality, political parties too have been associated with religious affiliations. It is not that only one singular formulation has been instrumental in forming political outfits, but rather it is a quest of aspirations that propelled the formation of religious groups into a political party. Diversity in the Indian society gets absorbed into political democratic process without shading its structured characteristics of hierarchy. Subrata Mitra has rightly observed that

> The political diversity of India is also enriched by its modern associations, trade unions, and all kinds of movements in which people come together for the purpose of obtaining material advantage. Group formation has frequently led to inter-community strife, initiated or exacerbated by groups promoting their shared interest. Social solidarity has become an important means of political mobilization.
>
> (Mitra 2014: 80)

The social mobilization has been a key to formation of the political group but religious mobilization also important means to form a political party without formal claims. Buddhist population in Ladakh, Assam and Arunachal had no political party and did not strive to have a political outfit whereas the neo-Buddhist floated many parties and remained visible only at conscious level and never entered into a conflict with constitution. Their religious sphere is governed by the idea of Dhamma understood by Ambedkar.

Memory becomes important means to remember as well as to understand the unique particulars associated with the representation. As political power is seen from the communitarian perspectives, the feudal rulers remained focus of attention in the colonial India, on the other hand, post-colonial India gave rise to many aspired communities to have their say in political sphere. One of the important means of becoming a group is based on caste as well as religion of the caste. Formation of such political parties through instrument of mobilization operates to consolidate their aspirations to political power. When it comes to the ethos of Buddhist logic, it is of rationality and creates a rational conscious being to be a '*samyak* society' (righteousness). In the philosophical sphere, rationality if often construed as 'relative'. Indeed, rationality is always relative. However, I submit that it depends on its objectives. If the objective of the rationality is to ward of ignorance then it becomes righteous rationality and if the objective of the rationality is not to kill ignorance, it becomes unrighteous rationality and hence it becomes 'protected ignorance'. Project of enlightenment in India during colonial rule always had religious sphere and continued in post-colonial India. The private is no more a private but a public entity. Buddhist ideas of celebrations had no mythological backup to display its public visuality as project of irrationalities whereas the dominant group of claimed Hinduness did not mind to display publicly any irrational celebrations. Hence, post-colonial India also witnessed spurts of religious holidays based on the Christian celebration of Christmas. Worth is also to take cognizance of Muslim League parties and the issue of Muslim representation in the recent times. Therefore, politics in colonial and post-colonial India has always been that of Ambedkar and anti-Ambedkar consciousness. The anti-Ambedkar consciousness is represented by Congress, BJP, left, Samajwadi Party, the whole of the Janata family and so forth. Political revolution is an unfinished agenda of the left as well as some groups such as *janata parivar* (JP). The JP movement is deemed as a political revolution, but in fact Jayaprakash Narayan was a devout Gandhian and hence transformation as alternative politics did not become a theme. It may be observed that the very political mobilization emanated from the religious caste position, the revival movement had a damning impact to think of an alternative.

What do I mean then by the Ambedkar and anti-Ambedkar consciousness of political sphere and a political memory? Ambedkar by adhering to the Buddhist logic always aspired to change the society and bring social transformation to create a '*samyak* society'. The 'anti-Ambedkar' has been represented by many political party in India has no agenda of social transformations as well as eradication of day-to-day sufferings of the masses. Shaping one's political sphere is very fundamental to investigate the nature of consciousness. Consciousness in Indian society being that of hatred, belief in hierarchy and absolute hold over any kind of resources as well as access to power, transformation becomes a difficult process. Here rational being becomes an 'aspired category' as well as a 'imagined category' as for the fact that without addressing presuppositions, it is being 'aspired for', holding the consciousness of self-desire structured in the social positioning. As noted earlier, the personal and non-personal merge and emerge as singular in order to be a functional entity embedded in a non-rational political consciousness to resolve to be a narrative of betterment. As there are inherent flaws in the religious sphere, the claimed enlightened political project becomes an alienated thought as it hits the root cause. Even after so many years of independence, hate, violence and poverty have neither vanished nor have the political parties strived to bring forth these issues or formalized such demand. Hence political reading/perception is also a mental construct that defines awareness as well as consciousness towards simple or basic traits of humanity defined in terms of righteousness. The perceptual inferences directs towards creating a realm of consciousness that come from the stored consciousness which a citizen of the republic of the Government of India always derives by claiming of tradition of sacred.

The aspect of mind-consciousness as has been elucidated in the *Abhidharmakoṣasaṅgraha*, Vasubandhu explains the inference through ālaya adds mind-consciousness (*manovijñāna*) and *manas* that gives rise to and the support of mind-consciousness. *Ālayavijnana* (stored consciousness) is the ground, or base, of the seventh consciousness (Hanh 2009: 150–1). Thus the politicality to remain aloof from constitutional morality is an ingrained factoring thought process that creates hindrances to create any kind of enabling process. Thus Ambedkar's definition of rule and principles is an essential tool that forbids creating political consciousness of rationality and aspirations to become '*samyak*'. As the object of perception is not a reality in itself but an image we have created. Propagation towards adherence of tradition and self-centred rules of caste and community are an example of 'protected ignorance' and bring us to the central ideas of representation. As the object of mind is thinking/ideas/imagination, its resultant category is a mind consciousness. When thinking and functioning is embedded in the sphere of rules and not in the sphere of principle, the result of consciousness directs towards violence, hate, anger and feeling of superiority, imagined consciousness of divinity.

The political parties and politics as is not centred on any agenda of social transformation, any perceptual change of righteous mind-consciousness are difficult to come forth. Public policy is an important means of empowering people to address their sufferings. Structural problems somehow do not get addressed through many public policies and the ways politics is played to get into driving power seat. It may be asked that 'where is not a transformation? Do we see any transformation? Don't we see our roads getting transformed into highways etc. Don't we see better amenities in place? Such questions are directed towards making claims of transformations and hence linguistic categories such as 'India is Indira', 'Shining India', '*Sabkā Sāth sabkā vikās*', '*nā khaunga nā khane dungā*', 'Make in India' and so forth, the list is too long where agenda of transformation is espoused to maintain ignorance of the masses to inflict self by the claimers of developments on the others. Emotive responses, managing social media, creating an image of influx, make citizen to imagine a mental image of greatness, comfort and not willing to accept anything beyond what is being served are part of an anti-Ambedkar agenda. Shock values in terms of capturing political imaginations by pervasive means by the political parties and political leaderships are all part of rules and not that of principle. It is in this context, one observes that political space, being fluid in nature, directed only towards votes without realization of the value of vote. It is a constant behavioural practice with utmost adherence to sacred and divine.

Recalling the issue of representation, being unique particular, to be part of the governance in political realm becomes a physical self. Therefore objective of representation becomes necessary means to interrogate the political self and the collective self. Through representations, power structure becomes accessible means, which translate to get into the structured fold to be not only part but also to be equal in gaining access to resources. The entrepreneurship and business houses that have emerged through political assertions and by capturing political power has become new means to break the shackles of 'wealth' as well as 'high-handedness'. Nevertheless, how do we understand such a phenomenon? Can we then call it a transformation? The political parties being rooted in maintaining normative, the idea of 'transforming India' becomes important to maintain the self-imposed by political authority and converting state into an agency of 'hegemony' rather than the 'agency of change'. Representation in this case becomes a self and not that of collective. Collective realm being located in shared aspiration, consciousness of being is a part of its embedded realities, often become a guiding factor but functions without any objectives. Hence, caste-Hinduness is being espoused as political normal. Psyche of caste behaviour as well as self-desired aspirations has created consciously the abject submissiveness in the political sphere.

Thus the objectives of transformations are converted into the materialist mode of visibility without any transformation of mind-consciousness of *samyak* principles. Political lust has been transformed into a 'political carrier' providing space for personal political position in the political sphere to full fill aspirations of self. There are many numerous examples. Intentionality being that of holding on presuppositions, the claims of modernism becomes a mere linguistic term than achieving the modernism itself. The political principle of modern is a much-desired sphere to be achieved. Modernity in India being cosmetic in nature, the thinking towards anything new is equally cosmetic. As and when political leaders use to visit Europe and observed as to how people have to pay for peeing, followed the similar model of 'use and pay', thus reducing the natures call into affordability as well as problem of access. The same leaders would never think of health and education system as part of replication, not making an effort of transformation.

In the field of education, many political parties resort to withdraw from education. Education has acquired the status of industry all over India. Being in the concurrent list in the Indian Constitution, both the state and centre governments has responsibilities. In the school curricula, mythological heroes are idealized to make children insensitive towards the historical past and the humanism propounded by the *Shraman* tradition. In a state like Maharashtra, the government has started giving permissions to open schools and those involved also use it as an industry to mint money and have acquired the tag of '*shikshan maharshi*'. Fundamentals of 'being' are addressed only in achieving the materialist show and not in the transformation of society. Manifestations of being are multifold in nature, embedded meanings is not a difficult process as it is completely inked with the idea of 'we' that has 'intentionality'. Self-revealing in the political voting process is a secret that creates politicality of intentionality. Intentionality often has no rational significance as it is rooted in the self-centric nature of the political functioning. The larger idea of the Hindu nation functions like a communitarian intentionality to be imposed and is located in factoring presuppositions. The nature of cause and effect gets manifested through the ballot box democracy is a testimony of consciousness of being adherence to Ambedkar and anti-Ambedkar political consciousness. Image representations on the posters, bill boards, newspapers are directed not only to communicate citizens but also to envisage the body type representation and constructs mental image of the political personas. They are regarded as – democratic *chakravartin*. They create a criterion of self like a *Mahapurushlkshanas* (i.e. signs of great beings; Walshe 1987). Interestingly, people hardly acknowledge those *mahapurushlakshanas* and prefer to sleep into the *short memory* as public at large are designed to shape their political memories in tune with the tenure of the political self-rule and hence functions as momentary.

These days there is an invisible doctrine of claim to *vote hamara Raj hamara* (i.e. our votes, our rule). Such a claim positions itself for transformation as the claimants are from the oppressed communities who are left without representation in the governing system of the country. At the same time, it acts as a method to generate a sense of consciousness that aspires to claim betterment for change in structural realms through political means. However, narrative played by the hegemonic political community is different in terms of its intentionality and working objectives. The dominance of doctrinal dissemination of consciousness is that of anarchy. How, who is maintaining anarchy, who is benefiting anarchy is essential to explain in public domain to make the political space that of political consciousness to claim constitutional functioning of the principles. Thus the conscious functioning of the state of mind is that of 'protected ignorance', hence the political morality is that of 'protected ignorance'.

References

Alone, Y.S. (2007). 'Historicism: Confrontations and Inquiries', in (eds.), Sukhadeo Thorat and Aryama, *Ambedkar in Retrospect*, New Delhi: Rawat Publication, pp. 261–91.

Ambedkar, B.R. (1979). 'Annihilation of Caste', in (ed.), Vasant Moon, *Dr. Babasaheb Ambedkar Writings and Speeches*, Vol. 1, Bombay: Government of Maharashtra Publications, pp. 23–96.

Ambedkar, B.R. (1987a). 'Buddha or Karl Marx', in (ed.), Vasant Moon, *Dr. Babasaheb Ambedkar Writings and Speeches*, Vol. 3, Bombay: Government of Maharashtra Publications, pp. 441–64.

Ambedkar, B.R. (1987b). 'Riddles in Hinduism', in (ed.), Vasant Moon, *Dr. Babasaheb Ambedkar Writings and Speeches*, Vol. 4, Bombay: Government of Maharashtra Publications.

Ambedkar, B.R. (1992). 'The Buddha and His Dhamma', in (ed.), Vasant Moon, *Dr. Babasaheb Ambedkar Writings and Speeches*, Vol. 11, Bombay: Government of Maharashtra Publication.

Ambedkar, B.R. (1995). 'Hindu Code Bill', in (ed.), Vasant Moon, *Dr. Babasaheb Ambedkar Writings and Speeches*, Vol. 14, Bombay: Government of Maharashtra Publications.

Foucault, Michel (1972). *Archaeology of Knowledge and the Discourse on Language*, [Translated], New York: Pantheon Books.

Hanh, Thich Nhat (2009). *Understanding Our Mind*, Noida: Harper Collins.

Jambulkar, Vikas (2017). 'Dr. B.R. Ambedkar, Uniform Civil Code and National Integration', in (ed.), M.L. Kasae, *Dr. Babasaheb Ambedkar: The Architect of Modern India*, Nagpur: RTM University, pp. 241–56.

Kumar, Deepak (2016). *The Trishanku Nation: Memory, Self, and Society in Contemporary India*, New Delhi: Oxford University Press.

Lourdunathan, S. (2017). *Foucault: Power/Knowledge Discourse, Department of Philosophy*, Karumathu-Madurai: Arul Anandar College.

Mitra, Subrata K. (2014). *Politics in India, Structure, Process, and Policy*, New Delhi: Oxford University Press (originally published by Routledge, 2011).

Nandy, Ashis (2004). 'The Politics of Secularism and the Recovery of Religious Toleration', in (ed.), Rajiv Bhargava, *Secularism and Its Critics*, New Delhi: Oxford University Press, pp. 321–44.

Rathore, Aakash Singh (2017). *Indian Political Theory: Laying the Groundwork for Svaraj*, London: Routledge.

Vundru Rajasekhar (2017). *Ambedkar, Gandhi and Patel, the Making of India's Electoral System*, New Delhi: Bloomsbury.

Walshe, Maurice (1987). *Digha Nikāya* [Translated], Boston: Wisdom Publication.

INDEX

Note: Page numbers in **bold** refer to tables, and those in *italics* refer to figures

Abdullah, Sheikh 162, 164, 165
Acharya, Ramanuja 110
Adamar matha 115
Adi Granth (Primal Scripture) *see* Guru Granth Sahib
Advani, Lal Krishna 9, 183
Agarkar, Gopal Ganesh 140
agonistic pluralism 197–8
Ahmad, Imtiaz 176
Ahmed, Hilal 181
Ahmedabad Labour Strike 198
Ain-i-Dharmarth 159–60
Ajmal, Maulana Badruddin 79
Akalis, meaning of 46
Akal Takh 44, 46
Akhbar-e-Mashriq 101
Akhil Bharatiya Vidyarthi Parishad 193
Alam, Sarfaraz 182
Ali, Idris 103
All Assam Student Union (AASU) 79
All India Congress Committee (AICC) 65
All India Muslim League *see* Muslim League
All India United Democratic Front (AIUDF) 67, 69–70, 71, 78, 79
All Jammu and Kashmir Auqaf Trust 163
All Jammu and Kashmir Muslim Conference 162
All Jammu and Kashmir Praja Parishad 167
Amarnath 169

Ambedkar, B. R. 13, 174, 205–6; Buddhism and 144; on Hinduism 2; religion and 2, 3
Amritdhari (initiated) Sikhs 46
Amritsar Treaty 157–8, 159, 171n1
Anandpur Sahib Resolutions 53, 56
Andhra Pradesh 28
Anglo-Indians 24
'Annihilation of Caste' (Ambedkar) 206, 208
anti-Sikh riots of 1984 8
appeasement 176
Araria, Bihar 35, 180, 181, 182, 184
Archaeological and Research Department 161
Aristotle 84
Armed Forces (Jammu and Kashmir) Special Power Act 170
Article 30 of the Indian Constitution 24–5
Article 35A of the Indian Constitution 170
Article 356 of the Indian Constitution 169–70
Article 370 of the Indian Constitution 6, 149, 166, 169, 170
Arya Samaj 44
Asom Gana Parishad (AGP) 66, 67, 68, 69, 70, 71, 74, 75, 79
Assadi, Muzaffar 113, 114
Assam 64–79; Assembly elections of 2001 67; Assembly polls of 1978 65; Assembly polls of 2016 64, 70–7; electoral politics since independence 65–7; Lok Sabha

polls (2014) 64, 67–70; migration into 64; population 65; regions 65; religion 77–9; socio-political setting 65
Assam Accord 66
Assam Agitation 65–6
Associated Press 161
Autonomous District Council (ADC) 93
Azad, Abul Kam 167
Azad Kashmir 164

Baba Budan 118
Baba Budangiri shrine, in Karnataka 118
Babri Mosque in Ayodhya 9, 11; demolition of 9, 183
Babu, Rajan 132
Badal, Parkash Singh 53, 56, 57
Badera, Ganesh Das 158
Baisakhi day 44
Bajrang Dal 113, 117, 175, 184, 185, 193
Balgokulam of Kerala 112
Balyan, Sanjeev 38
Banerjee, Mamata 103
Bannerji, Albion 161
Barak Valley 65
Barnala, Surjit Singh 56–7
Basaveshwara 110
Basu, Amrita 37
Bedi, Khem Singh 45
Bengal Legislative Council 21–2
Bhagalpur riot of 1989 179, 180, 182
Bhagwat, Mohan 74
Bhambhri, C. P. 5, 12
Bharat Dharma Jana Sena (BDJS) 132
Bharati, Uma 116
Bharatiya Jana Sangh (BJS) 5; in Bihar 177, 182; cow protection and 5; election manifesto in 1951 108; general election of 1967 5; in Gujarat 200; Hindu Code Bill 145; in Karnataka 5; in Maharashtra 144, 145, 147–8; in Punjab 52–3, **54**; SAD and 53; *see also* Bharatiya Janata Party (BJP)
Bharatiya Janata Party (BJP) 6, 193; anti-Ambedkar consciousness 211; in Bihar 179, 180–1, 182, 183, 184; Election Manifesto of 1998 109; in Goa 30; in Kerala **126**, 128, 132–3, **133**, *133*, **134**, 134–5; key objective 33; in Maharashtra 139, 140, 150–3; Parliamentary election of 1984 179; Parliamentary election of 1989 179; Parliamentary election of 2014 108; religious mobilization 178; riots and 38–40; Shiv Sena and 140, 150–3; in Uttar Pradesh 6, 11

Bharatiya Janata Party (BJP) in Assam 66; AGP and 67, 70, 71, 79; Assembly elections of 2001 67; Assembly elections of 2016 70–7, *76*, **77**, 79; 'bottom-up' approach 75; Lok Sabha polls of 2014 64, 67–70, **68**, *68*, **69**, 78; panchayat election of 2018 77, **78**; rainbow alliance 79; region-wise performance in Assam Assembly elections (1985–2016) **77**; RSS and 72, 73–4; social coalition 75
Bharatiya Janata Party (BJP) in Karnataka 109, 118, 119; Assembly elections of 2004 111; Assembly elections of 2008 111; Assembly elections of 2013 111; Assembly elections of 2018 109; coastal districts 113; communal riots 116–17; popularity of 109; regional parties and 109
Bharatiya Kisan Sangh 193
Bharatiya Mazdoor Sangh 193
Bharti, Indu 179
Bhatkal, Karnataka 114; Muslim radicals 114; riots 114, 116
Bhattacharjee, Malini 72–3
Bhattacharya, Buddadheb 99, 102
Bhave, Vinoba 144
Big Estates Abolition Act (1950) 166
Bihar 15, 174–84; communal polarizations 178–80; electoral democracy 175–7; Jan Sangh 177; religion as tool of political mobilization 182–4; Seemanchal 180–2
BIMARU states 98
Blair, Harry W. 175–6
Bodo Peoples' Front (BPF) 67, 68, 69, 70, 71, 75, 76–7, 78, 79
Bohras 189
Bortaman 101
Brahmaputra Valley 65
Brass, P. 4, 9
British 5, 22–3, 153; Amritsar Treaty 157–8, 159, 171n1; communal electorates in 1909 3–4; divide and rule policy 2; division of India 5; gurdwara reform movement 46–8; leaders of national movement against 1; Maharashtra and 140–3, 144; manipulated religious identities of Hindu and Muslim 3; mobilization of people against 4; Muslim minority 21–2; SAD and 50; Sikh nationalism and 45–6; Simon Commission 48; Tipu Sultan and 118; Treaty of Lahore 157
Brus (Hindu Reangs), in Mizoram 92–3
Buddha 204

'Buddha and Karl Marx' (Ambedkar) 206
Buddhism 144; Hinduism *vs.* 2; Mahayana 110; Theravada 110
Buddhist theories 204

capitalism 27
cause and effect theory 204
Census of India (2011) 65
Central Sikh League (CSL) 46, 49
Centre for Development Studies 130
Channakeshavapura Kannada Sangha 117
Chatterjee, Partha 97, 207
chetana (consciousness) 205
Chief Khalsa Diwan (CKD) 45–6
Chirag-i-Panjab (Badera) 158
Chittaranjan, U. 116
Chowdhury, Maulana Siddiqullah 102, 103
Christians: in Goa 29–30; in Karnataka 110, 111; in Kerala 124, 125, **125**, 126, **126**, **127**, 129–30
church: in Goa 29–30; Nilakkal Church dispute in Kerala 129–30
church, in Mizoram 30–1; as an election watchdog 87–9; confrontation between state and 86; ecclesial citizenship and 89–90; ethnic role of 86–7; genesis of political action 86–7; overview 84–5; religious morality over political morality 91–2; selective political action 92–3; without political authority 90–1
civil rights, colonial state 21
coalition government 11
Common Era 159
communalism 8, 12, 17, 35, 36, 129
communal polarizations, in Bihar 178–80
communal violence 174–5
Communist Party of India (CPI) 18n1, 66, 71, **126**
Communist Party of India (Marxist) 66, 95, **126**, 128, 129, 130, 131
The Concept of Political (Schmitt) 191
Congress 12, 18n1, 22–3, 178; anti-Ambedkar consciousness 211; anti-Sikh riots 8; appeasement of Muslims 147, 149–50; in Assam 64, 65–71, 72, 75–7, 78–9; in Bihar 179, 180, 182; elections (general and Assembly) of 1967 5; Emergency (1975–77) 5–6, 111, 113, 147–8; in Goa 30; incumbency effect on Hindu-Muslim riot 36; in Jammu and Kashmir 162, 163, 164; in Karnataka 109, 111, 113, 117, 118–19; in Kerala 125, **126**, 127–8, 129, 131, 132, 133; Lucknow Pact (1916) 45, 142; in Maharashtra 139, 142, 143, 144, 145, 147–51, 152; minorities and 5, 6; in Mizoram 31; NCP and 139, 140; OBC reservation 150–1; in Punjab 43, 45, 47, 48–9, 50–3, 56, 57, 58; secular credentials of 36; soft Hindutva 7–8, 118–19; transformation as mass organization 142; in West Bengal 96, 98, 100, 101
Constituent Assembly and minorities 24–7; Advisory Committee of 1947 25–6; Article 30 24–5; classification of minorities 24
Constitution Act 1939 166
Constitution of India 213; Article 30 24–5; Article 35A 170; Article 356 169–70; Article 370 6, 149, 166, 169, 170
co-option strategy of TMC 103–4
cow protection 5
cow slaughter 5
CPI(ML) 181, 182
Cripps, Stafford 50

Daily Vitasha 162
Das, Shankar 74
Dasha Mata 194
Dastur-al-Amal 159
Dattatreya Swamy 118
Delhi Agreement 166
democracy: agonistic pluralism and 197–8; political identity and 64
Deoras, Bhavoo Rao 111
Devnagari 163
Dhamma of Buddha 2, 3
Digha Nikaya 205
Distressed Debtors Relief Act (1950) 166
diversity 210
DMK 43
Dogra community 158
Dogra dynasty 158–60
dominion status 48, 142

Ecclesial Authority (EA) 89–90
ecclesial citizenship, in Mizoram 89–90
economic reforms 11
Economic Times 36
economy: liberalization of 11
education: as an industry 214
Education Reorganisation Committee 163
Election Commission of India 89; Model Code of Conduct 88, 89
election watchdog, church in Mizoram as 87–9
Emergency (1975–77) 5–6, 111, 113, 147–8
essentialization of religion 5–9
ethnic-regionalist coalition 79

ethnic role of church in Mizoram 86–7
Ezhava, in Kerala 124, 125, **125**, **126**, 130, 132, **134**

Fatherland 189–90
Fernandes, Sujatha 87–8, 93, 94
feudalism 200
First Post 74
forced family planning 5
Foucault, M. 206–7
Furfura Sharif, West Bengal 99–101, 103

Ganashakti Party 75
Gandhi, Indira: assassination of 178
Gandhi, M. K. 2, 142; assassination of 144; Congress under 142, 143
Gandhi, Rahul 119
Gandhi, Rajiv 9, 11
Gandhi, Varun 35
Gandhian ideology 144
Gandhian organizations and institutions 144
Ganeshotsav 141
ghar wapsi 103, 104, 112–13
Glancy, Bertrand J. 162
Goa: bi-coalitional politics 30; Christianity in 29–30; legislative assembly 30; Portuguese colonial rule 29
Godse, Nathuram 112
Gogoi, Tarun 67, 70
Gokhale, Gopal Krishna 140, 142
Golden Temple 46
Golwalkar, M. S. 108, 112, 142
Goria 65
Government of India Act 1935 166
Govindacharya, K. N. 9
Gowhar, Ghulam Nabi 172n10
Gujarat: anti-Muslim violence 35, 37, 39; corporate and media 194, 196; dissenting masses 198, **199**; growth model 196; political economy of 193; religious organizations 194, **195**; riots in 2002 35, 39; sects and dominant caste 193–4
Gulabnama (Ram) 158
Gurdwara Rakab Ganj 45
gurdwara reform movement 46–8
'Guru, Granth, and Gurdwara' 44
Guru Granth Sahib 44, 45
Gurumukhi script 51
Guttenar system 113

Haidt, Jonathan 13
Hajj (pilgrimage), government subsidy to 150
Hargobind, Guru 44
Haryana 5
Hasan, Mahmood 101

Hasan, Mushirul 95
Hasan, Zoya 34–5, 95
Hedgewar, K. B. 108, 111, 142
Himachal Pradesh 8; anti-Muslim violence 37
Hindu Code Bill 145, 205
Hinduism: Ambedkar on 2; Buddhism *vs.* 2; Kerala and 130; political influence of 11; sects and 194
Hindu Jagarana Vedike 113
Hindu Mahasabha 44, 50, 108, 112, 142, 143–6, 149, 154
Hindu Munnani 112
Hinduness 211
Hindu politics 188–200; absence of political opposition 196–8, **197**; constitutional standpoint 190–1; defined 192; marginalization of minorities 200; social formation 193; study of 193
Hindu Rashtra 2
Hindu right's politics of polarization 35
Hindus: categorical criteria for being 189; communities/sub-communities 189; essentials 189; Savarkar's theory 188–90
Hindu Samajotsavas 112
Hindu Samhati 103–4
Hindu Seva Pratishthana 112
Hindusthan 189
Hindutva 2; in Karnataka 111–19; mathas 114–15; Savarkar's theory of 188–90; sects and 194; upper castes alignment with 194; *see also* Bharatiya Jana Sangh (BJS); Bharatiya Janata Party (BJP); Hindu Mahasabha; Rashtriya Swayamsevak Sangh (RSS); Vishwa Hindu Parishad (VHP)
Hindu Yuva Sene 113
History of the Reigning Family of Lahore, with Some Account of the Jummoo Rajahs, the Seik Soldiers and their Sirdars, A (Smyth) 158
Hofstader, Richard 34
holyland 189, 190
home rule 142
Hubli, Karnataka 116

identity 188; anti-Hindu 33; Christian 94; cultural 207; ethnic 64, 72, 86–7; Hindu 33–4, 35, 135, 148, 151, 194; Mizos 86–7; movements based on 10; Muslim 8, 33, 98–9, 100; partisan 36; religious 8, 10, 14, 15, 78, 94, 131, 135; Sikh 8, 44–6
Ilaiah, Kancha 33
Imran, Ahmed Hassan 103
Independent India 28
Indian Council of Social Science Research (ICSSR) 97
Indian Mujahideen (IM) 114

Indian Muslims (Mujeeb) 34
Indian National Congress (INC) *see* Congress
Indian Union Muslim League (IUML) 125, **126**, 127, 128, 130, 131, 132, 133
Instrument of Accession 164, 166
Instrument of Merger 166
Inter-Services Intelligence (ISI) 114
ISKCON 194
Islamic State (IS) 114

Jaffrelot, Christophe 73
Jafri, Ehsan 200
Jagarana Prakashan 112
Jamaat-e-Islami 131
Jamiat-e-Ulama-e-Hind (JUH) 101–3; anti-land grab movement 102; demands for reservation 102; network 101–2
Jammu and Kashmir 9, 157–70; accession to India 164–5, 166, 170; Amritsar Treaty 157–8, 159, 171n1; autonomous bodies 169; civil society organizations 168–9; colonial-induced reforms 160–3; Constituent Assembly 166; constitution of 167–8; denial and discrimination of Muslims 161–2; divisions/regions 168; Dogra dynasty 158–60; governor rule 169–70; Hindu polity during Dogra dynasty 159–60; Instrument of Merger and 166; land reform 166; mass education 162–3; as a Muslim majority state 169; population 168; post-accession politics 170; responsible government 162–4; socio-economic overlapping divisions 165
Jammu and Kashmir Disturbed Areas Act 170
Jammu and Kashmir State (Delegation of Powers) Act 170
Jamwal Rajput 158
Jana Seva Vidya Kendra 112
Janata Dal (JD) 11, 18n1, 111
Janata Dal (S) 111
Janata Dal (United) 185; Muslim community and 183–4
Janata Party 65, 148
Janathipathiya Samrakshana Samithy 132
Jan Sangh *see* Bharatiya Jana Sangh (BJS)
Jenkins, Rob 11
Jodhka, Surinder 99
Joshi, Sharad 150
Joshi, Yadav Rao 111–12

Kairon, Partap Singh 50
Kalighat Temple development 103
Kalom 101
Kannada Chaluvaligar movement 117
Kannada Rajyotsava day 117
Kannada Shakti Kendra 117
Kannada Yuvajana Sabha (KYS) 117
Karachi Agreement 166
Karbi Anglong 65
Karnataka: Baba Budangiri shrine 118; Buddhism 110; Christians 110, 111; communal riots 115–17; Congress in 111; demography 110; exodus of 'non-Kannadigas' from 117; formation 109–10; Hindutva 111–19; IT boom in 117; Janata Dal (S) 111; linguistic chauvinism 116–17; mathas 114–15; Muslims 110–11; political scenario 111; pro-Kannada movement 117; Ram Janmabhoomi movement 116; reformist movement 110; religious traditions 110–11; Saivism 110; Tipu Sultan 118; Virasaivism 110
Karnataka Forum for Dignity (KFD) 114
Karnataka Rakshana Vedike 117
Kashmiri Pandits: Dogra dynasty and 160; migration of 9; Tantric Shaivism-Shaktism 160
Kerala 15, 124–35; Assembly election in 2016 132–5, **134**; caste and religious base of political parties **126**; Christians 124, 125, **125**, 126, **126**, **127**, 129–30; coalition governments 127–9; communal tensions and polarization 129–32; demographic composition 124–6, **125–6**, **127**; district-religious profile **126**; electoral performance 132–5, **133**, **134**; love jihad in 129, 130, 136n5; minorities in 124–6, **125–6**, **127**; Muslims 124, 125, **125**, **126**, **127**, 127–8, 129, 130–1; Nilakkal Church dispute 129–30; population growth 130; radical Muslim organizations 131; religion-wise population **127**; social reform movements 124; voting behaviour in Assembly elections (2011 and 2016) 133, **134**
Kerala Congress (KC) 125, **126**, 127–8, 129, 131, 132, 133
Khalandar, Dada Hayath Meer 118
Khalistan movement 8
Khalsa Advocate 45
Khalsa Akhbar 45
Khalsa College 45
Khalsa Panth 44, 45
Khalsa Samachar 45
Khan, Aga 4
Khan, Sikander Hayat 49
Khan, Sir Syed Ahmad 22
Khilonjia Muslims 65

Khojas 189
Kidwai, Rafi Ahmad 167
Kolar, Karnataka 117
Kumar, Deepak 209
Kumar, Nitish 183–4
Kumar, Sanjay 175
Kumaraswamy, H. D. 111
Kumbha melas 208

Laclau, Ernesto 197
Ladakh 157, 168, 170, 171n1; Buddhist population in 168, 210; Buddhist religionist politics 170; scheduled tribe status 170
Ladakh Buddhist Association (LBA) 167
'Lahore Singh Sabha' 45
Lahore state 157, 158
Lalhlimpui, K. 92
Lawrence, H. M. 159
Lawrence, Walter 161
Left Democratic Front (LDF) 125, 127, 128, 132, 133–5, **134**
Left Front Government (LFG), in West Bengal 95, 97, 98, 100; Assembly election of 2011 103; land acquisition 102; reservation for Muslims 99, 102
Leh 167, 170; *see also* Jammu and Kashmir
liberal democracy 191
liberalization of economy 11
Lingappa 117
Lingayats 110, 115
linguistic chauvinism, in Karnataka 116–17
Lok Janshakti Party 132
Lokmanya Tilak *see* Tilak, Bal Gangadhar
Lord Ayyappa 129
Lorrain, J. H. 86
Lourdunathan, S. 207
love jihad 104, 113, 129, 130, 136n5, 185
Lucknow Pact (1916) 45, 142
Luit Poriya Hindu Sammelan 74

Madhavacharya 110
Madhok, Balraj 171–2n6
Madhwa mathas 115
Maha-aratis, in Mumbai 152
Mahanta, Prafulla Kumar 66, 74
mahaparinibbansutta 205
mahapurushlakshanas 214
Maharashtra 139–53; Assembly election of 1995 152; Assembly elections of 2014 139, 140, 153; BJS 147–8; farmers' movement 150; Hindutva politics 149–53; historical context 140–3; Lok Sabha election of 2014 139, 153; *Maha-aratis* 152; Marxist movement 145; OBC reservation and 150–1; party-wise Lok Sabha seats (1952–54) in **141**; Patanjali's branches in 153; post-independence developments 143–6; Shiv Sena 146–53; upper-caste consolidation 151; urbanization 151–2
Mahayana 110
Mahjoor (Kashmiri poet) 164
Majithia, Sunder Singh 49
Majoor Mahajan Sangh (TLA) 198
Majuli, Assam 73
Malayalai Memorial 124
Malik, Umesh 38
Malviya, Pandit Madan Mohan 205
Mandal Commission Report 11
MAO *see* Muhammadan Anglo-Oriental Defence Association (MAO)
Marathawada University 147
Marathi Manus agenda of Shiv Sena 148, 149
Marcuse, Herbert 192
Masani, Minoo 200
mathas, in Karnataka 114–15
McDonald, Ramsay 49
Media Research and Development Foundation 130
Menon, Parvathy 114–15
Mewat, Haryana 5
Mico Kannada Sangha 117
minorities: Constituent Assembly and 24–7; in Kerala 124–6, **125–6**, **127**; mobilization of 176
Misra, Udayon 75
mission schools, Punjab 44
Mitra, Subrata 210
Mizo Accord 87
Mizo National Front 31
Mizo National Front (MNF) 86, 87, 92, 94
Mizo Peoples Forum (MPF) 88
Mizoram: Christianity in 30–1; conversion of local tribes 30; legislature 31; as a Union Territory 92
Mizoram Liquor Total Prohibition and Control Act 86
mobilization of Muslims 97; Furfura Sharif 99–101; Jamiat-e-Ulama-e-Hind (JUH) 101–3; Sachar Committee Report (SCR) 98–9, 100
modernity 213
Modi, Narendra 33; Trump compared with 34–5
Mody, Piloo 200
'Mohammed the Idiot' (Deccan herald story) 116
Moltmann, Jurgen 85

Montague-Chelmsford Scheme 48
Moral Code of Conduct 88, 89
morality 2
Moria 65
Mouffe, Chantal 197
Mughal dynasty 21
Muhammad (Prophet) 118
Muhammadan Anglo-Oriental Defence Association (MAO) 22, 23
Mujeeb, Mohammed 34
Munshi, K. M. 200
Musafir, Giani Gurmukh Singh 50
Muslim League 49–50; Lucknow Pact (1916) 45, 142; partition of India and 50; Shiromani Akali Dal (SAD) and 49–50
Muslim Rashtriya Manch 193
Muslim representation: in Bihar 176–7, **177**, 180, 181–2; in Lok Sabha from Gujarat 200, **201**; in Punjab Legislative Council 48; in West Bengal 98
Muslims: in Assam 65; en bloc voting 175, 176, 181; forced family planning and 5; in Kerala 124, 125, **125**, **126**, **127**, 127–8, 129, 130–1; as minority 21–2; Sachar Committee Report (SCR) 16, 95–6, 97, 98–9, 100, 103; Shah Bano case/judgment 8–9, 149–50; as villains of history 33
Muslims, in West Bengal: Congress and 96; educational condition 97; Furfura Sharif 99–101; *Jamiat-e-Ulama-e-Hind* (JUH) 101–3; left parties and 96–7; mobilization of 97, 98–103; population 96; representation of 97; reservation for 99, 102; rural concentration 96; Sachar Committee Report (SCR) 95–6, 97, 98–9, 100, 103; secular politics and 96–7; socio-economic backwardness 97; Trinamool Congress (TMC) 95–6, 103–4
Muslim Waqf board 169
Muthalik, Pramod 113
Muzaffarnagar riots (2013) 35, 38, 40
Mysore 109; communal conflagration 116

Nagalim 94
Nagaon, Assam 78
Nagoke, Udham Singh 50
Naidu, Sarojini 205
Nairs, in Kerala 124, 125, **125**, **126**, 133, **134**
Nair Service Society (NSS) 125
Namdharis 114
Nandy, Ashis 3, 208

Narayan, Jayaprakash 211
Nastalique 163
National Conference (NC) 9, 43, 162, 163–4, 167
National Crime Records Bureau 115
National Development Front 114, 131
Nationalist Congress Party (NCP) 139, 140
National Socialist Council of Nagalim (NSCN) 94
Nauroji, Dadabhai 140, 142
Navayaths 114
Nazi Party 191
Nehru, Jawaharlal 2, 145, 208; Instrument of Accession 164
Nehru Committee Report (1928) 48–9
Neilsen, Kenneth Bo 97–8, 100
Nellis, Gareth 36
neo-media 196
Nilakkal Church dispute, in Kerala 129–30
Nivarthan Movement, in Kerala 124
Nizam of Hyderabad 143
North Cachar (Dima Hasao) 65
North-West Frontier Legislative Council 49
nothingness *see shunyata* (nothingness)
Notun Gati 101
Nussbaum, Martha 34–5

Odisha 14
Other Backward Classes (OBC) 98; mobilization 11; reservation for 150–1
othering, concept of 188

Pahari Sewa Sangh 73
Pai, Sudha 35
Pakistan: demand for 50; Inter-Services Intelligence (ISI) 114
Pakistan Occupied Kashmir (PoK) 157
Palshikar, Suhas 72, 74
Panj Pyare 44
Panun Kashmir 170
Paramarth, Dadarao 111
The Paranoid Style in American Politics (Hofstader) 34
partition of Bengal 4
partition of India 2, 3, 4, 5, 23, 24–6, 50, 51, 80, 81, 143, 145
Paswan, Ramvilas 184
Patanjali 153
Patel, Ahmed 35, 200
Patel, Sardar 205
Pawar, Sharad 148
Pejavar matha 115
People's Democratic Party 9

Persian 21
Pheruman, Darshan Singh 50
Phule, Jyotirao 140, 141
Pir Sahebs of Furfura Sharif 99–101
polarization 33–40; overview 33–4; research on 36–8; riots and 38–40
political perpetuation of religious rights 27
political sphere: agenda of transformation 212; consciousness 205–6
Political Theology (Schmitt) 191
Popular Front of India (PFI) 114, 130, 131
Portuguese colonial rule, in Goa 29
Praja Sabha 162
Praja Socialist Party 132
Pratichi Trust 97
pratityasamvutpada 204–5
Pravasi Nivasi Party 132
Presbyterian Church 87
presuppositions 206
pro-Kannada movement 117
protected ignorance 209–10
public policy 212
Pungava Jagarana 112
Punjab: Anandpur Sahib Resolutions 53, 56; anti-Sikh riots 8; demand for Punjabi Suba 51; division of 8; gurdwara reform movement 46–8; Khalistan movement 8; *see also* Sikhs, in Punjab
Punjab Legislative Council 48

Quit India movement 50, 164
Quit Kashmir Movement 164
Quraishi, S.Y. 89

Rai, Nityanand 182
Rajagopalachari, C. 200
Rajasthan 37
Rajdarshani (Badera) 158
Rajkumar fans' associations 117
Ram, Kripa 158
Ramdev, Baba 153
Ram Janmabhoomi movement 11
Ram Mandir 9, 11
Ranade, Mahadev 140
Ranganath Mishra Commission 102
Rashtra Sevika Samiti 193
Rashtriya Janata Dal (RJD) 35, 71, 180, 182, 183, 184
Rashtriya Swayamsevak Sangh (RSS) 6, 9, 37, 193; in Assam 72–5; in Bihar 175, 178, 180, 184; on Buddhism 144; country-wide regional presence 108; cow protection vigilante groups 185; Emergency and 6; in Gujarat 193; Hindu Rashtra and 108; in Jammu and Kashmir 167; in Karnataka 108, 109, 111–19; in Kerala 128, 129–30, 131–2, 134–5; in Maharashtra 142–8, 151, 152–3; Nilakkal Church and 129–30; in West Bengal 103–4; *see also* Bharatiya Jana Sangh (BJS); Bharatiya Janata Party (BJP)
Rashtrotthana Parishat 112
Rathore, Aakash Singh 207–8
Rath Yatra from Somnath to Kolkata 9
Rehat Maryada (Sikh discipline/code of conduct) 44
religion: essentialization of 5–9; indispensability of 12–13; political economy and 11; resurgence of 10–12; separation of state from 1–2
religion and politics 188
religious mobilization 11, 174
religious rights: political perpetuation of 27
religious social categories 23
reservation for minorities 25–6, 27
Responsible Government Day 162
riots: in Gujarat (2002) 35, 39; in Kandhamal (2008) 35, 38–9; in Muzaffarnagar (2013) 35, 40
Rise of Saffron Power (Rehman) 38
Rosenzweig, Steven 36
Roy, M. N. 28
Roy, Rammohan 21

Sabarimal Ayyappa Temple 131
Sachar Committee Report (SCR) 16, 95–6, 97, 100, 103; language of mobilization 98–9; Muslims politics and 99
Sadhujana Paripalana Sangham 124
Sahajdhari (clean shaven) 45
Sahib, Harmandir 44
Saivism 110
Samajwadi Party 11
Samata Party 183
Sandhanwalia, Thakur Singh 45
Sangbad Pratidin 101
Sankardev (socio-religious reformer) 73
Sankardev Shisu Kunj 73
Sanyukt Maharashtra Movement 146
Sapru, C. S. 172n8
Saraswati Shishu Mandir 193
Sarb Hind Shiromani Akali Dal (SHSAD) 57
Sarma, Himanta Biswa 74
Sarvajanika Ganesh Samiti 116
Savarkar, V. D. 2, 3, 108, 112; Hindu Mahasabha 44, 50, 108, 112, 142, 143–6, 149, 154; Hindutva and 142, 143,

188–90; Marathi language and 143; 'two nations' theory 142
Savidge, F. W. 86
Sawant, Datta 149
Schmitt, Carl 191–2
sects 193–4, **195**; Hinduism and 194; identities of 194; sociology of 194
secularism 207; Nandy on 208
secular state 5–9
Seemanchal, Bihar 180–2; Assembly polls of 2015 181; Assembly seats in 180; BJP 180–1; by-election of 2018 182; Muslims 180, 181, 182
selective political action, of church in Mizoram 92–3
Seva Bharti 193
SGPC *see* Shiromani Gurdwara Parbandhak Committee (SGPC)
Shah, Amit 35
Shah Bano case/judgment 8–9, 149–50
Shankardev Sangh 73
Shariat Act (1937) 23
Shetty, Jagannatha 116
Shiksha Bharati 193
Shiromani Akali Dal (SAD) 5, 14–15, 43, 44; demands 51; formation 46; gurdwara reform movement 46–8; Muslim League and 49–50; objectives 46; as a 'Panthic' party 43; political support base 43; provincial elections results 50
Shiromani Gurdwara Parbandhak Committee (SGPC) 3, 43, 47–8, 53, 57, 58, 59
Shishu Shikha Samiti 73
Shivalik Ranges 157
Shiv-Jayanti 141
Shiv Sena: anti-reservation stand 150; BJP and 140, 150–3; formation 146; Hindutva politics 150–3; local conflicts and riots 147; *Maha-aratis* 152; *Marathi Manus* agenda 148, 149; minority bashing 147, 149; reincarnation of 148–9; rise of 146–7; tag line of 148–9
Shuddhi movement 44
shunyata (nothingness) 204
Siddaganga matha 115
Siddaramaiah 111, 118, 119
Siddique, Pirzada Toyeb 100–1
Siddique, Toha 100
Sikhs, in Punjab 43–60; Anandpur Sahib Resolutions 53, 56; conversion to Christianity 44; demand for Punjabi Suba 51; electoral shift 58; electoral support base 51–3; gurdwara reform movement 46–8; martial order of 44; overview 43; as political community 44–6; political representation 48–50; radical elements 56–7; return to mainstream politics 57–8
Sikhs, killings of 178
Sikh Secessionism 8
Simon Commission 48
Singh, Baba Kharak 48, 49
Singh, Beant 8
Singh, Giani Ditt 45
Singh, Giani Gian 45
Singh, Giani Zail 53
Singh, Giriraj 35
Singh, Gulab 157–9
Singh, Gurmukh 45
Singh, Guru Gobind 44, 46
Singh, Hari 161–5
Singh, Jit 157
Singh, Karan 166
Singh, Maharaja Ranjit 44, 157
Singh, Pradeep Kumar 182
Singh, Pratap 158–9
Singh, Ranbir 159–60
Singh, Sampuran 49
Singh, Santosh 184
Singh, Ujjal 49
Singh, V. P. 11, 150
Singh Sabha 45, 46
SKF Sangha 117
Smyth, G. Carmichael 158
social cleavages 15, 80
Social Democratic Party of India (SDPI) 114, 131
social divisions 1
Socialist Party 117
social media 185
Somashekara, B. K. 117
Sonkhaloghu Unnoyon (minority development) 100
Sonowal, Sarbananda 74
sovereign 192
Sree Dattatreya Bababudan Swamy Dargah 118
Sree Narayana Dharma Paripalana Yogam (SNDP) 124, 125
Sri Krishna Math, Udupi, Karnataka 112
Srinivasiah, K. R. 116
Sri Rama Sene 113
state as an agency of change 208
Student's Islamic Movement of India (SIMI) 114
Sultan, Tipu 118

Supreme Court: Baba Budangiri shrine 118; Shah Bano judgment 8–9, 149–50
Suryavanshi Rajputs 158
Swadeshi Jagaran Manch 193
Swadesh Sanhati Sangbad 104
Swami, Teertha 112–13
Swamy, Shivakumar 115

Tarapit Temple Development Authority 103
Taslimuddin, Md. 182
Tat Khalsa 45, 46
Telangana 15
Thackeray, Bal 146–9, 150, 152; *see also* Shiv Sena
Thackeray, Prabodhankar 146
Thakur, Manindra Nath 181
Thanmawi 92
Thansiami, K. 92
Theravada 110
Thiruvananthapuram, Kerala 130
Thomas, P. C. 132
Tilak, Bal Gangadhar 4, 140, 141–2
Tocqueville, Alexis de 84–5
Tod, James 158
Treaty of Amritsar *see* Amritsar Treaty
Treaty of Lahore 157
Trinamool Congress (TMC) 95–6, 101, 103–4
Tripathi, V. 75
Trump, Donald 34–5
two-nation theory 2

Unionist Party 49–50
United Democratic Front (UDF) 125, 127, 128, 133–5, **134**
United Liberation Front of Assam (ULFA) 66–7
United Minorities' Front (UMF) 66
Upadhyaya, Deendayal 108
upper castes, in Gujarat 194
urbanization, in Maharashtra 151–2
Uttar Pradesh 15, 98; anti-Muslim violence 37; BJP in 6, 11; election of 1993 11; Hindutva politics 14; Muzaffarnagar riots (2013) 35, 38, 40; Ramjanma Bhumi and Babri Masjid dispute 182; religious mobilization 11

Vaidya, M. G. 112
Vaikom and Guruvayoor Satyagrahas, Kerala 124

Vaishno Devi 169
Vajpayee, Atal Bihari 9
The Valley of Kashmir (Lawrence) 161
Vanavasi Kalyan Ashram 193
Varshney, Ashutosh 36
Vedanta Hinduism 110
Veerashaiva mathas 115
Vibrant Gujarat Global Investor Summit (VGGIS) 194, 196
Vidya Bharati 193
vigilante groups 113
Virasaiva/Lingayat movement 110
Virasaivism 110
Vishnuvardhana 110
Vishwa Hindu Parishad (VHP) 6, 185, 193; anti-Muslim violence and 37; in Bihar 175, 178, 180, 184; communal riots and 116; Dattatreya shrine and 118; Ekatmata Yatra 7; formation 112; in Karnatka 112–13, 116, 118; national executive meeting 112
Vokkaligas 115
voting, as a fundamental right 205

Waheguru 44
Wakf Board 118
waz-mahfil (religious gathering) 99, 100
Weaver, Michael 36
Weber, Max 84
West Bengal 95–104; Assembly election of 2011 103; Furfura Sharif 99–101, 103; Hindu Samhati in 103–4; Hindutva forces in 103–4; *Jamiat-e-Ulama-e-Hind* (JUH) 101–3; mobilization of Muslims 97, 98–103; Ram Navami celebration in 104; Sachar Committee Report (SCR) 95–6, 97, 98–9
Why I Am Not a Hindu (Ilaiah) 33
Wilkinson, Steve 36, 183
Wilson, James 34
Witsoe, Jeffrey 183
women's movement 145
World Value Survey **10**, 10–11

Yadav, Lalu Prasad 9, 182–3
Yedyurappa, B. S. 111
Yoga 153
Yogas Kshema Sabha and Nair Samajam 124
Young Mizo Association (YMA) 91, 93
Yusuf Shah, Mirwaiz 163, 164
Yuti 152

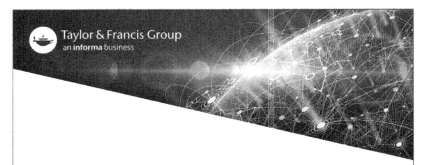